ORGANIZING HISTORY

Organizing History

Studies in Honour of Jan Glete

Edited by
Anna Maria Forssberg, Mats Hallenberg,
Orsi Husz & Jonas Nordin

NORDIC ACADEMIC PRESS

Nordic Academic Press
P.O. Box 1206
SE-221 05 Lund, Sweden
www.nordicacademicpress.com

Typesetting: Frederic Täckström, www.sbmolle.com
Copy editing: Karyn McGettigan & Charlotte Merton
Cover: Jacob Wiberg
Cover image: *Tower of Babel*, 1563 (oil on panel) Pieter Brueghel the Elder (*c.*1515–69). Bridgeman Art Library/IBL Bildbyrå
Printed by ScandBook AB, Falun 2011
ISBN: 978-91-85509-64-5

Contents

II. NORM SYSTEMS

III. INSTITUTIONAL CHANGE

Jan Glete

Preface

This book had been on our mind for a long time. As Jan kept a rather low profile in our university department, we especially wanted to give him the warmest token of friendship in academia: a Festschrift. We thought that he would be pleasantly surprised. As a scholar, of course, Jan did not keep a low profile at all. Not only did he publish an impressive number of seminal articles and books, he held lectures around the world and cultivated important contacts with historians in a host of other countries. In our department, however, Jan often kept a bit to himself. This permitted him to indulge in his greatest interest of all: research. If Jan was not working at Riksarkivet or Krigsarkivet, he could be found in his room: from early morning until very late at night. Regardless of how busy he was, he would always find time for a chat about my doctoral thesis or his latest thoughts on the navy or state formation or some other interesting topic. I always listened with great interest. I have spent many hours in his not-too-comfortable armchair, talking not only about history, but also about his beloved wife and daughter and about my own family. Jan and I also spoke about future research projects, especially about a comparative study we wanted to conduct together. However, he began to have reservations. 'I am growing old,' he would say. 'I don't know how long I'll be working.' Those statements seemed absurd to me. Jan was only in his late fifties and was full of energy and ideas – I foresaw that he would be doing research for at least another fruitful decade, if not many more. Yet our plans came to a halt when he was diagnosed with cancer in 2008. My colleagues and I immediately began to work on the book we wanted to give to him; however, it was not long before we came sadly to understand that Jan would not live to see the result. About a month prior to his passing, we presented the table of contents to him. He was so touched to see the names of his devoted friends and colleagues. I believe that he would have also appreciated the book. Each time that I work with my seventeenth-century sources in Riksarkivet, I look at the place were Jan used to sit. I am left with a sadness knowing that we will no longer be able to discuss our findings over a lunch; however, I feel deeply grateful for all the things I learned in his company.

The editorial group would like to thank the Department of History at Stockholm University, Delegationen för militärhistorisk forskning, and Riksbankens jubileumsfond for their generous financial support of this book. We also would like to thank our language editors Karyn McGettigan and Charlotte Merton for their dedication to the project.

For the editorial group
Anna Maria Forssberg

Introduction

Organizing history

Mats Hallenberg & Anna Maria Forssberg

To a large extent, the history of man is the history of organizations. For as long as there have been written records to study, people have cooperated to make use of scant resources in a more effective way. From churches and states to firms and trade unions, hierarchical organizations have been conspicuous throughout history. However, there are other forms of organization as well: market relationships that are shaped by the balance between supply and demand, and horizontal network relationships based upon trust and friendship. Institutions and norm systems have regulated organizations, just as individuals have been compelled to adjust their behaviour in order to participate in organized activities. Institutions are understood as formalized rules that structure human interaction, such as law and accepted custom. They are based upon norm systems, but custom also includes less formalized ideas, values, and cultural practices. Law and custom have shaped organizational behaviour, as have widely shared norms that are based upon conceptions of honour, godliness, and tradition. This interplay has been dynamic rather than static: effective organization has influenced the character of human institutions, while norms and values have propelled institutional change and organizational reform.

The dynamic interaction of organizations, norm systems, and institutional change is the theme of this book. Fittingly, it highlights the need to organize historical knowledge through the critical use of theory, for one of Jan Glete's strengths as a historian was his ability to adapt theories of modern firms and institutions, and to apply them in a premodern context. According to Glete, history was best viewed as the dynamic growth of complex organizations that ultimately changed the rules of human behaviour. People in traditional and medieval societies mainly interacted within their local community, and trusted only those whom they met in direct, eye-to-eye encounters. This is no longer the case in the modern world, as people are compelled to rely upon large organizations and put their trust in impersonal relationships. The dynamics of this process can be studied with the appropriate analytical tools. The organizational perspective may be just as fruitful for the study of medieval ironworks as in analysing modern marketing campaigns.

In the first chapter of this book, *Jonas Nordin* provides a general survey of Jan Glete's historical writings. Glete's work was driven by theoretical questions; however, his massive empirical research was of equal importance. He based his broad international comparisons upon a variety of material that he compiled from different sources. Friends and colleagues in this anthology continue the discussion on the patterns of historical change. Here you will find chapters that address theoretical and methodological, as well as empirical, points of view. We want to demonstrate the benefits of applying modern theories to medieval and early modern sources. We also wish to provide examples of comparative studies and long-term perspectives on human history. What is of importance to us is that the variety of chapters treats many different parts of the world. As Jan Glete so eloquently proved, theoretical insight opens the way for important studies of all times and all places.

Organizations

Jan Glete's way of applying theories of organization to the analysis of state formation in early modern Europe was at the very heart of his work. The dynastic princes of the period were seen as entrepreneurs rising to the challenge of competition from rival contenders for power. They had to be innovative to conclude lasting alliances with local elites in order to support organizational reform. Economic theory provided the inspiration for this perspective. Joseph Schumpeter considered the entrepreneur to be the prime mover of economic growth, due to his capacity to combine existing resources in new and innovative ways. Edith Penrose developed a model for how modern firms utilize managerial resources to promote expansion into new areas. Although these models are well known to economists, they are seldom recognized by historians interested in state formation.

Mats Hallenberg examines how the theories of Schumpeter and Penrose may be applied to modern states. By using Sweden as an example,

Hallenberg finds both benefits and problems with this perspective. He argues that the focus upon entrepreneurship is less productive when exploring the complex structures of the modern state. The organizational perspective must be combined with notions of legitimacy and voice in order to understand the transformation from dynastic rule to democratic regimes. However, the focus upon organizational growth does, indeed, provide interesting possibilities for studying modern states as producers of knowledge.

Gunner Lind demonstrates the importance of trust when introducing organizational reform. The Danish king's commissaries were important agents of what was a complex state as well as brokers of organizational reform. One of their main tasks was to serve as an interface between the ruler and the army. This is not to say that they were all supporters of the ruling monarch; many of them actually supported the idea of a mixed constitution. However, in the end, their existence was of great benefit to both the king and the army. The monarch gained a means to extend his control of the armed forces, while the army was provided with greater resources. The commissaries were predominantly agents of trust. As the army organization became institutionalized, the need for commissaries declined and their status and power diminished. Nevertheless, these royal agents played an important part in the state-building process.

Creating national navies was an important part of state formation and, as Jan Glete pointed out, naval forces were complex organizations in themselves. The chapters by Jeremy Black and Jaap Bruijn highlight the importance of effective institutional support in facilitating reform and preventing inertia in naval regimes. *Jeremy Black* discusses the development of the British navy in the period 1689–1815. He argues that organizational reform was not initiated as a direct response to naval warfare; rather, it was a long-term effect of international competition during peacetime. The success of the British navy must be attributed to a combination of well-established political institutions and strong interest groups that favoured the maintenance of a powerful navy. According to Black, British supremacy at sea was less the result of radical innovation than a product of sustained political effort and the successful adaptation to geopolitical realities.

The chapter by *Jaap Bruijn* offers a striking contrast, as it describes the decline of the once powerful Dutch navy. The Dutch naval organization that was so effective for most of the seventeenth century had begun to deteriorate by the start of the eighteenth century. Bruijn provides an illustrative example of a conflict between a Dutch admiral and his British colleagues during the War of the Spanish Succession (1701–1714). He demonstrates that what might appear to be an insignificant conflict of rank in fact mirrors the decline of the Dutch Republic as a sea power. Dutch naval organization, which was based upon a decentralized structure of five regional admiralties, suffered from a lack of money and competent leadership. Meanwhile, national pride and vested interests among naval officers combined to block any attempts at organizational reform. Dutch naval officers still clung to the memory of their glorious past; in reality, however, they could no longer compare to the effective organization of their English allies. A lack of institutional support and the resulting organizational inertia had eventually proved fatal.

The warship *Vasa*, which is on display in Stockholm, is a symbol of both organizational power and dismal failure. Built in 1628, the magnificent *Vasa* foundered on her maiden voyage after sailing a mere mile from the Stockholm Castle. She was salvaged from the bottom of the sea in 1961 and an ambitious restoration programme was launched. The *Vasa* is now one of Stockholm's most popular tourist attrations: a reminder of the time when the Swedish navy dominated the Baltic and of the countless lives that were sacrificed in the process. The director of the Vasa Museum, *Marika Hedin*, gives her view on the appeal of this cultural icon and discusses how to increase the allure of maritime heritage while still providing important material for research. The display of the warship might be seen as an attempt to reorganize history: to make the cultural icon of the past communicate directly with the present.

The chapters in the *Organizations* section of the book demonstrate the delicate balance between demands for organizational reform and the necessity of recognizing the traditional status and vested interests of elite groups. Effective organization is only achievable as long as the benefits can be harmonized with the values and norm systems that are prevalent in society. While entrepreneurial vision may be the trigger that initiates organizational growth, successive adaptation to a changing environment seems to be the key to sustaining complex organizations over long periods.

Norm systems

Organizational legitimacy – the ability to aggregate interests and justify collective action within the existing norm systems – is a key factor in the success of both states and enterprises. Jan Glete focused upon local elites when discussing the state-building process but the scope may well be extended to include other groups. *Anna Maria Forssberg* analyses the official declarations of war that Sweden and France published when entering the Thirty Years War. She argues they should be understood with regard to their functions and political context. The official proclamations were, indeed, integrated parts of sophisticated information systems, and clearly demonstrate the impact of norm systems in seventeenth-century France and Sweden. The comparative approach suggests that the ideological concept of just war (*bellum iustum*) was just as important in Richelieu's France as it was in Protestant Sweden. However, the declarations differed substantially since their purpose and intended audiences were not the same. What was described as a war against Spain in France was not represented as a war at all in the Swedish texts.

Prevailing norm systems might well obstruct organizational reform. *Enrique Martínez Ruiz* and *Magdalena de Pazzis Pi Corrales* describe the history of the Castilian Guards: a military institution that, in spite of losing most of its military function, persisted in essentially the same form throughout the sixteenth and seventeenth centuries. The heavy cavalry troops that constituted the Guards were essentially kept as a domestic army reserve, unlike the celebrated *tercios* that were constantly deployed to fight on foreign soil. The aristocracy wanted to preserve the mounted companies as part of a noble tradition, which may explain the survival of the Castilian Guards. Lack of pressure from the outside made the Guards less responsive to reform, while the aristocrats were reluctant to contribute to the war effort. Funds were often scant. Gradually, the local elite lost interest in buying the state's protection and concentrated instead upon defending their historical privileges. Thus institutional inertia may be understood from a normative perspective.

Some say that norm systems make up the foundation upon which societies are based and are vital to the understanding of human interaction. *Arne Jarrick* and *Maria Wallenberg Bondesson* address the history of legislation from an evolutionary perspective, offering operational tools for comparing law codes from widely different places and periods of time. The authors argue that human institutions are created and transformed through a process of cumulative change, as new generations seek to modify and reconstruct existing regulations. Law codes are particularly well suited to illustrate this process; they can be found in nearly all civilized societies and explicitly regulate human interaction. Careful classification of their contents may solve the methodological problems of comparing two sources as vastly different as the Laws of Hammurabi (*c.*1760 BC) and the Tang code from the seventh century AD. By structuring data into classificatory trees, the authors demonstrate that differences and similarities may be easily determined. This approach presents interesting possibilities for studying the interplay between norm systems and institutional change.

Christer Ericsson also carries out a comparison of value systems, although in an entirely different context. Ericsson studies how industrial companies in both Sweden and Japan promoted organized sport as a way to establish cooperation between employers and employees. The sporting ethos held positive connotations of teamwork and physical soundness; thus sport functioned as an important free zone for creating consensus in a capitalist society. Ericsson demonstrates that the sports movement was a highly flexible institution: in Sweden, it was regarded as a popular democratic movement that company managers could use; in Japan, the companies themselves organized it directly. Sport was used in company strategies in both countries as a way of strengthening company spirit: an effective means of inspiring workers to be more willing to accept authority and to increase productivity. Therefore, Ericsson provides support for Jarrick and Wallenberg's thesis that institutions are, indeed, 'cultural constructs' that function only as long as the people (or culture) involved recognize them.

The *Norm Systems* section maintains that the interaction between norm systems and human institutions can have widely different outcomes. As with propaganda systems and even law codes, institutions must be flexible in order to accommodate different sets of norms. Thus the organizational inertia that plagued the Castilian Guards may be attributed to it being an aristocratic enclave, clearly detached from the norms and demands that permeated other parts of the Spanish armed forces. On the other hand, organized sport has proven flexible enough to be a lasting success in widely different contexts: industrialists in both Sweden and Japan have adapted and utilized its norms and values to promote corporate cohesion.

Institutional change

Historians take a great interest in change. Since history is nothing if not the investigation of the past, it must come up with plausible answers to the problem of why some things change, while others remain. Explaining institutional change poses an intellectual challenge since institutions have often been analysed in terms of function (that is to say, an institution exists because it fulfils a present need in human society). However, institutions in modern society are clearly very different from their medieval counterparts. Therefore, how do we identify the important passages in time that created the systems we have today? What were the incentives for institutional change?

Johan Söderberg and Leos Müller analyse the dynamic growth of sea-borne trade in the early modern era. Many scholars have attributed the expansion of overseas shipping to the impact of the steam engine. These chapters suggest that important changes occurred long before the Industrial Revolution; the authors discuss different variables that may have contributed to this development. *Johan Söderberg* maintains that, since overseas shipping facilitated human contact and ultimately stimulated the price revolution as well as the globalization of the world economy, it must be seen as an important component of modernity. Söderberg finds that both improved safety (lower protection costs) and increased productivity (the construction of larger vessels) were important for the expansion of Swedish maritime trade during the late medieval period up to the nineteenth century. Söderberg suggests that the Swedish state played a pivotal role up to the eighteenth century in the success of Swedish merchant shipping by providing naval protection and the necessary knowledge for constructing larger vessels. Eventually, ship-owners learned how to operate medium-sized vessels with smaller crews. Therefore, the increase in productivity from the eighteenth century was the cumulative effect of private entrepreneurs learning how to optimize their resources.

Leos Müller has studied the records of the Swedish Convoy Office, which organized the protection of the merchant marine in the eighteenth century. He argues that low protection costs may explain why Sweden's mercantile fleet was the fifth largest in Europe by 1800. Unlike Britain or France, Sweden lacked the necessary means to guarantee naval protection for her mercantile fleet. However, while the great maritime powers were busy attacking each other's merchantmen, Swedish neutrality in the great Anglo–French conflicts provided ship owners with an opportunity to win a share of the market. The Swedish Convoy Office specialized in concluding bilateral agreements with the Barbary pirates of North Africa, thus providing the necessary security for Swedish shipping to expand in the Mediterranean. Ironically, the collapse of Sweden's imperial ambitions at the beginning of the eighteenth century allowed the merchant marine to be dynamic and innovative in the following period.

Ulf Jonsson's chapter also concerns trade relations, but in the globalized context of the late twentieth century. While focusing upon soybean production in the Southern Cone of Latin America, Jonsson discusses the emergence of a new food regime to challenge the hegemony of Europe and North America. By concentrating upon the large-scale production of agricultural products aimed at foreign markets, Brazil particularly seems to have strengthened its position in global trade. This development holds an important paradox: while European food producers have become increasingly sensitive to ecological factors, countries such as Brazil have focused upon industrial production with little regard for the environmental costs. Changing norms seem to trigger institutional changes in the geopolitics of food, as when European consumers demand sustainable food production. However, large-scale producers in South America may well be those who benefit from this kind of shift, and not the environmentally aware farmers of Western Europe.

Bo Franzén studies institutional changes in medieval iron production. Iron-mining and steel manufacturing holds a special place in Swedish history, and scholars have often emphasized its local, small-scale character. Franzén argues the late medieval iron industry was, in fact, highly capital-intensive: it required large quantities of both fixed and floating capital. While production units (smelting-houses) seem to have fallen in price during the period 1385–1504, large investments were still needed to cover transport, labour, and raw materials. Iron production was a complicated process that involved different stages and transactions; therefore, access to credit was crucial. Smelting-house returns were generally higher than the yield from farmland, which signifies the development of a credit market that could provide the means for procuring a sufficient work-force.

The diffusion of military reform is the subject of *Gunnar Åselius*' chapter. The divisional system that was introduced in the French army in the middle of the eighteenth century facilitated the effective organization of mass armies of conscripted soldiers. Åselius studies how this system was introduced in the Swedish army in 1813–1814. Sweden's involvement in the international coalition against Napoleon served as the impetus for institutional change. The introduction of general conscription in 1812 provided the army with the necessary manpower; however, a lack of educated officers obstructed the reform process. Informal contact between officers still played an important part in the organization, even though the new more bureaucratic system was implemented during successive campaigns. The commander-in-chief was dependent upon receiving correct information, and he therefore preferred to have personal adjutants report directly from different parts of the battlefield. Thus the introduction of a more hierarchical organization could be harmonized with the informal networks that were already in place within the officer corps.

Klas Åmark concludes the discussions about organization, norm systems, and institutional change by analysing the introduction of individual social security systems in Sweden and Norway. Åmark finds important similarities as well as differences when comparing the welfare systems of the two Nordic countries. As the Social Democratic Party came to dominate domestic politics in Sweden starting in the late 1940s, the changes appeared to be more far-reaching in that country. The social security system was designed to include all wage-earners whatever their profession. In Norway, this process was more cautious. Modifications were often introduced using the Swedish system as a model. Åmark stresses the importance of path dependency to institutional change. Pragmatism and existing norms and institutions heavily influenced new solutions in both countries; this characterized the reform process. The welfare systems that eventually emerged were hardly products of a radical reform spirit; they were the outcome of a series of compromises that involved a number of agents and organizations.

The chapters addressing *Institutional Change* all point to the same conclusion: lasting reform is not always the direct result of radical innovation; it is more often the net result of a process that involves several agents interacting within the existing structures. This does not mean that the outcome may not be radical; however, the process of history is often more complex than one might assume. Human institutions generally carry with them important traits from their antecedants. The chapters in this volume all stress the dynamic interplay between systems. Organizational reform may well be initiated from above. However, any proposed scheme will have to be adjusted to prevailing norm systems in order to achieve lasting institutional change. Organizations seem to be generally sensitive to changes in adjoining systems, while many institutions and norm systems are durable structures with great continuity over time.

The purpose of this book is to demonstrate the benefits of organizing history according to a specific model: the institutional theory that pervaded so much of Jan Glete's work. The interplay between organizations, norm systems, and institutional change clearly provides a useful perspective on the process of history. This is obviously not the only way to organize history, nor is it necessarily the best. However, the authors of this volume have endeavoured to pay their respects to a sorely missed colleague by addressing not only the tenor but the range of his work. We have applied some of Jan Glete's methods and theories to our own research in order to pose new questions and, hopefully, provide some new answers as well. If we inspire other historians to do likewise, then we will certainly consider this work to have been a success.

CHAPTER 1

The Historian Jan Glete

A brief overview

Jonas Nordin

Jan Glete was born on 1 September 1947 in Västerås, Sweden. Although the city is not particularly large, it is nevertheless old and significant in Swedish history. Västerås is also an important industrial centre, with Sweden's largest inland deep-water port. Formerly it also held the head office of Allmänna svenska elektriska aktiebolaget, ASEA. In 1988 ASEA merged with Brown Boveri and became today's ABB. The ABB Group still dominates the city's industry and has also deeply influenced the research of Jan Glete.

Jan was the only child of Allan and Mary Glete. Allan Glete was a technical engineer at ASEA. In the preface to Jan Glete's survey marking the centenary of ASEA, he recapitulates how he, as a child, asked his father what was hidden inside the tower of the corporation's main building in Västerås. 'It houses an archive,' his father replied. Little did he know that, a quarter of a century later, his son would plough through this archive as an established academic historian.

In 1966 Jan Glete graduated from Västerås Gymnasium, which was founded in 1623, making it Sweden's first and oldest senior high school. He began his academic studies at Stockholm University in the autumn term of 1967, and received his M.A. at the Faculty of Social Sciences in October 1969. Glete completed courses in political science, history, and macroeconomics. His undergraduate dissertation on social science was submitted to his advisor, Associate Professor Elmar Nyman, and dealt with the dissolution of the union between Sweden and Norway and its influence on the Swedish armament.[1] Glete also wrote an undergraduate dissertation under the tutorship of Professor Sven-Ulric Palme on the Social Democratic Women's Federation's views on military defence in the 1930s.[2] Glete was involved in the SSU, the Social Democratic Youth Organization, and later wrote a book about its Stockholm branch.

Although Glete had received his first degree and had already begun his postgraduate studies, he also presented yet another undergraduate dissertation in October 1972, this time in economic history. In this research, he investigated the Boliden Metalwork's relations to Ivar Kreuger and the Swedish Match Company. Glete came to pursue this investigation in his doctoral thesis, which he presented on 12 December 1975. Glete's thesis was the first book to be published in the research project 'The Kreuger Group on the Swedish and international capital market' (*Kreugerkoncernen på svensk och internationell kapitalmarknad*), headed by Sven-Ulric Palme and financed by the Bank of Sweden Tercentenary Foundation. Kreuger, the Match King and financial demon, had expanded his companies in the 1920s using borrowed capital from the US. This capital was re-lended to European governments that were short of foreign currency, in exchange for monopoly rights on the production of matches. Glete investigated in his thesis Kreuger's involvement with the Swedish mining company Boliden, which had been seriously affected by the financial kingpin's downfall. The collaboration between Swedish Match and Boliden brought about a collision between two opposing corporate cultures: Kreuger's quest for short-term profits through financial speculation; and the mining company's technical and long-term investment concerns. The collapse of the Kreuger Group revealed obscure ownership conditions among its component companies; one of the consequences was Lex Boliden, the law which until 1983 limited foreigners' rights to acquire properties and natural resources in Sweden.[3]

Glete's thesis drew strong criticism from the polemic literary critic Sven Stolpe in a newspaper review. Stolpe thought the book was a low-water-mark in Swedish scholarship: 'The book is, thus, an unscientific lampoon, which admits with unusual sincerity that no literature that does not support the view of Ivar Kreuger's enemies will even be considered!'[4] The reason for Stolpe's critique was that Glete ignored some of the studies, notably professor Robert Kristensson's, which tried to prove that Kreuger had done nothing illegal and that the court's verdict stemmed from a lack of insight into modern bookkeeping. According to Stolpe, Glete had dismissed the apologetic literature 'with customary academic snootiness' (*i känd akademisk snorkstil*). Stolpe's review ended with a call for a thorough intellectual house-cleaning at Swedish universities.[5] Associate Professor of Business Economics Anders Edström gave a much more positive assessment in another newspaper review. He thought that Glete's detailed investigation offered valuable insights into the role of mutual trust on a personal level in modern business enterprises. Since Kreuger was the only person to have full overview, his decisions could never be challenged. Business partners put unconditional faith in his judgements, which proved to be fatal. According to Edström, the same lack of safety valves could be seen even in modern, large-scale enterprises.[6]

Later examinations have affirmed Glete's prudence in not engaging in polemics over 'Kreuger propaganda', as it has been labelled. These studies have been proven to be of little or no value. Kreuger's biographer Lars-Erik Thunholm concluded: 'The only thing that needs to be said about Kristensson's way of counting stocks and debentures as "structural assets" is that there is no support whatsoever for this method of account in the Companies Act, nor in its preparatory work or the current commentaries. [...] What Kristensson is up to have is actually a cheap conjuring trick, which is all the more surprising when it comes from a professor of industrial economy.'[7]

Glete returned to Ivar Kreuger on several occasions in his research, most notably in the book *Kreugerkoncernen och krisen på svensk aktiemarknad* (The Kreuger Group and the Swedish stock market crisis). This voluminous investigation consists of four separate studies that can each be read separately. The first outlines the development and crisis of the Swedish stock market, banking, and industry until the mid 1920s. The second study examines the origin, early development, and, especially, the financing of the Kreuger Group, 1908–1924. This is followed by an extensive investigation of the Kreuger Group's financial involvement as a shareholder in other Swedish companies, 1925–1932. Finally, Glete studies the credit extended by the Swedish banks to the Kreuger Group 1917–1932. As can be deduced from this brief summary, his main purpose with the book was to investigate the importance of venture capital in the entrepreneurial process. When the Kreuger Group collapsed in 1932, it was not only due to Ivar Kreuger's personal conduct; he happened to be the biggest actor in an unrestrained capitalist economy and, as such, only behaved in a way that was expected of him. Nevertheless, he helped to shape liberal opinion in a period of industrial recovery and growth after the crisis of the early 1920s. It was generally assumed that growth would be durable, and the progress of Sweden's economy boosted national self-esteem. Glete concluded: 'It was a time when it seemed both less necessary and less opportune to recommend active and planned state interventions in the Swedish economy.'[8]

The disintegration of the Kreuger Group in 1932 had spawned endless myths and sensationalist writing in Sweden. With his study, Glete tried to set things to rights. Kreuger was undoubtedly a key figure because of the size of his corporation and the influence of his capital; however, as an economic theorist, he was more archetypal than unique. He could not comprehend that the fundamental problems in both politics and the economy of the early 1920s were still unsolved, and his bold gambles on future profits did not save him from an unpleasant awakening in the early 1930s. Although the losses for Swedish shareholders were much more limited in the 1930s than they had been in the 1920s, the dramatic collapse of the Kreuger Group became a legend that affected public opinion for decades to come.

Author and former film director Kenne Fant reviewed the book in the leading Swedish morning newspaper *Dagens Nyheter*. He was duly impressed: 'The eminently organized material, the lucid tables, and, not least, the clear language' made the intricate topic easy to grasp, especially if one had some prior acquaintance with the subject.[9] Fant also stressed the pioneering quality of Glete's work. Although the personality of Ivar Kreuger had continued to attract the attention of later generations, few serious studies had seen the light of day and his character, therefore, remained elusive. However, speculations about Kreuger's personality were alien to Glete and his altogether rational approach to the subject. He left this topic for others to explore.

Associate professor

Jan Glete was appointed associate professor at Stockholm University on 12 October 1977. Professor of Economic History Karl-Gustaf Hildebrand reviewed the application, and was highly appreciative. Glete's thesis was described as 'unexpectedly lucid, perspicuous, and generally convincing. It should be considered a pioneering effort, and the result gives evidence not only of significant insight and painstaking research, but also of a clear sense of proportion and an unbiased common sense'.[10]

Although Glete's second book, *Kreugerkoncernen och krisen på svensk aktiemarknad*, was not yet finished, Hildebrand was positive about the manuscript, which was handed in for assessment. 'On the whole, the manuscript denotes a broadening of Glete's competence; considering the time at his disposal, what is noteworthy is not that it is unfinished, but how far he has got with it.'[11]

Glete's broad competence became even more conspicuous with another work handed in for assessment, and which revealed another of his main interests as a scholar: naval history. The extensive study 'Svenska örlogsfartyg 1521–1560: flottans uppbyggnad under ett tekniskt brytningsskede' (Swedish warships 1521–1560: the expansion of the navy in a period of technological transition) was published in *Forum navale* (yearbook for *Sjöhistoriska samfundet*, the Swedish Society for Maritime History). Along with extensive appendices, the writing nearly filled two consecutive volumes. It was a ground-breaking study of the naval expansion of King Gustav I in the first half of the sixteenth century. The development of the navy during this period was only sketchily known until Glete's investigation. He was able to illustrate, using the registers of shipping, a tremendous naval expansion that had previously been largely ignored by historians. This expansion was carried through prudently, without overstraining the state coffers, which was otherwise so common in this period of general military growth in Europe. With the building of a galley fleet, a new kind of vessel was introduced in the Baltic; this demonstrates the innovativeness of Gustav I. The strengthening of the navy served the purpose of securing Sweden's borders, but it also enabled Gustav I to pursue a more active policy of controlling trade routes in the Baltic. Although Gustav I was able to restrain his desire for conquest, he nevertheless handed over to his successors a tool for military expansion. The origins of the Swedish imperial experience in the seventeenth century, therefore, should be traced back to the era of Gustav I.[12] Glete in his appendices revised, corrected, and completed the existing register of shipping for the period, thereby demonstrating his often-repeated conviction: systematically presented empirical findings are of intrinsic value to other scholars.[13]

Hildebrand was impressed by Glete's laborious work on the fiscal sources and his ability to draw valuable conclusions on general issues from detailed empirical studies. He found the investigation pioneering in method and fruitful in approach. Hildebrand was certain that the necessary requirements for becoming an associate professor were already demonstrated in Glete's thesis; nevertheless, he went on to note that Glete had prepared further treatises, which made his nomination undisputable.

The ASEA project and network studies

In the years that followed, Glete was involved in writing the history of ASEA, which also financed the project. However, in order to ensure the independence of his research, the study was carried out at the Stockholm School of Economics (*Handelshögskolan*) and the Institute for Economic and Business History Research (*Ekonomisk-historiska forskningsinstitutet*). The research grant lasted over five years (1977–1983) and led to a voluminous official monograph and a smaller book that summarized Glete's conclusions as well as broadened the perspective.[14] His results were not revolutionary, although the two books contained a lot of new empirical findings. In many respects, the book tells the story of the modernization of Sweden through large-scale projects such as the introduction of street lighting, the building of electrical tramways and railways, the construction of hydro-electric power stations, the development of nuclear power, and so on. Many of these long-term, large-scale projects were state funded, which explains how ASEA could continue to develop even during times of recession.

People's stories were never central to Glete's research, and one commentator, Erik Zander, a former employee of ASEA, criticized him for not leaving any room in his work for the industrial workers and clerks.[15] Instead, Glete had seized the opportunity to enter more deeply into questions about the role of technique in complex organizations. Technique and organizations are two of the main traits in his research; the third was power – or, rather, influence, since he paid a lot of attention to informal power structures. His special talent lay in the ability to combine observations from his various fields of research. When he later centred his attention on European state-formation, his earlier focus led him to original conclusions.

Glete remained at the Institute for Economic and Business History Research following the completion of the ASEA project. During this period, Jan Glete also met his wife, Sang Kum Yeo. Together they had a daughter, Jihi, born in 1983. For another two years he continued to study organizational structures in trade and industry. Glete analysed the differences in business cultures between the financial and the industrial sectors in the book *Ägande och industriell omvandling: Ägargrupper, skogsindustri och verkstadsindustri, 1850–1880* (Ownership and industrial transformation: proprietary groups, the forestry industry, and manufacturing industry, 1850–1880). This study was later revisited in *Nätverk i näringslivet: Ägande och industriell omvandling i det mogna industrisamhället, 1920–1990* (Networks in the economy: ownership and industrial transformation in the developed industrial society, 1920–1990). He examined in this book how an industrial society could continue to develop even though no new major corporations were established, and whether existent structures hamper new initiatives and block new entrepreneurs.

Glete had observed that when financial operators ran industrial enterprises, the actors' differing experiences created tension. He found that business economists had largely ignored this problem, which had not been explained in traditional economic theory. Therefore, he combined theories on path dependency (Joseph Schumpeter); on limited rationality and the incomplete cognitive capacity of both individuals and organizations (Herbert Simon); on the importance of transactional costs in the founding of companies (Coase & Williamson); and different assumptions on networking developed by economic theorists (Gunnar Eliasson, among others). Glete concluded that behaviour varied between branches due to varying experiences and networks. The different understandings of business-owners, executives and credit agencies can lead to tension, yet they can also serve as an impetus for transformation. As a by-product, he also developed hypotheses on how supply and demand has shaped companies with different priorities; this is a perspective that he found was surprisingly neglected in traditional business history. He also made important remarks on how the ownership structures and large-scale companies of the industrial breakthrough (*c.*1890–1920) have marked Swedish economy up to the present day.

The business historian Hans Sjögren commended *Nätverk i näringslivet* in the leading Swedish historical journal *Historisk tidskrift*; however, he regretted the book's lack of international comparison. Above all, Sjögren criticized Glete for his somewhat one-sided focus on large companies. Sjögren wrote that big industrial concerns are becoming an anachronism in the modern economy, and subsidiary companies with substantial growth potential can be concealed in old structures in the same way that small, seemingly independent companies can be part of major corporations.[16] Glete later responded to this criticism in a way that was typical for him.

He admitted that there could be theoretical difficulties in fixing the borders between various types of company. However, he maintained that, in this case, he had made a division that was unequivocally supported by the empirical evidence. He did not make theoretical assumptions; he interpreted and tried to explain what the sources revealed.[17]

Nätverk i näringslivet was widely discussed outside the academy as well. Nils-Eric Sandberg, editorial writer in the Liberal morning newspaper *Dagens Nyheter*, used the book to criticize Swedish monetary policy and the Social Democrats' jaundiced view on enterprise. At the same time, he rejected Glete's talk of the power of the corporate proprietors. Sandberg claimed that it is always the consumers – or perhaps the politicians – who hold the power in an economy subject to competition.[18] This was, of course, a political cliché, which hardly won the support of Jan Glete.

Official and political engagements

During the years 1985–1990, a committee appointed by the Swedish Government worked on a major survey on democracy and the distribution of power in Sweden. This project was generally referred to as *Maktutredningen* (the Power Inquiry), and involved well over a hundred scholars. The committee produced some twenty books and more than a hundred articles before presenting its final report to the Government. Glete contributed to the investigation with a study on the merger of companies into large corporations with a few principal owners, by revealing how this agglomeration affected the functioning of democracy. His conclusions made their way into the committee's final report; he found that two separate elite groups had dominated business and politics in twentieth-century Sweden. This observation was not, in itself, original. However, he further remarked that these two distinct groups had been formed during the industrial breakthrough, and had replaced a more homogenous bourgeoisie who had dominated not only trade and industry, but also politics and the bureaucracy. Glete asked: Did the large industrial owners still exercise informal influence over politics? He argued that this was, indeed, a potential threat, but, above all, he argued that control over capital when restricted to narrow groups could severely obstruct industrial initiative and enterprise.[19]

Glete was politically engaged in the Social Democratic movement. Especially in his younger days, he had been active in the youth and student organizations of the dominant political party in Sweden. He had left Västerås and moved to the capital to pursue his studies, and he contributed to the history written for the centenary of the Stockholm branch of the Social Democratic Youth Organization. The book has a picture of a young and animated Jan Glete in his 'favourite place', as the caption reads: on the rostrum.[20]

There are two kinds of lecturer in academe. There are those who are the travelling salesmen of speech, moving restlessly from one performance to the next and delivering more or less the same talk, thus advertising themselves and some particular aspect of their research. And then there are those who take lecturing just as seriously as they do publishing, carefully preparing their appearances, always taking pains to deliver new and original findings, and rarely repeating themselves. Glete was the latter. Compared to many other scholars of similar status, Glete's appearances might seem moderate in number. However, he only accepted invitations to conferences and seminars if he was certain that he could deliver a weighty contribution to the topic at hand. Or, when he was appealed to by organizers, he made it very clear that he had no insight whatsoever into the subject and, if he were to participate, he would only talk about matters that he mastered – take it or leave it. In the end, it always turned out that his off-topic speech was very much to the point and added quite substantially to the discussion. The great share of his speeches that have later been published bears testimony to how rigorously he prepared his appearances. It is also revealing that he listed speeches in his own bibliography alongside his printed works – without discrimination. For Glete, a lecture was just another medium of presenting original research.

Indulgence in naval history

Jan Glete had already received a large grant from the Swedish Council for Social Science Research (*Humanistisk-samhällsvetenskapliga forskningsrådet*, HSFR) while he was finishing his studies on ASEA. This gave him the opportunity to indulge his interest in maritime history. This was where his heart truly lay and, although his work had been very successful, his excursions into business history have to be characterized as a detour from his real passion. He had been keeping abreast of the literature and collecting data since the 1960s on early modern navies, with special interest in their quantitative and technological development. Although not maritime history, *stricto sensu*, the same aspects were central to a study he wrote in 1985 on Sweden's invasion security in 1850–1880: *Kustförsvar i omvandling* (Coastal defence in transformation). Here he showed interest in the novel armed structures and operational units that had been developed during the industrial transformation of the nineteenth century, and how they affected military doctrine.

His thorough studies in various European archives and literature in several languages resulted in an authoritative two-volume monograph: *Navies and Nations: Warships, Navies, and State Building in Europe and America, 1500–1860* (1993). The title already reveals its imposing scope. His ambition was to survey naval development in the Western World during three and a half centuries, the era of the great sailing-ships. The study was based upon an impressive set of statistics, presented in an extensive appendix with data on all navies in Europe and the Americas.

Glete rejected the term Military Revolution for several reasons. For navies, he preferred to use two other concepts: the Gunpowder Revolution and the Bureaucratic Revolution, thus once again pointing to technique and organization. The first occurred in approximately 1500, when the type of great, heavily armed sailing-ship that would dominate the seas for centuries to come had found its recognized form. The second took place some 150 years later when the state established a monopoly on violence at sea, and so superseded cities, trading companies, and privateers.

Navies were crucial to the advent of the modern state for Glete. They preceded both the army and the civil administration in becoming the first wholly state-controlled professional organizations. State control was necessitated by previously unheard-of demands for money, preparation, coordination, and leadership. In short, technical needs imposed organizational change. Glete assessed the states' abilities by their organizational efficiency. In a classification that he himself introduced, this could be either static or dynamic. Static efficiency was proven by the ability to make optimal use of existing resources. Dynamic efficiency was demonstrated by the capacity for creative improvement.

Naval history had long been the province of specialists and was rarely subjected to syntheses speaking to larger historical processes. The general picture was also incomplete, not to say distorted, due to an excessive number of studies on navies at war. In reality, navies were not easily dismantled during peacetime and, in contrast to armies, their success was not mainly measured in battle triumphs. Accordingly, Glete could prove that, up until the 1780s, the Royal Danish Navy remained the largest in the Baltic, although Denmark had not been involved in war since the early 1720s. Its main objective was to act as a deterrent and to protect the Danish merchant fleet.

The historian Ole Feldbæk reviewed the two volumes for the Danish journal *Historisk tidsskrift*, and was impressed by Glete's accomplishment. He wrote:

> Large syntheses can only rarely withstand critical examination of the raw data. Can the author really maintain exact sets of data, when he is incessantly moving between Russian coastal flotillas, Algerian corsairs, Venetian galleys, the Atlantic powers' high-sea fleets and the Sultanate of Oman's marine? A spot check in an area where this reviewer feels himself competent – the Danish Navy – suggests that Jan Glete is actually able to do that. He is well acquainted with the Danish literature, even the very latest; furthermore, he has treated a fair amount of Danish archival sources; his data has to be characterized as reliable and his accounts as satisfactory. And not least through his comparative quantifications he is able to reach new and interesting conclusions. [...] Both as a narrative and as a reference work, *Navies and Nations* is a monumental accomplishment, which fills all the requirements of becoming the standard work in international scholarship.[21]

Another commentator, W. J. R. Gardner at the naval historical branch of the UK Ministry of Defence, was equally impressed. In a review article, he pointed out the regrettable lack of academic interest in naval history. This was a field left to amateurs with a profound insight into naval technique and less insight into general historiography, or to academic historians who liked to generalize about marine issues, yet had only a shallow understanding of the technical side of the subject. Glete, he contended, managed to bridge the gap between these two opposites – his two-volume set had 'an aim breathtaking in its ambitions by any standards' and it was a book 'of great importance'.[22] Gardner was unreservedly impressed by Glete's collection of data, which he thought would prove useful to other scholars for a long time to come. He also applauded Glete's wider objective to connect the rise of the sailing navies with that of the states they served. He found Glete's suggestions interesting enough to stimulate further discussion, and although he was not totally convinced, his conclusion was that 'Glete deserves considerable plaudits for his great industry in collating and to a large extent standardizing such a large amount of useful data. That he falls short of being able to substantiate fully his general theory should not blind us to the worth of the attempt.'[23]

Richard Dowling made much the same point in a short and mostly descriptive notice in *History*: 'The labour that has gone into [the book] is clearly immense, and fellow toilers in the field will have had their efforts made that much easier by the consolidation of information from so many sources. Glete wishes his work to stimulate further research; I believe he will achieve his aim.'[24]

Nicholas Rodger at the National Maritime Museum in Greenwich joined the chorus of praise: 'The combination of a powerful theoretical instrument and a statistical base of unique range and detail makes a book of great importance. It is a work of high seriousness in the Germanic academic tradition, rich and laden, and it will undoubtedly take some time to have its full effect, but it is safe to predict that it will transform the study of naval history, and the understanding of naval history by non-specialist historians.' Rodger's review ended with the statement: 'It is simply the most important book in naval history for twenty years, and will leave the subject transformed.'[25]

A colleague among colleagues

By this time, Jan Glete had returned to his alma mater, Stockholm University. He continued his study of early modern navies with a special research grant awarded by the Faculty of Humanities for the years 1992–1998. During the same period Glete took up teaching for the first time. Although he had held occasional courses for postgraduate students, he had never had the opportunity or the inclination to teach at undergraduate level.

The tuition of postgraduate students in the Department of History mainly took place in special seminars that were led by an expert from the department's senior staff. One of the seminars entitled *Stat och samhälle* (State and Society) was devoted to the political history of the seventeenth and eighteenth centuries. Glete had attended it as a guest, not as a teacher. This was when I first met Jan Glete. I was a young postgraduate student, insecure about my position and all the new routines and individuals whom I did not know at the time. Glete was just one of all those unfamiliar faces and he seemed especially mysterious to me. As I recall, he generally sat silent during the discussions, rarely looking up, and even occasionally falling asleep. Our seminar administrator, Harald Gustafsson, nevertheless treated him with great respect and, at the end of the seminar, he always let Glete have the final say. Although he had appeared quite uninterested and aloof during the seminar, he would always deliver cogent and carefully prepared remarks that concluded the discussion and cut any Gordian knots. I soon realized that his opinions very much deserved my attention.

Harald Gustafsson left Stockholm in the autumn of 1993 for a new position in Lund, leaving the seminar without its administrator and a handful of doctoral students without a supervisor. The situation needed to be resolved quickly, and there were no teachers with the right qualifications among the ordinary staff. Glete was the only person on hand with proper knowledge of the political history of the seventeenth and eighteenth centuries. However, he had no steady position and no teaching experience to speak of. In addition, many of his colleagues who had never had reason to examine his work considered him somewhat unconventional. Therefore, the head of the department held an informal meeting where he asked whether we, the postgraduates, were willing to accept Glete as our administrator and supervisor. We, who had got to know him through the seminar, were not at all hesitant, and willingly went along with the proposition.

This solution surprised some of Glete's colleagues. Working at a university department not only involves teaching and doing research, it is also about administration and politics. Glete had never taken part in the latter, and this was a fact that could appear provoking to some. However, since Glete had always been employed on temporary grants, he had not had much time for anything other than keeping his benefactors satisfied by producing research. At a much later stage, when he was drawn into the administration, he proved his capability in this area as well. For example, early on he saw the necessity to respond to the new demands of research politics. In Sweden, as elsewhere, state authorities have begun to ask for measurable results and accountability from the scholarly community. As Glete argued, regardless of whether or not one likes this development, it is better to act rather than to react to what is unavoidable. The new and unified research programme that was adopted by the Department of History in 2009 was, thus, by and large his invention.

Glete was a humble person. Although he received ever-growing attention for his work, he never let his successes go to his head. He could talk enthusiastically for hours about new findings or the various theories he was developing, but he rarely, if ever, mentioned that he had published a new book or had received a good review. This was an appealing side to his character, but one that also affected his pupils. He was always supportive of his postgraduate students' research, but he never was one for promoting them in scholarly competition. Whereas some supervisors push their protégés forward in every possible situation and drag them into various networks, Glete put his trust in the hope that brilliance and hard work would always prevail in the end – as it had done for him. He never quite understood the importance of politics in such affairs. On a private level, however, he was always very loyal toward the young postgraduate students at the department, even those with whom he had no professional connection. He always showed up at conferences to listen when a junior colleague was to present a paper, regardless of the topic. Of all the senior staff, Glete probably had the best overview of what the young scholars in the department were actually doing.

Glete's interest in naval history naturally led him to *Sjöhistoriska samfundet*, where he was a board member since 1993 and vice-president between 1996 and 2009. He took a leading role in the society's activities, not to mention its publications. Glete kept an eye open for interesting works within the scope of the society, and several publications were the product of his initiative. Through the Sune Örtendahl Foundation, *Sjöhistoriska samfundet* also managed a large donation to support its publishing activities. Glete, with his understanding of finance, was well suited to administer the foundation's endowment.[26]

More on navies, warfare, and state-building

Glete was made a professor at Stockholm University in 1999. By that time, he had become a major international authority on naval history. When Jeremy Black, general editor of the series *Warfare and History*, wanted a survey on early modern maritime warfare, Glete was the natural choice for the assignment.

In *Warfare at Sea, 1500–1650*, Glete examined the technical progress of naval warfare and demonstrated how this development became a key factor in the global dominion of the European powers. However, in line with his general ambition, he did not confine his study to the technical side of warfare; he also related it to large-scale processes, especially state-building. Apart from stressing technical progress, Glete maintained that the transformation of naval warfare was economic, political and social, and that adaptability to change was decisive for success. Merchant fleets were protected by naval force to an increasing degree, and states that succeeded in securing a monopoly on violence were not only best at securing, they were also leaders at promoting trade. For instance, the Habsburgs and the Ottomans were powers that relied upon traditional galley technology, and they were unable to extend their trade outside the Mediterranean. The opposite was true of the Dutch Republic that, through technical and entrepreneurial skill, managed even to infiltrate the Spanish overseas empire. An important consequence was that the economic and political centre of the Continent was transferred from the Mediterranean to North-Western Europe.

In a review of the book, David Loades found the explanation for this change both interesting and suggestive. He praised Glete's command of the material, especially on the Low Countries and the Baltic. Loades felt that France and the Iberian Peninsula were more conventionally treated, and he thought that England was given a less than satisfactory role in the book. He also criticized Glete for the lack of detail and concrete examples to support his statements, and, in his view, the claims to originality were not always convincing. In spite of this, his overall assessment was positive: 'The author succeeds, within the modest compass decreed by the series, in introducing some sharp new insights into what, in terms of its outcome, is a familiar story.'[27]

Another reviewer, Carla Rahn Phillips, did not find Glete's explanations of the rise of North-Western Europe equally compelling. In her view, his conclusions rested upon too many traditional assumptions that have never been effectively proven. She also questioned one of his main arguments, namely the effectiveness of a large standing navy compared to a smaller navy combined with ships leased in time of need. Both systems had their disadvantages, she contended, and it was not self-evident which of them was best. Rahn Phillips also questioned Glete's time-frame. By ending the story in 1650, he was unable to follow the maturation of important processes that, had they been studied more closely, would have most certainly led to different conclusions. On the other hand, this allowed Glete to take an original view on many issues, and Rahn Phillips figured that this would make Glete's book appealing to many readers.[28]

Having written extensively on naval warfare on a global scale, Glete both widened and limited the scope in his next book. In *War and the State in Early Modern Europe*, he turned his attention to warfare in general and how it helped to shape the modern state. Although he described a more or less universal process, he confined his examples to three cases: the Spanish Monarchy, the Dutch Republic, and Sweden. According to Glete these were the first European states to develop strong, permanent armies and navies, and the monopoly on violence so acquired fundamentally changed the relation between state and society. Protection became a commodity that could be bought and sold. Glete did not want to form a general theory from these case-studies; he wanted to describe three different paths to what he labelled the fiscal-military state. A fiscal-military state was characterized by the maintenance of standing armies and navies that, in turn, required an effective organizational structure and steady taxes in peacetime. The different territorial conditions, socio-economic structures, and political and constitutional traditions of Glete's cases helped to explain both similarities and differences in this process.

For Glete, state formation was a question of negotiation rather than of subversion. He found that many explanations for the advent of the modern state were one-sidedly engaged with resource extraction through coercion and with the suppression of subjects and representative institutions. The formation of fiscal-military states in Glete's account was effected by bargaining; this demanded active participation from estates and traditional elites. Strong estates did not imply weak states; rather the contrary. The transformation was dependent upon various innovations, which made the fiscal-military state far more efficient than the medieval state. The new institutions and combined assets were at the disposal of various interest groups in exchange for the channelling of their knowledge and resources through the state's administration. Thus older power structures were transformed rather than suppressed. The groups that opened their ranks to talent and innovators gained, whereas those who resisted change lost. Their ability to transform natural and human resources into commodities and services at lower cost explain the overall effectiveness of the fiscal-military state.

The book was well received; however, by tackling this huge topic, Glete naturally exposed himself to criticism. One reviewer, Björn Asker, questioned his fundamental assumption of protection selling. Asker asked: While it is correct that states strived for a monopoly on violence, to what extent were the 'buyers' of protection free to choose between various 'suppliers'? Populations were certainly willing to pay for safety, yet they could not turn to a free market. Instead, they had to concede to protection offered in a Mafia-like manner. Besides these and some other objections, Asker nevertheless found *War and the State in Early Modern Europe* to be an important contribution to an issue of great concern to international historiography.[29]

Another reviewer, Clifford Rogers, found Glete's market analogy misleading for the same reason as Asker. Subjects were often compelled to pay for protection. Moreover, protection should equally often be labelled oppression instead. Rogers further remarked that Glete did not support his argument with primary or archival sources. This comment appears somewhat ironic in view of the empirical character of Swedish historiography in general – and Glete's research in particular. Equally surprising is Rogers's remark that Glete downplays the importance of Gustavus Adolphus. 'The book nonetheless remains a significant one', Rogers concluded, 'containing many challenging ideas and useful insights, and is well worth reading by anyone interested in early modern international history.'[30]

Last works

While finishing these books, Glete was also at work on his major synthesis on the Swedish maritime force, 1521–1721. The size and scope of this book is almost as impressive as *Navies and Nations*. Glete sets out to describe in detail the development of the Swedish navy over nearly two centuries of imperial expansion. The book is in part a detailed survey of the strength of the Swedish navy (the number of guns and warships, the equipment, and the personnel) and in part an attempt to explain how Sweden, with its non-maritime history and mainly peasant-based economy, managed to become a major power in the Baltic – with not only a powerful army, but with a strong navy as well. As before, Glete's explanations were mainly about the organizational capabilities of the Swedish state, or its 'power through organization'. Thanks to the administrative, fiscal, and military measures of the early Vasas in the sixteenth century, the dynasty's later kings had a surplus to employ in warfare (or 'protection selling') around the Baltic. The old explanation of a North European power vacuum exploited by the Swedish rulers was given a new twist. A state's ability to integrate external resources with its own core competence gave it decisive advantages over its competitors. Organizational proficiency was a key factor in this competition; something which could be easily proven by looking at the navy. Sweden had a comparatively small population and little maritime experience, but the country had vast natural resources at its disposal. An input of innovative technology copied from abroad, coupled with men disposed to change, secured the advantageous use of these resources. 'Because competitive naval power was scarce, the ability to create naval power gave the Swedish state a comparative advantage. It could attack or put pressure on most powers in the Baltic with little risk of counterattacks on its own territory.'[31]

Apart from new interpretations of the Swedish imperial experience and an extensive account of its naval operations, the book contains thorough investigations of the quantity, quality, and technology of the Swedish navy. Throughout his career, Glete followed his belief in solid empirical research.

In a review, Lars Ericson Wolke labelled Glete's book both a standard reference work and an inspiration for further research. He emphasized Glete's important studies on the Swedish galley fleet, long neglected by scholars. A one-sided focus on the men-of-war gives a false image of the Swedish navy's striking power and underestimates its capacity for amphibious operations. Wolke also underlined Glete's discussion of naval manpower. The perception that the Danish navy was manned by experienced Norwegian fishermen, whereas the Swedish navy had to rely upon peasant boys, has so often been repeated that the superiority of the Danish boatswain has become an uncontested truism. On the one hand, Glete accentuated the many traps in such assumptions; on the other, he called attention to the fact that a warship was a much more complex vessel than a merchantman, and that it called for much more specialized talents. Therefore, the men's experience of the sea and ability to swim were far from sufficient qualities to look for when manning a warship. Wolke concluded by commending Glete's talent in keeping an eye on the whole picture even when focusing on the fine detail.[32]

Swedish Naval Administration, 1521–1721 marks a worthy end to a distinguished academic authorship. The historian Marx Charles Fissel has called it 'a major contribution to our understanding of the evolution of the modern state'.[33] Nonetheless, one cannot help regret the works that will remain unwritten. Glete had been planning several big book projects – on Swedish naval technology, on Swedish imperial expansion, and on the importance of organizational capabilities in early modern state formation. 'Increasing age and declining health makes it unlikely that these books ever will be written', he wrote in the preface to his last book. By late 2008, Glete had been diagnosed with cancer. The severe treatment left him very weak, but finishing the book script kept him busy during his last months alive. The preface is dated in April 2009, some three months before his untimely death on 13 July 2009.

There is an anecdote that is revealing of Jan Glete both as a person and as a professional. In the early 2000s, the National Defence College (*Försvarshögskolan*) arranged a discussion in Karlskrona, home of one of Sweden's main naval bases. There was an informal gathering in the evening at Skärva, the country manor of the celebrated eighteenth-century shipbuilder Fredrik Henrik af Chapman. Among the guests was Jan Glete who quite unintentionally became the focus of attention and entertained the company with his conversation, both serious and light-hearted. He even managed to impress a high-ranking officer with his knowledge of weaponry and military technology. 'You know a surprising amount for being an arts type,' the officer remarked somewhat superciliously. 'I'm not an arts type,' replied Glete unassumingly: 'I'm a historian, and I take an interest in many things.'[34]

Acknowledgement

In addition to my personal recollections and the references mentioned in the notes, I have received valuable comments from my fellow editors of this book, all of whom knew Jan Glete professionally as well as privately. An earlier version was read and commented upon by Jan Glete's wife, Sang Kum Yeo.

Notes

1 *Unionsstridens betydelse för den svenska militära upprustningen, juni 1895–1899*, see Bibliography no. 162.
2 *Socialdemokratiska Kvinnoförbundet och Försvaret: Från 1930-talets början till andra världskrigets slut*, see Bibliography no. 164.
3 Jan Glete, *Kreugerkoncernen och Boliden* (Stockholm 1975).
4 'Boken är alltså en ovetenskaplig nidskrift som med sällsynt öppenhet erkänner, att ingen litteratur som inte styrker den uppfattning Ivar Kreugers fiender hävdar ens kommer att behandlas!'
5 Sven Stolpe, 'Sanningen om Ivar Kreuger?', *Norrköpings tidningar*, 16 January 1976.
6 Anders Edström, 'Kreugerkoncernen och Boliden, avhandling med dagsanknytning', *Göteborgs-Posten*, 3 February 1976.
7 'Om Kristensons [sic] sätt att räkna aktier och obligationer som "anläggningstill-

gångar" behöver bara sägas, att det inte finns något som helst stöd i aktiebolagslagen för en sådan redovisningsmetod, ej heller i förarbetena till denna lag eller i gängse kommentarer till denna [...] Vad Kristenson ägnar sig år är helt enkelt ett billigt illusionstrick, som man är förvånad över att en professor i industriell ekonomi kan hemfalla till'; Lars-Erik Thunholm, 'Ivar Kreuger – myter och verklighet', *Historisk tidskrift*, 113 (1993), pp. 105–130, quote p. 116.

8 Jan Glete, *Kreugerkoncernen och krisen på svensk aktiemarknad: studier om svenskt och internationellt riskkapital under mellankrigstiden* (Stockholm 1981), quote, pp. 611–612.

9 'Det föredömligt disponerade materialet, de överskådliga tabellerna samt inte minst det raka språket bidrar till att minska verkets svårtillgänglighet.' Kenne Fant, 'Genial svindlare och visionärt geni: nyanserad avhandling om Kreugerkraschen', *Dagens Nyheter*, 13 January 1982.

10 'Denna konturteckning [...] är förvånande klar, åskådlig och i allmänhet övertygande. Den får därmed anses utgöra en pionjärinsats, och resultatet vittnar inte bara om betydande insikt och forskarmöda utan också om proportionssinne och oförvillat förnuft.' Karl Gustaf Hildebrand's report to the history–philosophy faculty board, 'Till Historisk-filosofiska sektionen vid Stockholms universitet', 29 April 1977, Dnr 410/1977, Stockholm University Archives.

11 Ibid. 'Över huvud betyder manuskriptet en breddning av Gletes kompetens; med tanke på den tid som stått honom till buds är det anmärkningsvärda inte att arbetet är oavslutat utan att han hunnit så relativt långt med det.'

12 Jan Glete, 'Svenska örlogsfartyg 1521–1560: flottans uppbyggnad under ett tekniskt brytningsskede', *Forum navale*, 30 (1976), pp. 7–74.

13 The appendices contained a register of shipping, 1521–1560; compilations of Swedish naval strength, 1522–1560; estimations of the navy's armament; a list of shipbuilders, 1527–1560; a list of shipbuilding sites together with the vessels produced there, 1540–1560. *Forum navale*, 31 (1977), pp. 23–119.

14 Jan Glete, *ASEA under hundra år, 1883–1983: en studie i ett storföretags organisatoriska, tekniska och ekonomiska utveckling* (Västerås 1983); id., *Ett storföretag i starkström: ett svenskt industriföretags omvärldsrelationer – en sammanfattning baserad på 'ASEA under hundra år'* (Västerås 1984).

15 Erik Zander, 'Asea-historiken halvmiss', *Vestmanlands läns tidning*, 1 September 1983. Otherwise, Zander praised Glete for his 'exemplarily lucid and pedagogic account' (*föredömligt klar och pedagogisk framställning*).

16 Hans Sjögren, 'Nätverk i näringlivet', *Historisk tidskrift*, 116 (1996), pp. 309–314.

17 Jan Glete, 'Replik till Hans Sjögren', *Historisk tidskrift*, 117 (1997), pp. 256–258; See also Hans Sjögren, 'Fortfarande fundersam och frågande', ibid. pp. 259–260.

18 Nils-Eric Sandberg, 'Varför inga nya entreprenörer?', *Dagens Nyheter*, 28 November 1994.

19 Jan Glete, 'Ägarkoncentrationen och den politiska demokratin', in Rolf Eidem & Rolf Skog (eds.), *Makten över företagen* (Stockholm 1991), pp. 201–44; *Demokrati och makt i Sverige: maktutredningens huvudrapport*, Statens offentliga utredningar 1990:44 (Stockholm 1990), pp. 161–165.

20 Jan Glete & Gunnar Söderholm, *Boken om sta'n: SSU i Stockholm 1917–1981* (Stockholm 1981) p. 134.

21 'Store synteser kan erfaringsmæssigt kun sjældent stå for en kritisk prøvelse af deres fremlagte data. Kan forfatteren virkelig fastholde et præcist dataniveau, når

han uafladeligt bevæger sig mellem Russlands skærgårdsflotiller, Algiers korsarer, Venedigs galejer, atlanterhavsmagternes linieskibsflåder och sultanatet Omans marine? En stikpøve på et område, hvor anmelderen føler sig kompetent – den danske flåde – viser, at det kan Jan Glete faktisk. Han er fortrolig med den danske litteratur, også den allernyeste; ydermere har han indraget et ret omfattende dansk arkivmateriale; og hans data må karakteriseres som pålidelige og hans referater dækkende. Og netop gennem sin komparative kvantificering når han her frem till nye og interessante resultater. [...] Både som fremstilling og som referenceværk er *Navies and Nations* et storværk, som har alle forudsættninger for at blive standardværket i den internationale forskning.' Ole Feldbæk, review of *Navies and Nations*, by Jan Glete, *Historisk tidsskrift* (Copenhagen), 93 (1993), pp. 441–443.

22 W. J. R. Gardner, 'The State of Naval History', *Historical Journal*, 38 (1995), pp. 696, 704.

23 Ibid. p. 705.

24 Richard Dowling, review of *Navies and Nations*, by Jan Glete, *History*, 81 (Jan. 1996) p. 113.

25 N. A. M. Rodger, review of *Navies and Nations*, by Jan Glete, *European History Quarterly*, 24 (1994), pp. 619–621.

26 Mats Kero & Leos Müller, 'In memoriam: Jan Glete 1947–2009', *Forum navale*, 66 (2010), pp. 8–11.

27 David Loades, review of *Warfare at Sea, 1500–1650*, by Jan Glete, *Sixteenth Century Journal*, 32 (2001), pp. 236–237.

28 Carla Rahn Phillips, review of *Warfare at Sea, 1500–1650*, by Jan Glete, *Journal of Military History*, 64 (2000), pp. 1144–1145.

29 Björn Asker, 'De starka staternas uppkomst', *Militärhistorisk tidskrift* (2003), pp. 225–229.

30 Clifford J. Rogers, review of *War and the State in Early Modern Europe*, by Jan Glete, *International History Review*, 25 (2003), pp. 397–399.

31 Jan Glete, *Swedish Naval Administration, 1521–1721: Resource Flows and Organisational Capabilities* (Leiden & Boston 2010) p. 667.

32 Lars Ericson Wolke, review of *Swedish Naval Administration, 1521–1721*, by Jan Glete, *Karolinska förbundets årsbok*, 2010, pp. 155–156.

33 Mark Charles Fissel, review of *Swedish Naval Administration, 1521–1721*, by Jan Glete, *American Historical Review*, 116 (2011) pp. 884–885.

34 'Du kan överraskande många saker för att vara humanist.' 'Jag är inte humanist, jag är historiker, och jag är intresserad av många saker.' This anecdote comes courtesy of Professor Gunnar Åselius of the National Defence College.

PART I

ORGANIZATIONS

CHAPTER 2

The State as Enterprise

Applying theories of organizational growth to the process of state formation

Mats Hallenberg

One of Jan Glete's substantial achievements was to introduce theories of organization to the historical study of state formation. Glete's work on the emerging fiscal-military states of early modern Europe has demonstrated that they may be analysed as complex organizations, managed by princely entrepreneurs. However, while this perspective has proved its value in explaining the initial expansion of state power, it remains less certain whether it can be successfully applied to the more mature states of the industrial and post-industrial eras. I will discuss the pros and cons of using economic theory to study political organization, as well as the implications of drawing analogies between states in history and modern business firms. It is not my aim here to construct a new, all-encompassing theory of the state. Rather, I wish to illuminate some of the hazards and benefits of using theory to understand the multi-layered facets of historical change.

The argument will be presented as follows: first, I will provide a brief survey of Glete's own work to demonstrate how organizational theory may be utilized as an analytical tool in the study of state formation; second, I will take a closer look at some of these theories, focusing primarily upon Edith Penrose's classic theory of the growth of the firm; third, the implications of adopting the organizational perspective on state formation will be further investigated by discussing the Swedish case for the period 1521–1721; fourth, I will discuss the need to account for the legitimacy of the organizational frame, before addressing the problem of applying organizational theory to the genesis of the modern Swedish state; and finally, I will discuss how organizational theory may be combined with other explanatory models for a better understanding of the long-term development of European states.

European state formation according to Jan Glete

Theories of state formation have generally focused upon the activities of rulers, and their ability to extract resources and convert them into military power. Following the German historian Otto Hintze (1861–1940), the creation of modern European states has been seen the result of a continuous geopolitical struggle.[1] War and competition between states also played a central role in the explanation offered by Charles Tilly (1929–2008). In *Coercion, Capital and European States, AD 990–1992*, Tilly outlined a millennium of European state formation in which the survivors were to be those rulers who managed to bargain successfully for resources to be allocated for war.[2] Both of these interpretations essentially treated state formation as a political problem, with special attention directed at either international conflicts or domestic relations between rulers and subjects.

While generally accepting the importance of armed conflict, Glete tackled the subject in a different way, asserting that state formation was also a matter of organization. Since scarce resources could be used in more or less rational ways, state formation also had a qualitative dimension, favouring those rulers who could come up with innovative solutions to organizational problems. Glete first outlined this approach in *Navies and Nations* (1993), a comparative study of naval organizations in Europe and North America in 1500–1860. One of the most important conclusions was that the creation of permanent, state-controlled naval forces in the early modern period meant a reduction in transaction costs, and that these new bureaucratic organizations were able to enjoy the benefits of economy of scale. Centralized organization was, therefore, a rational economic solution as much as a political one.[3]

This perspective was further developed in *War and the State in Early Modern Europe*. Here, Glete progressed from studying navies to analysing state organizations. The key concept in this analysis was the *fiscal-military state*, which was characterized as 'a social innovation that increased the division of labour and made it possible to take advantage of economies of scale and specialization'.[4] In forming his own theory of state formation, Jan Glete drew inspiration from leading economic scholars such as Joseph Schumpeter, Edith Penrose, and Oliver Williamson. The first fiscal-military states of early modern Europe were formed by entrepreneurial rulers who succeeded in breaking free from the restrictions imposed by traditional society to create their own organizations for fund-raising and violence control. To implement reform, the rulers depended upon a core of loyal officials, whose interests had to be closely linked to the state. Thus the ability of state organizations to act as *social containers* became crucial. By concentrating technical, commercial, and administrative competences, the fiscal-military states came to house a corps of specialists whose expertise could be utilized to further expansion. The formation and growth of European states could thus be analysed in accordance with Edith Penrose's classic thesis on twentieth-century businesses.[5]

The growth of state organizations was intimately linked to the problem of interest aggregation. According to Frederic Lane's theory, the state can be seen as a protection-selling organization where the ruler had a contract to protect the population.[6] Consequently, rulers needed the support and participation of elite groups; this political dimension is strongly emphasized in Glete's last major work, *Swedish Naval Administration*. The fact that the rulers of Sweden (a country with little maritime tradition) could deploy the strongest naval power in the Baltic was very much the outcome of a royal policy that effectively harnessed aristocratic interests to work with the state. The success of this policy depended upon the monarchs' ability to master the means of organization. The creation of new organizational capabilities promoted the growth of state power, and thus gave rulers a strong advantage when bargaining with their wealthier subjects over resources.[7]

Glete places the Swedish experience firmly in a European context. State formation is regarded as a general process that affected all parts of Europe; however, some rulers were better equipped than others to adapt to changing circumstances. In Sweden's case, the innovative measures introduced by the first rulers of the Vasa dynasty meant that the state had a large, unused capacity for armed conflict, which could be deployed for overseas warfare. Glete characterizes the Swedish state as a dynastic enterprise, led by a series of royal entrepreneurs who successfully established a large-scale protection-selling operation in the Baltic during the sixteenth and seventeenth centuries. This dynastic enterprise, however, eventually ended in a failure of entrepreneurship as Sweden's military powers were effectively crushed by Russia in the Great Northern War (1700–1721).[8]

Glete concludes: 'States continue to grow as long as they have surplus managerial capacity to organise resources more efficiently than competitors.'[9] Glete's wide-ranging comparative studies have demonstrated the benefits of this theory in explaining the growth of state organizations in Europe (*c.*1500–1800). But what about the perseverance of early modern polities, and their eventual transformation into modern states? The Swedish state did not cease to exist in 1721; it has successfully maintained its autonomy until the present day. Also, since larger organizations will be able to command more managerial resources, the focus upon entrepreneurship suggests that the eventual outcome of this process must be the multinational super-state. While there is little evidence of such super-states in the making, we clearly need to re-examine the theoretical implications of this perspective. Let us, therefore, return to some of the original works that inspired Jan Glete.

The growth of firms and states

Quite a few scholars have recognised the analogy between the state and the modern business firm. Alfred Chandler analysed the development of great industrial enterprises in 1962, concluding that these companies, by transforming themselves into multidivisional corporations, had in fact adopted structures resembling the modern state.[10] Evidence thus suggested that, while business firms shared many characteristics with the state, the state might be subject to the same logic as business firms. Economists advocating the so-called new economic history during the 1960s and 1970s insisted on deploying classic economic theory for a better understanding of the history of states and nations. Douglass North asserted that the economic history of the world was not so much a problem of production as a matter of finding the most effective organization. The state, just like any other enterprise, was dependent on minimizing its transaction costs and creating stable institutions in order to promote economic growth.[11]

While economic historians focused on the macro-level impact of institutions, other theorists before them had concentrated on the pre-requisites for organizational growth within the firm. Joseph Schumpeter, the Austrian economist who studied the origins of the tax state, argued that entrepreneurship was the key to lasting success in a business enterprise. Schumpeter defined the entrepreneur as a creative leader capable of combining available resources in a more innovative way, creating new business possibilities in the process. In his earlier works, Schumpeter pictured the entrepreneur as an outstanding individual who relished the chance to create a business empire of his own. Later, he recognised that big companies might well fill the same function, investing capital in research and the development of new products.[12] This latter perspective was utilized by Edith Penrose to formulate what is perhaps the most influential theory of organizational growth in business firms.

Penrose published her seminal work *The Theory of the Growth of the Firm* in 1959. Her purpose was to explain why firms diversify in order to grow as organizations, rather than just expanding their output. The firm is treated as a collection of productive resources representing a number of potential services. In Penrose's analysis, growth is essentially a function of managerial competence; by supervising and executing entrepreneurial ideas, management may identify productive opportunities to expand the firm's operations into new areas. As the managerial group becomes more experienced, knowledge is accumulated and new productive services become available to the firm. The need to utilize these services becomes a strong incentive for expansion.[13] Penrose thus demonstrates that there are internal inducements for expansion as well as external ones, the latter being exemplified by growing demand and/or changes in technology. She also identifies the fundamental obstacles to growth: a lack of specialized services within the firm (internal); and strong market competition (external).[14]

In spite of having been written more than half a century ago, Penrose's theory of the growth of the firm has maintained its status as a modern classic: it puts the focus on the firm's ability to gather and process information, and is, in essence, a theory of knowledge.[15] The emphasis upon the creation of knowledge within the firm may be seen as an equivalent to Glete's use of the term 'power container' to describe the state's generation of administrative power.[16] Penrose also maintains that the overall ambition of the firm does not have to be profit maximization; rather, it is to achieve a healthy balance between long-term profits and growth.[17] These observations make it all the more tempting to apply her model to the development of state organizations.

European states expanded their power from the late medieval period by incorporating resources and activities that had previously been controlled by other segments of society: the church, the nobility, and urban and peasant communities. The process of state formation might then be analysed as one of organizational growth, in terms of both the quantity (accumulated resources, the number of state servants) and diversity (administrative, military and educational services) of state administration.[18] While the ruling prince may, thus, be compared to a chief executive, his top bureaucrats may be equalled to the managerial group of the company. Their major purpose would be to marshal the information that local officials gathered into new productive services, in the way Glete has described. External inducements for state expansion might come from general disorder caused by warfare, social conflict and/or economic recession, for example. Technological changes might also trigger state expansion, as was the case when firearms became readily available during the late medieval and early modern periods.[19]

Figure 1: Factors explaining organizational growth, according to Edith Penrose

	Inducements	*Obstacles*
External	Growing demand Changes in technology	Competition Patent rights
Internal	Unused productive services	Specialized services lacking

Source: Penrose, *The Theory of the Growth of the Firm* (1993), p. 66

Obstacles to state growth will certainly emerge if there is a lack of entrepreneurial services available to the rulers (that is to say, when they fail to attract competent administrators). The most pressing problem for rulers in premodern societies, however, would have been competition from other power-holders. The rulers of neighbouring states would always represent a potential threat, as would domestic rivals such as powerful aristocrats and other members of local or regional elites. Last but not least, we must account for the supranational competition posed by the Roman Catholic Church and by multi-territorial polities such as the Holy Roman Empire and the Hanseatic League.[20]

There are, however, some obvious flaws to this story that we must address. First of all, most states in history have claimed to be sovereign within their own territory, recognizing no external superior legislator;

while firms are always subject to rules set up by the state, the state, in a sense, makes its own rules. On the other hand, states have seldom or never been able to expand without facing restrictions. Religious leaders could at least put pressure on rulers in the medieval and early modern periods to comply with generally accepted norms. The creation of a European state system following the Peace of Westphalia in 1648 meant that territorial expansion became harder to achieve. A system of international law eventually emerged to place restraints upon even the domestic activities of rulers.[21] Then there is the problem of legitimacy. While business firms may concentrate on maintaining good relations with their customers (who may constitute only a small part of the total population), the state must appear legitimate to all its subjects/citizens all the time. Therefore, state organizations may be much more sensitive to the voice of social protest.[22]

Clearly, the answer to all these problems cannot be extracted from a macro-analysis encompassing all European states. In the following, I will concentrate on the example of the Swedish state to test the benefits and flaws of applying the Penrosean model to state organizations. Since the state-formation process became conspicuous in the sixteenth century, I will start there, before proceeding to later periods.

The Swedish state (*c.*1521–1721): A dynastic enterprise and its competitors

In my thesis, I explored the growth of the state organization in sixteenth-century Sweden. Gustav I (1523–1560) created an extensive local administration, with non-noble bailiffs serving in all provinces of the realm. This process occurred in three distinct (and partly overlapping) phases. At first, the prime reason to organize was political control and interest aggregation, as the new regime had to strengthen its legitimacy after a period of civil war. In the second phase, the bailiffs systematically gathered information about local sources of revenue, compiling it in tax registers (*jordeböcker*), which were then delivered to the King's Chamber in Stockholm. In the third and decisive phase, the King and his councillors could utilize this bank of information to expand the state organization. Subsequent years saw the incorporation of further sources of revenue, the transformation of the peasant militia into a rudimentary standing army, and the establishment of several new production facilities in the regions (manors, mines, and building projects).[23]

The initial expansion of the Swedish state thus followed the same curve growth that Edith Penrose described. The king recruited a core of state servants, acquiring the competence to collect and analyse large amounts of information, which was then used to expand the reach of the state organization. State expansion was realized at the expense of local and regional power-holders, who had to cede control of economic resources that were incorporated by the state. This, however, was a slow and cumbersome process, and the opposition of aristocrats, church lords, and incensed peasants repeatedly thwarted organizational growth. Maria Ågren has pointed out that one must pay more attention to these limiting factors when applying the Penrose model *in extenso*. She has also provided a modified version of the theory, specially designed to explain the growth of states.[24]

Figure 2: Factors promoting/limiting state growth

	Inducements	*Obstacles*
External	State of war	Powerful aristocracy
Internal	Unused productive services	Lack of competent leadership

Source: Adapted from Maria Ågren (2003).

The obstacles to state growth became more prominent in the period 1560–1611, as the Swedish state suffered from weakened monarchical leadership due to repeated dynastic in-fighting and the revitalization of a strong aristocratic opposition. However, the Swedish state still managed to expand its territory eastwards even as domestic conflicts resulted in a stagnating civil administration, for the collapse of the Teutonic Order (in conjunction with periods of widespread unrest in Muscovite Russia) created a window of opportunity that the Vasa rulers were eager to exploit. Territorial expansion provided Sweden's rulers with further inducements for organizational reform and growth. The military organization needed competent leaders and well-equipped soldiers as well as an effective system for logistics. New administrative structures had to be created for the conquered provinces in the Eastern Baltic. However, the unwillingness of the Swedish aristocracy to support the expansionist dynastic project obstructed further expansion of the state.[25]

It was down to Gustav II Adolf (1611–1632) to forge a lasting alliance with the aristocracy, now led by the ambitious organizer Axel Oxenstierna, who served as Chancellor from 1612. Together, the King and the Chancellor managed to win the support of the nobility for a political programme that was centred upon increased taxation and military conquest. This transformation of the Swedish state into a dynastic–aristocratic enterprise turned out to be remarkably efficient as Gustav II Adolf carved out a Swedish Empire by military force, encompassing both the northern, eastern and southern shores of the Baltic.[26]

The support of the aristocracy provided the state organization with a new generation of noble administrators who were eager to prove themselves in state service. However, bourgeois entrepreneurs who created their own enterprises on the basis of state privilege may have provided the most significant influx of productive resources. Tax-farming was introduced to the Swedish realm on a large scale during the 1620s, and the system provided the incentive for both domestic and foreign merchants to invest their capital in the Swedish state.[27]

Organizational growth during this period was both intensive and extensive. Territorial conquest went hand in hand with administrative reforms intended to make the Swedish state less dependent upon a monarch who was absent leading the army in foreign wars. The new constitution of 1634 was the crowning achievement, introducing hierarchical structures and a system of government based upon five departments: it strengthened the central administration and, while most of the production facilities eventually passed into private hands, the state retained full control over the local administration and the sources of revenue. In line with the Penrose model, the Swedish state diversified its operations by establishing new administrative departments for the mining industry and the commercial sector. However, organizational growth was ultimately dependent upon territorial conquest, and when military victories dried up the Swedish state organization was bound to face new problems.[28]

The Peace of Westphalia in 1648 and the Peace of Copenhagen in 1660 confirmed the profits of military expansion. Territorial expansion came at high cost, however, for Sweden now had foreign provinces to defend as well as her new-found status as a European superpower. During the regencies of Queen Christina (1632–1644) and Charles XI (1660–1672), the Swedish state was forced to operate without a strong monarchical ruler. Axel Oxenstierna, who led the government during the first of these regencies, skilfully managed to sustain Sweden's engagement in the Thirty Years War. While reorganizing the state administration, Oxenstierna secured the top positions for members of his own family. The dynastic enterprise was thus transformed into something resembling a joint venture, engaging leading aristocratic families as well as the ruling dynasty.[29]

Aristocrats with little interest in expanding the state organization ruled during the minority of Charles XI (1672–1697). The Lord High Chancellor, Magnus Gabriel de la Gardie, and his fellow aristocrats were generous in dispensing favours to their followers as well as themselves. Consequently, the Swedish state slipped into organizational inertia, derailed by the vested interests of the aristocracy and a lack of dynamic leadership. However, a series of military setbacks, which culminated in the bitter experience of the Scanian War (1675–1680), initiated a new wave of reform. Charles XI purposed to rule as an autocrat after the war; low-rank office-holders and the three commoner Estates in the Swedish Diet supported this. The provinces that had previously been conquered from Denmark were fully incorporated into the realm. The bureaucracy was restructured at all levels, and noble land once alienated by the Crown was confiscated in order to support a large standing army and a growing cadre of civil servants.[30]

There were three distinctive phases of state expansion in 1521–1721, led by Gustav I, Gustav II Adolf, and Charles XI, respectively. All of them seem to follow the pattern that Penrose has suggested: the Swedish state acquired knowledge through a set of administrative practices, which were then used to expand the organization into a variety of fields. Organizational decline, however, is a different matter. Glete attributed the final breakdown of this neo-dynastic enterprise to the rise of Russia. The Swedish state had lost its initial advantage as a pioneer of fiscal-military organization and was forced to succumb to superior competition.[31] However, we need to reconsider the shift of direction from external expansion to internal reorganization in the late seventeenth century. The dynastic–aristocratic alliance that had sustained the growth of the Swedish state since the days of Gustav II Adolf eventually crumbled when territorial conquest was no longer an option. The revival of the organization could only be achieved by a concentration of power in the hands of the king. Charles XII (1697–1718) effectively established a military dictatorship in order to fight his enemies in the Great Northern War. The state organization may have benefited from an influx of new blood as a corps of non-noble careerists made their way towards high office, but autocratic rule, however, effectively blocked noble participation in the management of the state. Consequently, when Charles XII fell in battle there was little support among the Swedish elite for reviving dynastic rule.[32]

The dynastic enterprise of the Vasas eventually fell prey to foreign competition. The scope for territorial expansion in post-Westphalian Europe was restricted. Thus, Sweden's conflicts with Denmark in 1658–1660 and 1675–1680 were concluded not so much by bellicose achievements as by deliberation on the post of France, England, and the Dutch Republic.[33] However, Sweden could not rely upon other European powers to maintain its status in the long run. As society grew more complex, the obstacles to state growth became progressively harder to overcome. The absolutist rulers had to stretch their resources to the limit in order to maintain Sweden's dominance of the Baltic region. In a modern capitalistic society, the opportunities in the Penrose model for expanding into new markets appear to be endless; the rulers of early modern Sweden, on the other hand, had considerably fewer options when territorial expansion was halted and most of the taxable resources had been tapped.[34]

Weak leadership and powerful competition may provide important clues in explaining the collapse of Sweden's imperial ambitions; however, there is clearly more to the story. Dynastic, aristocratic and merchant interests became progressively entwined during the course of the seventeenth century. As governments all around Europe became dependent upon the financial support of its wealthier subjects, this mixture of public and private interest was, indeed, a distinctive feature of the early modern state. Inevitably, the scope for royal entrepreneurs narrowed when kings became more concerned with rewarding their followers.[35] Organizational growth was not necessarily the main target for all rulers, a fact that sets them apart from most business managers in capitalist societies. This leads us back to the problem of voice.

State formation, legitimacy, and voice

The traditional view of the state as an aggressive organization intent on eliminating competition leaves us with a somewhat distorted picture. The experience of seventeenth-century Sweden points to the fact that a powerful aristocracy might be an asset rather than an obstacle to state growth. However, the input from noble and non-noble office-holders was not enough. In order to produce the political, military and jurisdictional services required by society, the Swedish state was dependent upon the participation of the larger part of its subjects. The commoner estates, and the peasantry in particular, had a vital part to play in the dynastic enterprise. Therefore, it became necessary for rulers to create durable institutions for political interaction.

According to David Beetham, legitimate power means that the ruler may expect active participation rather than stubborn recalcitrance from his or her subjects. Thus, legitimacy has a qualitative dimension that becomes increasingly important as the state organization grows more complex.[36] The authority of the Swedish state was to a large extent dependent upon the interaction between local office-holders and the peasant institutions of self-government: the district courts. Taxes and levies were negotiated in these public arenas and adjusted to conform to local practice. The district courts were also where grievances were formulated and submitted to the Diet in Stockholm. These grievances were often met by a favourable royal response: a fact that helped to bolster the legitimacy of the regime.[37] The Swedish Diet had medieval roots, and developed into a permanent national institution during the sixteenth century. As the monarchy was weakened by dynastic conflict, the Diet became the central arena for aggregating interest and forging political alliances.[38]

The original dynastic enterprise, therefore, developed a strong capacity for interest aggregation, with institutions for political bargaining established at both the central and local levels. This provided the incitement for various interest groups – the nobility as well as the commoner estates – to invest social status and economic resources in the state organization. On the one hand, rulers became increasingly dependent upon the support of domestic interest groups. On the other hand, rulers would eventually command a larger proportion of the available resources in society if they could maintain a strong bargaining position. Thus, the leaders of the state became progressively more exposed to the political factors promoting or restraining organizational growth.[39]

Albert Hirschman has identified *exit* and *voice* as the two most effective instruments of revival available to modern organizations. A business firm in decline may be promted to improve its output if faced by a massive exodus of clients. Correspondingly, the leaders of a trade union or a political party may change their policy when confronted with widespread protest from their members. In fact, all organizations are sensitive to both mechanisms, albeit to a different degree. Exit is hardly a realistic alternative for most members in traditional organizations such as states, churches, and families. Hirschman, therefore, introduces the concept of *loyalty* as an instrument for managers to hold exit at bay and activate voice. Loyalty may push customers/members into 'creativity-requiring courses of action' while, simultaneously, constituting an effective barrier to exit.[40]

Hirschman's theory, supported by Beetham's analysis of legitimacy, may supply the link we need to understand the interaction of the economic and political factors affecting state growth. In the weakly organized medieval polities, the threat of exit constituted an important political instrument. A less popular ruler might well be deposed by a coalition of discontented magnates. There was also considerable scope for local communities to act independently of the king. However, as state organizations grew more complex, rulers appropriated repressive resources, and exit (in the form of open insurrection) became a less viable alternative. The struggle for legitimacy, however, meant that rulers had to create loyalty-promoting institutions to ensure the cooperation of elite groups. Exit in modern states is virtually impossible, while voice – in the form of popular opinion – has become a most important factor imposing restrictions on the leaders of the state.

Sweden's short period of absolute rule represented the end of the state as a dynastic enterprise. However, the state organization managed to survive the turmoil and, within a couple of years, a constitutional regime based upon a parliamentary system was established. I would argue that this metamorphosis was made possible by the existence of political institutions created by the dynastic state to maintain loyalty and to sustain expansion. In essence, the dynastic enterprise was transformed from inside, albeit with assistance from the foreign powers who were engaged in maintaining Sweden's sovereignty.[41] Unlike most modern firms, the Swedish state could reorganize in the hope of maintaining equilibrium, rather than promoting further expansion.

From dynastic enterprise to modern welfare state

The early modern period might well be characterized as the golden age of dynastic expansion. While many polities perished in the process, others – such as Sweden – eventually had to adjust to their existence as minor states in a world dominated by a few great powers. However, this did not mean that state organizations generally lacked inducements to expand after 1718. The Swedish state – as with many of its European contemporaries – grew increasingly more complex, creating new functions and branches of government in the course of the eighteenth and nineteenth centuries.

Coping with stronger competition in the emerging international state system meant that available resources had to be used more effectively. In a changing society, economic growth became less dependent upon the extensive accumulation of farmland and other natural resources. Instead, new methods in agriculture, manufacture, transport, and commerce became crucial for creating a higher surplus. The state organization came to rely upon a small, yet growing, number of independent entrepreneurs, whose expertise could not easily be integrated in the state administration. Thus, rulers became increasingly focused upon regulating and coordinating the activities of other economic actors, rather than operating local enterprises of their own. Since the function of creating and maintaining viable institutions could not simply be filled by anyone else, this meant that the state organization had to distinguish itself more clearly from other types of organization.[42] However, political legitimacy and organizational strength still constituted the necessary means for spurring institutional change.

The Swedish government occasionally tried handing over parts of its organization to private interests: such was the case with customs and excise in 1726 and the Salt Office in 1750. These experiments were largely unsuccessful, however, and the general trend was that institutions for securing trade and commerce had to be maintained by the state.[43] Unused managerial services might still provide an important inducement to expand the state organization. As rulers found their freedom of action increasingly curtailed, entrepreneurial functions were delegated to the middle and lower levels of the now complex organization. Important agricultural and infrastructural reforms – such as the nationwide redistribution (*skiften*) of farmlands and the construction of roads, canals, and (later) railways – were accomplished by a small number of centrally placed officials in close collaboration with a large contingent of specialists (that is to say, land-surveyors and engineers). The state successively acquired new abilities and skills while planning and implementing such projects. More than ever, the coordination of local operations was dependent upon a continuous accumulation of knowledge.[44]

Meanwhile, voice continued to play a fundamental role in the development of the Swedish state. New legal institutions – the National Law of 1734 and the peripatetic Attorney General – were set up during the eighteenth century to handle the increasing number of disputes in a society troubled by population growth and social stratification.[45] As the functions of central and regional administrative bodies multiplied, more tasks were delegated and eventually appropriated by local institutions of self-government such as the town council or the parish meeting.[46] Thus, voice could serve both as an inducement for, and an obstacle to, state growth. Local assemblies could recapture public functions that had once been appropriated by the state; this points to the growing interdependence of state and society. The fact that the Swedish state had acquired the power to delegate bears testimony to its transformation from a dynastic enterprise into a public institution.

The politics of the conservative governments of nineteenth-century Sweden have been described as those of a nightwatchman state: limiting its activities to the preservation of law and order. The central bureaucracy, however, maintained its position, and the economic regulations of the old regime were not finally abolished until midcentury. The initiative for administrative reform, investment in infrastructure, and the reinforcement of financial institutions still belonged to the state. The Industrial Revolution did not take off until the 1870s; however, the subsequent development was all the more rapid. In the course of this transformation the rising elite of bourgeois businessmen and industrialists put new demands on state intervention. In order to be able to exploit natural resources and compete on the world market, Swedish capitalists needed the state to invest in large infrastructural projects such as the railways and electrification. External demands from the capitalist elite thus provided the inducement to transform the state into a more ambitious and profit-generating organization.[47]

The rulers of Sweden had succeeded in developing political institutions to accommodate the interests of the nobility, the church, the burghers, and the peasants. We have observed that political demands from some of these groups might serve as an inducement to expand the state, effectively pulling the organization out of inertia. However, the appearance of a large proletariat of landless labourers in the countryside (eventually followed by a mass of industrial wage-earners in the cities) did not fit well into this traditional system. The rise of new classes generated new types of social conflict, and the government had to establish ways to handle the groups who lacked a political voice of their own. The social problem became paramount around 1900; however, vested interests seem to have paralysed the ruling bureaucracy, which generally lacked the leadership qualities needed to reform the political system from within.[48]

Ultimately, the threat of social upheaval compelled the leaders of the Swedish state to open up its organization to more broadly defined social interests. Following decades of political strife, universal suffrage was finally established in 1921. As Liberals and Social Democrats extended their political leverage, state policy came to be directed by different norms. The twentieth century saw the most conspicuous growth of the Swedish state. A new generation of social reformers and technical experts led the expansion into new areas, transforming public institutions into a dynamic welfare state with a marked ambition to intervene on all levels of society. The government successively created new bodies for the promotion and administration of social welfare, often by incorporating functions that had previously been filled by voluntary associations. While some have heralded the Swedish welfare state as a role model, recent commentators have often been more critical, pointing to the vulnerable position of the individual in a society dominated by state-controlled, collective institutions. The growth of the welfare state that facilitated social reforms, such as full income support and state pensions, also entailed the exclusion – and even persecution – of marginalized groups who did not qualify as citizens.[49]

At first glance, we may recognize some well-known mechanisms at work: the pull of popular demand for social reform, reinforced by the push of a new generation of social engineers. The growth of the welfare state would, thus, be the effect of a growing demand for state intervention combined with new productive services becoming available to a government dedicated to social change. This phase of expansion, however, seems to have been halted and even reversed in the late twentieth century. Discontent with the control systems associated with the welfare state has initiated a wave of privatization and the delegation of state functions in a globalized economy. The entrepreneurial qualities required for improving public institutions, such as schools, hospitals, and day-care centres, are thus increasingly found in private firms rather than integrated in the state organization.[50]

Voice seems to be the decisive factor at work here. The state organization may well expand in response to popular action, inciting the state to shoulder new responsibilities. However, when there is a change in demand, when citizens no longer require public organizations to provide them with all the necessary services, some operations may be outsourced to be run by private entrepreneurs. The public character of the modern welfare state seems to make it less inclined to long-term organizational growth. In this way, the modern state clearly distinguishes itself from the dynastic enterprise of the Vasa monarchs. Meanwhile, the international state system and the global economy have introduced new obstacles to the expansion of states, thus providing less scope for entrepreneurship within state organizations.

We need to consider the more cynical view of modern society that has been presented by Michel Foucault and his followers in order to balance this somewhat optimistic estimation of the limits of state power. According to Foucault, power is not primarily located at the centre of government; rather, it presents itself in the daily practices of officials and the ordinary people subject to their surveillance. The state organization from this perspective will be less sensitive to popular voice; instead, it feeds upon the inherent need to monitor and control the actions of individuals. This image of the state as an organization driven by technocrats and bureaucrats has a lot in common with the Penrose model of organizational growth. Expansion remains the overall goal in both cases: seeking to further profit-seeking ventures on the one hand, to obtain full control over individuals on the other.[51]

Perhaps the growth of modern state organizations is best understood as a dialectic process involving both governance and voice. We may recognize an inherent drive within the state organization to promote expansion into new directions, inventing new forms of governance to facilitate state control. However, this incentive may be channelled into productive services or even be completely halted by the collective use of voice. Unlike its early modern ancestors, the modern state is less likely to be provoked into expanding by the emergence or non-emergence of external competition. The effective check on organizational growth that public voice provides, therefore, seems to constitute a fundamental difference between modern and premodern states. On the other hand, the rise of new global challenges (such as climate change and food crises) may yet form inducements for expanding states as well as for organizations operating on the supranational level.

Conclusion

The purpose of this chapter was to evaluate the pros and cons of applying economic theories of organizational growth to the development of the modern state. Jan Glete's analysis of the early modern Swedish state organization as a dynastic enterprise has been taken as a point of departure. However, discussing the implications of this theory for the development of the Swedish state between the eighteenth and twentieth centuries enables a better understanding of the transformation from dynastic enterprise to modern welfare state.

I have suggested that the Edith Penrose model might be combined with theories discussing legitimacy and voice. Clearly, the Penrose model has much to offer the study of state formation. The focus upon both inducements and obstacles provides us with instruments to understand the dynamics of political conflict. One of the main benefits of Penrose's theory is that it draws attention to the accumulation of knowledge and the creation of new competences within the organization. While the external obstacles to expansion may be easy to identify for a political historian, the internal inducements are often less conspicuous. From this perspective the relative successes and failures of early modern Swedish rulers may be explained as effects of managerial planning (intentional or unintentional), rather than of the random workings of coincidence. The state/firm analogy may also provide a check on the economic determinism of meta-historians such as Perry Anderson and Charles Tilly, who have both tended to regard state structures as merely reflecting the economic conditions within society.

The model of course needs some modification in order to be successfully applied to a historical analysis. As states are territorially confined, the distinction between internal and external inducements or obstacles must be clarified. Obstacles to organizational growth may stem from domestic contenders (aristocrats, burghers, or even disregarded peasants) as well as from outside competition (rulers of foreign polities). As more groups are integrated in the organization, the risk of intrastate conflict is notably increased (that is, disputes between the various branches of state administration). When it comes to the productive resources of the state, they can be found both at the centre (rulers, ministers, and top bureaucrats) and the local or regional levels (officeholders and other specialists). For rulers, the coordination of activities and the implementation of policy decisions pose a serious challenge, as the loyalty of local agents might be swayed by local elites. The elites, on the other hand, might welcome state expansion if its operations can be controlled to suit their own interests. As the organization grows more complex, drawing a sharp line between the state and its environment becomes increasingly difficult.

The flaws of the state/firm analogy become conspicuous when we follow the long-term historical development of a given European state – in our case, Sweden. The theory does not provide accurate tools for explaining the transformation of the dynastic state into to a modern public institution. I would argue that there are three points where the Penrose model seems to leave us at a loss. *First*, while most business firms operate within the multitude of opportunities provided by the capitalist system, state growth has become increasingly constrained by the power of vested interests. Elite groups, as well as popular movements, have become wary of the state, demanding that it must confine its operations to the provision of basic stability and security. Consequently, the leaders of the state have shifted focus from organizing their own enterprise to regulating and coordinating the activities of others. *Second*, the emergence of an international state system has raised a new kind of obstacle to state expansion. Within a system designed to preserve the existing balance of power, eliminating competitors by territorial conquest is no longer possible. Again, this is radically different to the competitive dynamics of the capitalist market, where firms are supposed to perish if they do not diversify or expand.

Third, while institutional constraints have hampered the expansion of the state, new technology has radically improved the conditions for accumulating knowledge. Rulers of modern state organizations have seized the opportunity to create more effective methods of control and repression. The expansion of the state, thus, has a sinister dimension; increasing the scope of governance may threaten civil rights as well as economic growth. Jan Glete has argued that the fiscal-military states created in the early modern period should not be seen as a burden on society. They provided security and protection; therefore, they acted as a precondition for political stability in Europe.[52] However, the growth of states since the nineteenth century has most often resulted in war, oppression, and meaningless destruction. There does not seem to be a general, positive connection between state growth and the welfare of its citizens. Rather, state power must be harnessed to serve the interest of the many – not just the few.

The organizational perspective, which recognizes the importance of the public voice, needs to be combined with a theory to overcome these flaws. The growth of the early modern Swedish state may well be analysed mainly as a function of dynastic ambition versus outside competition. However, the expansion of the modern welfare state rather depends upon the dialectics of governance and voice. The emergence of a new generation of administrative experts has provided the state with new productive resources and, thus, with inducements for expanding state control. The abiding importance of voice, however, serves as a check on such ambitions on the part of state officials. Democratic institutions may also articulate the demand for state intervention and social reform in times of crisis. Likewise, popular movements have an important function for revitalizing state policy by addressing new solutions to pressing problems.

Jan Glete regarded the historical development of fiscal-military states as a catalyst for institutional change; people eventually learned to put their trust in impersonal organizations rather than in the people they met in day-to-day encounters. This process today seems to have been reversed as states are more exposed to exogenous economic factors. Even the most complex of state organizations in a globalized world finds it hard to live up to the expectations of its citizens. A change of norms seems to have taken place in Europe and North America: people are becoming increasingly suspicious of the state's ambition to intervene in and regulate their daily lives. On the other hand, the global challenges posed by climate change, armed conflict, and financial instability still call for states to act as guarantees of institutional stability. However, expansion of the state organization as such will hardly be the object for future statesmen; rather, it will be to create viable institutions in accordance with the norm systems prevalent in civil society.

Notes

1 *The Historical Essays of Otto Hintze*, ed. F. Gilbert (New York 1975); Philippe Contamine (ed.), *War and Competition Between States* (Oxford 2000); Jeremy Black, *Great Powers and the Quest for Hegemony: the World Order Since 1500* (Oxford 2007).

2 Charles Tilly, *Coercion, Capital and European States, AD 990–1992* (Oxford 1992).

3 Jan Glete, *Navies and Nations: Warships, Navies and State Building in Europe and America, 1500–1860*, 2 (Stockholm 1993), pp. 486–487.

4 Jan Glete, *War and the State in Early Modern Europe: Spain, the Dutch Republic and Sweden as Fiscal-Military states, 1500–1600* (London 2002) p. 3.

5 Glete (2002), pp. 55–66.
6 Frederic C. Lane, *Profits from Power: Readings in Protection Rent and Violence-controlling Enterprises* (Albany 1979).
7 Jan Glete, *Swedish Naval Administration, 1521–1721: Resource Flows and Organisational Capabilities* (Leiden 2010) p. 649.
8 Glete (2010), pp. 651–661.
9 Glete (2010), pp. 667.
10 Alfred D. Chandler, *Strategy and Structure: Chapters in the History of the Industrial Enterprise* (New York 1962), p. 396.
11 Douglass C. North & Robert Paul Thomas, *The Rise of the Western World: A New Economic History* (Cambridge 1973) ch. 1.
12 Joseph A. Schumpeter, *Capitalism, Socialism and Democracy* (New York & London 1942).
13 Edith T. Penrose, *The Theory of the Growth of the Firm*, 3rd edn. (Oxford 1995), pp. 31–37, 44–56.
14 Penrose (1995), pp. 65–87.
15 Christos Pitelis, 'On the Garden of Edith: Some Themes', in: Christos Pitelis (ed.), *The Growth of the Firm: The Legacy of Edith Penrose* (Oxford 2002), pp. 1–15; Margherita Turvani, 'Mismatching by Design: Explaining the Dynamics of Innovative Capabilities of the Firm With a Penrosean Mark', ibid. pp. 195–213.
16 Glete (2002), pp. 63–66. Anthony Giddens, *A Contemporary Critique of Historical Materialism, 2: The Nation-state and Violence* (Cambridge 1985), pp. 12–17.
17 Penrose (1995), pp. 29–30.
18 For European state formation, see Hendrik Spruyt, *The Sovereign State and its Competitors: An Analysis of Systems Change* (Princeton 1994); Thomas Ertman, *Birth of the Leviathan: Building States and Regimes in Medieval and Early Modern Europe* (Cambridge 1997); Philip S. Gorski, *The Disciplinary Revolution: Calvinism and the Rise of the State in Early Modern Europe* (New York 2003); John Watts, *The Making of Polities: Europe, 1300–1500*, (Cambridge 2009); Harald Gustafsson, *Makt och människor: Europeisk statsbildning från medeltiden till franska revolutionen* (Gothenburg 2010).
19 William Hardy McNeill, *The Age of Gunpowder Empires, 1450–1800* (Washington DC 1989); Clifford J. Rogers (ed.), *The Military Revolution Debate: Readings on the Military Transformation of Early Modern Europe* (Boulder 1995); Brenda J. Buchanan (ed.), *Gunpowder, Explosives and the State: A Technological history* (Aldershot 2006).
20 Tilly (1992), pp. 1–5, 62–65; Spruyt (1994), pp. 34–57, 146–150; Harald Gustafsson, 'A State That Failed? On the Union of Kalmar, Especially its Dissolution', *Scandinavian Journal of History*, 31 (2006), pp. 205–220.
21 Jeremy Black, *European International Relations, 1648–1815* (London 2002); Benno Teschke, *The Myth of 1648: Class, Geopolitics and the Making of Modern International Relations* (London 2003).
22 Barrington Moore, *Injustice: The Social Bases of Obedience and Revolt* (London 1978); David Beetham, *The Legitimation of Power* (Basingstoke 1991); Michael Braddick, *State Formation in Early Modern England* (Cambridge 2000), pp. 11–46.
23 Mats Hallenberg, *Kungen, fogdarna och riket: Lokalförvaltning och statsbyggande under tidig Vasatid* (Eslöv 2001), pp. 266–268, 408–414.
24 Maria Ågren, 'Gustav Vasas fogdar – centralmaktens förlängda arm', *Historisk tidskrift*, 123 (2003) p. 596.

25 Michael Roberts, *The Early Vasas: A History of Sweden 1523–1611*, (Cambridge 1968); Glete (2002), pp. 181–195; Gary Dean Peterson, *Warrior Kings of Sweden: The Rise of an Empire in the Sixteenth and Seventeenth Centuries* (Jefferson 2007), pp. 53–115; Mats Hallenberg, Johan Holm & Dan Johansson, 'Organization, Legitimation, Participation: State Formation as a Dynamic Process – the Swedish Example, *c.*1523–1680', *Scandinavian Journal of History*, 33 (2008), pp. 247–268.

26 Michael Roberts, *The Swedish Imperial Experience, 1560–1718* (Cambridge 1979); Erik Ringmar, *Identity, Interest and Action: A Cultural Explanation of Sweden's Intervention in the Thirty Years War* (Cambridge 1996); Glete (2002), pp. 196–212; Paul Douglas Lockhart, *Sweden in the Seventeenth Century* (Basingstoke 2004).

27 Mats Hallenberg, 'Peasants and Tax-farmers in 17th-Century Sweden: Local Conflict and Institutional Change', in: Wim Blockmans et al. (eds.), *Empowering Interactions: Political Cultures and the Emergence of the State in Europe 1300–1900* (Aldershot 2009), pp. 253–266.

28 Jan Lindegren, 'The Swedish "Military State", 1560–1720', *Scandinavian Journal of History*, 10 (1985), pp. 305–336; Johan Holm, 'Skyldig plicht och trohet: Militärstaten och 1634 års regeringsform', *Historisk tidskrift*, 119 (1999), pp. 161–195.

29 Lockhart (2004), pp. 106–122; Glete (2010), pp. 287–305.

30 Göran Rystad, 'The King, The Nobility and the Growth of the Bureaucracy in 17th Century Sweden', in: id., (ed.), *Europe and Scandinavia: Aspects of the Process of Integration in the 17th century* (Solna 1983), pp. 59–70; Lockhart (2004), pp. 123–144.

31 Glete (2010), pp. 123–133.

32 Jan Lindegren, 'Karl XII', in: *Kungar och krigare: Tre essäer om Karl X Gustav, Karl XI och Karl XII* (Stockholm 1992), pp. 149–225; Peterson (2007), pp. 242–277.

33 Karl-Erik Frandsen, 'Da Østdanmark blev til Sydsverige 1645–1720: En oversigt over den politiske baggrund og historikernes vurdering av den', in: id. & Jens Christian Vesterskov Johansen (eds.), *Da Østdanmark blev Sydsverige: Otte studier i dansk–svenske relationer under 1600-tallet* (Skippershoved 2003).

34 On mobilization for war, see Jan Lindegren, 'Men, Money and Means', in: Contamine (ed.), (2000), pp. 129–162.

35 Wolfgang Reinhard (ed.), *Power Elites and State Building* (Oxford 1996); Julia Adams, *The Familial State: Ruling Families and Merchant Capitalism in Early Modern Europe* (Ithaca 2005).

36 David Beetham, *The Legitimation of Power* (Basingstoke 1991), pp. 25–33.

37 Eva Österberg, 'State Formation and the People', in id., *Mentalities and Other Realities: Essays in Medieval and Early Modern Scandinavian History* (Lund 1991); Hallenberg et al. (2008); Johan Holm, *Konstruktionen av en stormakt: Kungamakt, skattebönder och statsbildning 1595 till 1640* (Stockholm 2007).

38 Michael F. Metcalf (ed.), *The Riksdag: A History of the Swedish Parliament* (Stockholm 1987).

39 For state formation as a demand-induced activity, see Douglas C. North, *Structure and Change in Economic History* (New York 1981), pp. 21–22; Michael Mann, 'The Autonomous Power of the State: Its Origins, Mechanisms and Results', in John A. Hall (ed.), *States in History* (Oxford 1986). For the early modern state and social movements, see Wayne te Brake, *Shaping History: Ordinary People in European Politics, 1500–1700* (Berkeley 1998).

40 Albert O. Hirschman, *Exit, Voice, and Loyalty: Responses to Decline in Firms, Organizations, and States* (Cambridge, Mass., 1970).

41 For a similar interpretation, see Erik Örjan Emilsson, *Before 'the European Miracles': Four Essays on Swedish Preconditions for Conquest, Growth and Voice* (Gothenburg 2005), pp. 56–72.

42 This may be compared to the 'Neo-classical theory of the state' suggested by Douglass C. North (1981) ch. 3; see also id., *Institutions, Institutional Change and Economic Performance* (Cambridge 1990), pp. 48–52.

43 Stefan Carlén, 'An Institutional Analysis of the Swedish Salt Market, 1720–1862', *Scandinavian Economic History Review*, 42 (1994), pp. 3–28; Mats Hallenberg, *Statsmakt till salu: Arrendesystemet och privatiseringen av skatteuppbärden i det svenska riket 1618–1635* (Lund 2008), pp. 224–226; Magnus Linnarsson, *Postgång på växlande villkor: Det svenska postväsendets organisation under stormaktstiden* (Lund 2010), pp. 199–203. See also Leos Müller on the Swedish Convoy Office in the present volume.

44 For agriculture, see Staffan Helmfrid, *The* Storskifte, Enskifte *and* Laga Skifte *in Sweden: General Features* (Stockholm 1961); Carl-Johan Gadd, 'The Agricultural Revolution in Sweden, ca. 1700–1900', in: Magnus Jerneck (ed.), *Different Paths to Modernity: A Nordic and Spanish Perspective* (Lund 2005), pp. 39–73. For infrastructure, see Hans Westlund, 'State and Market Forces in Swedish Infrastructure History', *Scandinavian Journal of History*, 23 (1998), pp. 65–88.

45 Gustafsson, Harald, *Political Interaction in the Old Regime: Central Power and Local Society in the Eighteenth-century Nordic States* (Lund 1994), pp. 105–153.

46 Torkel Jansson, 'The Age of Associations: Principles and Forms of Organization between Corporations and Mass Organizations. A Comparative Nordic Survey from a Swedish Viewpoint', *Scandinavian Journal of History*, 13 (1988), pp. 321–343; Peter Aronsson, 'Local Politics: The Invisible Political Culture', in: Øystein Sørensen & Bo Stråth (eds.), *The Cultural Construction of Norden* (Oslo 1997), pp. 172–205.

47 Per T. Ohlsson, *100 år av tillväxt: Johan August Gripenstedt och den liberala revolutionen* (Stockholm 1994); Lars Magnusson, *Den synliga handen: Nation, stat och det industriella bygget* (Stockholm 2005), pp. 161–186; Lars Magnusson, *Nation, State and the Industrial Revolution: The Visible Hand* (New York 2009), pp. 114–121.

48 Svenbjörn Kilander, *Den nya staten och den gamla: En studie i ideologisk förändring* (Uppsala 1991); Torbjörn Nilsson, *Elitens svängrum: Första kammaren, staten och moderniseringen 1867–1886* (Stockholm 1994); Lennart Lundqvist, *Fattigvårdsfolket: Ett nätverk i den sociala frågan 1900–1920* (Lund 1997).

49 Sven E. Olsson, *Social Policy and Welfare State in Sweden* (Lund 1990); Urban Lundberg & Klas Åmark, 'Social Rights and Social Security: The Swedish Welfare State, 1900–2000', *Scandinavian Journal of History*, 26 (2001), pp. 157–176; see also Åmark in this volume. For critical interpretations, see Maija Runcis, *Steriliseringar i folkhemmet* (Stockholm 1998); Gunnar Broberg & Mattias Tydén, 'Eugenics in Sweden: Efficient Care', in: Gunnar Broberg & Nils Roll-Hansen (eds.), *Eugenics and the Welfare State: Sterilization Policy in Denmark, Sweden, Norway, and Finland* (East Lansing 2005), pp. 77–149; Jenny Andersson, 'Nordic Nostalgia and Nordic Light: The Swedish Model as Utopia 1930–2007', *Scandinavian Journal of History*, 34 (2009), pp. 229–245.

50 Richard B. Freeman, Robert H. Topel & Birgitta Swedenborg (eds.), *The Welfare State in Transition: Reforming the Swedish Model* (Chicago 1997); Stefan Svallfors, 'The Middle Class and Welfare State Retrenchment: Attitudes to Swedish Welfare

Policies', in id. & Peter Taylor-Gooby (eds.), *The End of the Welfare State: Responses to State Retrenchment* (London 2007), pp. 34–51.

51 Michel Foucault, *Discipline and Punish: The Birth of the Prison* (New York 1979); Mitchell Dean, *The Constitution of Poverty: Toward a Genealogy of Liberal Governance* (London 1991); Roddy Nilsson, *Kontroll, makt och omsorg: Sociala problem och socialpolitik i Sverige 1780–1940* (Lund 2003).

52 Glete (2002) p. 217.

CHAPTER 3

Commissaries, Officers, and Politics in an Early Modern Army

Denmark-Norway (1614–1660)

Gunner Lind

Commissaries could be exasperating to the early modern army officer. Otto Ludwig, Count of the Rhine, a Royal Danish colonel, complained in 1628 that the commissaries 'do now command my regiment according to their ideas, and my authority as a colonel has been taken away from me'.[1] Commissaries may also baffle the historian. According to the Oxford English Dictionary, a commissary is 'an officer or official who has charge of the supply of food, stores, and transport, for a body of soldiers', and formerly also inspected the musters of men.[2] Early modern armies, however, had commissaries with more tasks and much greater authority than this modest job description implies. This has been clear since the ground-breaking study by Otto Hintze on *Der Commissarius* (1910).[3] So, commissaries were a far from uniform group; however, the range of variation is not well known.

The label itself contributes to the confusion. A commission was a letter conferring special authority for a specific task of a temporary character (such as during a war). Hence, the title 'commissary'. Commissarial appointments and the title of commissary had been widespread since the Middle Ages; however, some commissarial agents both inside and outside the military had other titles, such as the French *intendants de guerre.*

The sparse literature assigns several important roles to commissaries. They are described along Weberian lines as crucial tools in the formation of centralized states with bureaucratic management. (This was Hintze's point.) Military commissaries are also depicted as agents of discipline towards both troops and commanders, as well as having a key role in supplying armies with money and materiel: tasks that were as important for success in the field as military command proper. In short, despite the air of bureaucratic boredom emanating from the OED description, it seems well worth adding to our knowledge of early modern military commissaries.

The commissaries treated in Hintze's survey can be divided into two main types. At the root, we find the *supervisory* commissary of the sixteenth and early seventeenth century. He managed the payment and provisioning of armies, and kept a check on the activities of the military men. European armies consisted of units deployed by military enterprisers with a high degree of autonomy and a reputation for cheating their customers. The power to supply and pay – and to withhold goods and money – was a potent instrument against irregularities; it was only natural if it tended to blend with other aspects of command and control. Under such circumstances, commissaries became the all-purpose representatives of the buyer of military services – the warring state – defending state interests from the suppliers – the military enterprisers. Douglas Baxter has shown how the *intendants de guerre* were instrumental in establishing civilian control – the control of the royal ministers – over the fiercely independent and often politically unreliable marshals of France.[4] John Lynn has described how the *intendants* and their subordinates contributed to disciplining the army in relation to civilians, both through the establishment of supply services and the hard hand of punishment.[5] Michael Mallett and John Hale have clarified how the proveditors and collaterals of Venice worked down the centuries to make intransigent condottieri and their men conform to the rules of the Republic.[6] In neither case was this without conflict.

Managing levies, supplies, quarters, and justice could transform supervisory commissaries into the second type, what might be called the *proconsular* commissary. The Prussian *Kriegskommissarien* gradually took over most of the administration of the state as a whole during the seventeenth century, while the territorially defined subgroup of French *intendants* became the mainstay of provincial administration. Both these groups lost most of their military character, concentrating instead upon the management of the provinces. According to Hintze, war and competition between states was a driving force in the early modern state formation process, and princely autocratic rule was the natural and superior form of government established as an integral part of this process. Commissaries (extraordinary executives with broad powers) were the natural agents of the monarchical police state, pushing aside aristocratic constitutionalism and the traditional rule of law in the name of military necessity. Not all commissaries served the interest of princes, however. In some German states, locally elected *Landkommissarien* mediated between princely wishes and local elites.[7] Commissaries might potentially represent the full range of power-holders within early modern composite states. The connection between commissaries and princely authoritarianism may be less self-evident than suggested by Hintze's main narrative, which rests upon French and Prussian evidence.

Seen from the point of view of military history rather than the history of state formation, the supervisory commissary is the most interesting type. The organization formed by such men and their helpers must have been the actual 'social container', as Jan Glete defined it,[8] for a crucial range of competences during the phase when armies were transformed into permanent state institutions. Their expertise was as important for military performance – and, hence, also for the state formation process – as that of the military officers; and it was in their field of work, at least as much as in military technology and tactics, that innovation was found.

In the long run, supervisory commissaries were transformed into a third type – the *subordinate* – manning an integrated, supporting branch of the military itself. This was a logical result when the enterpriser aspect of military organization declined. As armies became bureaucratically managed state organizations, supply and payment became the province of humble and practical men who did not form a control structure independent of the military hierarchy. This seems to have been a fairly universal development, even in states where commissaries of high rank spawned successors of the proconsular type. In the well-studied French case, this development even happened twice. The sixteenth-century *commissaires de guerre* had been transformed into subordinate officials by the first decades of the seventeenth century, and the *intendants de guerre* introduced during these decades had lost their extraordinary character a century later. In the meantime, the *commissaires* were enrolled as helpers to the *intendants;* however, the service was only transformed into a corps with military grades as late as 1767–1772.[9] Such a corps allowed for the full integration of expertise into a stable organization. It is less clear how, and how successfully, earlier supervisory commissaries were able to perform this task.

Early modern military commissaries were, therefore, very far from being of one kind: their political role may prove to have been more complex than assumed; they did not yet form an integrated support branch of the military organization as such; and their field of work was crucial. Having a clearer picture of commissaries is central to a better understanding of early modern military organizations and early modern war. This chapter explores a new case, the Danish state from 1614 to 1660. These were the years between the establishment of the first permanent regiments of the Danish army and the absolutist revolution; a period marked by rapid military expansion and organizational development, severe wars, and political conflict.

The Danish state and the Danish army

Until the absolutist revolution in 1660, 'Denmark' was a union of two unions. The united kingdom of Denmark and Norway was connected with the united duchies of Schleswig and Holstein in a personal union as well as by a treaty of eternal union, which included a military alliance covering all just wars, offensive or defensive.[10]

Political power was distributed within each unit. In the kingdoms, the elective king was dependent upon the Council of the Realm. This was both the royal council with members appointed by the king and an upper house considered to represent the Danish nobility and the realm in general. The Council elected the king and was consulted on legislation, and its consent was required for taxes and declarations of war. As Bodin deplored, Danish kings shared sovereignty with the nobility.[11] When grave decisions were at hand, the Estates might be called. Meetings of the Estates became increasingly frequent during this period, often confronting both king and Council with demands from below, mostly coming from the nobility outside the Council.

In the duchies, the 'duke' himself was a composite. From 1544 to 1773, rule was shared between the royal branch of the house of Oldenburg and the cadet branch residing at Gottorp castle. Demesne income and lordship over commoners was territorially divided in the seventeenth century, while lordship over nobles as well as major decisions concerning the land as a whole were held in common. The composite 'duke' was strongly hemmed in by the Estates of the duchies: notably, the rich and powerful nobility. The duchies had no permanent noble representation such as the Council in Denmark-Norway, even if leading nobles were traditionally conferred with the title of provincial councillor (*Landrat*). At the head of the nobility stood the king's representative, the Viceroy, for generations appointed from the leading branch of the Rantzau family. He was both the embodiment of the duchies as a political unit and the linchpin connecting the land with the royal dynasty. The political power that empowered Danish commissaries was, indeed, split and combined in many ways.

The Danish form of aristocratic constitutionalism gave the elites in both parts of the state a strong voice in central government; however, there was no separate power vested in the administration. Danish state officials were not regulated by law, did not possess their office as saleable property, or exist as a corporate body. Compared with parts of Europe where such phenomena were common, *all* Danish administrators resembled commissaries rather than regular officials. Those labelled commissaries were similar to the commissaries of other states insofar as their appointment was seen as temporary and often came in addition to an existing post in royal service. These were characteristics shared by extraordinary envoys, for example. However, there was no dramatic difference in legal status or degree of independence between such men and other classes of high official.[12]

The Danish state fought three wars in the period in question: one against the Emperor and the Catholic League in 1625–1629, and two against Sweden in 1643–1645 and 1657–1660. The last war was in reality two, separated by six months of peace in 1658. Apart from the campaign of 1658–1660, all the wars were unsuccessful, and the war of 1657–1658 was a real disaster leading to major loss of territory.

A permanent army was created in 1614: initially, only two regiments were conscripted on a Swedish-inspired pattern; however, the army continued to grow, both in war and peace, throughout the period under study and well beyond. Maximum strength during the German War of 1625–1629 seems to have been approximately 40,000; during the war of 1657–1658 it amounted to 45,000. Maximum strength in peacetime – guarding Denmark–Norway's neutrality while war raged in Germany – was reached in the early 1640s with approximately 35,000, partly in a low level of readiness.[13] These were large forces considering that the Danish state had only two million inhabitants. Compared with the standards of the age, this was a rapid military build-up to a high level, interspersed with vicious wars with major powers. The challenges to organization and leadership alike were immense.

The commissaries

Commissaries came to Denmark along with other institutions of the well-developed German military mould. This makes them easy to identify by label. Only a few cases are ambiguous. At the top we find a handful of men of government rank who performed commissary tasks without the title. They are included here. At the bottom, there is some vagueness in the distinctions between subordinate commissaries such as 'commissaries for payment' (*zahlkommissær*) and lower ranking personnel with titles such as 'clerk of the musters' (*mønsterskriver*) or 'master of victuals' (*proviantmester*). The ambition here has been to exclude the clerks (even if men similar to them might have been called commissaries in other states) and include those who contemporaries labelled as 'commissary'. This means accepting that, despite their title, a small number of those included did only serve as clerks to more powerful commissaries. Ad hoc orders occasionally directed specific men to do specific tasks, such as when the county governor in Segeberg, Caspar von Buchwald, was commissioned to muster the regiment of Henrik Holck before it was transferred into Dutch service in 1629.[14] Such occasional 'commissaries' are not covered by this study.

Between 1618 and 1660, 189 men were active as commissaries, sharing 291 separate positions. As a comparison, 2,026 men were commissioned with the rank of captain or higher in the army.[15] So, commissaries were quite numerous: approximately one for every ten of the officers they were to support and monitor. Naturally, most positions were filled in wartime (for example, 68 during the war of 1625–1629 and 93 during the wars of 1657–1660). Still, the growing peacetime army did also demand commissaries. None were in service during the peace years of 1615–1618; however, 48 appointments were made in the inter-war years of 1630–1642, and 45 from 1646 to 1656. Seen as a group, the commissaries developed into a stable element comprising a considerable part of the ranking personnel of the army.

Being a commissary was rarely a dominant phase in an individual career. The typical commissary only received one such appointment. Eight men had 4 appointments, however, and twenty-three obtained 3. The average duration of a single appointment as commissary was slightly longer than three years and the average total time amounted to slightly less than five years, yet twenty-three of them logged more than ten years of service. Their combined years of service accounted for four out of ten of all years served by Danish commissaries in 1615–1660. It would be exaggerated to speak of a corps of commissaries or a commissary career track; only a handful of those who served many years had full-time positions, and almost all combined their commissaryship with other offices. Seen from the point of view of the individual, very few could have regarded their commissaryship as the dominant element in a professional identity. Seen from the point of view of military organization, however, professional specialization was pronounced enough to enable this group to assemble much expertise and experience and keep it alive for the future. A few became trusted experts who kept reappearing in new positions, such as the Dane Knud Ulfeldt (commissary-general 1639–1646 and general 1657) or the Holsteiner Cay von Ahlefeldt (commissary-general 1627–1629, 1636–1647, and 1657–1660).

The commissaries were mostly noblemen and few were foreigners. Fully 87 per cent of the posts went to indigenous men and 80 per cent to the nobilities of Denmark-Norway or Schleswig-Holstein. The non-nobles were almost exclusively found in subordinate, functionally specific posts. This stands in glaring contrast to the regular officers. During this period of expansion, approximately half of the officer commissions (of or over the rank of captain) went to foreigners, and the indigenous noblemen took only a quarter.[16]

Quite surprisingly, given the degree of trust involved, one in six is not on record as having been a servant of the Danish crown before their first appointment as commissary. The background of these new men may be suggested from the cases of Heinrich von Stöcken, who came from the personal service of Commissary-General Cay von Ahlefeldt, or Tönnies von Buchwald, who worked during a year of crisis along with his brother Detlev, who was well established in royal service.[17]

The most common previous employment was in the army. More than half of the commissaries were also military officers. Out of those 189 military officers, 97 served as commissioned officers in the Danish army at some point in their career (and two in the navy). This includes 84 who had served as army officers before their first assignment as a commissary and 47 who served afterwards. A number who had seen military service in foreign armies must be added to the 97 Danish officers. A considerable proportion of the officers cannot be described as professional military men. Their military commissions might lie far back, be modest, or concern the noble cavalry, which was only partly integrated into the army. A sizable fraction, however, were military men of some standing. Only one had reached the rank of general; however, 30 of the 84 had served as regimental officers (13 colonels, 13 lieutenant colonels, and 4 majors).

The proportion who had served as civilian administrators was also a little more than half: 96 of the 189 commissaries had some such service on record before their first commissaryship, often in more than one post. By far the most common was service as *lensmand* (*Amtmann* in the duchies) – 73 of the 189 men – the county governorship that was the backbone of local administration, while 21 had been secretaries in the chancellery, although only two in the financial administration. Of these men, 21 had reached the highest level as councillors of the realm or provincial councillors in the duchies. Being a secretary in the royal chancellery was a job for young men and mostly a thing in their past. The other civilian posts were almost always kept during commissary service.

All civilian posts implied contact with the court and the king. A spell as gentleman of the court or as secretary in the closely integrated chancellery was a typical early career step for a nobleman. Most of those who had served at court had gone on to other posts before their first commissary appointment; however, in 25 cases (13 per cent) such service (typically taking place some years prior) was the only earlier employment. The young gentlemen of the court were organized as a cavalry unit. A career starting here could go on to encompass military as well as civilian posts – in some cases, both. Almost one in four commissaries had served both as an army officer and a civilian administrator.

If we compare the Danish commissaries with their best-known European counterparts, few were delegates from the central administration. Only half had any previous connections to the civilian administration, and these were mostly local administrators. The careers of Danish commissaries points to the importance of two more general characteristics, which they shared with delegates from the central administration: connectedness and experience. However, connectedness was, by birth, to the hereditary nobility of the Danish crown and, by service, to the crown in general – not to its central administration – and their experience was not necessarily as an administrator. Familiarity with war seems to have been seen as desirable. The high proportion of former military officers is surprising. Quite a few commissaries were even serving officers at the same time. They might have been suspected of the worst sin of any commissary: collusion with the officers; however, men with strong military experience might serve well both as supervisors and in the army leadership if their loyalty to their employer was unwavering. The commissarial career was one where diverse forms of expertise mingled and combined.

Patterns of appointment

Two-thirds of foreign-born commissaries were commissioned during the campaign in Germany (1625–1629). This was one of many clear patterns in the selection of commissaries. The German War provides several good examples of such patterns.

Christian IV, as Duke of Holstein and *Kreisoberst* of the Lower Saxon Circle, formed an army in Germany during the summer of 1625. His generals were all German princes and nobles attached to the Protestant party in the Empire. The same went for a number of specialist civil–military administrators, such as the quartermaster-general or the master of victuals, and a few commissaries without special designation who mainly seem to have been attached to the separate corps. These Germans were all new in the Danish service. Against normal procedure, some of them seem to have been commissaries and officers at the same time. The three leading commissaries, however, were all noblemen from Holstein: both natural subjects of the King and born on the soil of a member of the Lower Saxon Circle. All had been previously employed as military officers or war commissaries. Even if Danes were active in the entourage of the King, there was not a single Dane in the army leadership.[18]

The Danes came at the beginning of 1626, and not simply any old Danes, but political and administrative heavyweights. Two councillors of the realm went to Germany as commissaries-general. A third was put in charge of the main war chest. A councillor from Holstein was made commissary-general of victuals. The most prominent German commissaries were, thus, replaced while the less prominent stayed on. This lasted until the summer of 1627, when the Danish commissaries-general were dismissed and sent home. In their stead, a number of colonels – all German – became commissaries. When prompted to appoint a new commissary-general, the King proclaimed: 'I am that myself, and I will not readily choose another'.[19] He was, indeed, active with commissary tasks, unifying the two lines of army control in the person of the commanding ruler.

In the autumn of 1627, the combined forces of Wallenstein and Tilly broke through the front line along the Elbe. Schleswig, Holstein, and Jutland were occupied except for a stretch of southern Holstein that was secured by a chain of fortresses and redoubts. Practically all senior German officers and commissaries were discharged when the army leadership was reconstructed. In their stead, a number of regional leaderships were appointed, consisting of officers and commissaries in close cooperation. The power to decide over the Holstein fortresses rested with a committee that consisted of a varying number of officers and commissaries. All came from the Holstein nobility, and all had served in the field army in Germany. In each of the main Danish provinces confronting the enemy, a committee of three were made joint leaders: one high-ranking officer and two noble administrators with military experience. All committee members were designated commissaries-general, including the serving officer. Lesser provinces also had joint leaderships of officers and commissaries. In these cases, however, the officers did not get commissaryship. Central leadership was sparsely manned: the King, the marshal of the realm (a traditional noble post resurrected at this time of crisis) and a commissary-general of payments (who was put in charge of all extraordinary taxes for the army). This organization lasted until the war ended.

The German War exemplifies a number of common traits. One of these is *change that is recurrent, often rapid, and radical.* Whole groups of commissaries came and went suddenly, both in times of war and of peace. As was the case in 1626 and 1628, most commissaries in Denmark were changed in 1658; and a number of administrative rearrangements produced wholesale changes in peacetime (1638–1639, 1645–1646). Another recurring trait is the *coexistence of separate groups of commissaries.* Most conspicuously, the kingdom of Denmark never share commissaries with Schleswig-Holstein, despite three wars with extensive fighting in both of these adjacent territories, and a lengthy period (1635–1648) when large forces from the kingdom were stationed in the duchies in order to safeguard the frontier. In this case, the troops from the kingdom were mustered and paid by Danish commissaries, while commissaries from the duchies paid their own contingent and were intermediaries with local authorities and communities. The *autochthonous nature of the majority of commissaries* was closely connected with this trait, especially the more important ones. Commissaries from the local nobility were preferred: Germans in Germany, Danes in Denmark, local *Ritterschaft* in the duchies, even Norwegian-born in Norway (despite the lack of a formal political border between Denmark and Norway).

Commissaries were, thus, an inchoate group geographically an temporally. New units of men might suddenly be introduced, and dif-

Control and Command, 1 September 1643

- Kingdom of Denmark
  - The King.
  - The Marshal of the Realm: direction of troops actually in the kingdom.
  - Commissary General for the troops raised according to the Union treaty: payment and control, in the kingdom or in the duchies alike.
  - Separate accountant at Court to pay the military household.
- The Danish province of Skåne
  - Two members of the Council of the Realm to pay and control border fortresses and their garrisons from separate income.
- Danish provinces
  - Eight provincial commissaries to control separate military funds from certain taxes.
  - Three commissaries to collect military customs duties assigned to the Commissary General.
- Norway
  - The Viceroy, serving as both supreme commander and commissary, using both military officers and provincial administrators for support.
- The duchies of Schleswig and Holstein
  - Commissary General of the King, assigned to the union troops of the duchies.
  - Commissary General of the Duke of Gottorp, assigned to the union troops.
  - Jointly appointed Major General for the union troops.
  - Three commissaries from the nobility to control the establishment and flow of money.
  - War commissary assigned to pay troops in the royal fortresses.

ferent parts of the state had their own men with local roots. This was an organization of the moment, prone to experimentation and only gradually developing more stable forms. Sensibility to changing conditions was great, and links to the political level were strong.

Politics and commissaries

Political links were occasionally made explicit. During the German War, one single appointment was directly linked to a political deal. This was the Commissary-General of Military Payments (*generalkrigszahlkommissær*) Niels Krag, whose post was created in June 1628. Seen from the army, Niels Krag delivered service. He paid money according to the directions of others – mostly commanders – and mostly through subordinate commissaries of payment. Accordingly, he had little responsibility for supervising the military men; he supervised the king instead. The extraordinary taxes were paid into his coffers, and members of the Council audited his accounts. This elderly appeals judge had been selected by the Council and the noble Estate before he received his royal commission, and his job was to monitor the stream of money so that taxes, voted for the defence of Denmark, were not diverted into the renewed offensive desired by the king.[20]

Krag's position was unique. No other commissary was made guardian of the bulk of the military budget. However, about a quarter of the commissary positions were dedicated to the custody of specific military funds that were fed by dedicated taxes. Other examples of commissaries with an explicit political agenda were the fortress commissaries in Skåne (1624–1647), the commissary-general of Schleswig-Holstein (1636–1646), the provincial commissaries (1638–1658), and two boards of councillor commissaries (1657–1658). The provincial commissaries (*landkommissær*) were the most numerous (61 positions); these were introduced in 1638 in order to handle military reserve funds approved by the Estates, and elected by the nobility of the provinces.[21] This is an exact parallel to some of the German *Landkommissarien*. In all these cases, the core agenda was to serve as a politically programmed money valve, designed with other political stakeholders in mind rather than the military. A standard feature was auditing by delegates of those who had granted the money.

Given the explicit political background of some appointments, it would be natural to expect that the general traits in recruitment were also politically determined. Political considerations could easily explain a preference for local noblemen, the division into different groups relating to different parts of the Danish lands, and the rapid changes when the political situation shifted. Indirect evidence is often strong, as in 1626, when Danish councillors were appointed as commissaries-general in Germany the moment the king had solicited financial support from Denmark for his German war.[22]

This direct, as well as indirect, evidence demonstrates how commissaries were agents in networks of trust and distrust. Every commissary had the trust of those who appointed him; however, it might be even more important that he had the trust of third parties. Traditionally, commissaries drew the distrust of those paying towards the military. However, they might also express the distrust of tax-voting bodies towards the executive or of allies towards one another, as in the joint union army put up by Denmark and Schleswig-Holstein in 1635–1648. Handling trust and distrust was so important that it trumped other considerations, such as individual experience or organizational coherence.

On the job

The commissary-general of military payments (1628–1629) is an example of a commissary with a limited range of duties. Krag had a lot to do as very large sums were received, paid out, and duly accounted for.[23] However, he did nothing except supervise the flow of money received from tax-collecting administrators, and pay out according to the requests of those in command. The other money-controlling commissaries had the same few duties, yet their task portfolio had a strong tendency to expand. This was immediately visible when committees of councillors were involved. The committee in Skåne rapidly developed into a regional command in charge of everything concerning the defence of this border province, from building bastions to running spies, only ceding operational command to proper generals in wartime. The committee operating in Copenhagen in 1657–1658 became heavily involved in operational decisions, the selection of personnel, and overall political guidance of the war effort. The range of activities of the provincial commissaries also grew in the long run. They handled more funds from more sources and became involved in disbursement, which inevitably involved supervision of the troops.[24]

Commissaries who existed to supervise the executive rather than the military must not be confused with the smaller group of specialized commissaries. A total of 36 positions had a clear functional specification as commissary of payments, victuals or the like. Their surviving accounts indicate that this was not only a difference in title.[25] Their work focused upon the control of money or goods: paying and delivering according to the directions of others who were supposed to keep tabs on the recipients. The use of specialized commissaries presumed the existence of other commissaries at the location, be it a fortress or a field army. A commissary-general of victuals or payments was always a nobleman; some of the commissaries of victuals were, but not many of those made commissaries of payments. These last had few responsibilities beyond the handling of money and accounts and, in some cases, may have been mislabelled clerks – not commissaries.

A third special group was attached to foreign armies. Ten Danish noblemen were appointed to be commissaries for the evacuation of Swedish units leaving Denmark after the peace of February 1658. There were seventeen commissaries to the allied troops from Brandenburg, Poland, and the Empire during the campaign of 1658–1659. Such commissaries mostly regulated quarters and other aspects of the interaction between the foreign troops and the population. Insofar as they supervised the military, they monitored adherence to the agreements between the Danish and foreign governments.[26]

Leaving aside all specialized groups we are left with about half of the positions (161). These were less specific 'commissaries', literally 'commissaries for war' (*krigskommissær* in Danish; *Kriegscommissarius* in German) or 'commissaries-general' (*generalkrigskommissær*). A few acted without any formal title; these were dignitaries of the highest level – councillors of the realm, the Viceroys in Norway or the duchies – who proceeded solely on the basis of orders concerning their assignment. They might even function jointly with true commissaries-general without a commission, as the Viceroy Christian Rantzau did with Friedrich and Detlev von Ahlefeldt in managing the army in Holstein (1657).[27]

The titles did of course express differences in rank; however, non-specialized commissaries only occasionally displayed much of a hierarchy. This was only the rule when a board of councillors had overall responsibility for a large area. Such boards acted through subordinates, including both ordinary commissaries and commissaries-general.[28] The typical configuration in the field or in garrison was either to have a commissary-general with a range of responsibilities comparable to a general officer, and aided by specialized commissaries for victuals and payments; or, ordinary commissaries allocated to a fortress, section or even a single regiment, and no specialized commissaries. The commissaries had no superiors below army central command in the second case or even at the level of government (which might be the same when the king was in command). Neither of these organizational models ordered non-specialized commissaries in a bureaucratic hierarchy.[29]

The duties of non-specific commissaries had a well-known core, officially described as 'the drawing up of muster rolls, distribution of victuals, payments, and the like'.[30] A system of rules guided these activities: either general rules such as ordinances on quartering or specific contracts made with enterprisers. Core duties tended to expand from this; discipline was often formally included. Ferdinand von Spiegell, judge advocate of a Scottish regiment arriving in Danish territory, was made commissary of this regiment. The royal letter specified that, among his new obligations, he should 'keep diligent care that the officers keep the soldiers in check and in good order, and not permit damage to be inflicted upon Our subjects in any matter'.[31] Discipline was essentially a job for officers in collaboration with the military juridical and penal system; however, commissaries were natural 'meta-disciplinarians', keeping an eye on those who were supposed to take action in the first instance. However, it was a step further when a commissary-general was instructed to 'keep good order' in the regiments that made up an army corps.[32] His role changed from supervising the officers to being a prime mover, activating officers and military justice personnel. The auditor became a superior.

As in the case of the Scottish regiment, one side of discipline was the treatment of civilians. Quarters, provisions, and so-called 'contributions' provided by the population all featured among the pay of the soldiers. This made commissaries the natural go-betweens in all matters concerning the relationship between the army and civilians: organizing passage and transport, collecting taxes and levies, allocating quarters, drawing up the complex accounts, and resolving the inevitable conflicts. These tasks were normally not specified in their instructions; however, they were often the subject of specific orders. It was clearly a standard expectation that commissaries should engage in such issues.[33]

In summary, the day-to-day activities of commissaries were less dependent upon a hierarchy of command than upon systems of rules. Any internal hierarchy among commissaries was only relevant for the commissaries-general with their subordinate specialists. The royal government or high commanders might order commissaries to muster, pay or provision bodies of troops according to military priorities. However, the execution was governed by the ordinances and contracts then in force, rather than orders.

Commissaries were rule-bound enforcers of regularity, yet they also constantly moved into areas where no rules applied. Their activities had a tendency to expand according to the needs of the day. Added to the core package of tasks, strongly ordered by rules and instructions, we find a second package governed by ad hoc orders and discretion. This second package keeps reappearing with similar content, indicating that these tasks were bound up with one another and not easily performed by, or entrusted to, the military officers. It is understandable that the all-round experience of county governors or regimental officers was more desirable than time spent in the central administration.

Commissaries and commanders

Supervision created an unavoidable field of tension between commissaries and officers. There were other zones of conflict. Commissaries and commanders were supposed to cooperate; however, no clear hierarchy existed in case of disagreement, and conflict became more likely the more the field of activity of commissaries expanded.

Commissaries, and especially commissaries-general, often issued operative orders in a restricted way both in war and in peace. Most of these orders concerned the dislocation of troops or equipment. This was a grey zone concerning preparation and readiness, rather than operational leadership in the full sense. Sometimes, however, the responsibility of command came to rest completely upon the shoulders of the commissaries. This happened by accident in 1627, when commissary Joachim von Mitzlaff took charge of the isolated army corps in Moravia and Silesia, following the death of both general officers. In 1637, commissary-general Tønne Friis sought and obtained instructions on what action to take 'if the Imperial troops insist on entering the land of Holstein', including taking up the fight with all troops in the province.[34] In both cases, the commissaries stepped into a gap created when no general officers were at hand. The commissaries were then the most distinguished royal servants, outranking the colonels.

A commissary-general was designated the commander of an army in a single case: Jørgen Bielke led the small army corps of northern Norway into the (formerly Norwegian) adjacent province in Sweden in 1657. A strange choice, as Bielke was a seasoned colonel and could well have been appointed general, as he was a few months later. His own regiment was also a part of his army; therefore, Bielke, the commissary, supervised Bielke, the military enterpriser.

A plausible explanation may be the isolation of the theatre of war where Bielke's corps was to operate. This made it desirable to have a leader with extraordinary independent powers. Another factor may have been the importance of interaction with the civilian population across the border during this campaign.[35] Relations with civilians were, after all, a commissary speciality.

Bielke's role seems to have been unique, insofar as he was appointed sole commissary and commander.[36] The distinction between commissary and commander was strongly blurred in a considerable number of other cases where leadership rested with a group. In a few instances, all members of the collective were commissaries. The Danish councillors active as commissaries-general in Germany in 1626–1627 may serve as an example. They operated as the high command in the sector where they resided. Here, they collected intelligence and worked hard on relations with the inhabitants. They corresponded with the enemy command. They gave orders on the occupation of key positions and other tactical operations. In short, the collective of commissaries-general had full responsibility in this sector. However, the sector was not much threatened by direct enemy action. There was little need for general officers to lead operations.[37] This seems to have been the rule where boards solely consisting of commissaries of government rank formed the high command.

A much more common model placed the direction of war with a committee where some members were commissaries and others were officers. Such solutions were numerous in the wars of 1625–1629 and 1643–1645 and during the period of readiness in 1635–1643. This model had two main varieties.

One variety was the large board, often called *Kriegsrat* or Council of War; this is not to be confused with the councils routinely summoned by commanders to deliberate. Good examples recur in Southern Holstein, where a chain of fortresses and redoubts protected the marshlands. A '*corpus* and *consilium*' was formed in December 1628 from two commissaries-general, who were also provincial councillors of Schleswig-Holstein, aided by two lawyer administrators.[38] This was soon expanded into its largest form, which included one commissary-general and councillor, two commissaries, one major-general, two colonels, a county governor, and two lawyers. These 'deputies to the regiment and council of war' obtained full authority to direct the war in the province, acting as a group in the name of the king. Only the special commissary tasks – musters, provisions, and payments – were excluded. They were the preserve of the commissaries acting alone directly under the king. The tasks of military officers were not specified; however, it is clear that the generals in the province were expected to act as field commanders under the direction of the board.[39] This council of war was not the council *of* a commander, as was usually the case; it was *the* commander.

The other variety was small committees of two or three persons in charge of a sector or an army corps. Such committees directed the defence of the Danish islands against the Imperial Army (1628–1629). One member was an officer of appropriate rank – from lieutenant general down to captain, depending upon the size of the sector – and the other one or two members were commissaries. However, all were officially termed commissaries or commissaries-general according to their level of responsibility; this included the officer. The authority to command rested with the commission, and not with the ranking officer included in it. In one case, it can be shown that a commissary with command responsibilities kept accounts of payments;[40] however, commanding commissaries seem to have acted as generals in most cases and only issued orders of payment to the Commissary-General of Military Payments Niels Krag and his staff.

These commanding committees greatly annoyed men like the colonel who was quoted at the beginning of this chapter. Commissaries acting as superiors, not only as supervisors, were clearly a strange and unwelcome addition to the international corps of officers. On the Danish side, however, commissaries were regarded as natural commanders. The King indicted Colonel Conway because he had disobeyed Commissary-General Claus Daa 'in his command, which His Majesty himself has entrusted to him'.[41] The same Claus Daa, in collaboration with Field Marshal von Thurn, had authored the royal ordinance a few months earlier, specifying the proper relationship in the event of a similar conflict: the ultimate decision in a joint leadership should rest with the commissary. The commander – the leading officer – should respect him and instruct his men to do the same. The commissary had sole responsibility for justice done between soldiers and the civilian population, and for passwords, musters, and the allocation of quarters. Together, they should both plan watches and fortification work and, as a rule, the commissary should decide 'with the counsel and deliberation of the commander, and also including other officers who may be present'.[42]

Distrust of the available generals led to these radical solutions. This is why leadership by committee predominated from 1628–1629, when the disorder accompanying the retreat of the royal army into Denmark had produced a major political crisis and the dismissal of most of the German high officers to be replaced with Danes, Scots, and Englishmen.

Leadership by committee produced a military organization that deviated substantially from the European tradition. Instead of two separate organizational strands, we find integration at the highest level, only branching out farther down. The repeated admonishments to other committee members not to interfere with the core commissary tasks demonstrated an awareness of the danger that collectivity could lead to the disintegration of supervision with the officers as enterprisers. The dangers inherent in the collectivization of operational command were not unrecognized, as disgruntled officers warned: 'those who have no experience usurp the command'.[43] However, if these dangers were not dismissed, then they were seen as secondary to securing strong control during the later stages of the war (1625–1629) with the remaining foreign-born officers in high command.

Organizational normalization

Leadership by committee only reappeared on a modest scale during the next war (1643–1645). Committees consisting solely of commissaries organized local defence in most Danish provinces; commissaries acted as subordinate leaders in the army in Norway. Nevertheless, the leadership did not like this solution. According to an Austrian diplomat, the Marshal of the Realm Anders Bille spoke badly of 'the commissaries, who manage affairs due to the lack of competent and seasoned officers.'[44] Higher command was no longer entrusted to committees. Along with the two ranking officers of the province, the seasoned Commissary-General and Councillor Cay von Ahlefeldt improvised a leadership committee in Southern Holstein immediately following the unexpected Swedish attack. However, Prince Frederik soon replaced the committee as *generalissimus*. High command came to rest with political–military leaders such as the Prince, the King, the Marshal of the Realm, and the Viceroy in Norway, Hannibal Sehested. They did not need to be chaperoned by indigenous commissaries. The use of commissaries was now clearly a stopgap in the abscence of high officers. Recruitment from abroad was difficult as it was a surprise attack and available funds were low. However, if generals had been imported, they might well have found themselves tightly controlled by commissaries as in 1628–1629.

The army was reduced in size following peace with Sweden in 1645 and the Peace of Westphalia in 1648. Still, the army was quite considerable and the number of experienced military men was high compared with previous generations. The marshal of the realm was now their leader: a traditional noble office held ex officio his membership of the Council of the Realm. As the permanent army expanded, the marshal had steadily gained in importance. There was a need for permanent management and this was an obvious place to find it.

Within Denmark proper, all commissary tasks were concentrated in the hands of the provincial commissaries. Most of the army's sources of income and most obligations to pay were transferred to them. At the same time, they were put under the direction of the marshal. The marshal had become a powerful minister of war as he also commanded the army officers; however, this was true for the kingdom of Denmark, and not the Danish state as a whole. The smaller military establishments in Norway and Schleswig-Holstein did not come under the authority of the marshal and did not develop a corresponding level of specialization in military leadership during the peace. Control in Norway was in the hands of the Viceroy. All remaining troops there were conscripts and the few commissary duties were passed onto the local administration. The most prominent commissaries in the duchies were also dismissed. A German-born commissary with one or two assistants served the troops in the fortresses.[45]

The tentative trend after 1629 was then towards the normalization of the army's organization with two separate branches of control: the military chain of command and the supporting, supervisory commissaries. The trend was clearly visible after 1648; however, it could also be discerned during the war years of 1643–1645 and in the final years of the army corps activities in the duchies (1638–1643). The limiting factor was the availability of able and trusted general officers: the word trusted equating to 'from the indigenous nobility'.

Countdown to revolution

As preparations for war progressed in 1657, it became apparent that decades with a permanent army and two recent wars had created new conditions. The number of men from all lands of the crown capable of taking up arms or shouldering higher command had grown enormously. More troops could be raised within Denmark–Norway's borders. More men were available who combined expertise and experience with the trustworthiness of the indigenous nobleman or the well-integrated immigrant. This applied to officers as well as commissaries.[46]

A strong field commissariat was created early on. In each of the four main armies, a commissary-general was in overall charge of supervision and pay. Subordinate commissaries assisted them with payment and victuals. Subordinates in Denmark included the provincial commissaries; in Norway, local commissaries appointed from among the resident nobility. Commissary boards with members of government rank were responsible in the base areas behind the frontlines: especially for the flow of money, as well as the issuing of directives to the commissaries-general. Two boards of councillors were set up in Denmark proper. The Viceroy of Norway had sole responsibility; the Viceroy of the duchies operated along with two commissaries-general (who were also councillors).

The roles of commissaries and commanders were, for the first time, clearly separated in most armies; the only exception was the double role of Jørgen Bielke in northern Norway. Elsewhere, each army had a purely military command structure consisting of a commanding general who was supported by general officers of lesser rank. The commanding generals were empowered to order commissaries to muster and issue pay without referring back to the government level.

A document from early 1657 defines the rights and duties of a commissary-general in this new organization. First of all, it states that he must be respected by everyone: he is the only man in the army empowered to allocate quarters or give civilians letters of protection; he may detail men for guard duty; he summons the council of war; he issues the password if no lieutenant-general or field marshal is present, even in the presence of a major-general; he conducts his own correspondence with superiors, foreigners, or the enemy; he is to inspect the provisions and has sole trust for payments 'and depends upon nobody but the king in this matter'.[47]

Despite the increased status of the commanding generals, the commissary-general retained his separate sphere of responsibility; he also kept a role in operative command. As convenor of the council of war he had a strong influence upon operative decisions and an implied duty to keep the commander from exercising his power without proper counsel. Still, this gave less direct control than the earlier commanding committees had done. Each commanding general was ultimately empowered to act according to his own 'rational consideration'.[48]

Compared with earlier wars, this distribution of responsibilities implied a specialization of the two branches of military leadership and a demotion of the commissary branch. What made this possible was the new crop of commanders. All commanding generals were both experienced military men and Danish noblemen, while the most important were the Marshal of the Realm and two other members of the Council. The commanders of the army were now men worthy of the same kind of trust as the commissaries and did not need the backing of a collective leadership.

The great army of 1657 collapsed within a year. The enemy destroyed the western corps; the eastern corps had to be severely reduced following the peace in 1658. The Marshal of the Realm died from his wounds and was not replaced. Only the army in Norway survived in good order. The commissaries-general and other commissaries appointed in 1657 ended their business. When war restarted after six months of peace, the Danish army was reconstructed under extreme conditions.

The bulk of the new regiments were raised using 'contributions' and unpaid quarters from the subjects of the duchies and Jutland following their liberation at the hands of Denmark's allies.

Renewed military expansion demanded more commissaries. The separate armies had very different solutions. Under the supervision of their heads of office acting as commissaries, book-keepers detailed from the financial administration took care of accounts and payments in besieged Copenhagen; the municipal administration looked after quarters; the large number of dignitaries present in the city took care of musters. The defence relied upon the participation of the estates of the besieged city: the burghers, the noblemen and court personnel, and the university and clergy. Dignitaries from all estates audited the accounts.[49] Such political control from below was natural when the estates took on extraordinary burdens to maintain the troops and provided a large part of the defending forces in person. The city was provided with a surplus of military officers, and commissaries were not involved in command.

The field armies used the same model as they had during the previous war: a commissary-general aided by local commissaries in Norway, who were all drawn from the regular Norwegian noble administrators, plus one or two subordinate commissaries; and the commissaries-general of the previous war were reappointed in the duchies, again supported by the same specialized commissaries. The new Danish field army also received a commissary-general who was supported by a few non-noble specialized commissaries and a handful of supporting regional commissaries. Most of these supporting commissaries were new men: former army officers who had never been commissaries before. They were first appointed as commissaries to the allied forces and their functions were later extended to cover the new Danish army. Even their titles were uncertain. On one occasion, they were called 'extraordinary commissaries'.[50]

The position of the commissaries was essentially the same as it had been during the previous war (1657–1658). They supported and supervised commanders without being directly involved in command. As the leading generals had changed, this represented a change in policy. In lieu of Danish councillors, the two main armies operating in Denmark and the duchies each had a foreign professional as leader. Both men had been brought in during the winter 1657–1658 when war losses made it imperative to find new generals. The most influential field marshal, Hans Schack, had connections to Schleswig and was rushed through naturalization as a Danish nobleman. Still, neither Schack nor his colleague were strongly attached to the Danish political system. Army leadership now rested with military professionals, all of whom were of foreign birth with the exception of Jørgen Bielke, who was now a lieutenant-general in charge of the main army in Norway. The lesser generals were also now experienced professionals born in the duchies or farther south in Germany, even if several had been naturalized. The Council of the Realm expressed their lack of confidence in 'the foreigners who have now been entrusted with the highest command'.[51] The councillors may have desired a return to command by committee; however, they had few instruments of power under the circumstances.

The strongest and most important army politically was that in the Danish provinces, which Schack and Pogwisch governed. Commissary-General Otto Pogwisch had been both a military officer and a provincial commissary, yet was first of all personally close to the king and the court.[52] Pogwisch obtained extraordinary powers when he was sent to the liberated provinces with orders to raise an army. He was authorized to claim all ordinary royal income, to draft soldiers, and to impose 'contributions' as needed. In combination with the commissary-generalship, these powers were assigned to Schack when he arrived to take command of the offensive against the Danish islands. The field marshal's instructions clearly placed him above Pogwisch even if collaboration, rather than outright command, was the expectation in the text. The correspondence between the two men reveals that they did collaborate well, and that the commissary-general was indeed the junior partner.[53] This was now the expectation everywhere: Field Marshal von Eberstein, the commander in the duchies, participated in the allocation of quarters, money and goods, and even complained when the commissaries-general mustered the troops without his participation.[54]

The powers given to Pogwisch and Schack demonstrated an extraordinary degree of trust. The two were given as free a hand as they would in occupied enemy territory. They had no real counterweight in Denmark; the successful offensive and the evacuation of enemy troops after the peace in 1660 extended their authority to the whole kingdom. No larger group shared their power: the other ranking commissary in Jutland, Councillor Henrik Rantzau, was assigned to liaise with the allies and the army in the duchies. Lastly, the King granted these powers without proper consultation. This provoked a conflict with the Council of the Realm; however, relations between King and Council had already broken down in the aftermath of the winter catastrophe (1657–1658). The Council could complain, yet had no leverage to enable it to challenge the fact that royal letters had been issued 'both for recruitment and taxes, the levying and mounting of troops, against privilege, and other extraordinary things under threat of military execution, which should not to happen without the approval of the Council and, in part, the consent of those concerned as well'.[55]

However, Schack and Pogwisch, as well as von Eberstein in the duchies, had the trust of the king – and with reason. They and their men proved to be loyal to him when the orders were given to apply military pressure at the crucial point of the political process leading to the introduction of absolute royal rule in the autumn of 1660.

Conclusion

During the build-up of a permanent army, the Danish military commissaries were a multitude who served many purposes. These were only partly military. Commissaries were a much more complex group than the military officers because of their core task as an interface between the army and the state at war, with all its peculiarities. Many resembling commissaries are to be found in other states; however, some of Denmark–Norway's solutions were unusual, if not unique (such as the use of commissary-dominated committees in command).

The ranking commissaries during these years belonged to the supervisory type. Commissaries of the subordinate type were mostly specialists under their control. Towards the end of the period, however, we do see a tendency to reduce the status of commissaries in relation to high command (that is to say, a small shift towards transforming all commissaries into the subordinate type typical of bureaucratically organized armies). This was a tendency that was to continue after 1660. With extensive influence outside the army, the proconsular type of commissary only makes a fleeting appearance during the last war under the old political system (1658–1660). This had political importance during the months when the absolutist revolution was carried through; however, it had no lasting influence upon the Danish administration.

We meet commissaries as crown agents in this singular context. The precondition was the breakdown of the normal political mechanisms due to defeat and occupation, for otherwise, Danish military commissaries were anything but natural agents of monarchical expansion; they were the tools and protectors of the mixed constitution in the composite state. Many powerful commissaries were not even delegates of central power; they represented estates in the social or territorial sense. As with the commissarial managers of the Venetian Republic, they were agents rather than enemies of aristocratic constitutionalism. Such commissaries constituted civilian control of the military, one with strong political overtones, yet they primarily enabled different political actors to control one another within constitutional arrangements or political compromises.

This did not block a rapid militarization of the state; it enabled it: politically, by making taxation easier, and practically, by mobilizing a large number of the best administrators in the service of the army. The Danish case demonstrates the importance of a silent assumption in Otto Hintze's model of monarchism driven by military needs; it rests upon the notion that traditional sharers of power would reject change necessitated by military developments. When this was true, a prince's commissaries might, indeed, offer a way to circumvent them. However, insofar as the traditional elites endorsed such change, their agents became agents in the development of the military as commissaries of another kind. This enabled the military side of the state-formation process in a political and administrative framework, which Hintze presumed would reject it.

Organizational ambiguity was the result when the supervisory role of the commissaries, mostly commissaries-general, was extended to operational command. They still operated as supervisors of the military enterprise and as agents of discipline and order; however, from an organizational point of view, the two neat lines of military control were entangled: the commanding officers and the supervising, supporting commissaries. Entanglement was most complete when command by committee was used in preference to unchaperoned foreign military professionals or as a remedy when such men were lacking. This made for very efficient civilian control of the military, probably at the expense of quality in command, as some contemporaries noted.

Organizational entanglement probably helped in producing entanglement on the level of personnel in the shape of the frequent use of former, or even active, military officers as commissaries. They may not have been perfect for the supervisory role; however, experience in command was useful in other respects, and became more useful the more the mission expanded. The range of tasks made it attractive to use men with all-round experience: county governors rather than bureaucrats from Copenhagen and, best of all, men combining experience in both military command and civilian administration.

Personnel stability did not develop to the point where it is appropriate to speak of a corps or career; the organization was always far from a state of bureaucratic order and permanence. Still, personnel stability markedly increased, and commissaries in Denmark proper did acquire a rudimentary organization that was partially integrated into the army's organization in general. Danish military commissaries could – and did – function as containers of expertise for the permanent army then being established. Due to entanglement, however, the commissary group was even more a vehicle for the *import* of expertise: from the international military business of the Thirty Years War into the budding Danish establishment, and from the civilian administration into the management of the army.

The difficult marriage of military and administrative competences was always the pressing task that shaped the characteristics of early modern commissaries. However, the Danish experience highlights the importance of their other mission: commissaries were agents of trust and expressions of distrust. This agenda obviously comprised civilian distrust of military enterprisers; however, it had more aspects than that: distrust of foreigners in command, distrust between power-holders inside the state, and so on. One important issue of trust in Denmark gradually became less pressing as a permanent army and recurring wars created an ever-larger group of dependable, indigenous nobles capable of higher command. This opened the road to supervisory commissaries becoming more of the subordinate type: a tendency that is visible from the middle of the period. Further steps along this road between1658–1660 were also made possible by trust. However, this was of another kind in a radically new political setting. Changes in the regime of trust transformed the nature of commissaryships more than anything else. Changes in who could trust commissaries might have significance far beyond the army.

Notes

1 Otto Ludwig to the King, 19 March 1628, Tyske Kancellis Indenrigske Afdeling [TKIA], A 93, Rigsarkivet, Copenhagen (Danish State Archives or RA).

2 *Oxford English Dictionary*, <http://dictionary.oed.com>, s.v. 'Commissary' (accessed March 2010).

3 Otto Hintze, 'Der Commissarius und seine Bedeutung in der allgemeinen Verwaltungsgeschichte: Eine vergleichende Studie', in: *Gesammelte Abhandlungen*, 1: *Staat und Verfassung*, ed. Gerhard Oestreich (Göttingen 1962), pp. 242–274.

4 Douglas Clark Baxter, *Servants of the Sword: French Intendants of the Army 1630–70* (Urbana, Ill., 1976), pp. 205–208.

5 John A. Lynn, 'How War Fed War: The Tax of Violence and Contributions During the *Grand Siècle*', *Journal of Modern History*, 65 (1993), pp. 286–310.

6 Michael E. Mallett & John R. Hale, *The Military Organisation of a Renaissance State: Venice c.1400 to 1617* (Cambridge 1984).

7 Hintze (1962), pp. 272, 243, 270.

8 Jan Glete, *War and the State in Early Modern Europe: Spain, the Dutch Republic and Sweden as Fiscal-Military States, 1500–1660* (London 2002), pp. 58–59.

9 Baxter (1976), pp. 11–12, 73–78; André Corvisier (ed.), *Histoire militaire de la France*, 2 (Paris 1992), pp. 32–33.

10 On the complexities of the union, see Gunner Lind, 'Krig, udenrigspolitik og statsdannelse i Oldenborg-monarkiet, 1533–1658: En analyse af unionen mellem Danmark, Norge og Slesvig-Holsten', in: Knud, p. Arstad (ed.), *Strategi, ledelse og samfunn 1588–1720* (Oslo 2000), pp. 8–38.

11 Jean Bodin, *Les six livres de la république* (Paris 1583), pp. 266–267.

12 Leon Jespersen, E. Ladewig Petersen & Ditlev Tamm (eds.), *Dansk Forvaltningshistorie*, 1: *Stat. Forvaltning og Samfund. Fra Middelalderen til 1901* (Copenhagen 2000), pp. 96–102, 140–142; Hintze (1962), pp. 272–274.

13 Gunner Lind, *Hæren og magten i Danmark 1614–1662* (Odense 1994), pp. 114, 481.

14 1 September 1629, TKIA A10, RA.

15 These and all following statistics are based upon a database of army officers, commissaries, etc., available from the Danish Data Archives <http://www.sa.dk/dda> as DDA-1573. On the sources, structure, and contents of this database, see Lind (1994), pp. 451–466.

16 Below the rank of captain, foreigners and non-nobles counted for much more. There is a considerable margin of error, as the origin of many officers is unknown.

17 *Dansk Biografisk Lexikon*, 16, ed. C. F. Bricka (Copenhagen 1902) p. 546; Database of officers etc. (see note 15).

18 On this war, see Paul Douglas Lockhart, *Denmark in the Thirty Years War 1618–1648: King Christian IV and the decline of the Oldenburg State* (Selinsgrove 1996), and still Julius Otto Opel, *Der niedersächsisch–dänische Krieg*, 1–3 (Halle/Magdeburg 1872–1894). For army leadership, see Lind (1994), pp. 296–315. For statistics, see Database of officers etc. (see note 15).

19 C. F. Bricka & J. A. Fridericia (eds.), *Kong Christian den Fjerdes egenhændige Breve 1589–1648*, 2 (Copenhagen 1889–1891), pp. 103–104.

20 Lind (1994), pp. 309–311.

21 Leon Jespersen, 'Landkommissærinstitutionen i Christian IVs tid: Rekruttering og funktion', *Historisk Tidsskrift*, 81 (1981), pp. 69–100.

22 Lind (1994), pp. 303–304.
23 Militære Regnskaber IIb 9, RA.
24 Lind (1994), pp. 293–294, 317–319, 327–329, 338–340, 348–357.
25 Accounts in RA Militære Regnskaber, section II–IV; auditor reports in RA Danske Kancelli B 217 and 219.
26 Lind (1994), pp. 368–369.
27 Joint orders March–May 1657, TKIA A22, RA.
28 Best known is the board of councillors in Copenhagen 1657–1658. Their archive has been preserved as Danske Kancelli B no. 154–155, 248–249, RA.
29 Lind (1994) part 4; Database of officers etc. (see note 15).
30 Undated January 1629, TKIA A13, RA.
31 28 February 1627, TKIA A13, RA.
32 Order for Cay von Ahlefeldt, 10 August 1641, TKIA A22, RA.
33 Royal orders are preserved in TKIA A20–A24, RA. Other papers from commissaries in A87, A93, A96, A147–149, and in Regeringskancelliet i Glückstadt, Militaria, RA. Orders in Danish are printed in *Kancelliets Brevbøger* (Copenhagen 1885–2005).
34 K. C. Rockstroh, 'Christian IVs hvervede Hær i Aarene 1638–43', *Historisk Tidsskrift*, 8, series 2 (1910), pp. 329–330.
35 Arne Odd Johnsen, *Krabbekrigen og gjenerobringen av Jämtland 1657–1658* (Oslo 1967).
36 Knud Ulfeldt may have led an army corps in Skåne as commissary-general the same year; however, it is not clear what charge he had; K. C. Rockstroh, 'Knud Ulfeld til Svenstrup: En adelig embedsmand de to sidste Aartier før Enevælden,' *Historisk Tidsskrift*, 8, series 1 (1907–1908), p. 475.
37 Lind (1994), p. 304.
38 23 December 1628, TKIA A 13, RA.
39 15 January 1629, TKIA A10, RA; 23 December 1628, undated January 1629, TKIA A13, RA.
40 Militære Regnskaber II:8, RA.
41 19 January 1629, TKIA A10, RA.
42 Ordinance, 30 May 1628, TKIA A46, RA.
43 Marquard von Rantzau, 6 July 1628, TKIA A88, RA.
44 Lind (1994), p. 337.
45 Lind (1994), pp. 338–347.
46 On the war 1657–1658, see Lind (1994), pp. 348–357.
47 Undated, *c.* February 1657, TKIA A93, RA.
48 Commissions 23 April and 25 May 1657, Danske Kancelli B 150, RA.
49 Gunner Lind, 'At forsvare København 1658–1660', *København: Kultur og Historie*, 1 (2009), pp. 57–78.
50 17 October 1659, Danske Kancelli B 81, RA.
51 Lind (1994), p. 364.
52 Lind (1994), pp. 361, 367–370.
53 Privatarkiver 6262: Hans Schack, RA.
54 Lind (1994), p. 368.
55 P. F. Suhm (ed.), 'Christen Skeels tvende Skrivelser, 1658 og 1659', in: *Nye Samlinger til den danske Historie*, 1 (Copenhagen 1792), p. 301.

CHAPTER 4

Responding to Challenges

The Royal Navy 1689–1815

Jeremy Black

One of Jan Glete's great achievements was to move beyond the customary account of naval power, with its emphasis upon the history of an individual state and, instead, to provide the naval history of an entire system. This led Glete to stress the role of relative naval power and to provide a statistical demonstration of its nature. Such a demonstration provided an abrupt lesson on the challenges facing the British Royal Navy[1] and, notably, a chronology that clarified the extent to which they varied.

Alongside this crucial statistical demonstration has come an awareness of the impact of diplomatic developments, and each needs to contribute to the general picture. These diplomatic developments created a major challenge to Britain in the period 1689–1815, ensuring that a powerful navy was a key aspect of the solution, thus providing a valuable instance of the challenge-and-response nature of military power, otherwise described in terms of a stress on tasking.

In the sixteenth and seventeenth centuries, England/Britain had benefited from the ability to fight sequentially rather than simultaneously: a key goal for any power, major or minor. Thus, in the sixteenth century, conflict had been with France or Spain, and in the seventeenth century, with France, Spain or the Dutch. A combination of opponents was unusual. In the 1620s, England had been at war with both France and Spain; however, the two had not been allied. In the late 1530s, the Habsburg Emperor, Charles V, and Francis I of France had allied against Henry VIII, and there had been grave concerns in England about the possibility of an invasion. These, indeed, had led to the construction of coastal fortifications, as well as to an effort to build up Henry VIII's navy. In the event, however, the alliance did not last and, instead, Henry was able to join with Charles against Francis.

Allies and enemies

This situation of sequential conflict helped England in its warfare with the leading European naval powers, whether Spain in the late sixteenth century, the Dutch in the three Anglo–Dutch Wars of 1652–1674, or the French in the early stages of the Nine Years War (1689–1697). In most cases, moreover, the English were allied to, or cooperating with, other naval powers: notably with the Dutch against Spain in 1585–1604; with Louis XIV against the Dutch in the Third Anglo–Dutch War (1672–1674); and with the Dutch (and Spain) against Louis XIV in the Nine Years War. The value of this cooperation helped explain the problems created by the threat of cooperation between France and the Dutch at the time of the Second Anglo–Dutch War.

The Royal Navy surpassed the size of the French navy in the 1690s; however, this achievement did not lead the other states to ally in an anti-hegemonic alliance, although the rhetoric of such an alliance was to play a role in French propaganda over the following century. Indeed, indicating the extent to which talk of threats was rhetoric as much as analysis, the British used this rhetoric when criticising Spanish attempts in 1738–1739 to exclude them from trade with the Spanish New World. The 9 February 1739 issue of *The Citizen, or, The Weekly Conversation of a Society of London Merchants on Trade, and other Public Affairs* claimed that 'the just Balance of Power amongst the European nations might as eventually be broken and destroyed, by an unjust and partial monopoly of the medium of commerce, as by any particular state engrossing to itself too large an extent of dominion, and other branches of power'.

Instead of uniting against Britain and, thus, prefiguring the situation in both early 1780s and late 1790s, the Dutch and Spain joined her in the 1690s in co-operating against France. The situation changed, however, during the War of the Spanish Succession, in which Britain was engaged from 1702 to 1713; however, this change occurred as a result of dynastic factors and not due to opposition to Britain's naval position. The accession in 1700 of Louis's grandson, Philip, Duke of Anjou, to the Spanish throne as Philip V, led to an alliance of France and Spain opposed to that of England, the Dutch, and Austria. However, this alliance disintegrated after the war, and Britain, France, Austria and the Dutch were united against Spain in the War of the Quadruple Alliance (1718–1720). Thus, the British were able to defeat a Spanish fleet off Sicily in 1718 (the Battle of Cape Passaro) and to mount an amphibious attack on the Spanish port of Vigo in 1719 without having to fear the opposition of France.

The same was true of British naval operations, and planned operations, against Spain in 1725–1729: France was allied with Britain and the Dutch, as part of the Alliance of Hanover. Therefore, it was possible for Britain to blockade the Spanish ports of Cadiz and Porto Bello without fear of French military action, despite major French investment in the cargoes due to be brought back from the Americas in the blockaded ships.

However, this situation changed in the 1730s with the collapse of the Anglo–French alliance in 1731 and the replacement in 1733 of the Anglo–Spanish alliance by co-operation between France and Spain. The basis of this alliance was dynastic: the first of three Family Compacts between the Bourbon rulers of France and Spain, this alliance established the diplomatic core of the challenge facing the Royal Navy. Allowing for periods of diplomatic co-operation between Britain and Spain, notably in the early 1750s when Ferdinand VI of Spain was unwilling to heed French pressure for joint action, and of Anglo–Spanish military co-operation against Revolutionary France in 1793–1795 (for example at Toulon in 1793), this alignment of France and Spain provided a basic naval challenge to Britain; one that lasted until wrecked by Napoleon when he tried to take over Spain in 1808. The combination of French and Spanish warships at Trafalgar in 1805 demonstrated this challenge, and also how it survived changes in regime, as such co-operation had been seen in the Battle of Toulon in 1744, and when Spanish warships joined the French at Brest in preparing for the unsuccessful invasion of England in 1779.

The impact of this Franco–Spanish challenge was exacerbated by the extent to which Anglo–Dutch naval co-operation became less significant from the 1710s and, indeed, ceased from 1748. This change transformed the naval situation in the English Channel, the North Sea, and the Indian Ocean and, thus, more generally. Instead, the two powers became enemies, fighting the Fourth Anglo–Dutch War in 1780–1784 and, again, after the French overran the Netherlands in 1795 during the French Revolutionary and Napoleonic Wars.

These shifts, as well as the individual problems of specific conjunctures, posed the key problem for the Royal Navy; however, they did not exhaust the diplomatic difficulties it confronted. In addition, two major rising naval powers were opposed to Britain in particular periods, although only one actually fought her. Russia became a key regional naval power under Peter the Great (1689–1725), although part of its navy was very different to that of Britain, as it had a galley component essentially restricted to Baltic waters. The British envoy, Sir Cyril Wych, reported in 1742 that there were 130 galleys in St Petersburg in 'constant good order', each with three cannons and able to carry 200 troops, and that 'with these they can make great and sudden [...] irruptions'.[2] Such a force was not a threat to Britain; however, it was to her allies. Russia came close to conflict with Britain in the early 1720s, both during the last stage of the Great Northern War and subsequently. However, war was avoided, as it was again in 1791 during the Ochakov Crisis and in the 1800s when Russia had periods of alliance with France, notably under Paul I in 1800–1801 and after Napoleon and Alexander I signed the Treaty of Tilsit in 1807. By then, Russia was a wide-ranging naval power: indeed, its fleet had been deployed to the Mediterranean against the Turks from 1769.

The British relationship with the US, in contrast, became more hostile. Aside from the War of Independence with Britain in 1775–1783, the two powers waged the War of 1812 in 1812–1815, and this conflict posed a challenge to British naval resources, not least as they struggled to develop a blockade of America's ports and to overcome American privateering while also fighting France.

The loss of the support of the Thirteen Colonies was not significant in terms of the arithmetic of ships of the line; however, it was important for the manpower that had been contributed to the Royal Navy – both directly and indirectly – through the role of the merchant marine of the American colonies in British imperial trade, notably of the West Indies. Indeed, manpower issues helped lead to the outbreak of the War of 1812. This point serves as a reminder that statistical measures of naval power in terms of numbers of warships need to be complemented by analysis of the manpower situation and also by an appreciation of the regional dynamics of naval power, not least if these dynamics related to far-flung empires.

If mention of America from 1775 does not exhaust the list of challenges facing the Royal Navy, it does provide an indication of their scale and range. The diplomatic dimension is crucial because it underlines the degree to which the navy had to cope with a situation shot through with unpredictability. Indeed, that was a key element in the peacetime British naval strategy for the prospect of war, as in 1733–1735 (when Britain was neutral in the War of the Polish Succession despite its Austrian alliance and sent a fleet in 1735 to the Tagus when Spain threatened Portugal); this might mean war with France or Spain, or both. In reacting to this situation of inherent uncertainty, the British, therefore, had to rely upon diplomacy (in order to lessen the build-up of an opposing coalition), intelligence (in order to ascertain what their opponents would do), and a strong navy. The three were linked, and it would be misleading to treat them separately.

New challenges

The navy itself responded within existing technological and institutional constraints. There was no marked change in either in this period: a point that serves as a reminder of the danger of assuming that hegemonic military strength necessarily reflects the availability of particular technological and institutional advantages. The Royal Navy had some comparative advantages, however, within a context of a system in which variations were relatively minor. French warships tended to be better built in the mid eighteenth century, while the British subsequently benefited from carronades and copper-bottoming; however, neither advantage was decisive. Instead, British fire-discipline was a key element – one shown to devastating effect during the French Revolutionary and Napoleonic Wars. This fire-discipline arose from training and experience, and not from technological advantage.

Challenges played a role in enhancing the British development of the advantages they possessed. Thus, the need to respond to the Seven Years War (1756–1763) helped ensure the emulation of French shipbuilding techniques, while copper-bottoming and carronades were pushed forward due to the War of American Independence (1775–1783), which was also an Anglo–French war from 1778: with Spain and the Dutch participating from 1779 and 1780, respectively. British fire-discipline benefited from the experience of frequent conflict.

In comparison, Britain only fought one naval war with a Western power between 1815 and 1914 – the Crimean War with Russia in 1854–1856 – and yet there was a massive transformation in the Royal

Navy between 1815 and 1870 and, again, subsequently. In large part, this transformation arose from competition with other naval powers, notably France and, from the early 1900s, Germany; however, the key point in comparing the eighteenth and nineteenth centuries is that challenge itself does not lead to transformation.

Nor did it, in the eighteenth or the nineteenth centuries, for opponents who lacked naval dominance. Indeed, the latter generally responded to their weaker position by seeking to build up strength, especially through a diffusion of the technology and personnel from the leading power or powers. Thus, for example, Russia recruited British captains, sailors, and shipwrights. It is notable that, in contrast, there was scant interest in the type of paradigm-shifting challenge presented by initiatives in mines and submarines. The latter were associated in particular with Robert Fulton, who posed a threat to British hegemony, pressing both France and the US to take his inventions as an opportunity to overcome the British position. Despite the fact that France was at war with Britain, this route was not taken, which was probably an appropriate response to the possibility of effectively manufacturing any new system. However, the net effect was to ensure that the Royal Navy was not challenged by any radically new system. During the War of 1812, Fulton found support for naval steam-power in his native US, yet his work did not threaten the British position, any more than David Bushnell's successful effort to create a workable submarine had done during the War of American Independence.

Nor was the Royal Navy confronted with any significant development in the tactical, operational or strategic spheres. Indeed, in contrast to the development in the seventeenth century of professional navies, specialised fighting ships (neither, of course, began in that century) and line-ahead tactics, there was remarkably little change in the eighteenth century. This point invites the question whether it is indeed appropriate to expect such change. Thus the US, having become the master of carrier warfare in the 1940s, has essentially maintained that paradigm of naval capability ever since. A similar point can be made about Britain and battleships earlier in the twentieth century.

There is scant sign of novelty being seen as the solution, which helps explain the emphasis placed by the British upon command skills and character. Indeed, command was regarded as the key, alongside the efforts of the crews. This emphasis upon command opens the question whether there were any particular efforts to teach command. The answer, in practice, was that the stress in all respects was on an incremental response to possibilities, and that this response accorded with the cultural norms of the period. Indeed, such a response can also be seen in governance and the army, although a different emphasis can be presented if the stress is upon the 'Financial Revolution' of the 1690s. At any rate, there was no comparison at sea, which indicates the limited responses available at sea in meeting the multiple challenges of the period: Britain has been seen as the setting for agricultural, industrial, financial, transport, and political revolutions in the period 1689–1815, yet not as one for a naval revolution.

The relevance of this point for the wider field of military change in this period is also suggestive. There is a tendency to argue that a military revolution arose from the French Revolution[3] and that, in combination with the supposed military revolution of 1560–1660, such military revolutions were possible, desirable, and the route to enhanced capability and success. These arguments, however, tell us more about contemporary and (later) scholarly discourses concerning military power and development, than they do concerning the far more complex processes involved. In particular, change tended to be incremental; the gaps in capability between armies (and navies) were smaller, and more contingent on circumstances, than is generally appreciated, and the nature of improvement was not always clear.

Similar points can be made about naval warfare in this period, and these points can be underlined by drawing attention to the variety of tasks that navies were expected to undertake. In particular, there was no one task, and thus no single measure of effectiveness. Britain's navy had the prime strategic requirement of protecting the homeland (as well as the colonies) from invasion. This role was also seen with the Dutch navy during the Third Anglo–Dutch War, but it was not a goal shared by the navies of France, Spain, Russia or the US, the last of which relied against invasion on the militia, on coastal fortifications, and on the vast extent of the country.

Again with the exception of the Dutch, the British navy had a role in preventing the interruption of trade routes that was not matched elsewhere. Such interruption posed a fundamental problem for the operation of the French and, to a lesser extent, Spanish economic systems; however, there was nothing to match the British dependence, in terms of its economy (of credit and public finances), on overseas trade. This situation again posed a fundamental challenge to the British navy, because trade protection, like the sea denial called for in invasion prevention, was fundamentally reactive. It was necessary to block or react to the sailing of hostile warships and privateers: under circumstances in which intelligence (especially prior intelligence) was limited and communications about any such sailing were slow and not readily subject to confirmation. Toward the close of the period, there was a degree of improvement with the introduction of semaphores, yet their impact was restricted. More serious was the extent to which balloons did not offer the capacity for aerial surveillance that later developments in powered flight were to provide.

Reactive patterns

Thus the British navy was trapped by a set of tasks that forced it into a reactive operational stance. In September 1756, the First Lord of the Admiralty drew the attention of 'his ministerial colleagues to the dire consequences of the problems posed by blockade: "My Lord Anson… represented the condition of the squadron under the command of Vice Admiral Boscawen, that the crews of the ships are very sickly, that the ships must necessarily return in order to be refitted, and that, upon the whole, the fleet would run the utmost hazard, were it to continue cruising off Brest, beyond the middle of the next month".'[4]

The following month, John, 4th Duke of Bedford and Lord-Lieutenant of Ireland, complained about ineffectiveness as well:

> What have we been doing with our fleet this summer, but endeavouring to hedge in the cuckow, which, as must always be the case, we have been utterly unable to effect? For many ships and forces have been stole away from the different ports of France to America, and with this additional disadvantage, that whilst we are wearing out our ships and sailors by keeping the French fleet within their harbours, they are, without any waste of men or ships, getting themselves into a condition of being able to drive us off their coasts in a very short time.[5]

Irritation with the blockade was seen in Charles Townshend's complaint that the navy was 'once more crying the hours off Brest under Lord Anson who, with the deportment, punctuality and terror of a London watchman, knocks every night at every French seaport in the Channel to see that all is at home and quiet within his station. The admiral is, I fear, better suited to this service than the fleet which might have been sent upon real duty'.[6]

Convoying trade provided another form of reaction: an arduous task that was important not only for commercial reasons, but also for maintaining related political links.[7] There was also the need to respond to enemy operations on land and the potential threat they posed to maritime interests. Thus, in 1757, Robert, 4th Earl of Holderness, Secretary of State for the Northern Department, wrote to William, Duke of Cumberland, who was then commander of the army of allied German forces entrusted with the defence of Hanover.

> In consequence of the hints thrown out in your Royal Highness's letters of the 6th and 11th instant, a man of war, a sloop, and two armed vessels are sent to the Ems, in order to see if they can choose such a position in that river as might (in case the enemy possess themselves of Emden), prevent the operation of any embarkation on board the small vessels of that country [...] proper care will also be taken to have cruisers so stationed as to keep the mouth of the Elbe, and the Weser, free from any annoyance from the enemy.[8]

The reactive stance is not the picture that generally emerges from popular accounts of naval operations, let alone battles; however, the latter devote insufficient attention to the strain involved in more commonplace blockading. That, in fact, many battles arose as a result of blockades, and thus are indicative of the essentially reactive strategy that was central to the use of British naval power, can readily be established by a consideration of the battles and, not least, their location.

Proactive patterns

However, the contemporary conception of British naval power was also very different. It was proactive, not reactive, and that assumption posed a different form of challenge; moreover, one that was accentuated by the nature of British public politics. The call to action was frequent, both in peacetime and during war, and there was scant sense of any limits on what the navy could achieve. Thus, the *Monitor*, an influential and populist London paper, declared in its issue of 24 December 1757:

> A fleet is our best security: but then it is not to lie by our walls; nor be confined to the navigation of our own coasts. The way to deliver Rome from the rival ship and hostilities of the Carthaginians was to carry fire and sword upon the African coast. Employ the enemy at home, and he will never project hazardous invasions. Our fleets are able to bid defiance to all the maritime forces of Europe. And as the surest and most rational means to humble the ambition of France is to destroy her power by sea, and her trade from America; no service, but what is directed towards this salutary object of British politics, can be worthy of the attention of a British ministry.[9]

Moreover, failure led to savage criticism, as Admiral Byng discovered in 1756; the press was very ready to condemn naval strategy and operations.[10]

Britain's allies could also expect much from the Royal Navy: Frederick II called in 1758 for expeditions against the French coast capable of making France withdraw troops from Germany.[11] To support such invasions, the *Monitor* of 29 April 1758 urged the construction of shallow-draft invasion boats, each armed with twenty cannons and able to carry a hundred marines.

The politics of strategy is a field that has attracted insufficient attention for the (long) eighteenth century, not least because of the focus upon the politics of naval command. Moreover, there has been a preference for focusing upon strategy in operational terms, particularly the location of fleets, as in the discussion of the strategic grasp of John, 4th Earl of Sandwich, First Lord of the Admiralty during the War of American Independence.[12] This scholarship is of considerable value, yet it does not exhaust the issue of strategy, and not least that of the wider politics of naval tasking and the rating of naval requirements within British public culture and government. As an instance of the challenges posed by the latter, the Glorious Revolution of 1688–1689 led to the replacement of a monarch, James II, with a deep personal commitment to the navy who by the first in a series had no such commitment. Although William III (1689–1702) came to Britain by sea, he was very much a general. This was even truer of George I (1714–1727) and George II (1727–1760). As young men, they had gained important military experience, but on land and not at sea. Moreover, both men had a powerful commitment to their native Electorate of Hanover, which was not a naval power and would not become one.

This attitude on the part of the Crown was taken further by the powerful and long-standing commitment to the army by royal princes, notably William, Duke of Cumberland and Frederick, Duke of York, the favourite sons of George II and George III, respectively. In contrast, there was no such politically charged commitment to the navy. William IV, as Duke of Clarence, followed a naval career; however, it proved abortive, and lacked weight.

Royal attitudes were not central to the political position of the navy, yet they were an element in the complex circumstances under which it had to operate. Parliament could prove more intrusive, not least when things went wrong, as they tended to in the early stages of most wars. The resulting controversies were in part an aspect of the problems stemming from an assumption of success. This assumption became more insistent because the Wars of the Spanish Succession (1702–1713) and Quadruple Alliance (1718–1720) did not leave any legacy of perceived failure.

As a result, the concerns of 1744–1746, 1756, 1759 and 1779 about projected or possible French invasions seemed unacceptable and the product of political and/or naval neglect. This situation underlined the political and thus strategic problems stemming from a reactive operational stance. The need to plan to fend off an attempted invasion was not necessarily a result of failure, however much that might have seemed to be the case to elements in British public politics.

If the operational and political issues posed by invasion threats provided a key strategic problem, it was not one that changed greatly during the period. There were anxieties about invasion for most of the period, although the extent to which any invasion was seen as likely to enjoy domestic support varied greatly. The last, indeed, constituted a key element in the political challenge to naval power, for anxiety about domestic backing for invaders, whether, in particular, from Jacobites (notably in the 1690s and 1740s) or Irish rebels, created greater pressure for naval security and at least the appearance of assured mastery. This situation lasted until the Irish risings of 1798 and, far less seriously, 1803; after that, the French naval threat was not seen in terms of exacerbating domestic disaffection. Thus in 1805 the French naval threat came, first, from an invasion of Britain and then from intervening in the Mediterranean; however, the domestic British response was far more uniformly hostile than on some previous occasions.

This last point serves as a reminder of the degree to which the (varied) response to the problems faced by British naval power in successive conflicts helped mould the politics of the following years. The Napoleonic Wars provided a show of British naval dominance not seen in the American Independence or French Revolutionary wars. There was no repetition of the large-scale, indecisive battles of the former (Ushant, 1778; Virginia Capes, 1781) or of the naval mutinies (1797) and strategic problems of the latter (the withdrawal from the Mediterranean in 1796 and failure to prevent French forces landing in Ireland in 1798). Instead, the arduous nature of the Mediterranean naval commitment after Trafalgar (1805), especially of the difficult blockade of Toulon, was overlooked in the post-war glow of remembered glory. Also there was the anxiety about France building up its navy after Trafalgar; an anxiety that focused upon the dockyards of Antwerp. This anxiety led to the Walcheren expedition of 1809, as well as to later concern to ensure that any subsequent peace did not leave France in control of the port, which had indeed been the intention of the Austrian Chancellor, Metternich. Indeed, a key element in the politics and strategy of naval power related to bases, and thus to the military operations, planning priorities, and international negotiations, was bound up with their capture from opponents.

There was the related question of the expansion – at home and, even more, abroad – of the British system of bases, a system that, in turn, saw the interplay of naval criteria with imperial and domestic policy and politics, as was to the fore in the bitter debate of 1786 over naval fortifications. The House of Commons then rejected the government's plan for fortifying Plymouth and Portsmouth, a measure that the ministry regarded as necessary not only to protect the key bases for a Western Squadron, but also to free the fleet for wartime offensive operations. This episode indicated the range of factors involved in naval politics and strategy, and also the danger of seeing results as a product of plans without noting the powerful mediation of these factors.

This emphasis upon politics directs attention to another important aspect of Glete's work: his stress on naval power as the product of co-operation between interest groups, notably those who controlled and could finance warships. Glete noted valuable variations on this head within Europe and on the world scale; thus, he provided an account of naval strength with a dynamic that was not simply located in the world of competition between naval powers. Instead, intentionality was linked to a structural assessment of the societies and political cultures of these powers.

This insight is a crucial one for understanding the challenges and responses of British naval power, as it locates this power in a different pattern of response to that affecting Britain's rivals. In particular, government support for other navies could be extensive, yet tended to lack the political, social, and institutional grounding seen in Britain. As a consequence, elsewhere there could be a mismatch between governmental decisions to expand resources and build up naval strength and, on the other hand, the limited achievement in terms of the delivery of effective naval power: a point clearly seen with Russia under Peter the Great.

Relating naval power and strategy to politics is appropriate. A key element in eighteenth-century Britain was the lack of any unpacking of strategy and policy; a lack that reflected the absence of any institutional body specifically for strategic planning and execution, and also the tendency in politics, government and political discussion to see strategy and policy as one, and necessarily so. As Glete showed so well, institutional practices and political assumptions rested upon important configurations reflecting linked constituencies of support. Britain's ability to respond to the challenges facing its naval power can, in large part, be explained by this situation. To an extent unmatched among the major European powers, British policymakers and the British political nation understood the implications of the remark in the *Monitor* of 18 March 1758: 'no prince nor state ever arrived to any great superiority of power without the assistance of a powerful navy'.

Notes

1 For the best introduction to the navy in this period, see N. A. M. Rodger, *The Command of the Ocean: A Naval History of Britain, 1649–1815* (London 2004).
2 Wych to John, Lord Carteret, Secretary of State for the Northern Department, 10 April 1742, London, National Archives, State Papers (hereafter NA SP) 91/31.
3 David A. Bell, *The First Total War: Napoleon's Europe and the Birth of Warfare as We Know It* (Boston 2007).
4 Cabinet Minute, 29 September 1756, London, British Library (hereafter BL) Additional Manuscripts, 51376 fols. 85–86.
5 Bedford to Henry Fox, 14 October 1756, Earl of Ilchester (ed.), *Letters to Henry Fox* (London 1915), p. 93.
6 Charles Townshend to his mother, Lady Townshend, BL Blakeney papers vol. I, no. 65.
7 Wych to Carteret, 10 April 1742, NA SP 91/31.
8 Holdernesse to Cumberland, 27 May 1757, BL Egerton MSS 3442 fols. 97–98.
9 See also issues of 11 March and 29 April 1758.
10 *Owen's Weekly Chronicle*, 15 April 1758.
11 Andrew Mitchell, envoy in Berlin, to Holdernesse, 9 February 1758, NA SP 90/71.
12 N. A. M. Rodger, *The Insatiable Earl: A Life of John Montagu, Fourth Earl of Sandwich, 1718–1792* (London 1993).

CHAPTER 5

A Little Incident in 1707

The demise of a once glorious Dutch naval organization

Jaap R. Bruijn

In 1707, a high-ranking Dutch naval officer and nobleman was involved in an incident that generated hardly any indignation or even interest in the Dutch Republic. A few similar events in the history of Anglo–Dutch naval cooperation were also little cause for concern there; however, the incident illustrates the degradation of the once glorious naval power of the Republic, a state with a federal and decentralized political structure and a peculiar naval organization very different from those of any other early modern European state. This present study touches upon the problems of inertia and the impossibility of institutional change.

Five admiralties, one decentralized naval organization

The history of the Republic of the Seven United Provinces is one of provincial sovereignty and decentralization in a small country. As such, it is a history with medieval and sixteenth-century roots. The Union of Utrecht of 1579 was originally a defensive alliance of rebellious provinces against Habsburg Spain; however, it was later used as a quasi-constitution. This had stipulated that the sovereign partners would have a number of common finances, one army and one navy, and coordinated foreign relations.

For concerted action, the Seven Provinces delegated sovereign powers to the States General in The Hague. That body was responsible for military and naval funding, in which the delegation of each province had one vote and in which unanimity was often required. One permanent source of income was allocated to the navy in 1582: the yield from the duties on incoming and outgoing ships and carts, and their cargoes. For any other additional sources, ad hoc decisions by the States General were required. A captain and admiral general was the commander of both the army and the navy. The States General appointed him. The command went mostly to the prince of Orange who was also the Stadtholder of Holland and of several other provinces. Holland was by far the wealthiest and most populous, and, therefore, the most important province.

After having had initial disputes over greater centralization, the Seven Provinces in 1597 decided to continue with five separate admiralties. Although this arrangement was considered only a temporary solution to managing naval forces, it remained unchanged until the end of the Republic in 1795. The admiralties were located in the maritime provinces of Zeeland, Friesland, and Holland (the latter with three of them). The most important of the admiralties was located in Amsterdam. This decentralized naval administration was split up into five largely autonomous organizations, and was the outcome of rivalries among the provinces and among cities in Holland.

A board of councillors, appointed by the States General, ruled each admiralty. Nominated by the provinces, these councillors were either selected from the province in which the admiralty was located, or they represented one of the six other provinces. An oath of allegiance to further the interests of the commonwealth above those of their province or city was required of them.

The admiralties in the Dutch Republic were given a wide variety of tasks that pertained to naval and merchant shipping. They were to adjudicate matters to do with the taking of prizes and were to collect certain taxes, which formed the source of their own direct income. All of these tasks were put into place at the formation of the Republic and, in essence, never changed. The organizational structures lasted until the end of the eighteenth century and were thought to be permanent. At times, suggestions for reforms were discussed; however, none were ever introduced.

Each admiralty thus levied taxes upon incoming and outgoing commodities and on the means of transport by sea and across the land borders of the Republic. The States General laid down the tariffs listed by commodity. This was a uniform system for the entire country; however, the economic potential of the five different districts was not the same.

The admiralty of Amsterdam collected most of the common duties, and soon became the economic metropolis for the Republic and for all of northern Europe. The intention was for the money to be spent specifically on the men-of-war that were used to escort the merchant fleet during peacetime. It was a sort of quid pro quo: a return for merchants on the taxes they paid.

The States General voted special subsidies for the battle fleets and squadrons; this was a practice that rendered the admiralties totally dependent upon the efforts of the provinces to provide funds. This budget required the provinces' consent and, according to its economic and demographic resources, each province was allocated a certain proportion of the funds for which it was responsible. In most cases, the money was collected from taxes on consumer goods. The system of quotas assessed Holland at 58 per cent, Friesland nearly 12 per cent, Zeeland 9 per cent, and the four inland provinces the rest. There was no guarantee that the admiralties would receive their part of the subsidies on time. Provinces were often in arrears with their instalments, and there was no sanction imposed for non-payment. The inland provinces considered the army more important than the navy, which influenced how quickly they paid their share of the cost of battle fleets.

The five admiralties had a number of facilities at their disposal for the proper execution of their tasks. Dockyards with several storehouses and workshops for the construction, repair, and the fitting-out of warships were among these. Amsterdam had a dockyard with five slips; the other admiralties' yards had fewer. The proliferation of facilities with their corresponding work-forces was the result of the great autonomy of the admiralties and the promotion of local interests. In principle, naval administration was the concern of all the provinces represented in the States General; this was reflected in the composition of the boards of councillors. In practice, however, matters did not work this way. Promotion of local interests was evidently a prime concern for the councillors representing the city in which an admiralty was established, and for the councillors from the local neighbourhood. Local suppliers were in charge of all kinds of deliveries to the dockyard, ropewalk, administrative offices, and other facilities. The three most important officials of each admiralty were always chosen from the local class of regents. These officials were appointed for life and represented continuity in board decisions, which they prepared themselves and were responsible for executing. By and large, this structure guaranteed the more than passing economic and social interest of the ruling class in their own admiralty.[1]

This fragmented naval organization presented a gloomy picture in those periods of the Republic when centralizing forces were lacking and few people took an interest in naval affairs. This was especially true of the eighteenth century. The States General could always order the admiralty boards to send delegates to The Hague to receive instructions and to discuss matters of common concern. The level of coordination reached at these gatherings depended upon the power exerted by the States General and the gravity of the particular matter. Such coordination was seldom a problem in the seventeenth century, when Europe and the Republic were ravaged by war and navies were, thus, extremely important assets. The Grand Pensionary of Holland in those times, particularly in the period from 1650 to 1672 when no Stadtholder or admiral general was available, wielded great influence as leader of Holland in the States General and as unofficial minister of foreign affairs. In cooperation with Lieutenant-Admiral Michiel de Ruyter, Grand Pensionary John de Witt achieved the highest level of coordination possible in the decentralized naval administration. This was in the period from 1653 to 1672.

Although the princes of Orange held the title of admiral general, they seldom played an active role in naval affairs. Their major interest was traditionally the army, which they commanded in many campaigns. They never went to sea; however, at times they stimulated the coordination of naval activities. King-Stadtholder William III took the greatest interest in the navy, which he very much needed in his lengthy wars against Louis XIV's France.

The achievements of this naval organization reached their pinnacle in the second half of the seventeenth century. The Republic then knew only few years of peace. It was almost continuously at war, mostly at sea. John de Witt himself and William III provided good leadership, the latter in the person of the secretary of the Amsterdam admiralty, Job de Wildt, who acted on his behalf. There was great involvement of the ruling class, several members of which still had a personal interest in commercial and industrial enterprises. Important and lasting naval changes took place, particularly in the 1650s and 1660s. The tactics of naval warfare were drastically altered, as was the design of warships. Naval officers closed ranks to achieve true professionalism. The years 1652 and 1713 can be considered as clear watersheds. The 'old' navy lasted until 1652, at which time a 'new' navy was born. The year 1713 saw the end of the period of intensive warfare and the beginning of a long, seventy-to eighty-year period in which the navy was rarely of prime importance in either Dutch politics or daily life.

Glete's observations

Jan Glete always took a great interest in the structure of the Dutch Republic and its armed forces, the army as well as the navy. He compared the federal Republic with absolutist states and demonstrated the strong points in its weak constitution. The last time he examined Dutch institutions was in a posthumously published chapter in a study, which placed Admiral De Ruyter in an international context.[2] Among other things, he stressed that the seventeenth century Republic was an extremely well-armed state, both absolutely and relative to the size of its population; its wartime efforts of mobilization reached higher levels than any other country. As for the navy – probably the most complex organization in early modern Europe – the officials of the admiralties provided links between the policy of the state and local maritime networks, interests, and resources. Or in other words, as formulated in an earlier publication, the socio-economic elite ran the state they had created from below during the revolt against Spain in the sixteenth century.[3] The Dutch political system was, to an unusually high degree, based upon the ability of local societies to use the central state in their interests and to coordinate their own activities through the state. This relation between state and society was a central feature of the institutional framework. The system of five admiralties proved able to raise far larger resources per capita for naval warfare than any other contemporary system in Europe. Glete also stated that urban environments made it easier for many individuals to develop personal contacts, and several cities geographically close to one another made it easier to develop regional networks: a situation very different from that prevailing in the other much larger European states. These contacts and networks were naturally superior to large, anonymous structures and organizations. The ruling elite met each other very frequently in the Dutch city councils and the gatherings of the provincial states and the States General.

This sketch of the peculiar structure of the Dutch Republic and Glete's interpretation of its benefits refers to the seventeenth century.

In the following century, the negative side of a federal and decentralized constitution came to full light. It was late in the seventeenth century that the hitherto reliable parts of the Dutch political, financial, and military system showed growing weaknesses: signs foretelling the Republic's fall from the position of a major player on the European scene. This happened almost imperceptibly – and irreversibly. This article is not the place to analyse this complex process. Here, I want to illustrate a number of aspects that went hand in hand with this breakdown. This is a little case-study dealing with the degradation of the navy and is connected to Anglo–Dutch naval cooperation during the War of the Spanish Succession (1702–1713).

A 1707 case-study

The case-study of 1707 shows explicitly and implicitly the absence of a strong naval administrator as in the days of John de Witt and the father and son of the De Wildt family (both of whom were naval administrators at different times in their lives). This also shows the lack of interest in far-off naval operations in the Mediterranean among the ruling elite, most of whom were no longer actively involved in trade and shipping.[4] The lack of adequate funds for naval equipment was also obvious. At the same time, however, this study provides insight into the pride and self-confidence of Dutch naval officers who, for political reasons, had been put in an inferior position relative to their English colleagues. The foundation was laid almost immediately after the end of the Third Anglo–Dutch War (1672–1674) for the later cooperation of the two 'maritime' powers – England and the Dutch Republic – in the wars against France. The two concluded a number of treaties: one on navigation and commerce in December 1674; a defensive alliance in January 1678; and, in March of the same year, a treaty signed at Westminster, in which both agreed to use all of their forces on sea and land to bring Louis XIV's France to heel. A final agreement in August 1678 specified that, for these combined forces, England was to furnish one-third more at sea than the Republic and the reverse on land.[5]

This understanding about the relative proportions of forces in wartime was further defined in the Treaty of London of May 1689, at the start of the Nine Years War (1689–1697). This document would govern Anglo–Dutch naval cooperation for this war and the War of the Spanish Succession. This was based upon mainly Dutch proposals, including a ratio of 3 to 5 in allied naval forces, which was a decrease from the earlier ratio of 2 to 3. An explicit arrangement on how a combined naval command would work was required. The English position prevailed: their senior officers, of whatever rank, would always have overall command. The Dutch suggestion that command should go to the officer with English or Dutch seniority was rejected. From 1689, an English officer was to command each squadron or any detachment from that squadron, even if a more senior Dutch officer were present. It proved difficult to establish satisfactory procedures for the councils of war during fleet operations, in particular how to take votes. Each council was composed of flag officers and captains from both countries in equal numbers. The English and Dutch had different systems of voting. The junior officer gave his opinion first and the senior officer last in the English navy; in the Dutch navy, it was the other way round. The English wanted Dutch officers to vote first. It was decided that each party would vote according to its own rules; however, nothing was officially stipulated as to seating and voting.[6] All matters before the councils were to be decided by majority. All these provisions were renewed on the eve of the War of the Spanish Succession in 1702.

During the first phase of the Nine Years War, the Dutch navy was able to establish a position of moral and professional superiority within the alliance: one that continued for the rest of this war. At the outset, the quality of English naval forces was open to question. There were some unfortunate actions and some uncertainty about loyalty of their officers' corps. Moreover, the Dutch admiralties were able to meet their annual naval quotas. By and large, cooperation at sea went smoothly. Both navies had an experienced command: capable flag officers such as Philips van Almonde and Gerard Callenburgh on the Dutch side and Edward Russell, George Rooke, and Clowdisley Shovell on the other side. They were not antagonistic in character, and they enjoyed mutual respect. For instance, the complete council of war accepted Van Almonde's suggestions for the attack at Vigo in 1702.[7] The flag officers somehow managed to understand each other despite the fact that hardly any of them could speak or understand the language of his opposite number. In 1692, Admiral Russell had an English and a Dutch secretary, the latter of whom also acted as an interpreter. Baron Jan Gerrit van Wassenaer, one of the more junior flag officers, was able to write a letter in English, although he did apologize for his 'broken English'.[8]

Always in the background, however, was Dutch sensitivity about the English taking overall command. That was most obvious in cases where a more junior English flag officer took precedence over a considerably senior Dutch colleague. This occurred twice during the Nine Years War – in 1694 and 1697 – and once the Dutch got their way. This happened early in 1694 when the English commander went down with three of his ships. Callenburg, the oldest and most senior man, then took command.[9]

Anglo–Dutch naval cooperation and actions followed a familiar course at the start of the War of the Spanish Succession in 1702. The Dutch again contributed their accorded share of three-eights. The contribution approached the quota in the first year; however, from 1703, the Dutch admiralties failed to meet their commitment for the Mediterranean. They supplied only half or less than the agreed share during 1704–1706. The situation hardly improved after that.[10] The main reason for the shortfall was the lack of money for the admiralties and for the Republic in general. The Republic was virtually bankrupt. There were differences of opinion about the best way to deploy the allied forces as well. This process weakened the position of the Dutch flag officers in the councils of war. The familiar admirals on both sides were still in command, including the likes of Shovell and Van Almonde; this helped in dealing with precarious situations where junior English flag officers had to command. The increasingly smaller Dutch contingent was initially top-heavy with flag officers. The initiative was with the English. The Dutch ships increasingly formed an auxiliary force, and were thought of in this way.

The year 1706 was a turning-point in this respect. The Mediterranean operation lost some of its priority for the English Admiralty. At the same time, the Admiralty Board's irritation about the inadequate Dutch contributions grew. Both sides had successfully avoided open confrontation over this point, and the English had shown sufficient awareness about Dutch sensitivity to the imposed command structure. That now ended. A vice-admiral – and not an admiral – would temporarily command the Mediterranean forces. This was announced to the Dutch authorities as a fait accompli. Admiral Van Almonde was already on his way to his usual destination in the Mediterranean. When he anchored at Lisbon in June 1706, he found an emergency order from The Hague to disembark from his flagship and to return home in order to prevent any disputes and embarrassments about the command. Within less than a fortnight, Van Almonde sailed home on board an English man-of-war, after having entrusted his command to vice-admiral Van Wassenaer. The 62-year old admiral never commanded again, and spent the rest of his life in his mansion 'Haeswijk' in Oegstgeest.[11]

The Dutch authorities and their naval officers considered this English decision degrading and a public affront to the Republic. This was unacceptable. The Dutch, however, glossed over the fact that they were not managing to meet their quotas. The English obviously gave full priority to their national interests in the deployment of senior flag officers. However, this was just the beginning. Van Wassenaer, Van Almonde's replacement, became another victim of English pettiness or *kleynachtingh* as the Dutch called it. Only one year later, Van Wassenaer came back from the Mediterranean in November 1706. He had been away for more than a year and a half, and had spent the winter with a detachment of the Dutch squadron on the river Tagus near Lisbon. The hibernation of the core of the allied Mediterranean forces in a Spanish or Portuguese port was part of the overall strategy. The other ships in the fleet were sent home, while fresh contingents completed the over-wintering forces in the spring. This way, the French Atlantic and Mediterranean fleets could be kept separated and the troops fighting on land in Catalonia and northern Italy could be supported in their earliest spring campaigns.

Baron Jan Gerrit van Wassenaer was not just any flag officer. Born in 1672, he was still relatively young, although his record was already a very distinguished one. He had seen a great deal of active service. He became a captain in 1690, a rear admiral in 1700 and a vice admiral in 1703, always serving the main admiralty: that of Amsterdam. The wars of 1689–1697 and 1702–1713 offered Van Wassenaer many opportunities for command. He was a daring and courageous man. He did not eschew fighting and even boarding a hostile ship. He was seriously wounded in 1697 and taken prisoner by the famous French privateer, Duguay Trouïn. Commanding a force of three smaller men-of-war escorting a homeward-bound convoy from Bilbao, he was no match for five heavily armed privateers. His opponent spoke so positively of Van Wassenaer's fighting qualities that, after he recovered from his wounds, he was immediately released and Louis XIV received him at court.[12]

From 1700 onwards, he was seldom at home. Still a bachelor, he was sent almost every year to the Mediterranean, building up an impressive fighting reputation and becoming one of the leading admirals of his day. He sailed under the command of either Van Almonde or Callenburgh. Iberian waters and ports held few secrets from him, Lisbon in particular. In that port, he headed the over-wintering fleet in 1703–1704 and in 1705–1706.[13]

Jan Gerrit belonged to the highest rank of the nobility. He was the third son of Jacob van Duvenvoorde, Baron van Wassenaer (1649–1697) and younger brother of Arent (1669–1721). Both were influential politicians. For instance, his father was ambassador to England in 1685 and a member of the admiralty board of Rotterdam during the 1690s. The famous Admiral Jacob van Wassenaer Obdam (1610–1665) was a very distant relative. Soon after his return from southern Europe in November 1706, Jan Gerrit married his cousin Maria Jacoba van Liere (1682–1718). The marriage took place on 31 May in Rosendael Castle near Arnhem, the property of Jan van Arnhem (1636–1716), who was Jan Gerrit's godfather and uncle. The young couple then bought the Rosenburg estate at Voorschoten, adjacent to the family property Duvenvoorde.[14] He was not able to enjoy a long honeymoon though. Jan Gerrit was called back to naval service in August.

In 1707, the Dutch contingent in the Mediterranean was slightly smaller than before, consisting of fifteen ships-of-the-line. Vice admiral Philips van der Goes was the only flag officer. This was a symptom of the now careless way Dutch officials handled the command structure of their most important naval squadron. The custom had been three flag officers, particularly in a force with several first- and second-rate warships. None of those who were responsible for the navy and for relations with their English ally showed any interest in this grave omission. The secretary of the Amsterdam admiralty Job de Wildt, an old hand, had died in 1704. The lack of concern among his less effective successors proved costly. On 9 July 1707 Van der Goes died after a six-day illness. Captain Johan van Convent became the highest-ranking Dutch officer in the combined fleet under Admiral Shovell. This had never happened before. Another Dutch flag officer had to be sent to Genoa. The Hague awoke to the need for action. Grand Pensionary Anthonie Heinsius moved immediately. On 4 August he informed the most prominent political figures of Amsterdam of the problem and suggested the name of Jan Gerrit van Wassenaer as the most capable officer with sufficient rank for the job; he thought Van Almonde and

Van Callenburgh, both in their sixties, were too old for the long overland journey. Moreover, rumour had it that Shovell would soon return to England. A vice admiral would be fine and Van Wassenaer had already presented himself for the assignment.[15] So, he departed on 22 August and arrived in Genoa on 12 September.

To Van Wassenaer's great surprise, the English fleet had sailed to Gibraltar for revictualling. Captain Van Convent had only been given notice of their departure and had received no further instructions. Van Wassenaer considered this outrageous and an affront to Dutch officers. He thought that such decisions ought to be taken in a council of war. The vice admiral did not hesitate; he sailed straight to Gibraltar, arriving on 10 October, just as Shovell was about to leave for England. Both men had known each other for years. Shovell, of a genial nature,[16] understood his colleague's anger, apologized, and called for an immediate council of war. Apart from Shovell, two English vice admirals and one rear admiral were present, while only a captain accompanied Van Wassenaer. As was the case later, the Dutch would be very much in the minority. The Admiral announced his immediate departure, the wind being too favourable to be missed.[17] Rear Admiral Thomas Dilkes would command the winter forces. Shovell assumed Van Wassenaer would become Dilkes' opposite number. However, that was not what the Dutchman thought. As a vice admiral he could not serve under a rear admiral; to do so would be a sign of disrespect for his masters, the States General. Most English officers were surprised by this refusal by the baron, and tried to change his mind; however, it was in vain. The baron said no. Shovell said it was now too late for another English command arrangement. It was clear: the Dutch had to accept the English arrangement because they did not have flag officers of the correct rank in their contingent.

Van Wassenaer assembled his ships after the meeting, gave instructions for the winter period, wrote to the States General, and sailed to Lisbon on board the first-rate *Prins* (92 guns) together with another warship. When he arrived on 19 November, he was in a desperate mood. His hurried trip to the Mediterranean and then the voyage to Gibraltar proved fruitless; the money spent uselessly. He hated the idea of spending another winter in Lisbon, this time as a real idler (*ledig ganger*). The need to maintain respect for the Dutch Republic had given him no other option. Van Wassenaer hoped to be recalled. This did not happen. The Hague fully approved his actions, yet let him stay in Lisbon.

The English vice admiral John Leake arrived on 7 April; however, it was not until 5 May that the two vice admirals sailed to the theatre of war in the Mediterranean. There, they were jointly involved in a very successful campaign against the French. The occupation of Minorca was one of the results. Early in November 1708, Van Wassenaer was back in the Republic.[18]

An officer of a higher rank serving under a lower-ranking allied colleague remains, even today, a touchy proposition. This was even more so in an era when the assumed honour of the state not to mention the personal pride of an officer were at stake. Baron Van Wassenaer's behaviour must also be placed in the perspective of the rapidly declining Dutch naval power, growing English irritation with the Dutch. The Republic was no longer an equal partner; it was evident that no Dutch admiral would ever again be present in the allied fleet: only a rear admiral in 1709–1710 and, once again, a vice admiral in 1711. In a nutshell, this little case-study demonstrates – was already obvious some years before 1707 – that the usual ability to run naval warfare smoothly was ebbing away. The complete military and financial breakdown of the Dutch Republic came soon. Public finances were completely exhausted. The state coffers at The Hague were shut for some time following the Peace of Utrecht in 1713. The shortage of funds meant little influence and a subordinate position for Dutch naval forces and their commanders.

The incident illustrates a number of more fundamental changes and problems in the naval organization and the political structure of the Dutch Republic. The conflict exposes the lack of willingness and indeed ability to invest more funds in the navy. The presence of adequate naval forces in the Mediterranean was considered of less importance than the safety of the mercantile fleet and fishing vessels in northern waters. A well-functioning naval apparatus of five different admiralties had always required a strong central leader, as in the days of John de Witt and the De Wildts during William's regime but there would never be another. As a consequence of unavoidable changes in the shipping movements in Dutch ports, three admiralties saw their annual income drastically shrink. In fact, they became superfluous institutions. However, adaptation to this new situation was impossible. This would have meant a complete overhaul of the Dutch political structure.

Notes

1 Based upon Jaap R. Bruijn, *The Dutch Navy of the Seventeenth and Eighteenth Centuries* (Columbia 1993; rev. edn. Research in Maritime History, St. John's 45, 2011), pp. 6–12, and id., *Varend Verleden: De Nederlandse oorlogsvloot in de 17de en 18de eeuw* (Amsterdam 1998), pp. 15–20.

2 Jan Glete, 'The Dutch Republic as a Great Power: Political Action and Armed Forces', in: Jaap R. Bruijn et al. (eds.), *De Ruyter, Dutch Admiral: Protagonists in International Perspective* (Rotterdam 2011).

3 Jan Glete, *Warfare at Sea 1500–1650: Maritime Conflicts and the Transformation of Europe* (London 2000), pp. 68–69, 75; id. *War and the State in Early Modern Europe: Spain, the Dutch Republic and Sweden as Fiscal-Military States, 1500–1660* (London & New York 2002), pp. 140–173.

4 This case-study was earlier published as 'A Baron says No: Jan Gerrit van Wassenaer and Anglo–Dutch Naval Cooperation in 1707', in: Jan Frans Dijkhuizen et al. (eds.), *Living in Posterity: Essays in Honour of Bart Westerweel* (Hilversum 2004), pp. 47–53.

5 James B. Hattendorf, '"To Aid and Assist the Other": Anglo–Dutch Cooperation in Coalition Warfare at Sea, 1689–1714', in: J. A. F. de Jongste & A. J. Veenendaal (ed.), *Anthonie Heinsius and the Dutch Republic 1688–1720: Politics, War, and Finance* (The Hague 2002), pp. 177–198; Jaap R. Bruijn, 'The Long Life of Treaties: The Dutch Republic and Great Britain in the Eighteenth Century', in: Rolf Hobson & Tom Kristiansen (eds.), *Navies in Northern Waters 1721–2000* (London 2004), pp. 41–58.

6 A. L. van Schelven, *Philips van Almonde: Admiraal in de gecombineerde vloot 1644–1711* (Amsterdam 1947), pp. 52–53; see Bruijn (1993/2011), pp. 89–98.

7 van Schelven (1947), pp. 135, 167–171.

8 Jaap R. Bruijn, 'William III and His Two Navies', *Notes and Records Royal Society of London*, 43 (1989), pp. 117–132, at 120; Hattendorf (2002) p. 190.

9 van Schelven (1947), pp. 108–109; Hattendorf (2002) p. 191.

10 Hattendorf (2002), pp. 192–193.

11 van Schelven (1947), pp. 196–202; *De briefwisseling van Anthonie Heinsius 1702–1720*, 5, ed. A. J. Veenendaal (Rijks Geschiedkundige Publicatiën, Grote Serie RGP, GS 183; The Hague 1983), pp. 442–443.

12 J. C. de Jonge, *Geschiedenis van het Nederlandsche zeewezen*, 3 (Haarlem 1860), pp. 520–526.

13 de Jonge (1860), p. 565 passim; van Schelven (1947), pp. 180–195.

14 H. M. Brokken (ed.), *Heren van stand: 1200 Van Wassenaer 2000: Achthonderd jaar Nederlandse adelsgeschiedenis* (Zoetermeer 2000), pp. 187–189, 267–270; J. C. Bierens de Haan, *Rosendael: Groen Hemeltjen op Aerd: Kasteel, tuinen en bewoners sedert 1579* (Zutphen 1994), pp. 28, 79, 307.

15 *De briefwisseling*, 6 (1984), pp. 402, 444, 450, 452, 455. My thanks to Julia M. Wixley who wrote a paper on the squadron of 1707/1708 for a maritime history seminar at the University of Leiden in 2000–2001.

16 van Schelven (1947) p. 181.

17 If Shovell had delayed his return, he might have missed the storm that swept his and three other ships to their destruction on the rocks of the Scilly Isles.

18 States General (1.01.05), 5719, 9343, Nationaal Archief, The Hague; ibid. Van Wassenaer van Duvenvoorde (3.20.87), 3272; *De briefwisseling*, 6 (1984), pp. 594–597, 618; ibid. 7 (1985), pp. 317–318, 436–437, (Rijks Geschiedkundige Publicatiën, Grote Serie RGP, GS 194; de Jonge, 4 (1861)), pp. 1–29.

CHAPTER 6

Exhibiting the Seventeenth Century

Maritime history made public through the Vasa royal warship

Marika Hedin

During the 2009 conference of the International Congress of Maritime Museums (ICMM), a workshop was held on the question of audiences. Participating museum professionals from all over the world reported a decline in visitor numbers, and foresaw an even bleaker future ahead. Various reasons for this diminished interest in the maritime cultural heritage were discussed; it was argued that the maritime experience does not play a central role in the life of the average museum visitor any more. Harbours and docks are mostly away from populated areas; people mainly travel by car or airplane; the decline of the small-scale fishing industry means that coastal areas no longer have a socio-economic maritime makeup. Moreover, the multinational character of the shipping business removes it from national self-image, even in countries whose economy in reality depends upon this sector. Therefore, the museum professionals argued, this lack of a personal relationship with the sea means that museum visitors simply choose to go elsewhere.

One could argue that total visitor numbers are not, or should not, be the decisive factor in judging the success of a museum. Governments hand out specific assignments to national museums in most countries today: a condition for receiving the yearly grant to cater to younger audiences, work with schools, develop new visitor groups, help to establish new or marginalized art forms, and so on. Time and money are invested in these assignments. However, at the end of the year, it is still total visitor numbers that are demanded, reported in the media, and cited by the politicians. Non-national museums, which are more dependent upon outside sources of revenue, are if anything even more focused upon visitor attendance. Aside from ticket revenues, being able to point to the crowds is an important tool in attracting sponsors. Therefore, increasing visitor numbers (regardless of who these visitors actually are and what they actually do in the museum) is a key asset for any museum today. Neil Cossons has pointed out that, although visitor figures are the common currency of the debate on the public value of museums, many museums in reality have repeat visits from a small segment of society.[1]

However, there were two main exceptions to the general gloomy picture presented at the ICMM conference. The first exception was the National Maritime Museum in Greenwich in London, where visitor numbers had grown following a successful campaign inviting visitors to have 'a great day out' in the museum grounds. This is interesting and calls for a separate paper on how to transform the image of maritime heritage sites. The second example was the Vasa Museum in Stockholm. Visitor numbers have continuously grown here over a number of years; even during a short-lived experiment with free entrance to other national museums in Sweden, from which the Vasa Museum was exempt.

Understanding the mechanisms of museum success

Why is it that certain heritage sites and museums capture the imagination of the visitor and others do not? Why did nearly 1.2 million people decide to visit this single-object museum in northern Europe in 2010, when other Swedish museums are more than satisfied with visitor numbers ten times smaller? What *is* the lure of the *Vasa*?

First, it is useful to establish some facts and figures. The Vasa Museum opened in 1990. This was following a long period during which the ship was being treated for conservation purposes in a large shed: the *Vasa* was salvaged in 1961, after 333 years under water. This shed gradually evolved into a museum of sorts, and many Swedes of earlier generations have vivid memories of seeing the *Vasa* being soaked in PEG (the conservation fluid used).[2] Visitors to the temporary museum amounted to several million over the years; therefore, when the new museum was being planned, designers and architects calculated for a yearly limit of 600,000 visitors. For a Swedish museum, this was an exceptionally high figure, so sceptics started talking about hubris. Some politicians expressed worries early on that the financial situation of the museum might quickly become troublesome, once the initial curiosity died down.[3] However, all predictions turned out to be inadequate. The Vasa Museum has never had fewer than 730,000 visitors in any given year.

In trying to explain why the museum is so successful in terms of visitor numbers, I think it is relevant to point to three equally important reasons that need to be taken into account: content, design, and day-to-day museum operation. Each of these reasons also places the Vasa Museum at the heart of the historic argument of what museums really are and what they should be.

Making history accessible

The first suggestion has to do with the story of the *Vasa* and her times. She was built in 1628. Perhaps the seventeenth century is distant enough for most people to qualify as intriguing and vague; it is possible to fill one's mind with fantasy images of the time. This was a century that witnessed the scientific revolution, the Baroque, and the rise of the omnipotent kings in Europe. However, there was also war just about everywhere; it was the dawn of colonization and cultural exploitation; and there was appalling poverty and disease among most people. The *Vasa* story makes all this quite tangible and still leaves room for that elusive, mythical quality that the past often evokes.

The ship was commissioned as part of the young king Gustavus Adolphus' drive to expand the Swedish realm, conquer neighbouring states, and establish Sweden as a player in world politics. Building the ship was difficult and very costly and, once it set sail, the *Vasa* turned out to be unstable and difficult to manoeuvre. She sank only thirty minutes into her maiden voyage, a great and embarrassing fiasco – which makes her story one of human hopes and human fallibility. This is something that transcends the historic dimension. (In fact, some scholars have recently pointed to the construction of the *Vasa* as a valid example of bad management: something from which lessons can be learned even today.[4])

The royal splendour, the magnificent early baroque wooden carvings (after their colouring was analysed, the sculptures of the *Vasa* can be described as perhaps closer to Medieval church drawings than to the artistry of the Versailles), the technical and scientific advances, and the complicated economic structure of the period are all present in the ship. This makes her a prism of her times. Equally present, of course, is the warfare of the early seventeenth century: so important in an era when trade and diplomacy were less usual routes of national expansion. The *Vasa* was built in a fashion that made her suitable to wage war in seas larger than the Baltic; it has been suggested that the Mediterranean and the Atlantic were in Gustavus Adolphus' future plans for her as well. This also connects *Vasa* with the expanding sea-trade and the early colonial ventures of the period.[5]

Since most of the crew assigned to the *Vasa* were not on board when she sank, the cost in human life was not as great as it could have been. A rough estimation is that around 25 people died. Their belongings show the simple but functional design of the clothes, cutlery, and leisure equipment of the Swedish seventeenth-century peasant, including pipes for smoking tobacco and board-games. Their remains tell the often forgotten story of undernourishment, chronic disease, toothache and badly healed wounds that were the reality for most people in those days, especially once they had reached middle age. Since it is so rare to have this kind of source material from the lower strata in society – and since peasants all over Northern Europe lived in much the same conditions – the collections at the Vasa Museum probably appeal to many museum visitors who might not otherwise be interested in Sweden's political, military, or economic history.

There is something accessible about the ship being one large object, in which many different meanings are embedded and, therefore, many different stories can be told.[6] Most of the museum displays were designed and texts were written with the average Swedish 11-year-old in mind; this is something that can characterize the storytelling in the museum as direct and inviting. (One interesting fact to ponder is how well this textual style works with a predominantly adult audience.) Little previous knowledge is needed to appreciate the story of the ship and her time, so the museum can be described as generous to first-time visitors, regardless of their educational or cultural background. Moreover, the experience of the *Vasa* differs from visitor to visitor; this is a good illustration of Jim Bennett's conclusion that 'objects have meanings that are differentiated across contexts both outside and inside the museum'.[7] Since the sinking was a disaster, the story appeals to all of us who have an interest in dramatic events, as long as they are distant enough not to affect us personally.[8]

This ties in well with one of the conclusions of the ICMM conference, namely that maritime history and cultural heritage often touch on the larger human experiences: life and death, victory and defeat, migration and hardship, hope and disappointment. The seventeenth century can be described as a historic period with sharp contrasts and many dramatic events. However, if one part of the storytelling rests upon a pillar of mystique and historic vagueness (many things from this era seem alien and strange to us today), then another is firmly placed upon recognition. One message that the museum sends is that human experience across centuries and cultures shares many traits. In this sense, museum visitors can approach history through the experience of the present; the museum, thus, thrives on a broad sense of identification.[9] However, since the story the curators tell is largely aimed at a different audience than the one actually present in the museum (the intended Swedish 11-year old has transmagnified into the adult from abroad), the 'past/present alignments' of the *Vasa* are multiple and unexpected.[10]

Telling the story of a cultural icon

There is of course more to the story of the *Vasa* and the factors that can explain her unprecedented success. The term 'cultural icon' is often used to define emblematic personalities; however, it can just as well describe objects that are embedded with specific meanings in our present culture.[11] These meanings, however, are social and ideological constructs; therefore, they differ depending upon who is relating to the icon. Describing the *Vasa* as a cultural icon places her within the current discussion on how cultural heritage is used and commodified.

For her Swedish audience, the *Vasa* can convey several different meanings; it has been argued that raising the ship was part of a need in post-war Sweden to reconstruct national pride. Swedish Second World War appeasement policies towards Nazi Germany and the Allied forces had hurt the self-image of certain conservative groups. Raising the *Vasa* would remind everyone of a time when Sweden really was an international player in world politics (in Swedish history, the seventeenth century is known as Sweden's Great Power era).[12] Another suggestion is that, since the procedure was a very complicated operation, the twentieth-century raising itself symbolizes the image of present-day

Sweden as a country in the forefront of scientific and technological development. As private and public sector joined forces in the project, it is also one where society as a whole works together toward great achievements.[13] For an international audience, these aspects might not carry much meaning; however, other aspects will. Furthermore, while there are today many other raised ships around the world, none is so big and, by the look of it at least, as well preserved as the *Vasa*. This has transformed the ship into a 'must-see' in the cultural sector, which is underlined by the museum's typical visitor profile: an urban resident in his or her mid-thirties who 'collects' a few cultural experiences each year.[14] It makes sense to call the *Vasa* a 'cultural icon' in the sense that Llorenç Prats has discussed cultural heritage: how certain objects (as well as places and realities) are evocative enough to produce a multitude of symbolic connections.[15]

Making maritime heritage tangible and spatial

As the average Vasa Museum visitor 'collects' a few cultural experiences each year, the lure of history, however accessible, cannot be the sole explanation for the lure of the ship. A second suggestion toward explaining the success of the museum, therefore, is the importance of the *Vasa* as *a ship*. A vital part of this has to do with how she is displayed.

The maritime aspect of the *Vasa* is tangible and evident. The visitor experiences a large warship seemingly crammed into a museum: it looks huge and imposing. There is a distinct smell of wood and tar in the cool, climate-controlled air. Visitor galleries invite contact up close, *almost* letting visitors touch the surface of the ship. Walking around the display makes it easier to imagine the 'micro-society' of a seventeenth-century warship: soldiers and boatmen stayed on board for months on end, living a confined and highly regulated existence, while making use of all available space. Yet again, the fact that the ship is itself the main museum object underlines this particular aspect of maritime history: the ship that then, and now, represents an alternative to ordinary society or ordinary life. Boarding the ship meant leaving your old life behind; it meant entering into a whole new set of rules and relationships. And, in the minds of most visitors, there is still an element of fascination and romance in this, which is crucial to experiencing the maritime heritage. However, in order to feel the scope of this alternative life, one needs something substantial to help your imagination. Here is where the grandeur of the *Vasa* as a museum object comes into play.

Experiencing the ship close up, from all sides and from the bottom up, is a different experience from studying rows of display cases with maritime artefacts. The Vasa Museum makes ample use of the fact that a ship is a *spatial experience*. Spatiality is a key factor in the design and architecture of the building and the construction was appropriately named 'Box' when first presented in the competition held in the 1980s. The architects, Månsson & Dahlbäck, were awarded the prestigious Kasper Salin Prize in 1990, and the building still attracts international attention.[16] The museum is asymmetrical and adjusted to the surrounding landscape with multiple layers of roofs; with thick concrete walls and few windows, it looks quite small and unassuming from the outside. Inside, the building opens up and the theatrical presence of the ship hits the visitor upon entering. The light is carefully designed, both for conservation purposes and to maximize the impact. There is a feeling of a cathedral or perhaps a temple in the open space with its slanted ceiling some seven stories high. All exhibition spaces within the building are subordinate to this spatial experience; few corners of the museum are closed off from the ship and all displays must work within the larger framework of the interior.

In this sense, the whole museum becomes one big exhibit, one in which to parade the 'wonder' and channel the 'resonance' of the *Vasa* – to stop visitors in their tracks and give them a different kind of maritime museum experience.[17] Museum buildings that can be described as attractions in themselves are of course not a new idea; in the past decade, a number of spectacular museums – often displaying art – have opened around the world.[18] However, the two ambitions of designing great architecture while displaying objects at the same time do not always sit comfortably together; this has been the topic of discussion for Kiasma, the museum of contemporary art in Helsinki.[19] In the case of the Vasa Museum, the force of the museum object itself can be described as working with the architecture, instead of the two competing with each other.

The discussion about the balance between design and content in museums is often unsatisfactory, as if it were a choice between (superficial) aesthetics and (boring) adherence to facts. Mattias Bäckström has argued for a more nuanced discussion, where design and content must be made to collaborate instead of existing within two separate realms of references; he argues that this is often the case today. In his view, museum professionals must be more comfortable in engaging with both the scholarly references needed to produce content and the current discussions trends and in design and architecture.[20]

At the ICMM conference, it was suggested that there were some key assets to maritime history that could, and should, be used to draw in new visitors to the museums: the experience of a different lifestyle, the adventure, the tangibility of boats and ships, and the almost separate world created in life at sea. However, the discussion did not really touch upon how this could be best conveyed to visitors. I would argue here that spatiality is a key element in projecting this feeling. All of these assets are present in the design of the Vasa Museum, precisely because the emphasis has been upon a careful yet powerful display of the ship itself.

Welcoming the visitor

Even so, an interest in maritime history cannot in itself account for all the visitors to the Vasa Museum. As mentioned, maritime heritage seems to have a diminishing appeal for the general public worldwide. In fact, a specific interest in boats is a rare answer when visitors are asked why they have chosen to come to the museum. This would suggest that it is not primarily visitors with a relationship to the sea who flock to the Vasa Museum. The suggestion here is that a third reason for its success is something else: something too rarely discussed when talking about museums and heritage, namely the professional handling of the visitors.

Of course all museums and heritage sites welcome their visitors. These venues aim to both educate and please, to cater to the uninformed, and preach to the converted. However, in the intellectual baggage of the museum world, there is certain ambivalence as to what this should mean.[21] Are museums meant to live up to visitors' expectations, regardless how ill informed they are? Is not research and preservation *really* what museums should invest time and money in? And are visitors *not* there to be educated? There have been numerous debates in the last twenty years or so about 'dumbing down' and 'selling out' in order to meet the new sensation-hungry, postmodern audiences with short attention spans.[22] At the same time, society now talks about meeting educational needs in new ways: about adjusting learning to the individual's preferences and abilities, about the breakdown of intellectual 'canons', and about inviting different interpretations of the past. Museums are at the heart of this debate because they have always been part amusement park, part educational facility, and part research centre.[23] This is what makes museums such fascinating places: vastly different from universities and schools, and also from fields of merry-go-rounds and rollercoaster rides. It is precisely this tension between knowledge and fun that explains the dynamic of the museum.[24]

Museum professionals are often interested in discussing collections, exhibition design, research issues, preservation techniques, and educational challenges. I find that it is rarer to touch upon the crucial questions of how visitors are received, how they pay their entrance fees, how they are met with information upon entering the museum, how easily they can find their way around the building, and so on. These are the logistics of any museum visit, and the experience of shops, restaurants, and restrooms play a big part in most museum visits – as much as the content and design of what is being displayed. The reality in the twenty-first century is that there are multiple choices for prospective museum visitors in what to do and where to go. Since a museum visit is a totality, the whole museum experience becomes important. (To borrow NMM's tagline, it is 'a great day out'.)

Therefore, it is appropriate also to discuss the Vasa Museum as a visitor attraction. One can be rather prosaic and point to the fact that, since the museum opened, Sweden has evolved into an established tourist destination. The country is not as expensive as it was in the 1970s and 1980s for most visitors. In 2009, for the first time, foreign tourists visiting Sweden spent more money than Swedes travelling abroad.[25] Neighbouring states around the Baltic have simultaneously evolved into countries with citizens who are not only *allowed* to go on holiday; they can actually afford it, too. This development has been evident in the Vasa Museum in the last decade. Visitors from former Eastern Europe countries make up a large proportion of museum visitors, especially in the winter holiday season. Since the museum opened, there has also been a significant increase in visitors from the Mediterranean to Northern Europe: especially in August. However, tourists now come not only from Europe, they come from all over the world. Some 75 per cent of the visitors to the Vasa Museum describe themselves as being 'from abroad' in visitor studies. Since most Swedish museums do not attract many visitors from other countries, merely pointing to the fact that Sweden has become a tourist destination is not a sufficient explanation for the Vasa Museum visitor numbers. In order to understand the lure of the ship, I think it helps to think about the museum as a major tourist attraction, rather than just as housing of collections with the aim of dispersing knowledge and educating the masses.

The unexpectedly large audiences in the museum has actually forced staff to develop the kind of professional visitor services that are normally reserved for amusement parks and the like. An efficient system of queuing and guiding practices has evolved in order to welcome as many people as possible in the building on any given day, regardless of climate restrictions. The entrance system is designed to let people in as quickly as possible. Opening hours are generous and groups are let in before opening or after closing. Guided tours in several languages are constantly being held by groups of students from multicultural backgrounds. Texts and films are also written and spoken in different languages. Museum staff employ various schemes to steer clusters of visitors away from the most crowded points in the museum. The visitors, most of them in the building for the first time, will find guides dressed in distinct clothing around the museum. There is a visitor services desk near the museum's entrance, which acts both as an information point on the *Vasa* and a central booking spot for taxis and the like. Despite visitor pressure in the summer months, the system seems to work well. The Vasa Museum was presented with the 'TRIP Global Award' in 2009 for being foreign tourists' best experience in Sweden – in competition with major hotels and amusement parks.[26]

Losing the essence of the museum?

The risk in this great visitor machinery of the Vasa Museum is losing essential parts of what a museum should be: a place not only for amusement but for education and research as well. There is little incentive during the summer season to do anything other than get people in and out of the museum in a way that the visitor perceives as generous but is as quick as possible. The in-depth tours, the thematic programming, the ideas for new exhibits, and the general resourcefulness that characterizes most good museum operations take a back seat. Slow, painstaking research with doubtful economic effectiveness has no place in this equation. The Vasa Museum has become a modern and efficient visitor attraction, but has perhaps lost something in the process. This development has been accentuated in the past decade when the museum has been integrated into the larger museum authority: the National Maritime Museums of Sweden (SMM).

The collaboration with experts has also been affected by the challenge of welcoming an increasing number of visitors, something which is currently being addressed. As the world's leading expert on the early modern Swedish navy, Jan Glete was vital for the museum's storytelling; we had just begun ambitious discussions together and we all looked forward to more systematically using Jan's vast knowledge in displays, books, and programming, when he became ill. The Vasa Museum initiated a historical research programme in 2003, when Fred Hocker was engaged to document and interpret the *Vasa*. The dialogue with Jan Glete became even more important when the museum began to plan a new exhibition on war at sea. These discussions eventually influenced the more formal research collaboration between SMM and Stockholm University that began in 2010. In retrospect, it is apparent that the museum should have involved Jan earlier and more continously.

The tension present in the Vasa Museum is part of a general trend. Museums all over the Western world have experienced an upsurge in interest since the 1980s, and have become a public concern. As Neil Cossons put it: 'Perhaps, for the first time, [museums are] being seen as the intellectual property of the people who use them and those people are increasingly wanting their likes and dislikes to be heard.'[27] Comparing the experience of the Vasa Museum with that of hotels and amusement parks has merit, since it takes into account one central aspect of a museum visit: the hospitality of cultural institutions. However, there is no other aim than to increase visitor numbers in an amusement park. In a museum, with its government funding and a responsibility for preserving cultural heritage, there must be other ambitions as well.

The Vasa museum and maritime heritage

As the Vasa Museum is part of the SMM, a government authority, one answer to the conundrum is to channel resources from its ticket revenues into two other museums of a more traditional type. Both the Naval Museum in Karlskrona and the Maritime Museum in Stockholm have, in recent years, opened large, research-based thematic exhibitions, offered generous family programming, and have supported an expansive development of maritime archaeology techniques. These are all things that would have been very difficult to achieve without the collaboration between all three museums. The two museums each have between 150,000 and 200,000 visitors per year; on their own, they would have been hard pressed for resources had they not been organizationally connected to the Vasa Museum.

Another development made possible by the success of the Vasa Museum is the collaboration between the three museums and Stockholm University in the form of a centre for Maritime Studies (CEMAS). This project, initiated in 2010, is an attempt to generate high-quality, relevant research on maritime history, which can raise the profile of the programming and exhibitions in all three museums. By connecting the university and the museums financially, and by having CEMAS governed by a board of directors made up from both bodies, the aim is that the museums, as visitor attractions, will also inspire university-based research projects of a wider public interest. The centre has attracted both national and international interest for its attempt to cross, in a new way, the boundaries between the academic world and the museum world. The successful nature of the Vasa Museum and its huge visitor numbers are an important factor in this discussion.[28] It remains to be seen how this collaboration will make its mark in the Vasa Museum visitor experience.

Conclusion

Attracting visitors is crucial to any heritage site. A current worry for the maritime museums of the world is that visitor numbers are dwindling. Now that people have a less personal relationship with the sea and with their maritime cultural heritage, something new needs to be offered. So, how can visitors be brought back? Here I have analysed the success of the Vasa Museum in order to explain why visitors continue to make this museum one of the most visited maritime museums in the world.

One such suggestion is the museum's approach to history and how it is made accessible, understandable, while still maintaining its mythical and elusive character. In making use of the dramatic story of the sinking of the ship and ordinary people's lives in the seventeenth century, the history of the *Vasa* becomes both intriguingly distant while, at the same time, very real and present. Characterizing the *Vasa* as a cultural icon also explains some of its drawing power and ability to convey different meanings to a diverse audience.

The tangible quality of the maritime aspect of the *Vasa* is another success factor. In many museums, the spatial aspects are underplayed. When separate exhibits are being designed, the urge is often to confine an area and make it thematically coherent, both in terms of layout and content. As a contrast, the Vasa Museum opens up and displays the ship as dramatically as possible, making use of space and size, along with smell and – almost – touch. Exhibits are conceived with respect for this larger museum space: something that is not always true in modern museum architecture and design. Thus, the maritime experience becomes something else: a sensory experience that is larger and more tangible than simply displaying objects in cases. Boats are big, the smell of the sea is upon them, and they represent a different kind of life – maritime museums should use this to their advantage.

Lastly, the visitor-oriented approach, aimed at welcoming as many people as possible in a smooth fashion, also goes a long way in explaining the success of the Vasa Museum. For parts of the year, this approach becomes a machinery of sorts, aiming to provide as many visitors as possible with a positive museum experience. Part of this welcoming approach also lies in the immediate experience of the museum content, its architecture, and the design. This is a museum where no one needs to wonder where to go, what to see, and what one is supposed to experience.

The accessibility and focus on visitor reception has, in some ways, made the Vasa Museum underplay other important features of a national museum displaying cultural heritage. As a result of developments in the last decade, new exhibitions, programming, and research have taken a backseat, at least for some of the year. Some of the resources not used at the Vasa Museum have been channelled into exhibitions and programming at the two other maritime museums connected to it; some into developing the discipline of maritime archaeology; and some into a research collaboration with Stockholm University. Thus, as a whole, Sweden's maritime heritage probably benefits from the extraordinary success of the Vasa Museum. The museum must, therefore, be seen within this larger context in order to be understood as a traditional museum.

It is true that the large museum institutions of the nineteenth century were designed for the masses; however, the viewpoint was different, the aim was to educate and transform the lower strata of society. As a consequence, some museums are still impatient with visitors who do not behave correctly or display the right kind of interest. This impatience shows, perhaps more than most museum professionals are aware of. The debate about the 'dumbing down' of museums to make them more visitor-friendly is part of this historic tension within museums. However, I believe the *Vasa* exemplifies that a museum *can* tell an interesting story in an accessible way, present objects in a spectacular fashion, and treat visitors in much the same way as the hospitality industry treats guests without losing its essential qualities. And in this, the Vasa Museum makes a strong argument for the museum as a separate medium: a powerful vehicle of learning and of experience.

Notes

1 'Museums in the New Millennium', in: Svante Lindqvist (ed.), *Museums of Modern Science: Nobel Symposium 112* (Canton, Maryland, 2000) p. 8.

2 For a brief summary of this history, see <http://www.vasamuseet.se/en/Preservation--Research/Conservation-1962-1979/>.

3 'Motion till riksdagen 1992/93:Kr288', by Ulla Tillander et al., <http://www.riksdagen.se/webbnav/?nid=410&doktyp=mot&rm=1992/93&bet=Kr288&dok_id=GG02Kr288>, (accessed 30 May 2011).

4 For example E. H. Kessler, 'Vasa Syndrome: Insights From a 17th-century New-product Disaster', *Academy of Management Executives* (August 2001) p. 80.

5 Although built for war in the Baltic, resent research has suggested that Vasa was even better suited for war in the Atlantic – which might indicate that Gustavus Adolphus had grander plans that just engaging in the Northern European theatre of war. See Fred Hocker, *Vasa* (Stockholm 2011) esp. ch. 1.

6 Robert Bud, 'Science, Meaning and Myth In the Museum', *Public Understanding of Science*, 4 (1995).

7 Jim Bennett, 'Beyond Understanding: Curatorship and Access In Science Museums', in: Lindqvist (ed.), (2000) p. 57.

8 There are thousands of visitor-made entries on websites such as Flickr and YouTube with images and films made in the museum, which are interesting sources on how today's more media-savvy audiences process their museum visit.

9 Tony Bennett, *The Birth of the Museum: History, Theory, Politics* (London 1998), pp. 130–131, discusses the various readings of the past that a museum can convey to visitors.

10 Bennet (1998), pp. 147–148.

11 James Park, *Cultural Icons* (London 1991), pp. 7–13.

12 Henrik Arnstad, 'Varför bärgades skeppet Vasa? Studie angående nätverk och historiekonstruktion under slutet av 1950-talet', undergaduate thesis, Department of History, Stockholm University, 2009.

13 Marika Hedin, 'Vraket som nationalsymbol', in: Marika Hedin, Åsa Linderborg & Torbjörn Nilsson, *Bilden av Sveriges historia: Fyrtio sätt att se på 1900-talet* (Stockholm 2005), pp. 260–263.

14 Visitor studies are archived at the museum; see 'Vasapersonen', internal report, Vasa Museum 2005.

15 Llorenç Prats, 'Heritage according to scale', in: Marta Anico & Elsa Peralta (eds.), *Heritage and Identity: Engagement and Demission in the Contemporary World* (London 2009), pp. 76–89.
16 See <http://www.arkitekt.se/s52866>, (accessed 30 May 2011) for a history of the Kasper Salin-prize and how the Vasa Museum was described.
17 Stephen Greenblatt, 'Resonance and Wonder' in: Ivan Karp & Steven D. Lavine, *Exhibiting Culture: The Poetics and Politics of Museum Display* (Washington & London 1991), p. 42.
18 Two well-known examples are Frank Gehry's Guggenheim in Bilbao and Daniel Libeskind's Jewish Museum in Berlin.
19 Kiasma was designed by Stephen Holl, and the building of the museum 1993–1998 was plagued by controversy over the design, the materials used, and the relation of the museum building to its surroundings.
20 Mattias Bäckström, 'Den snygga utställningen', *Utställningsestetiskt forum* (July 2008), <http://www.ueforum.se/2005-2009/forum05-09/0806snyggutstallning.php>, (accessed 30 May 2011).
21 On the ambivalent identity of museums, see Eilean Hooper-Greenhill, *Museums and the Shaping of Knowledge* (London & New York 1992), pp. 191–193.
22 'Today's museums aim to be genuinely populist', Caroline Reinhardt, 'History With an Attitude: Elitism Is Out, Populism Is In,' *The Spectator*, 4 April 1998; 'smirking irony, cultural relativism, celebration of putative victims, [and] facile attacks on science' at the Smithsonian, according to Heather MacDonald, 'Revisionist Lust: The Smithsonian Today', *The New Criterion* (May 1997); 'museums today are trying to become like theme parks or upscale shopping malls [...] a lot of the people that you see popping in and out of the Louvre have been dumped there with no foreknowledge', said Philippe de Montebello in an interview (Calvin Tomkins, 'The Importance of Being Elitist', *The New Yorker*, 24 November 1997).
23 The most emblematic of display techniques, the glass case, was in fact appropriated by museums from elegant shops (Chantal George, 'The Museum as Metaphor in Nineteenth-Century France', in: Daniel J. Sherman & Irit Rogoff (ed.), *Museum Culture: Histories, Discourses, Spectacles* (London 1994)).
24 Museums 'as entertainment is simply a return to the astonishment and delight associated with the first private Renaissance museums' (Victoria Newhouse, *Towards a New Museum* (New York 2006) p. 191).
25 Swedish Agency for Economic and Regional Growth, *Tourism in Sweden: Effects of Tourism on the Economy and Employment, Volumes, Behaviour and Supply and Demand: Facts and Statistics 2009*, (Stockholm 2010), available for download at <http://publikationer.tillvaxtverket.se/ProductView.aspx?ID=1507>, (accessed 30 May 2011).
26 <http://www.turistgalan.se/2009-10-22/vasamuseet-aer-den-baesta-upplevelsen-i-sverige>, (accessed 30 May 2011).
27 Neil Cossons, 'Museums in the New Millennium', in: Lindqvist (ed.), (2000) p. 4.
28 In fact, when first approached, Stockholm University was interested in starting a partnership with the Vasa Museum; however, it still showed initial reluctance to collaborate with the National Maritime Museums of Sweden; Stefan Lundblad & Leos Müller, 'Centre for Maritime Studies (CEMAS): A New Hub of Maritime Historical Research in Sweden', *International Journal of Maritime History*, 22:1 (2010), pp. 79–82.

PART II

NORM SYSTEMS

CHAPTER 7

Arguments of War

Norm and information systems in Sweden and France during the Thirty Years War

Anna Maria Forssberg

Entering what was to be known as the Thirty Years War, both Sweden and France felt the need to justify their actions. As the King of Sweden, Gustavus Adolphus, and his soldiers set foot upon German soil in June 1630, a manifesto explaining his intervention was published in German and Latin; editions in French, English, and Dutch soon followed. France declared war upon Spain a few years later, yet chose to proceed in a more traditional manner.[1] A herald accompanied by a trumpeter was sent to Brussels in May 1635 to declare war upon the Spanish Cardinal-Infante.[2] Since the latter understood the purpose of the visit, he and his servants refused to see the herald, who in the end attached the declaration of war to a post on the border. A more lengthy French war declaration was soon published. War manifestos were important documents that could serve a variety of purposes. They are not only interesting sources on notions of war; they also shed light upon information and norm systems in the seventeenth century.

The first, and perhaps surprising, question to ask is why war had to be explained at all. As we all know, war was more common than peace during the seventeenth century. However, this does not mean that it was not controversial. There was a general understanding that war brought misery. The discussions on the right to wage war, and the attempts to define just war – *bellum iustum* – were multiple. In accordance with these ideas, war had to be explained on an international level even though there was no undisputed doctrine at hand. On a national level, offensive wars had to be explained because they potentially cost the subjects both lives and livelihood; defensive wars also needed to be explained because their mere existence proved that the king had failed his most important duty: to protect his subjects. Still, it is probable that the idea of war and the apprehended roles of ruler and subjects varied between different countries. In Jan Glete's last work on the Swedish naval administration, he discusses norm systems.[3] According to Glete, Sweden underwent a significant change under the Vasa dynasty, a period that concluded in the 1620s. From being reluctant to pay taxes and contribute to the military system in the early sixteenth century, Swedes now accepted paying considerable taxes for the maintenance of an efficient navy and a standing army. In exchange for protection, the people had agreed to contribute substantial sums to the military system and, thus, to the state. The norm system had changed. However, this does not mean that war did not need to be explained; rather, it meant that a system was in place that simplified legitimation. The question also remains whether the Swedish population was prepared to support offensive warfare, such as Sweden's entry into the Thirty Years War. A quick glance at France, with its multiple peasant uprisings during the seventeenth century, suffices to conclude that they were far from eager to support the expensive warfare with high taxes. Were the norm systems concerning war different in the two countries?

In this chapter, I will analyse the arguments presented when Sweden and France entered the Thirty Years War. A close reading of the different war manifestos will be in focus; I will argue that they were written for immediate distribution and focused upon the best argument for the day. They were political documents written for their time and not for posterity. They can only be fully understood in the context of a greater information system. I will especially focus upon the *function* of the manifestos, and upon the question of what audience was intended. I will investigate what arguments were used to explain war, and how the roles of the rulers, subjects, enemies, and religion were portrayed. A thorough analysis from this perspective can elicit important information not only about the war arguments, but also on the norm systems of war in France and Sweden.

Explaining war

In 1985 Konrad Repgen initiated the discussion about declarations of war by pointing to the fact that these documents are not helpful in understanding the real reasons for war, but for our understanding of which arguments were seen as legitimate. Repgen claimed that war manifestos should be read as war advocacy directed at the ruler's own subjects, to the enemy, and to those parties not involved in the war. Repgen also divided declarations of war into twelve different categories.[4] Pärtel Piirimäe has discussed the arguments of the Swedish manifesto, and has analysed them in the context of the idea of *bellum iustum*. The right to wage war was widely discussed at the end of the sixteenth and the beginning of the seventeenth centuries. The question had been treated already by Augustine, who had tried to bridge the pacifist message of the New Testament with the idea of the Christian sovereign's right to wage war; Aquinas and others further discussed this during the Middle Ages. The basic idea was that war could be rightful and even necessary, if it fulfilled some important criteria. Most thinkers agreed that three types of war were acceptable: defensive war, war that was started to take back what had been taken, and punitive war. One had the right to wage war to help one's allies, but never for the sake of glory or for the purpose of spreading religion. It was never right to start a war unless one had first tried to peacefully resolve the conflict. Before entering a war, the belligerent also had to consider whether the expected suffering was in proportion to the wrongdoings committed by the enemy. The traditional ideas of war and peace were challenged by both the colonization of the New World and by the state-building process. New thinkers appeared who sought to adjust the rules of war to the pragmatic reality of the early modern era. Richard Tuck has made a division between the more traditional and restrictive theological thinkers and the humanists who substantially extended the list of reasons for a just war. According to the humanists, pre-emptive war was to be considered defensive war; therefore, it was acceptable. They also claimed that it was right to wage war for humanitarian reasons. These new thoughts were of great importance for European behaviour in the New World, as well as in the old continent.

Pärtel Piirimäe argues that, although Gustavus Adolphus and Axel Oxenstierna were familiar with the humanist arguments (and used them in domestic propaganda), they chose to argue in a more traditional way. Instead of claiming that the war was either pre-emptive or a humanitarian intervention, they avoided the word 'war' altogether and described the intervention as a 'police action'.[5] This line of argument later caused trouble when Sweden turned out to be victorious in a war in which it did not officially take part. Randall Lesaffer, meanwhile, contends there was no uniform or undisputed doctrine of just war at the time, and has partly challenged the description presented by Piriimäe. In the existing judicial vacuum, the most powerful nations could themselves define just war; issuing a war manifesto was one way of doing so.[6]

It could be said that war manifestos constitute a genre: there are some arguments or phrases that seem to have been considered indispensable. Since rhetoric was very important in the Baroque age – more for practical, than aesthetic reasons – it is also likely that the manifestos followed the basic rhetoric rule. As Aristotle once described it, the most important notions in classical rhetoric are ethos, logos, and pathos. To simplify, one could say that ethos is persuading by showing that the speaker has a good character; logos is persuading by logical arguments; and, pathos is persuading by appealing to the emotions of the audience. All of these elements are visible in the war manifestos; however, the most important rhetorical rule in this context was the adjustment of the message to the audience.[7] Or, to quote Aristotle: 'Rhetoric may be defined as the faculty of observing in any given case the available means of persuasion.'[8] 'The available means of persuasion' naturally depended upon the goal of the persuasion as well as the political situation at hand, which audience was targeted, and the beliefs and norms of that audience. We can expect that the authors of the war manifestos carefully chose arguments that they believed would appeal to the intended audience.

What do we know about the norm systems of war in France and Sweden? In both countries, the defence of the inhabitants against invasion was considered one of the king's most important duties.[9] However, there was a difference of opinion regarding the king's right to start war and to demand taxes for warfare. During the first half of the seventeenth century in Sweden, the general idea was that the king had no right to wage offensive war and to tax his subjects without the approval of the *Riksdag* (Diet).[10] France was not a constitutional regime; therefore, there was no reason for the king to ask permission to decide upon war and peace or to write laws.[11] He could do as he wished; the formula was 'car tel est nostre plaisir'. However, it is likely that the situation was much more complicated since France had been shattered by civil war, and royal authority had been called into question. According to Glete, interest aggregation was an important part of the formation of the fiscal-military state; that is to say, the rulers managed to persuade elites and broader strata of society to participate in the expansion of the complex organization that the state really was. This meant persuading them that they had something to gain from the new system: peace within national borders, important positions in the bureaucracy, and/or money. Even though conflict was not entirely over, it seems reasonable to agree with Glete that such a system was in place in the 1620s in Sweden, yet hardly in France. France was ravaged by severe, internal armed conflicts during the same period, and it is evident that no aggregation of interest was at hand. According to Glete, it was only in 1661 that France could start a more efficient state-building.[12]

In this context, something should also be said about the different information systems in the two countries. I have shown elsewhere that the ruling elite of Sweden was very eager to legitimize war to the common people during the second half of the seventeenth century, and had an efficient information system at its disposal.[13] Research indicates that this was also the case at the time of the Thirty Years War.[14] The two most important means of reaching Sweden's subjects was the church (that is to say, getting the priests to read decrees and propaganda texts from the pulpits) and the regional administration, in which both governors and bailiffs could receive the task of orally disseminating information. The Swedish Diet was another arena for legitimation, and its decisions were normally printed and circulated. The printing press still primarily reached the elites; this is probably also true of the state newspaper, *Post- och inrikes tidningar*, which Axel Oxenstierna founded in 1645.[15]

When it comes to France, the situation is quite complicated. The rulers of France understood very early on the importance of the printing press, and engaged in pamphlet war and created state organs such as *La Gazette de France* (1631) and *Le Mercure François* (1611; the latter was not created by state officials, yet gradually came under state control).[16] Richelieu is known as a master of propaganda, and different kinds of power legitimization during the reign of Louis XIV have also been studied.[17] Nevertheless, most scholars seem to agree that French propaganda was aimed, first and foremost, at the elites, foreign countries, and posterity.[18] The peasants were considered ignorant; politics was none of their business. Furthermore, high politics was supposed to be secret: 'the truth is the duty of the subjects, whereas the secret is a privilege of the Prince.'[19] All of this might very well be true for the personal reign of Louis XIV, yet is more doubtful for the earlier seventeenth century. France was shaken by several civil wars and peasant uprisings, and war affected the subjects through ever-increasing taxes and by the unwelcome presence of soldiers on their way to the different theatres of war. Is it really true that the state felt no wish to explain the war to the common people? As for the information system, the printing press played an important role in France, and this is especially true for the newspapers when it concerned the stately diffusion of information. The role of the church is disputed. The French priests quite successfully fought to get rid of the burden of reading decrees from the pulpit, yet they had an obligation to read royal letters and the like until the end of the seventeenth century. There are examples of other texts being read as well; it also seems that bailiffs and others could read proclamations at the church gate after service. Laws had to be registered at the *Parlements* and in the courts below them, and were often proclaimed in the towns. This was also true for war declarations; however, it changed during the seventeenth century. Days of thanksgiving or 'Te Deum' were celebrated in both Sweden and France after victories, or other important events; these ceremonies also were important parts of the information system.[20]

Sweden enters the Thirty Years War

Sweden was occupied by a lengthy war with Poland during the first years of the Thirty Years War. However, this did not prevent Axel Oxenstierna and Gustavus Adolphus from paying close attention to the course of events in Germany. Even though Sweden did not enter the war until 1630, preparations were made much earlier.[21] The legitimization of the war was considered very important since multiple wars had left Swedish inhabitants longing for peace and tax reductions. The wars in Germany were already being described in the announcements of Intercession Days (*böndagsplakat*) in the early 1620s; these were important documents signed by the king and read yearly from all pulpits in Sweden. According to these texts, the Catholics were pursuing the Protestants and waging a religious war. The threat seemed to grow yearly and to come ever closer. The ambition of the Catholics was said to be to oppress all 'true worshippers of the name of God'.[22] The possibility of war was discussed at no fewer than four Diets. The main argument was that war could easily spread to Sweden and that it was better to attack first in enemy land. The Diet of 1627 accepted the war and the taxes that came with it, stating that it was better to bind the horse in someone else's pen and keep war as far from the border as possible.[23] The Swedish intervention, however, was slow to come. The King of Denmark had entered the war in 1625, yet had to withdraw in 1629 after a number of serious setbacks. Sweden decided to interfere in 1628 in favour of the besieged town of Stralsund. In a discussion with the Council on the eventuality of war in December 1628, the Swedish King argued that Wallenstein's criticism of this intervention meant that a state of war was already at hand. The King, however, claimed that the intervention in Stralsund had not been directed at the Emperor, but rather at his wilful commanders. However, according to the King, there were other just reasons for going to war: imperial support for Poland, the Habsburg attempt at universal monarchy, the oppression of Lutherans in Germany and, lastly, the planning of an imperial fleet in the Baltic. The council decided after numerous discussions that Sweden should go to war, and that the war should take place on German soil. The members of Council promised to 'prompt, advise, lecture, and encourage all His Majesty's subjects to patience, concordance, benevolence, and obedience'.[24] A few days later, decrees for conscription were sent in which the danger of the invasion of Sweden was heavily accentuated.[25] In spite of this, it took well over a year and two meetings with the Estates before the Swedish intervention could occur. The Swedish attack was carried out in June 1630. Aboard ship, state secretary Johan Adler Salvius wrote a Swedish explanation of the war to Germany.[26] Its title did not indicate that it was a declaration of war; it was more an explanation of the reasons that had forced the Swedish King to come to Germany with his soldiers. The manifesto was published in several languages, yet not in Swedish – a circumstance to which we shall return later. It should also be noted that the French translation (which was also the basis for the English translation) differs significantly from the original version.

France enters the Thirty Years War

The beginning of the seventeenth century had been turbulent in France. Both dynastic and religious conflicts had shaken the country, ending only with the royal victory over the Huguenots at La Rochelle in 1628. France was also marked by the fact that Spain was strengthening its position in Europe as a colonial power. The double wedding in 1615 of Louis XIII and Anne of Austria and Philip IV and Elisabeth of France was intended to strengthen the relationship between the two dynasties; however, it had not really worked its magic. The Habsburgs held power not only in Madrid and Vienna; they also controlled Prague, Naples, Milan, Lisbon, and Brussels. France felt surrounded and was especially sensitive about the so-called Spanish Road: the marching route from Italy to the Spanish Netherlands. Another area of conflict was the passage over to Austria: France and Spain fought several times for control of the Valtelline valley in the Alps.[27] France also took part in 1629 in what appeared to be an internal Italian affair. The last duke of Mantua had died and France interfered to put the French Duke of Nevers on the throne. After the intervention of the Emperor and some French setbacks, peace was concluded to France's advantage in Cherasco in 1631. During that same year, the Archbishop Elector of Trier came under French protection. When he was attacked by Spanish troops in 1635, this gave France (who had been considering war for some years, and had already given important subsidies to Sweden and the Netherlands) a possible reason for war. France entered the war in May 1635 after having secured several alliances. The eventuality of a war with Spain had been discussed among the French elite for several years before France officially entered the war, but it is likely that it was less known among the common people. Nevertheless, the conflict was made known (for instance, the celebration of a Te Deum for the culmination of the Spanish siege of Casale in 1629).[28] Another indication of the level of conflict is that censorship was sharpened: no texts could be printed or sold without being stamped with the Great Seal, or having the chancellor's permission.[29] An even clearer sign of what was happening was the prohibition of all trade with Spain, which was issued on 30 April 1635.[30]

When the herald reached Brussels with his declaration on 19 May, the war had already begun; the first battle took place in Avein the day after. This was a victory for the French, and it was soon celebrated in the churches of France.[31] A more detailed *Déclaration du Roy* was issued on 6 June 1635, which was later to be registered at the *Parlements* and published in the *Gazette de France* and the *Mercure François*.[32] After being registered in the *Parlement* of Paris, it was proclaimed in the streets of Paris on 23 June. Simon le Duc, the juré-crieur attested that he proclaimed it 'with the sound of trumpet and public cries' (*à son de trompe et cry publiq*) at crossings and in the faubourgs.[33] The declaration was also registered at other *Parlements* and was further disseminated by the French administration. In Aix, it was first registered in the *Parlement* in June; orders were given that it should be proclaimed in the streets of Aix.[34] The declaration was sent from the *Parlement* to the *Sénéchaussé*, the Admiralty, and the 'ressort de la cour' for further registration. The declaration was registered at the *Sénéchaussé* in July, and it was ordered that extracts should be sent for registration and publication in lesser royal towns and places.[35] This is to say that it reached quite a significant level of circulation. Nevertheless, yet another justifying text was published only a few days later: *Manifeste du Roy contenant les justes causes que Sa Majesté a euës de déclarer la guerre au Roy d'Espagne*.[36] This same letter was also sent to governors.[37]

As I have shown, information on the war entry was widely diffused in both countries; however, the information systems differed. The questions then remain: how was the war justified and what norm systems can be discerned from a close reading of the different war manifestos? I will analyse *Ursachen* and *Déclaration du Roy* and address the following categories: reasons for war, the King, and the Enemy. I will also explore in the same paragraphs how religion and the rulers' subjects were treated in the texts. All of these elements are certainly mixed together in the documents; however, I will attempt to keep them apart for analytical purposes.

Reasons for war

The 'Declaration of War', that the herald had unsuccessfully attempted to give to The Cardinal-Infante was quite brief. According to the text, the French King was taking up arms because the Cardinal-Infante 'has refused to restore the Archbishop of Trier, Elector of the Empire, to liberty, who has been placed under the King's protection in the impossibility of the Emperor or any other prince to bestow their protection onto him, and as he holds a sovereign prince prisoner who was not at war with him, against the dignity of the Empire and against the law of nations'.[38] The imprisonment of the elector remained the main reason in the more wide-ranging *Déclaration du Roy*; however, it was embellished and a number of substitutions made. The *Déclaration* started with a classic rhetorical figure: 'The large and serious outrages that this Monarchy has had to suffer at divers times from Spain are so well known to everyone that it is futile to bring them to memory.'[39] Documents of this kind often refer to the fact that 'everyone knows' or 'all enlightened people know'; this is a way both of underlining that the statement is uncontroversial and to make the reader feel important. The Swedish manifesto also started with a reference to common knowledge: 'It is an old saying that no one can keep his peace longer than his neighbour wishes or wants', and the remark that this was also certainly the experience of the Swedish King.[40]

According to the French text, the main reason for war was that the Spanish, driven by their ambition, had started to openly oppress France's allies. Spain had violated the law of nations (*droit de gens*) in their actions against the Elector of Trier. War was in the interest of all princes of Christianity, and was also perceived as an offence to the French King. The reference to the law of nations is interesting since no such law really existed at the time. Evidently, the notion itself had a strong impact, even though it did not correspond to real law.

The treatment of the Elector of Trier is in focus; however, other events are mentioned as well. Spain's actions have forced the French King to use his God-given powers to wage a pre-emptive and just war in the country of the enemy rather than wait for the war to come to his own Kingdom.[41] Therefore, according to the text, the King is not really starting the war; he is simply responding to the Spanish war preparations: 'Among all the just causes that force us to start the war, or rather to defend ourselves from those who prepare it for us'.[42] As mentioned, the idea of pre-emptive war was quite new at the time, and was quickly put to use.

The Declaration deals with the different conflicts between Spain and France: the conflict over Valtelline, and how Spain tried to obstruct the peace conditions afterwards, and the Spanish actions against the dukes of Savoy and Mantua. According to the Declaration, the Duke of Lorraine has taken up arms against France five times because of Spain, and Spain has done all it can to plant heresy and rebellion in France. They have even attempted to disrupt the French royal family. They tried to 'arm France against herself'.[43] Until this point, France has refrained from action other than trying to diminish any harm; however, this has only served to strengthen Spain and increase its audacity. According to the text, the relationship with Spain is an undercover war disguised as peace, which allows Spain to enjoy peace within its borders whereas France suffers from all the dangers of war. The French King has started the war only to defend himself and to obtain peace.

The reasons for war in the French text focus upon Spanish wrongdoings, and especially the incident in Trier. The Swedish text is far more vague. As I have underlined, the Swedish intervention is not described as a war, and the Emperor is not portrayed as an enemy. A main reason for war is not presented, although there is a long catalogue of wrongdoings committed against the Swedish King, especially in the context of the Swedes' war with Poland. According to *Ursachen*, the Swedish King had always tried to maintain good relations with his neighbours, particularly the German states. One of his reasons for doing so had been to preserve free trade to the benefit of all. However, peace-haters who ravaged Germany with murder and fire had destroyed the peace. The intention of the peace-haters was to prolong the war, and they promised the Poles to help them invade and occupy Sweden.[44] They forbade the Swedish King to recruit soldiers in Germany, yet willingly let the enemies of Sweden do so. When this plan failed and German soldiers enlisted in the Swedish army, the enemies mustered an army under the command of the Duke of Holstein, which would fight under the flags of the Holy Roman Emperor. They also forbade the commerce in the Baltic and confiscated Swedish ships. This was even more serious since the protection of the Baltic, by tradition, belonged to the Swedish King.[45] A letter from the Swedish King to the Prince of Siebenbürgen was also said to have been taken, opened and its contents published, while the poor messenger was incarcerated – which was a violation of international law (*Völcker Recht*).

Here again, we find references to an international law that did not really exist. Both manifestos also make reference to other abstract but commendable goals, especially public freedom. This is also a reference to the religious conflict; however, religion is not mentioned as an argument for war in either text. First of all, as we have seen, religion was not considered a just reason for war; secondly, it was in the interest of both countries to downplay the importance of religion. Sweden did not want to create conflicts with potential allies, and France evidently did not want to brag about joining the Protestant side. When religion was mentioned, it was always when denigrating the enemy. I shall discuss this below.

It was important for Sweden to explain the intervention in Stralsund in 1628. According to *Ursachen*, the Swedish King intervened only because the inhabitants of the town had asked him. Stralsund had done nothing wrong – the Emperor himself had even declared it innocent – yet it had been ravaged by Wallenstein's troops. The town's inhabitants and those in the surrounding countryside had been subject to enormous cruelties. Stralsund received no help and was forced to ask for assistance to save itself from ruin. The Swedish King could not refrain from intervening – this would have been a violation of his honour and conscience. Stralsund had always been one of Sweden's allies because it was seen as a neighbour that shared similar views on religion, freedom, and trade. The goal for the Swedish King was to ensure that the imperial decree concerning Stralsund was respected and that commerce in the Baltic was made free and safe for his allies.

The main arguments were repeated at the end: the King's letters had been opened, his soldiers and servants robbed, commerce that should by nature be free had been prohibited, and the enemies of Sweden had been discouraged in the peace process. Furthermore, hostile armies had been sent twice toward the Swedes. This leads to the perhaps surprising conclusion that the King has been forced to act in consideration of humanity, reason, and nature itself. Piriimäe has pointed out that the Swedes did not argue that they were waging a pre-emptive war. It is true that no such explicit references are made; however, it is implied. According to the text, there were plans, threats, and preparations on land and at sea that were all aimed at the King's ruin. The texts say that, in this context, it is right to meet violence with violence. All Christianity is invited to judge and to consider that it is only extreme necessity that has forced His Majesty to this measure. This is a way of describing the threats toward Sweden as a reason for a just war, even though they were perhaps not made explicit enough to be convincing.

The peace-loving king

The reasons for war were the main contents of the manifestos (the equivalents of logos); they also contained parts that can be referred to as ethos and pathos. As a matter of fact, quite a substantial part of the texts was devoted to show the good character of the king. Both the French and the Swedish texts state over and over again that the monarch wants peace and has done everything in his power to avoid war. This is exemplified by the fact that allies, advisors, and wise man have recommended that they should take up arms at an earlier stage, yet they have refrained from doing so.

There are descriptions in *Déclaration* of all the efforts of the French King to improve France's relations with Spain and to forget old conflicts.

The double wedding between France and Spain is given as an example. He has tried to avoid conflict and has preferred 'public peace, rather than a just revenge'.[46] According to the text, the French King has also tried to appease the troubles in Germany and disarm those who had chosen to take up arms against the Emperor. He intervenes in the war only because he is forced to. The King wants peace; however, he is also part of a honourable warrior tradition. The text describes the glorious French past, in which the ancestors of the King had fought dangerous wars in defence of their allies.

Nothing is said about Sweden's war history; however, the text is rife with examples of Gustavus Adolphus' reluctance to intervene in the war. In *Ursachen,* several German states are described as waging the King to take up arms and to interfere in Germany. His Majesty had every reason to do so: both state reasons since the inhabitants had asked for his help, and moral reasons, since his own friends were being oppressed. However, the King chose to proceed mildly, leaving the matter in the hands of God, rather than to act prematurely. This is a recurring theme and also a reference to the most important cardinal virtue: *prudentia* or prudence. The peaceful mind of the Swedish King is really the main point of *Ursachen*. He has worked for peace and for the common good (*allgemeiner Nutzen*). He takes up arms only as a way of protecting the common freedom (*Der allgemeinen Freyheit*), to restore his friends and neighbours to their previous positions, for the city of Stralsund, and for the safety of the Swedish kingdom. The safety of Sweden, however, is not the focus of the text, nor is the Swedish subjects who appear vaguely in the phrase 'zu seiner vnd der seinigen Schutz die Waffen genommen'. Otherwise, they do not feature.

The French text, on the other hand, harps on the role of the subjects; it is obviously an important part of the King's ethos to care for his subordinates. According to the text, Spain is about to attack: 'We believe that we would, in a way, be accessory to the evils that our people could suffer, did we not act to find powerful cures in time.'[47] The King is prepared to expose himself to danger in order to defend his people; it is also said that a war will cause less suffering to the people than a doubtful peace. The King fights for his people, and also has expectations of his subjects: 'We would no longer command this warrior nation, which has always been the retreat of distressed and the support of oppressed Princes, if we did not know that our good subjects would take part in the indignation and help us to get restitution for the offences made to us so openly.'[48] The subjects are then explicitly ordered to wage war.[49] The *Déclaration* also contains instructions about its diffusion to *Parlements* and lower courts, and its public publication.[50] All servants and officers were ordered to carry it out. Even though the King's concern for his subjects is addressed, the ending is the usual one: 'because this is our desire' ('Car tel est nostre plaisir').[51]

The enemy

The enemy is given completely different descriptions in the two manifestos. Reading the Swedish manifesto, it is not evident who *is* the enemy. The enemy is mostly not mentioned by name other than 'enemy', 'peace-hater', 'turbator pacis', and so on. There are few concrete examples of his ferocity other than the siege of Stralsund, during which the inhabitants were apparently exposed to enormous cruelties. Reading the text carefully, it becomes evident that the Emperor and his troops are the enemy; however, it is underlined in the document that the Swedish King does not hold any grudge against the Emperor. It seems as though Salvius did not want to make this explicit. The Swedish King is not waging war against the Emperor; rather against certain warlords within the Empire. This is understandable, since many of the German princes who Sweden so eagerly wanted to befriend were not prepared to take part in open hostilities against the Emperor.

The French text, on the other hand, carefully describes the vices of the enemy. And the enemy is Spain. According to *Déclaration*, the reason for the Spanish behaviour is 'the hatred and natural jealousy that the Spaniards have against the Frenchmen.'[52] This was a common figure in early modern propaganda, taken from the Old Testament enemies of Israel, who God had sent, and who are always driven by hatred and jealousy, and never by geopolitical or economic goals. The Biblical enemies are also often described as cunning and arrogant.[53] During this same period, a number of broadsheets and other prints in France made fun of the Spanish as being poor, arrogant gluttons.[54] This was part of the understanding that Spain had tried to create a Universal Monarchy – something that was also underlined in the *Déclaration*. Spain was also accused of working against Catholic interests; this was a statement that was meant to blur the fact that France had participated on the wrong side in the war.

A new text and a new translation

Sweden's and France's entry into the war had been justified in *Ursachen* and *Déclaration*; however, the legitimization continued. I will briefly discuss the translation of *Ursachen* into French and a new French manifesto, since they both contribute to our understanding of the function of war manifestos.

Only three days after signing the *Déclaration*, the King signed a *Manifeste contenant les justes causes que sa Majesté a euës de declarer la guerre au Roy d'Espagne*. This was published as a separate print as well as in the *Mercure François*, and seems to have been sent to the governors. The letter to the Duke of Mont Bazon, the Governor of Paris and Île-de-France, did also find its way to the printers. In addition to the text itself, it contains an introduction, wherein the King explains the purpose of the text and what the governor is supposed to do with it. According to its preamble, the Governor has been informed before about the war with Spain. The reason for the letter is to show what pressing reasons have forced the King to take this step despite the fact that all he ever wanted was 'to keep good relationships with my neighbours, in order to secure peace for my people.'[55] As in the *Déclaration*, the people are referred to using the plural form: 'mes peuples'. The task assigned to the governor is to circulate the text to all royal servants in his charge, so that they understand that it was necessary, and therefore just to take up arms. Everyone will understand that the King has good reason to expect support from God. In fact, according to the text, God has already helped. This is in reference to the Battle of Avein and the Te Deum that followed; however, it is not made explicit. The King expects 'that all my good subjects will contribute to the war not only with their wishes, but with their persons according the need that I might have on such an important and legitimate occasion'.[56] It is the governor's task to make this happen. 'To what end you know how to exhort them according to the fidelity and affection that you have always used to serve my interests, and the greatness and prosperity of this Crown'.[57] Thus, it is made clear that the text was intended for wider diffusion for propaganda purposes.

There are substantial similarities between the *Déclaration* and the *Manifeste*. The same Spanish wrongdoings are mentioned, although not in the same order, and the King is once again portrayed as a lover of peace who tries to avoid war at all costs. However, there are also some interesting differences. First of all, the question of religion is more evident. The French King is said to have support from God, and one of his goals is described as a calming Christianity. The Spanish are described as disturbers of peace who have cooperated with the Protestants of France (referred to here by the demeaning phrase 'those of the so-called reformed religion') and made them revolt.[58] By their secret plotting, the Spanish managed to spread suspicion among the French Protestants. This forced the King to take action: to punish the instigators and to seek them out in their fortresses. Spain tried to take advantage of the fact that the King was busy at La Rochelle, and besieged Casal. This was their way of perturbing the King in his righteous decision to bring the Protestants back to the happiness that they enjoy under his reign.[59] It is noteworthy that the text claims that the Spanish caused the French civil war. Moreover, according to the text, the Spanish only use religion as a pretext to cover their real plans.[60] On the other hand, the French King wants to avoid conflict with other Catholics and has been in contact with the Papacy. In reality, this was a very delicate question, and the Pope was less happy about it than was admitted in the text.

Secondly, the King's concern for the wellbeing of his subjects is accented even more strongly than in the *Déclaration*. The very first sentence of the *Manifeste* states that the French King has always had a passionate desire to keep 'the calm of his people and the peace with his neighbours'.[61] The subjects are then mentioned several times in the text, and are also the focus of the last paragraph. The King expresses his hopes of Divine protection and the chance to relieve his poor subjects of the burdens that he has put upon them in order to protect them. Their wellbeing is as dear to him as his own life, which he has put at risk before and is prepared to do so again when it comes to acting to protect the honour of his Divine Majesty or the serenity of his State, or the preservation of his good neighbours and allies.[62]

The Swedish manifesto was first published in German and in Latin; it was also translated into many other languages after a couple of months. The French translation was published in the *Mercure François* and later translated into English with a new introduction.[63] What is interesting is that the translation is less careful and more straightforward than the original texts; the new introduction emphasises this.[64] According to the text, one should always ask whether or not a war was just; since those who lack correct information of the Swedish King's righteous motives have questioned them, Gustavus Adolphus as decided to make them known to the world. A large part of the introduction is devoted to describing a heroic Swedish King who is prudent, courageous and has power, strength, and resources. The translator adds the 'ethos' that was lacking in the original version. The Swedish King has been troubled by war with three enemies and the Swedish King has tried to end each war in turn. He now controls almost all of Pomerania: something he has achieved at his own expense, risking his own life, to help his friends from oppression. This is already well known to the public and it has made him famous in the entire universe.[65] He has defended the free towns and duchies of Germany against the Spanish and their partisans in their quest for Universal Monarchy.[66] According to the text, this is part of the prince's duties towards his subjects and allies; however, he had never imagined that the enemies of public freedom would proceed with such violence. The translator made the Spanish the most important enemies, which was hardly the case in reality, and raised the question of Universal Monarchy, which was not mentioned in the original texts. In this way, the text more resembles the French *Manifeste*; the ethos of the Swedish King was added along with Spanish enemies and a concern for the King's subjects.

The function of war manifestos

War manifestos are easily lumped together and seen as a genre with common features.[67] This is also reasonable to some extent, since they seem to have followed some unspoken rules and patterns. However, they could also differ significantly, as is the case with *Ursachen* and *Déclaration*. Or they could differ less, yet in quite important ways. They were intended for immediate circulation, and used the best argument of the day. They were also intended for different audiences, and their messages were adjusted accordingly. They did fill different functions, which is why the Swedish *Ursachen* hardly mentioned religion, the King's subjects or, for that matter, his enemies. The function of the text was to explain the Swedish intervention to the German princes and hopefully turn them into Swedish allies. The text was not even published in Swedish, because it was not aimed at the Swedish subjects at all; they had already received information and propaganda from other sources. However, the target audience changed when the text was translated into French, and therefore so did the message. For France, it was important to portray the ally Gustavus Adolphus as a strong, honourable and sworn enemy of Spain – and so they did.

Scholars before have discussed the two French texts *Déclaration* and *Manifeste*. Herman Weber has argued that they differ because they had different authors, whereas Anuschka Tischer has claimed they were intended for different audiences: the *Déclaration* mainly for the French power elite and the *Manifeste* for foreign audiences.[68] My close reading of the texts, however, points to a different conclusion. According to my analysis, it is especially in the *Manifeste* that great efforts are made to prove that the King cares about his subjects and that Spain caused the French civil wars. Therefore, it seems more likely that the *Déclaration* was written both for a national and international audience, while the *Manifeste* was primarily written for the French. Why did French authorities publish this new war manifesto only a few days after the first one? This all depended upon the information system. The *Déclaration* was to be duly registered in the *Parlements* and lower courts, and ultimately proclaimed on street corners in towns around France. However, the *Parlements* tended to be quite slow to register decrees they did not like, which potentially made the diffusion of information very slow, and people already knew about the war. There were those who knew about the war from rumours or from being affected by the military sector, or from having heard about the decree of stopping all trade with Spain. Those who were not part of any of the aforementioned knew about the war because of the Te Deum that had been celebrated for the first French victory over Spain in Avein in May. I believe this is why the King issued yet another manifesto, and sent it to the governors with the explicit order to rouse the people. The rulers needed the people's support; therefore, they wanted to justify the war. The function of the *Manifeste* was to win the subjects' support for the war as soon as possible, stepping outside the normal information system.

Norm and information systems

The rulers of both Sweden and France felt obliged to justify embarking on war to their subjects even though both information systems and norm systems were different in the two countries. War propaganda in Sweden was spread to the broader layers of society long before the actual war began. The publication of the French *Déclaration* and *Manifeste* within a few days of each other reveals that, perhaps more surprisingly, the French government felt this same need. This chapter has shown that the manifestos targeted separate audiences; therefore, they used different arguments. Both Sweden and France used the oppression of their allies as a main argument when they turned to other countries. *Ursachen* was mainly written for potential German allies, and was to be changed in order to appeal to an intended French audience. A more detailed and heroic description of Gustavus Adolphus was added to the French translation, and Spain was made the most important enemy. Invasion threats and religious propaganda were of greater importance in domestic propaganda. Swedish subjects seem to have accepted the system as such; however, it is evident that the King and his Council did not expect them to embrace the new war with enthusiasm. An exhaustive propaganda campaign was arranged. According the French norm system, the King could start wars as he pleased – and he did. However, both the *Déclaration* and the *Manifeste* show how eager the rulers were to demonstrate the King's love of peace and especially his concern for his subjects. The Thirty Years War would turn out to be extremely costly for the French; taxes went up considerably during the war. The lack of a Diet made it all the more important to present the reasons for war and taxes to the *Parlements* and to the inhabitants in general. Both French and Swedish Kings had a long way to go before they could do as they pleased without justifying themselves. 'Car tel est nostre plaisir' did not yet suffice to motivate French or Swedish peasants to fight and pay taxes. And the question remains whether it ever would.

Notes

1 All quotations from the seventeenth century appear as in the original sources; they have not been modernized or corrected.

2 Christophe Parry, 'Les hérauts d'armes dans les relations internationales', *Revue d'histoire diplomatique*, 114 (2000), pp. 252–253; see also Christophe Parry, *Les hérauts d'armes à l'époque moderne* (Paris 2005).

3 Jan Glete, *Swedish Naval Administration, 1521–1721: Resource Flows and Organisational Capabilities* (Leiden & Boston 2010), ch. 9.

4 Konrad Repgen, 'Kriegslegitimation in Alteuropa: Entwurf einer historischen Typologie', *Historische Zeitschrift*, 241 (1985), pp. 41–43.

5 Pärtel Piirimäe, 'Just War in Theory and Practice: The Legitimation of Swedish Intervention in The Thirty Years War', *Historical Journal*, 45:3 (2002).

6 Randall Lesaffer, 'Defensive Warfare, Prevention and Hegemony: The Justifications for the Franco–Spanish War of 1635', *Journal of the History of International Law*, 8 (2006), pp. 7–17.

7 Rolf Hugoson, *Krig och retorik: En introduktion* (Lund 2004).

8 As translated by W. Rhys Roberts, and published online: <http://www2.iastate.edu/~honeyl/Rhetoric/rhet1-2.html> (accessed 17 June 2011).

9 Anna Maria Forssberg, *Att hålla folket på gott humör: Informationsspridning, krigspropaganda och mobilisering i Sverige 1655–1680* (Stockholm 2005), pp. 19–22; Denis Richet, *La France moderne: L'Èsprit des institutions* (Paris 1973), p. 41.

10 Johan Holm, *Konstruktionen av en stormakt: Kungamakt, skattebönder och statsbildning 1595–1640* (Stockholm 2007), pp. 49, 85–88.

11 Richet (1973), pp. 41–52.

12 Jan Glete, *War and the State in Early Modern Europe: Spain, the Dutch Republic and Sweden as Fiscal-Military States, 1500–1660* (London & New York 2002), p. 22.

13 Forssberg (2005).

14 Sverker Arnoldsson, 'Krigspropagandan i Sverige före 30-åriga kriget', *Göteborgs högskolas årsskrift*, 7 (1941).

15 Forssberg (2005), pp. 50–73.

16 Jeffrey K. Sawyer, *Printed Poison: Pamphlet Propaganda, Faction Politics, and the Public Sphere in Early Seventeenth-Century France* (Berkeley 1990); Christian Jouhaud, *Mazarinades: La Fronde des mots* (Paris 1985); Howard M. Solomon, *Public Welfare, Science and Propaganda in Seventeenth-Century France: The Innovations of Théophraste Renaudot* (Princeton 1972); Hélène Duccini, *Faire voire, faire croire: L'opinion publique sous Louis XIII* (Paris 2003).

17 Joseph Klaits, *Printed Propaganda Under Louis XIV: Absolute Monarchy and Public Opinion* (Princeton 1976); Gérard Sabatier, *Versailles ou la figure du roi* (Paris 1999); Peter Burke, *The Fabrication of Louis XIV* (Yale & New Haven 1992).

18 Joël Cornette, *Le roi de guerre: Essai sur la souveraineté dans la France du Grand Siècle* (Paris 2000), pp. 272–275; Burke (1992), pp. 152–165.

19 Françoise Hildesheimer & Michèle Bimbenet-Privat, *État des sources de la première modernité (1589–1661) conservées dans les Archives et bibliothèques parisisiennes* (Paris 2006); quotation from Yves-Marie Bercé, *Complots et conjurations à l'époque moderne* (Rome 1996) p. 3.

20 On the information system in France and especially on the Te Deum, see Michèle Fogel, *Les cérémonies de l'information dans la France du XVIe au milieu du XVIII siècle* (Paris 1989).

21 Nils Ahnlund, *Gustaf Adolf inför tyska kriget* (Stockholm 1918). For another perspective on Sweden's entry into the war, see Erik Ringmar, *Identity, Interest and Action: A Cultural Explanation of Sweden's Intervention in The Thirty Years War* (Cambridge 1996).

22 Arnoldsson (1941), p. 10.

23 Arnoldsson (1941), p. 15.

24 Ahnlund (1918), p. 112.

25 Arnoldsson (1941), p. 20.

26 *Ursachen, dahero Der Durchleuchtigste unnd Großmächtigste Fürst unnd Herr, Herr GUSTAVUS ADOLPHUS Der Schweden, Gothen unnd Wenden König, GroßFürst in Finland, Herzog zu Esthen und Carelen, Herr zu Ingermanland, etc. Endlich Gleichfals gezwungen worden, mit dem kriegsvolck in Deutschland über zu setzen unnd zuverzucken* (Stralsund 1630), quoted in Sverker Oredsson, *Gustav Adolf, Sverige och Trettioåriga kriget: Historieskrivning och kult* (Lund 1992), pp. 284–294.

For Salvius, see Sune Lundgren, *Johan Adler Salvius: Problem kring freden, krigsekonomien och maktkampen* (Lund 1945) esp., pp. 26–27.

27 For the Thirty Years War, see Geoffrey Parker (ed.), *The Thirty Years War*, 2nd edn. (London & New York 1997); Lars Ericson Wolke, Göran Larsson & Nils Erik Villstrand, *Trettioåriga kriget: Europa i brand 1618–1648* (Lund 2006).

28 *Lettres du Roy à sa Cour de Parlement de Provence, sur l'heureux progrez de ses armes en Italie, où les Espagnols ont esté contraincts de laisser avitailler Cazal et d'oster le siège* (Aix 1629).

29 Duccini (2003), p. 451.

30 *[Ordonnance portant] rupture de commerce entre la France et l'Espagne* (Compiègne 1635).

31 Guillaume Lasconjarias, 'Avein, 20 Mai 1635: La France entre dans la guerre de trente ans', *Revue internationale d'histoire militaire*, 82 (2002).

32 *Déclaration [...] sur l'ouverture de la guerre contre le Roy d'Espagne, Vérifié en Parlement le 18 juin 1635* (Paris 1635) Archives Nationales (AN) AD + 237; see, *Le Mercure François*, 20 (1635), pp. 933–948. The research group GRIHL at l'École des Hautes Études en Sciences Sociales in Paris has made the *Mercure François* accessible on the Internet: <http://mercurefrancois.ehess.fr/>.

33 Manuscrits français, Ms fr 11693, fols. 2–6, Département des manuscrits, Bibliothèque Nationale Française.

34 Lettres royaux 1635–1636, B 3350, fols. 200 ff., Parlement de Provence, Centre d'Aix en Provence, Archives Départementales des Bouches-Du-Rhône.

35 Sénéchaussé d'Aix, Enregistrement des lettres royaux 1627–1645, 4 B 9, fol. 373, Centre d'Aix en Provence, Archives Départementales des Bouches-Du-Rhône.

36 It was published separately as well as in *Le Mercure François* (1635); see <http://mercurefrancois.ehess.fr/picture.php?/23149/category/118> (accessed 17 June 2011).

37 'Lettre du Roy, escrite à Monseigneur le duc de Mont-Bazon, [...] gouuerneur et lieutenant général pour le Roy de Paris et Isle de France, contenant les justes causes que Sa Majesté a euës de déclarer la guerre au roy d'Espagne'. Bibliothèque Nationale Française, Lb 3058, available online at <http://gallica.bnf.fr/ark:/12148/bpt6k747876> (accessed 17 June 2011).

38 As quoted in Lesaffer (2006), pp. 3–4. The text was published in *Gazette de France*, 272 (1635) under the title 'Sommation envoyée de la part du Roy par un Héraut au Cardinal-Infante'.

39 'Les grandes & sensibles offenses que ceste Monarchie a receuës en diuers temps de celle d'Espagne, sont si cognuës de tout le monde, qu'il est inutile d'en renoueler la memoire', *Déclaration* (1635), p. 3.

40 'Es ist eines altes Sprichwort, dass niemand länger Frieden haben könne, als seinem Nachbar beliebe oder gefalle', Oredsson (1992), p. 284.

41 'mais pour tâcher de les preuenir par une juste guerre, que toutes sortes de raisons & de Lois, nous obligent de porter plûtost dans leurs Pays, que de l'attendre dans nostre Royaume', *Déclaration* (1635), p. 5.

42 'Parmy tant de justes sujets qui nous obligent à commencer la guerre, ou plûtot à nous defendre de celle qu'ils nous preparent', *Déclaration* (1635), p. 17.

43 'd'armer la France contre elle mesme', *Déclaration* (1635), p. 10.

44 'Das Königreich Schweden einzunehmen und unter das Joch zubringen', Oredsson (1992), p. 285.

45 'weil die rechtmässige Beschützung dieses Meers von undenklichen Jahren her, der Königen in Schweden eygenthumb verblieben', Oredsson (1992), pp. 286–287.
46 'la paix public, à celuy d'une juste vengeance', *Déclaration* (1635), p. 13.
47 'Nous croirions estre en quelque façon complices des maux que nos peuples en pourroient souffrir, si par une juste préuoyance nous n'employions de bonne heure les plus puissants remèdes qui soient en nostre pouuoir, pour les en garentir', *Déclaration* (1635), p. 15.
48 'Et ne penserions plus commander à ceste Nation belliqueuse, qui a toûjours esté la retraite des affligez & l'appuy des Princes opprimez, si tous nos bons & fideles subjects ne prenoient part au ressentiment d'une offense qui nous a esté faite si publiquement, pour nous ayder à en tirer raison', *Déclaration* (1635), p. 20.
49 'Et cependant ordonnons, & tres expréssement enjoignons à tous nos Subjets, Vassaux, & Serviteurs, de faire cy-apres la guerre par terre & par mer audit Roy d'Espagne, ses Pays, Subjets, Vassaux, & adherants', *Déclaration* (1635), p. 24.
50 'Si donnons en mandement à nos amez & feaux, les gens tenans nos Cours de Parlement, Baillifs, Senéchaux, ou leurs Lieutenans, que ces presentes ils facent lire, publier & registrer chacun en l'estenduë de son resort & iurisdiction, & le contenu en icelles, garder, obseruer & entretenir selon leur forme & teneur, sans y contreuenir, ny permettres qu'il y soit contreuenu en aucune maniere', *Déclaration* (1635), p. 30.
51 *Déclaration* (1635), p. 31.
52 'la hayne, & jalousie naturelle que les Espagnols ont contre les François', *Déclaration* (1635), p. 4.
53 Forssberg (2005), pp. 78–80.
54 Duccini (2003), pp. 476–501.
55 'de conseruer la bonne intelligence auec mes voisins, pour affermir le repos de mes peuples', *Manifeste* (1635), p. 3.
56 'que tous mes bons subjets en general y contribueront, non seulement leurs veux; mais aussi leurs personnes selon le besoin que j'en pourray auoir dans une si legitime & importante occasion', *Manifeste* (1635), p. 4.
57 'À qouy vous les sçaurez bien exhorter selon la fidelité & affection que vous auez tous-jours apportée à ce qui est du bien de mon seruice, & de la grandeur & prosperité de cette Couronne', *Manifeste* (1635), p. 4
58 'Ce pendant par leurs secrettes menees dans la France, ils trouuerent moyen de couler des soubçons dans les esprits de ceux de la Religion pretenduë Reformee, & les ayans portez à une rebellion ouuerte', *Manifeste* (1635), p. 6; Brian E. Strayer, *Huguenots and Camisards as Aliens in France, 1598–1789: The Struggle for Religious Toleration* (New York 2001), p. 3.
59 'ce qu'ils feirent aussi, pour diuertir le Roy de ses justes resolutions, qu'il auoit prise de ramener ses sujects de la Religion au bon-heur qu'ils trouuent aujourd'huy en l'obeyssance qu'ils luy ont renduë', *Manifeste* (1635), p. 6.
60 'que l'on voict éuidemment que le pretexte de la Religion dont ils ont voulu se seruir jusques icy ne leur sert plus que d'un manteau pour couurir leur desseins dereglez', *Manifeste* (1635), pp. 14–15.
61 'en conseruant le repos à ses peuples, de maintenir aussi la paix auec ses voisins', *Manifeste* (1635), p. 5.
62 'Ce que sa Majesté souhaitte de toute son affection pour l'aduancement de la gloire de Dieu, & pour auoir plus de moyen de soulager ses pauures sujets des charges

qu'il a falu imposer sur eux pour leur conseruation, laquelle luy est aussi chere que sa propre vie, qu'elle a souuent exposé & exposera tousjours tres-volontiers en toutes occasions, où il s'agira de l'honneur de sa Diuine Majesté, ou repos de cet Estat, & de la Conseruation de ses bons Voisins & Alliez.' *Manifeste* (1635), p. 16.

63 *Manifeste ou Declaration des causes principalles qui ont meu le tres Auguste Roy de Suède à prendre les armes & entrer en l'Allemagne*, Traduict d'Alleman en François (1630); see also <http://mercurefrancois.ehess.fr/picture.php?/17936/category/102> (accessed 17 June 2011).

64 Piirimäe (2002), p. 519; Repgen (1985) p. 17.

65 'fait eclatter sa renommee par tout l'Vnivers', *Manifeste* (1630), p. 4.

66 *Manifeste* (1630), pp. 4–5.

67 In his commendable attempt to categorize the manifestos, this was also in a way what Repgen (1985) did.

68 Herman Weber 'Zur Legitimation der fransösischen Kriegserklärung von 1635', *Historisches Jahrbuch*, 108 (1988); the statement by Tischer is quoted by Lesaffer (2006), p. 66. See also Anuschka Tischer, 'Offizielle Kriegsbegründungen in der frühen Neuzeit – Funktionen, Formen, Inhalte', *Militär und Gesellschaft in der Frühen Neuzeit*, 8 (2004).

CHAPTER 8

The Castilian Guards in the Hispanic Monarchy's Military Structure

Enrique Martínez Ruiz & Magdalena de Pazzis Pi Corrales

Between 1482, which marked the beginning of the war against the Muslims of the kingdom of Granada, and 1503, when the conquest of Naples was complete, the Catholic Monarchs' military ambitions underwent a profound change. Ferdinand King of Castile (as Ferdinand V) and of Aragon (as Ferdinand II) and his wife, Isabella I of Castile, lifted their sights beyond the Iberian Peninsula and embarked on a rivalry with France that would last centuries. This extension of their military commitments called for reforms and a restructuring of the Spanish royal army that would be continued in subsequent decades by their grandson, Charles V, the son of Philip the Fair and Joanna the Mad.

Charles V inherited the kingdoms of Spain in 1516, and a few years later the domains of his paternal grandfather, the Holy Roman Emperor Maximilian I. This inheritance made Charles the most fortunate grandson in Spain's history. However, along with the territories, he also acquired the problems and rivalries that come with such privilege. Among other things, he was obliged to improve a military apparatus that already had a dual structure: one part, which we will call the domestic army, was deployed within the Iberian Peninsula; the other, which we will call the foreign army, was to fight abroad. This dual structure remained in place until the end of the Spanish Habsburgs in 1700.[1]

Despite the fact that changes in military practise had already made the heavy cavalry obsolete in the sixteenth century, the Castilian Guards survived until the end of the seventeenth century. How can this be explained? As Jan Glete pointed out, Spain might be called 'the first fiscal-military state'. Yet while the organization of the Spanish army at the beginning of the sixteenth century was pioneering, by the seventeenth century the state was in a rapid military decline. According to Glete, one of the main reasons for Spain's decline as a military state was that local elites were too strong for the monarch to impose his will. The rulers also failed to explain to the people of Spain why they should contribute to the military effort. The elite, who had willingly cooperated with the state to achieve domestic peace, were less eager to support warfare outside the Iberian Peninsula.[2] Can the fate of the Castilian Guards be explained in the same way? What do the Castilian Guards tell us about the Spanish state as an organization?

The configuration of Habsburg military power

The War of Granada, which ended in 1492, was the last large-scale, feudal, military engagement in Spain. Throughout the conflict, Ferdinand the Catholic could see the difficulty of commanding such a mosaic of military forces that were heterogeneous in origin, organization, and command structure. The nucleus of the operation was the royal guard (a permanent force comprising mostly heavy cavalry, recruited and paid for by the king), the continos (also royal guards), and the light cavalry (jinetas). Additionally, there was an army of vassals on horseback who could quickly be mobilized, for which the King also paid on an annual basis. There were the cavalry and infantry forces of the Hermandad, which Ferdinand had wanted to convert into the core of his army so as not to be dependent upon the Cortes or the aristocracy, but this was a project the King would have to abandon. Seigneurial contingents were also there; particularly, as the monarch was paying. Cities and towns also offered their militias and some artillery.

The conquest of the Nasrid Kingdom of Granada marked the end of the Reconquest; it also marked a crucial shift in the use and conception of military force. For eight hundred years, the enemy had been indigenous. As the new monarchy, starting with Charles V, played an increasingly important role in Europe and the world, and was nearly always at war, military action after 1492 would take place on the borders and abroad. Very quickly, Ferdinand had realized that defending his lands in Italy would entail a confrontation with France and, if he wanted to triumph, he would have to implement sweeping military reforms with two primary objectives: first, to dismantle the system in existence until 1492; and second, to make himself the sole commander of the army, with sufficient means to free him from having to turn to the Cortes or the nobility in order to mobilize, organize, and command his military forces.

The Castilian Guards, created on 2 May 1493 as a part of this reform, would last approximately two centuries. The new body comprised 25 companies (capitanías) of 100 men each, a total of 2,500 men, of whom four-fifths were men-at-arms, each with two horses and full armour, and the remainder were cavalry equipped with helmet, breast-plate, and leg protection and armed with spear, bow, dagger, and sword.[3] With these forces, the Catholic King hoped to rival the French. Yet while their respective armies may have been similar on paper, the French troops were far more homogeneous; the French cavalry, in particular, was widely acclaimed.

An important step in the reorganization of the royal army came in 1503, when the various contingents lost their autonomy. From that point on, the king would be in charge. The new structure was based upon the pre-eminence of heavy cavalry, which became one of the basic elements of Hispanic military organization for the next two hundred years and constituted the first permanent Spanish army: the Castilian Guards. The Guards were a fundamental part of the Spanish military until 1525, when fresh reforms were introduced, the result of developments in warfare that clearly pointed to the importance of infantry, and motivated by a desire both to block a potential land invasion by France over the Pyrenees and to secure victory in Italy and elsewhere.

The Italian Wars saw far greater role for the infantry thanks to their mobility and the growing presence of light firearms that favoured coordinated action by pikemen and musketeers to neutralize cavalry charges and defeat them at a distance. The capture of Francis I at the Battle of Pavia on 24 February 1525 is illustrative of the changes: infantry captured the commander of the most elegant cavalry of the times when both he and his horse fell. Charles V's ordinance was issued forty days later.[4] Not only was it clear that warfare was no longer conducted as it had been, Charles V was now experiencing financial difficulties. Both circumstances undermined the Guards' position. A reduction in their number was an appropriate response to the financial squeeze and the Guards' diminishing importance in battle. The Guards' hombres de armas were reduced by 45 per cent (820 of the 1,800 were dismissed) and the jinetes were cut by 40 per cent (433 of 1,072 were dismissed).[5]

In the years that followed, war determined Charles's policies.[6] He had to neutralize the League of Cognac of 1526, which led him to concentrate on his forces in Italy. Starting in 1529, the Turks' pressure on Vienna showed how seriously one had to take the Infidel.[7] Following the collapse of the Diet of Augsburg in 1530 and the establishment by imperial Protestants of the Schmalkaldic League, Charles had new military fronts to which to attend. The growing 'internationalization of imperial warfare' called for new tools, to which end the Emperor himself oversaw a new reorganization that resulted in an ordinance (or instruction) of 15 November 1536.[8] This aimed to restructure a contingent comprising 10,000 Spaniards, 24,000 Germans, and 26,000 Italians, with a clear predominance of infantry over cavalry. Thus the situation of the armed forces in Italy was solidified, and the binding function of the Spanish forces within the imperial army (soon to be called tercios) was confirmed.[9] From then on, the tercios would be the administrative, tactical, and organic units of the Spanish infantry and the clearest examples of the heterogeneous whole that was the army of Charles V and his successors. A whole, indeed, known incorrectly by the name of one of its parts.

Starting with this latest reorganization, the military model that the Hispanic monarchy would use for the rest of its existence was in place. It was based upon two distinct organizations, definitively structured in the ordinances of 1525 and 1536. The first of the organizations was that of the Guards, which became the key element in the various forces that operated mostly within the Iberian Peninsula (Castile, Navarre, and Perpignan, yet not in the kingdom of Aragon).[10] The second was directed outwards; among these forces the tercios were central. There was a contradiction, however, beneath this dual reform; the Guards' medieval origins as heavy cavalry was conspicuous, whereas the tercios, whose distinguishing weapons were the pike and the musket, represented a more modern conception of warfare in which infantry dominated. This was a fundamental difference. In many ways, the Guards were anachronistic, while the tercios were perfectly adapted to their times, and until the mid seventeenth century their influence and prestige on the battlefield was unparalleled. Therefore, we must speak once again of a 'domestic' or 'reserve' army, whose main component was the Guards, and a 'foreign army' (whose most representative Spanish units were the tercios).

The reasons for this dualism are not clear, and it is even less clear why it was maintained despite the obvious advantages of the infantry. The Guards' survival can possibly be explained by the fact that they were never the decisive element in any Spanish army; instead, they were complementary, and their Hidalgo members conjured up chivalric memories among aristocratic society. One must also remember that the monarchy lacked the resources to undertake a clear and decisive reform. Instead, the Guards, poorly paid, were retained on the off-chance they might be needed. Equally, it is possible no one kept an eye on whether, and how, the ordinances were implemented, and that the publication of the reform did not lead to any improvements. The only characteristic the two armies shared was that they were conceived, created, organized, and used as permanent instruments of the monarchy. This was a huge innovation in Europe, where princes raised armies as the need presented itself and dissolved them as soon as the need vanished.

Between reform and inertia

Charles V enjoyed his greatest military splendour in the years that followed the conquest of Tunis in 1535. It soon faded, however, as international circumstances once again pushed him into war with his three traditional enemies: France, the German Protestants, and the Turks. During the last years of his reign, military reform was once again a pressing concern, and the Guards were a frequent reference point in both political and military affairs. However, the Emperor's well-known financial straits would prove to be an obstacle.[11]

By this point in Charles's reign, it was clear that the Iberian Peninsula was in no danger of a sustained invasion, for even if enemy forces were massive and well equipped the native population would not support them and troops raised by lords and towns would be able to stop their advance. The wars with France and the attacks by North Africans demonstrated this, which we must take into account when considering the contemporary understanding of the military scenarios.[12] If there was no pressing danger to the peninsula, then the necessary task of improving the Guards could be postponed until external circumstances permitted a closer examination. Improvement was obviously necessary: there had been no follow-up after the 1525 ordinance, and royal attention had been directed abroad. It was under these circumstances that serious, and quite possibly the most painstaking, reform of the Guards was undertaken. The 1525 ordinance remained in effect until 1551, at which point a new ordinance (that had been at least two years in the making) was issued. Another followed in 1554 that would have a lasting impact upon subsequent regulations.

The Guards' ordinances of 1554 would become the most widely known.[13] This long and detailed text emphasizes the administrative means of ensuring well-managed finances, and particularly salaries and payments to suppliers. As was the case in the army as a whole, fraud by captains who inflated the number of their men and vendors who inflated their prices was a drain on the royal treasury. The guardsmen's equipment, gear, and weapons were also a concern. The ordinance instructed captains to act as fathers to their men by instilling in them a sense of Christian obligation. These new norms were put into practice in the early years of Philip II's reign. However, the new monarch continued his father's policies when it came to deploying his forces abroad – Flanders was especially costly in men and resources – and matters relating to the defence of the Iberian Peninsula were systematically postponed. The reform became an ever-receding target, attended to only when circumstances permitted, such as after the Alpujarras Revolt of 1570–2, in the wake of the Turkish defeat at the Battle of Lepanto in 1571, and during the most tense moments of the Revolt of the Netherlands.

When Philip II asked cities, lords, and the Church how many men they could raise and what their resources were in case military mobilization was necessary, the answers were disappointing. Military capacity was practically non-existent. After years of internal peace, weapons were rusted; worse, no one knew how to use them. The possibility of raising a general militia was also nil, so the king turned once again to the Guards.[14] A new ordinance was duly issued in 1573 to replace that of 1554. The text was shorter this time, consisting of just twenty articles and eliminating most of the administrative and organizational aspects. Judging from the document's introduction, the reform attempt was a serious one: it states that the Guards were badly paid, badly armed, and got along badly with those who provided them with quarters; that they were too few in number; and those that there were were old, unfit, and ill equipped.

Once again, the Guards ceased to be an object of attention. Although the Mediterranean diminished in importance after Lepanto, the Atlantic axis loomed even more significantly following the 1580 annexation of Portugal, in which the Guards participated, because of the worsening of the Dutch Revolt and the growing conflict with England.[15] Once again, events abroad consumed the monarch's attention, energy, and resources, and this remained the case until his death. Orders, edicts, and instructions multiplied for the arming and mobilization of military units and navy alike. The sea increasingly became the setting for these new commitments; this was where differences were settled and interests collided.[16]

The military needs of Philip II caused him to seek other resources and mobilize the institutions he had. This helps to explain the Guards' new ordinance, the raising of new tercios, and the measures the King took from the 1570s to the end of his reign, with which he sought (with little success) to make the available workforce more effective. He also sought to increase troop numbers by mobilizing the lay and secular forces provided by the cities, and tried several times to instil a general interest in military matters amongst the gentry.

Philip II's great military reforms, however, were left undone. His projects and initiatives were gathered in large folders in the Council of War and Secretariat of War, who much later (during the reign of Philip III) would carry all the reforms through. Once again, the Guards would be one of the objects of reform, although the results turned out to be equally disappointing.[17] From that point on, although general military legislation occasionally affected them, the Guards adhered to their own particular norms and became gradually obsolete, evolving into a locus of aristocratic clientage and little more. The Guards disappeared without a whimper at the end of the seventeenth century, having travelled a long road from being one of the monarchy's most important military tools to having no relevance whatsoever.

Obsolescence and disbandment

Peace was the greatest concern in the waning years of Philip II's reign. This continued in the early seventeenth century with the appearance of what has been called – erroneously, in our opinion – a 'pacifist generation.'[18] The change in the monarchy had no impact upon land-based military deployment, and priorities remained the same. This meant that positional defence continued to be the fundamental goal, and the army became the principal means of attaining it. Throughout the seventeenth century, the vertices of an imaginary triangle governed from Madrid comprised Flanders to the north, Milan and Naples to the south, and the Peninsular kingdoms in the west. There were, however, substantial variations as a result of the Portuguese Revolt and the independence of Holland. Portents of what was to come, these two events together heralded the diplomatic and strategic modifications that waited.

In general, however, the approach adopted during the reign of Philip III was a continuation of his predecessors'. The Flemish question was the most complicated. Archduke Albert and his wife, Isabel Clara Eugenia (Philip's daughter) to whom Philip had given those territories, had no issue. This meant that Madrid could not avoid the problem that had been temporarily put aside by the signing of the Twelve Years Truce in 1609. Generally speaking, it would appear that Philip III and his favourite, the Duke of Lerma, lost an opportunity to rejuvenate the military structure. Despite the evidence of what Henry IV was doing in France and the turbulent winds that blew from the Empire, which would culminate in the storm of 1618, inertia and lassitude appear to have sunk the plans for military reform. The ultimate reason might simply have been the lack of cash. The Council of War reform received propositions that had been prepared during the reign of Philip II; military reform would have been based upon these plans. Archduke Albert was among those in the 'line of fire' who indirectly and intermittently requested such changes, as his letters from Brussels dated 6 March 1602 reveal.[19]

However, attending to the needs of the Archduke were only of relative importance because broader reform was on the horizon. On 8 June 1603, following Council of War deliberations, a new ordinance was issued to put an end to the failings of the infantry of which Madrid was fully aware. From then on, we see a clear tendency to legislate separately for each military branch, as if the Crown wished to address only the most urgent problems or to implement reform piecemeal. The fact is that, a few months later on 13 November 1603, this latest ordinance was followed by a royal decree (cédula) regarding the cavalry whose reformist content was a far cry from that concerning the infantry: it only created one new position – that of Commissioner-General – and established a few unimportant new regulations.

It did not take long for Madrid to hear the reaction to these measures. One of the most important replies came from Albert himself, who had received the ordinance on 31 August. His letter dated 10 December said that many of the regulations would be 'not only difficult to comply with, but awkward to order.' Similar reactions came from Carlos Coloma in Milan.[20] As a result, the King consulted with the Councils of State (Flanders and Naples), as well as the councils devoted to Milan and Sicily. At the suggestion of members of these councils and the Council of War, yet another ordinance, consisting of fifty-three articles, was published on 17 April 1611: a somewhat modified version of that of 1603.[21]

Another dimension to these nominal reforms concerned the ability to raise a general militia in Castile – a possibility that never moved beyond the proposal stage – and the state of the provincial militias, to which district commanders had been already appointed in 1597. However, nothing substantial had taken place since then, even though several attempts were made during the late sixteenth and early seventeenth centuries to conduct a census in order to determine how many soldiers could be raised.[22]

The Guards were not completely neglected in this reformist campaign. Indeed, the government did consider them, albeit only near the end of the first reformist wave when confronted by their manifest deficiencies. The companies were in bad shape: for example, the companies based in Navarre in the early seventeenth century, tired of never being paid on time, were forced to work at a variety of tasks to survive. They not only worked; they also begged and committed acts of violence, which exacerbated contact with the locals.[23] Billeting troops on small villages and towns, such as those in Navarre, inevitably led to a dangerous imbalance in community life and insufficient resources to go round. The situation in 1612 was such that a member of the Cortes of Navarre asked that the Guards be withdrawn from the kingdom and replaced with native Navarrese hidalgos who would pay for themselves and were obliged to serve whenever the king summoned them. The request in effect sought to reinstate the ancient practice of local defence, which surely would have been a relief for those forced to lodge the Guards. The Council of War, convinced that the problem in Navarre was the lack of funds with which to pay the soldiers, declined the petition. As there was no money in Madrid, the council told the viceroy to seek funds wherever he could, pay the Guards, and order them to cease their disorderliness and violence.[24]

As part of this general reformist wave, a new ordinance aimed at regulating the Guards appeared in 1613.[25] Consisting of eighty-six articles, it was an attempt to modernize the corps. The preamble set the tone by referring to previous ordinances and the gap between their wording and the Guards' actual situation. The stated objective was to bring past ordinances into line with the needs of 'the present moment'; however, it sounded more like self-justifying official rhetoric than a well-thought-out reform. This was particularly true since many articles from old ordinances were simply copied verbatim into the new one. Such passages emphasized the need to avoid fraud, which harmed the royal treasury; that the corps should be complete; that all guardsmen should possess the required equipment and behave like good Christians; and that conflicts with locals should be avoided. None of this was new. There were many similarities to the ordinance of 1554, which makes us wonder whether the reforms might have actually worked if the 1554 document had been implemented. The kind of people linked to the control of the companies had not changed either: they were still influential individuals of social standing, aristocrats who enjoyed influence as the owners of the estates where their power lay. This made them the employees of the monarchy without really binding them strongly to it, although both parties were interested in maintaining those bonds. The guardsmen, however, did not experience any change in career and continued down the road that led to a total decline.

Inertia, together with a lack of resources and the relentless pressure of military demands, all seemed once again to conspire to ensure that the Guards would continue on a course that guaranteed their obsolescence. This became even more obvious after 1621, as the war in Flanders continued and the international situation became even more complicated with the start of the Thirty Years War, in which France was increasingly involved, leading to a direct confrontation with the Hispanic monarchy. Far greater military participation and coordination on the part of the Peninsular kingdoms was needed, to which end the Count-Duke of Olivares in 1624 drew up a proposal for Philip IV to establish what had become known as the Union of Arms: a general defensive plan that would incorporate all his kingdoms and subjects in a common effort.[26] However, the results were disappointing, and it became clear in 1626 that without money or men it would not be put into effect. It was believed at the end of the 1620s that 200,000 men could be raised,[27] yet this was an estimate that ignored the fact that not only did the men not exist, but in some regions there were no horses either.[28] Reform of the Guards was mooted once again. As usual, a new (and final) ordinance was published, this time in 1628. This was noticeably similar to those that preceded it; in fact, it amounted to little more than a copy, for even those portions that were not lifted from its predecessors still conveyed the same meaning. There was no question of following up on the implementation of the ordinance. The only solution appeared to be the mere publication of an ordinance that repeated previous ones.

The situation did not change much in subsequent decades, though some attempts were made to modernize the army in part or in its entirety. For example, an order was issued on 11 July 1632 to reform the cavalry by updating its uniforms and weaponry, which had remained unchanged since the reign of Philip II. At least one study considers this to be one of the most meaningful cavalry reforms in the seventeenth century.[29] The Guards were affected by a similar measure when it was ordered that each company should now number of 60 men. What were known as caballos-corazas were created, in which most hombres de armas could do without their second horse, and pistols replaced lances as individual weapons. Each hombre de armas was given two pistols, while the jinetes had only one; a helmet and part armour replaced their full armour.

From 1635 to the end of the century, the war with France provided constant complications and required that the northern front and all Peninsular borders were permanently active. This entailed both human and financial costs. Salaries and supplies were delayed, and only the most urgent needs were prioritized. This would work against the Guards, who as usual were working without basic supplies and pay. Various orders were issued at the end of the 1640s and throughout the 1650s, some of which affected the Guards cavalry. For example, the order of 15 September 1656 declared that the cavalry in Spain, Flanders, and the Italian possessions would be organized in twelve companies consisting of 50 men each.

The biggest problem for the Guards was the constant lack of money, which meant that salaries were always in arrears. During the critical mid seventeenth century, things could not have been more parlous. A document dated 10 June 1652 noted that the accounts of the inspector-general of the Castilian Guards, the ordinary infantry, sea captains, and retired captains showed that no revenue had been received since 1642.[30] As a result, many men had not been paid. It is easy to imagine their lamentable state: either they had to beg or they had to live off the people where they were quartered. Not even the Guards' participation in the Catalan Revolt (1640–52) was to alleviate the Guards' plight. By 1670, the situation had worsened, and then deteriorated further as the end of the century approached. In response to the situation on the Roussillon border, the cavalry underwent some reorganization –

some 2,800 Spanish cavalry were posted, in addition to dragoons and other units – but as these forces were insufficient, twelve of the Guards' nineteen companies were sent; they were inspected in Madrid's Casa de Campo on 7 and 8 January 1694.

This was their last inspection that we know of. Although no written order survives, the Guards were officially disbanded in 1703. We know they ceased to exist thanks to a report dated 23 April 1703 and additional documents that the Council of War's secretary, José Carrillo, gave to Philip V when the he and his aides embarked on a remodelling of the seventeenth-century army they had inherited.[31] In essence, the report was an epitaph. After two centuries, no one did anything to stop the Guards from disappearing: a statement of tacit recognition that they were inoperative and inadequate to meet the new challenges war presented. They could no longer serve as an effective military force or as a means to exercise local power and control. The gentlemen who had long maintained company command were not dependent upon the Guards to preserve their social status.

The Castilian Guards played a special role throughout two long centuries in the various armies that were at the service of the Hispanic monarchy. Their survival can be explained by several factors; however, due to the many theatres of war abroad, they were never given priority. The mere fact that the Guards were never a decisive element in any Spanish army might have contributed, as did the fact they were part of an aristocratic tradition. To follow Jan Glete, it seems likely that strong local elites made it difficult for the state to implement reform. The building of a complex organization had worked very well; however, once the organization was in place, its members started to look to their own interests.[32] Plagued by institutional inertia and hampered by poor fiscal and military organization, the Guards lacked the resources necessary for thorough-going reform, not to mention the energy to set their own house in order.

Notes

1 On the Habsburgs' military policies, see Enrique Martínez Ruiz, *Los soldados del Rey: Los ejércitos de la Monarquía Hispánica (1480–1700)* (Madrid 2008).

2 Jan Glete, *War and the State In Early Modern Europe: Spain, the Dutch Republic and Sweden as Fiscal-Military States, 1500–1660* (London & New York 2002), pp. 68–139.

3 On the birth of the Guards in the reign of Ferdinand and Isabella, and the origins

of the 'military revolution' in the Spanish monarchy, see René Quatrefages, *The Modern Military Revolution: The Crucible Spanish* (Madrid 1996). Miguel Angel Quesada Ladero has recently raised interesting points in his book *Armies and Navies of the Catholic Kings, Naples and The Roussillon (1494–1504)* (Madrid 2010) esp. pp. 141–178 which links the existing forces to the Royal Guards: 'The core of the royal troops were standing companies of cavalry the Royal Guards, whose origin was not very distant in time of the Catholic Monarchs and still in 1406, when Henry III died, there were more than three companies of one hundred "throw" each, but in 1426 the figure rose to 1,000.' (p. 141)

4 The Ordinance, cited below, can be found in Archivo General de Simancas (AGS), Consejos Suprimidos, 1st series, leg. 1; AGS, Contaduría del Sueldo, 2nd series, leg. 1; Servicio Histórico Militar, Colección Aparici, Microfilm nº 3, Document 1402, pp. 310–333.

5 Obviously, the original contingent of 2,500 had grown, which was highly unusual, as was the fact that the force had no vacancies. Research in AGS indicates there were always vacancies, especially among the *hombres de armas*, for whom the expense of the equipment, uncomfortable lodging, long idle periods, and frequent delays in payment were all disincentives. Our forthcoming monograph on the Guards will elaborate upon this information.

6 These are the years that we can consider to have been the threshold of the 'military revolution', a topic that has generated abundant literature, notably Michael Roberts, *The Military Revolution 1560–1660* (Belfast 1956); Geoffrey Parker, *The Military Revolution: Military Innovations and the Height of the West, 1500–1800* (Barcelona 1990); id., 'The Military Revolution, 1560–1660: A Myth?', in: *Spain and the Netherlands, 1559–1659* (Madrid 1986); René Quatrefages, *La revolución militar modern: El crisol española* (Madrid 1996); id., 'La Specifité militaire espagnole', in: Jean-Pierre Amalric, *Pouvoirs et société dans l'Espagne moderne: Hommage à Bartholomé Bennassar* (Toulouse 1993); B. M. Downing, *The Military Revolution and Political Change: Origins of Democracy and Autocracy in Early Modern Europe* (Princeton 1992); Jeremy Black, *A Military Revolution? Military Change in European Society, 1500–1800* (Basingstoke 1991); Clifford J. Rogers (ed.), *The Military Revolution Debate: Military Readings on the Transformation of Early Modern Europe* (Boulder 1995). It is also noteworthy that the Spanish contribution to the military revolution, ignored for decades, has in recent years caught historians' attention, among them Jan Glete: 'As far as our present state of knowledge allows us to make generalisations, the Spanish monarchy was the most important innovating force behind the development of large-scale and complex military organisations in sixteenth -century Europe. Other states contributed parts of innovation, and some made it more efficient in certain aspects; however, organising state-run armed forces into something really large and complex that changed Europe was achieved primarily by Spain.' (Glete (2002), p. 127)

7 On Italy and the Mediterranean, see G. Galazo & A. Musi (eds.) *Carlo V, Napoli e il Mediterráneo* (Naples 2002).

8 Antonio Vallecillo, *Legislación militar de España antigua y moderna*, 11 (Madrid 1853), pp. 549 ff.; 'Instrucción dada en Génova por el Emperador Carlos V a 15 de noviembre de 1536 para el régimen y organización de su ejército en Italia', Biblioteca Nacional, Cód. E. 136, fol. 41.

9 There is a large historiography on the *tercios*, most of it laudatory. See, for example,

Julio Albi de la Cuesta, *De Pavía a Rocroi: Los tercios de infantería española en los siglos XVI y XVII* (Madrid 1999).

10 Although a portion of the Guards would be deployed in Italy under the command of Fernández de Córdoba, *el gran capitán*, its principal mission was to protect borders and suppress internal revolts (as in the case of the 1568 Revolt of the Alpujarras or the Aragonese disturbances owing to Antonio Pérez's presence in Zaragoza in the 1590s). The Guards also participated in the 1580 occupation of Portugal.

11 Ramón Carande, *Los banqueros de Carlos V*, 1–3 (Barcelona 1990).

12 See Martínez Ruiz, *Los soldados del rey: Los ejércitos de la monarquía hispánica, 1480–1700* (Madrid 2008), pp. 420 ff.

13 We cannot say if the ordinance of 1551, if it even existed as such, was more important than that of 1554, though we are inclined to believe that the 1554 version was more important, given the references to it in subsequent ordinances.

14 I. A. A. Thompson, *Guerra y decadencia: gobierno y administración en la España de los Austrias, 1560–1620* (Barcelona 1981).

15 There are many works about Lepanto and the circumstances surrounding the battle, for example, David & Enrique García Hernán, *Lepanto: el día después* (Madrid 1999).

16 On the Dutch revolt, see Geoffrey Parker, *El ejército de Flandes y el camino español, 1567–1659: la logística de la victoria y derrota de España en las guerras de los Países Bajos* (Madrid 2000).

17 Although the Armada has drawn the attention of many historians (for example, Jorge Calvar Gross, et al. *La batalla del Mar Océano*, 1–3 (Madrid 1988–2009), there are other notable episodes in the Anglo–Spanish conflict. Among other sources, see Magdalena de Pazzis Pi Corrales, *La 'otra Invencible': España y las potencias nórdicas* (Madrid 1983).

18 Magdalena de Pazzis Pi Corrales (ed.), *'Armar y "marear" en los siglos modernos: XV–XVIII': Cuadernos de Historia Moderna* (Madrid 2006).

19 Enrique Martínez Ruiz, 'El ejército español en el siglo XVII', in: José Alcalá-Zamora & Ernest Belenguer Cebriá (eds.), *Calderón de la Barca y la España del Barroco*, 2 (Madrid 2001), pp. 97–120.

20 Enrique Martínez Ruiz. 'Palacios, cuadros y batallas: un ambiente para un pintor: Velázquez, el Buen Retiro y la guerra', *Revista de Arte, Geografía e Historia*, 2 (1999), pp. 125–170.

21 Sérafin Maria de Sotto, conde de Clonard, *Historia orgánica de las armas de infantería y caballería espanolas desde la creación del ejército permanente hasta el dia*, 4 (Madrid 1853), pp. 269–272.

22 Ibid. pp. 269–272.

23 AGS Secretaría de Guerra, lib. 111.

24 Several of these censuses are in AGS Guerra Antigua leg. 529.

25 Javier Gallastegui Ucín, *Navarra a través de la correspondencia de los Virreyes (1598–1648)* (Pamplona 1990) p. 215.

26 This sample is actually quite widespread in the Hispanic Monarchy, as Thompson (1981) has stated. Jan Glete also noted the same: 'The Spanish decline in the seventeenth century cannot be explained by exhaustion or lack of resources. The Spanish monarchy was Europe's second largest political entity in terms of inhabitants, and it controlled the world's largest transoceanic empire. But the rulers' ability to extract and organise resources had efficiently diminished. Unlike in the sixteenth century,

resources raised for war were not used for the creation of dynamic organisational structures that could act independently of society. Instead, resources could be raised mainly on the condition that the society and its elites retained control over them in a fashion that was more typical of medieval Europe. Rather than a modern fiscal-military state structured by the central government, Spain had a military structure connected to and shaped by networks of entrepreneurs, aristocrats, and city elites by the late seventeenth century.' (Glete (2002) p. 137)

27 'Ordenanzas de las guardas de Castilla, por las quales se an de regir y gouernar, librar y pagar la gente dellas desde VIII de febrero de MDCXIII en adelante por el tpo. que la voluntad de S.M. fuere.' AGS Contaduría del Sueldo, 2nd series, leg. 2. See Enrique Martínez Ruiz & Magdalena de Pazzis Pi Corrales, 'Los perfiles de un ejército de reserva español: Las Ordenanzas de las Guardas de 1613', in: id., (eds.) *España y Suecia en la época del Barroco (1600–1660)*, (Madrid 1998), pp. 341–374 (in English: Madrid 2000).

28 This is not the place to elaborate upon Olivares's famous memorandum and the Union of Arms. See John H. Elliott, *El conde-duque de Olivares: El político en una época de decadencia* (Madrid 2004); Gregorio Marañón, *El conde-duque de Olivares: (La pasión de mandar)* (Madrid 1952); and J. H. Elliott & J. F. de la Peña (eds.) *Memoriales y cartas del Conde Duque de Olivares*, 1 (Madrid 1988).

29 Elliott (2004), p. 277, reduces the number to 170,000. On the other hand, Jan Glete (2002) rejects the possibility altogether.

30 R. A. Stradling. *Spain's Struggle for Europe, 1598–1668* (London 1994).

31 Julio Albi de la Cuesta, 'La Caballería de los Austrias', in: Julio Albi de la Cuesta, Leopoldo Stampa Piñeiro & Juan Silvela Milans del Bosch, *Un eco de clarines: La Caballería española* (Madrid 1992) pp. 21–23.

32 AGS Contaduría del Sueldo, second series, '1652 Sueldo. Intervención de la entrada y salida en las Arcas [...] de las Guardas de Castilla [...] desde 10 de junio de 1652 en adelante'.

33 *Colección de Ordenanzas Militares, Compañías Viejas de Castilla*, 1 (Madrid 1768) p. 13.

34 Glete (2002), pp. 90–91.

CHAPTER 9

Flexible Comparativeness

Towards better cultural-historical methods for the study of law codes and other aspects of human culture

Arne Jarrick & Maria Wallenberg Bondesson

The main purpose of this chapter is to offer a set of operational tools with which comparative research in the humanities could be significantly improved. Such a methodological change for the better is long overdue, for the quality of comparative research in the humanities is not the best; another reason is that systematic comparative work is rarely seen in our field. With luck, by offering better and more attractive tools for comparative research than have been applied to date, we can contribute to overcoming the general reluctance among researchers in the humanities to go down this particular road of scholarly enquiry.

That said, our primary motive was the methodological problems that we ourselves have faced when attempting a large-scale, comparative study of law codes from the dawn of human civilization in Mesopotamia to the present. Indeed, our difficulties began with the very first sources we had studied with comparison in mind: the Babylonian law code of Hammurabi of the eighteenth century BC and the Tang Code of seventh-century China.

The specific purpose of our general study of the history of legislation is to come to grips with certain social phenomena that have been of essential importance for human interaction and for long-term cultural change: the emergence and cumulative development of institutions and human self-regulation. As this indicates, this undertaking is intrinsically related to a wider attempt to arrive at a general understanding of the species-specific, cultural dynamism of human society. For this reason, we begin here by providing a general background to this enterprise. We also want to stress that despite the fact that the examples we provide are mainly about our particular case – that of legislation – our methodological innovation is intended to be generally applicable in comparative research. For example, our model is currently being tested on the global and long-term history of eating habits.

The dynamics of the human society

Our general point of departure is the basic observation that mankind has a unique capacity for producing and sustaining culture – this being the ultimate explanation of the unparalleled dynamism that characterizes human society. Being a uniquely cultural species implies, firstly, that humans are naturally innovative. This means they have an innate urge to find ever-new solutions to old and new problems; this is also the case when the subjects of this innovation are spatially and temporally distinct from the setting as such. Humans have an extraordinary ability to consciously and deliberately handle past experience as well as contemporaneous events elsewhere – and to make plans for the future. These are only some of the many expressions of the uniquely human capacity to handle what is not present – the second implication of the uniqueness of human culture – another example of which is the clearly demonstrated ability to build social networks across vast distances. Thirdly, humans as a rule deliberately transmit their innovations to one another, either vertically down *and up* the generational ladder, or horizontally within generations. Concomitantly, humans are also prone to learning what others intend to teach them, although often in a creative and rarely straightforward way. In truth, since the circumstances in which people live are in constant flux, the transmission of knowledge would fail in the long run if humans only aimed at its exact replication. On the contrary, in order to copy faithfully, they simply have to be creative learners.[1]

By cultural dynamism, we mean that human society has gone through an unparalleled degree of cumulative change down the ages, conditioned by the cultural capacity of its human carriers. This dynamism is ongoing and substantiated by innumerable observations, be they of diversification and loss (for instance of languages) or of the generalization and diffusion of cultural traits (such as equality before the law, for example in marital law) or the spread of eating habits.

All this means that mankind is an innovative, teaching, and learning species that sets up goals for its own future, largely based upon a more or less systematic grasp of past experience. This gives rise to the self-promoting, ever-ongoing process that has made it possible for humans to colonize and adapt to almost any kind of terrestrial environment and live in societies with population densities never observed in any other species of similar size.

A basic question of particular relevance to this context is whether the unremitting process of cultural change is accompanied by a steadily growing complexity of human interaction. Many scholars – from Herbert Spencer onwards – have claimed this.[2] With the emergence and development of civilizations and population growth, it would be natural to expect the gradual growth, differentiation, and coordination of social activities, as much as a steady or even exponential rise in the quantity of artefacts. Furthermore, when expanding civilizations incorporate ever-new groups of people, cultural and moral codes must then be renegotiated, possibly adding to the complexity.[3] However, this is not necessarily the whole story. There may also be forces at work that tend to make things rather less complex; more so the more social interaction in large and growing societies becomes increasingly abstract, and people who never meet in real life are connected.

The importance of institutions to mankind

Being social creatures, humans simply have to interact. If a certain group of people do so on a permanent basis, their interaction is worthy of being called a society. For a society to persist, interaction must be regulated in some way or another. Where they are deliberately introduced and maintained we call such regulations *institutions*, irrespective of the way they emerged or whether they were formally or only informally established, with or without support of written documents.

Without going into the details of the process of institutionalization, let us just point out one thing that is of relevance for any discussion about law-making: the introduction of an institution implies not only the codification of power by those with power to codify, but also the depersonification of power, which accordingly tends to become less arbitrary than it was prior to its codification. The result is that the power of the powerful is left more restricted than it would otherwise have been.[4]

Any institution can be seen as a means by which an innovation is sustained. Consequently, an institutionalized innovation is not only a sign of change; it is also a sign of an intention to block further change in the particular area where the institutionalization took place. This is what the upholding of tradition is all about.[5] Institutions are meant to survive the men and women who invented them. And yet again the making of institutions testifies to man's ability to think strategically about the destiny of his own society by planning for a situation far beyond the present and far beyond his own expected lifetime.

And yet, no institution will last forever, at least not as it was set up and intended to work.[6] Building, maintaining, modifying, dismantling, and reconstructing institutions are essential aspects of human interaction. This non-stop social metabolism is of profound importance for culture and thus for the dynamics of human societies. This is the case whether there are written documents institutionalizing the regulations, or whether they are established by an oral agreement that is then transmitted by word of mouth down the generations.[7]

Since the need for institutions seems to be felt in all societies in all times, they could be considered an essential or natural ingredient in all human dealings. Equally, such naturally emerging institutions could be seen as 'cultural constructs', given that from a certain point of view they are agreements between certain individuals about certain regulations and, crucially, only exist as long as they are recognized as such by the people concerned, and will perish at the very moment when this recognition is withdrawn.[8] Nevertheless, despite the fact that institutions can be seen as interactive processes, they are normally conceived of as existing even when they are not currently operating – when the people whose specific interactions constitute the institution are not interacting.

The latter leads us to conclude that the existence of institutions is dependent upon the uniquely human ability to handle what is either not visible or not present, be it temporally or spatially. Since institutions are a certain form of interaction, it is hardly possible to see them directly or to experience them physically. This is even more the case when they are not in operation; when they exist only in the minds of those who recognize them as existing.

The importance of laws and law courts in particular

Human societies abound in institutional arrangements. While some (such as the division of labour) appeared almost at the dawn of human society, others were introduced much later (as was the case with money).

If some institutions have survived (money again – at least thus far), others have risen only to fall (such as freemasons, whose numbers peaked in the eighteenth century and have been gradually crumbling ever since).

There is thus a considerable repertoire of institutions that could have been suitable for our study. However, our choice has fallen on law codes because they better serve our purpose than most other relics of institution-building.[9] Firstly, law codes are an explicit regulation of human interaction, thereby substantiating the fact that values have been set up and obligations have been defined; this signifies a degree of self-awareness among those who took charge of these regulations.[10] These aspects are of crucial importance for our understanding of the cultural dynamics of human society. Secondly, law codes testify to a conscious attempt to regulate this interaction permanently, indicating that they were meant to outlive those who designed them. This also implies a depersonification of power, which eventually also limits the power of the power-holders themselves.[11] Thirdly, the existence of law codes points to the fact that the legislators operated with potential – not yet materialized – conditions (albeit differing in their degree of generalization), thereby displaying the ability, so essential for the dynamism of human societies, to handle non-present phenomena. Finally, laws have been codified in all societies where there are also political elites and a central bureaucracy.[12]

Of course, there are other reasons for the study of laws. As a rule, historical or archaeological studies in our field have been biased towards studies of material culture. This is perhaps not primarily for scholarly reasons; rather, it is because material remains may be easier to access and easier to interpret than traces of non-material culture. Such is the state of the field, despite the fact that non-material culture has been of profound importance for the evolution of human society. In order to provide a fuller picture of cultural development, it behoves us to add time-series of non-material culture to the many time-series that already depict the development of material culture. Moreover, laws should be considered part of non-material culture, as remains of past norms, despite the fact they also have survived as artefacts.

To describe, explain, and understand

A systematic study of the very long history of law codes will enable us to discern age-old components – the 'universals' of legislation – as well as general trends over time as to what emerges and what disappears.[13]

As we have already alluded to, an issue of profound importance in this respect concerns the fate of complexity in law-making. On the one hand, the continuous enlargement and differentiation of social interaction indicate growing complexity, and thus that more aspects of social life must be regulated. On the other hand, the 'virtualization' of interaction brought about by the selfsame process, by which people belonging to a given society no longer meet more than a tiny minority of their fellow citizens, points in the opposite direction. Laws in small-scale societies mirror physically concrete and varied interaction. In large societies, they tend to become generalized and all-encompassing; thus they are also less specific, less casuistic, and are consequently fewer.[14]

Furthermore, it is likely that a study such as ours will also make it possible to establish whether similar legislative traits, present in many places and at many times throughout history, were established independently or through processes of diffusion. Finally, we will also get a glimpse of the specific traits that were only of limited importance for a brief time or in one place. More specifically, the questions that we ask concern the following aspects of the law codes to be studied:

- What aspects of social life were regulated?
- How was the regulation done? (For example, by resort to civil law, penal law, or both?)
- Were people considered unequal or equal before the law?
- What principles of sanction were proclaimed: retaliation, revenge, reformation/rectification, and so on?
- What were the legitimizing principles of the law? What kind of authority did it invoke?
- What was the balance, if any, between obligations and rights?
- To what degree, if at all, were the subjects of the law assigned personal responsibility for their deeds?

These questions were selected because, at least when it comes to secular trends in law-making, they will particularly enable us to capture the essence of the cultural dynamics of human society.

The systematic comparative approach here stands for experimentation in the service as much of explanatory purposes as of descriptive ones.[15] Moreover, law codes promise to be suitable for a comparative approach aimed at answering our basic questions as to the structure of cultural dynamics: they have existed for a reasonably long time, at least when compared to other cultural traits in human civilizations (probably rather more than four thousand years); and almost all societies have written laws, many of which have been preserved in intelligible forms, thus exposing them to meaningful comparison. Law codes provide a good picture of those recurring and sometimes timeless (as well as time-bound) occupations that have been subject to regulation in different cultures and at different times. They express mutual obligations between humans to varying degrees, making it possible to assess the measure of legislative self-awareness involved (one aspect being the extent to which the legislator was ready, or forced, to circumscribe his or her own power).

The lack of comparative studies

In our experience, comparative work is infrequently attempted in the human sciences. Scholars know perfectly well that all conceptualized knowledge is dependent upon some sort of comparison, be it in the humanities or in other sciences, in everyday life or in academic research. However, traces of more-or-less rudimentary and more-or-less conscious comparisons can be seen everywhere, while systematic comparative work cannot.

This relative paucity of systematic, long-term comparative research is sometimes visible even in contexts explicitly devoted to comparative research. The journal *Comparative Studies in Society and History* is a case in point. A cross-sectional survey of this journal from its inception in 1958 to the present day reveals that, on the whole, the findings presented there are less comparative than one would expect.[16] First, around one-quarter of the articles are either not comparative at all or only remotely so. Secondly, while most of the essentially comparative articles show evidence of a systematic approach, in general they are descriptive rather than causal, and verbal rather than statistical in execution. Only rarely are the analyses arranged so as to allow for generalizing conclusions. Thirdly, there seems to be a trade-off between truly long-term, secular, or even millennial studies and systematic comparisons; that is to say, the more long-term they are, the more impressionistic they become. A remedy for this is badly needed. The methodological suggestions and examples presented below are intended to point the way. As far as we know, nothing similar has ever been tried before.

A similar observation could be made about historical scholarship in particular. A certain number of historical studies have appeared over the years, explicitly designed and carried out according to a comparative scheme, where all observations are organized the same way, and where the aim is to enable and improve causal reasoning. However, they are relatively few.[17] And where there are comparisons, far too often they are brought in at a late stage in the research process as supplementary information gained from other studies in order to bring what is often vaguely called a comparative *perspective* to the case in question. This usually means that the case-study is related to other more-or-less similar case-studies conducted by other researchers applying concepts, operational definitions, and methods that may *or may not* be similar to those applied in the study in question. One example of this is social history of criminality, which was a flourishing field of research in the 1990s. Although addressing similar issues and being largely acquainted with one another's research, many researchers applied different methods and categorized the panorama of crimes without coordinating their efforts all that much.

Moreover, the objectives of such comparisons are rarely spelled out; they most often seem to be descriptive rather than explanatory. Similarly, in the historical sciences one almost never sees interdisciplinary validity and reliability checks where researchers replicate studies that other researchers have already done.

Therefore, given the state of the field, what is needed? First of all, humanists should broaden their comparative ambitions. The loose use of comparative *perspectives* should be replaced by a systematic approach characterized by conceptual and classificatory coherence that ensures real comparativeness. Second, systematized flexibility is also needed while upholding classificatory coherence. This means that the comparative work should be arranged so as to allow for continuous revisions of the classifications (when new sources result in observations that were not originally foreseen, such revisions become desirable or necessary). Third, as in all good science, methodological transparency must be maintained in order to enable anyone to replicate the study; systematic, interdisciplinary procedures should be adopted from the outset. We will give some specific suggestions in the following sections regarding how these comparative objectives might be met.

The Code of Hammurabi and the Tang Code

The Code of Hammurabi is the oldest of the law codes considered here; it is also one of the oldest collections of law extant, and while those of Ur-Namma and Lipit-Ishtar (from the same cultural area) are older, they are much less complete.[18] The laws in question were established in approximately 1760 BC, during the reign of King Hammurabi (*c.*1792–1750 BC), the ruler of the city-state of Babylon. Hammurabi had recently conquered a number of other city-states, thus substantially enlarging his territory and changing its character. This was the beginning of the transition from a system of competing city-states to that of one territorial state in Sumer and Babylonia.[19] The code was originally displayed on at least three stone steles in central locations in Hammurabi's realm.[20] The regulations present specific cases and are almost exclusively casuistic in character ('If a slave kills a member of the noble class ...') and are not generalized to abstract moral rules ('Thou shall not kill'). Furthermore, the code is not divided into chapters or parts. The code was originally not divided into articles either; it was later editors who gave the articles numbers (in the English edition by Martha Roth that we have used, the laws are divided into 282 articles).[21]

The Tang Code was established in the early days of the Tang dynasty; it is the first Chinese code that has been preserved in its entirety, although a number of codes preceded it, for there are remnants of both the Qin (*c.*220 BC) and the Han codes (*c.*200 BC), and several other dynasties prior to the Tang are known to have produced codes.[22] The Tang Code builds upon a code that was issued during the early Sui dynasty, and appeared in several editions during the seventh and eighth centuries AD. The most notable edition is that of 653; extensive commentaries were added to the original text during a revision in that same year. However, all extant versions of the code build upon an edition from 737.[23] The Tang Code is divided into two main parts: the first contains general principles (for example, concerning the treatment of specific groups in society); the second deals with specific crimes. Together, it comprises 502 articles; originally they were not numbered, and were referred to by their headings (Wallace Johnson has provided them with numbers in his English translation.) The articles, in turn, consist of several parts: first, the article as such, then commentaries and subcommentaries follow. In some cases, rhetorical questions and answers are also included.[24] The regulations of the code are generally casuistic;

however, it is substantially more structured and systematized when compared to the Code of Hammurabi.

We have examined two kinds of information in these codes – the types of human action that are regulated and the prescribed punishments or other stipulations – both of which display the differences and similarities between the codes. With regard to the issues treated, a substantial overlap is visible: 41 per cent of the regulations in the Tang Code and 91 per cent in the Code of Hammurabi concern regulations that are present in both codes. At times, certain regulations have a similar frequency in both codes: for instance, about 17 per cent of the regulations in both codes concern property crimes and 11 and 14 per cent respectively concern crimes of violence.[25]

However, there are also striking differences between the codes in the prioritization of regulations. The Code of Hammurabi is characterized by a high frequency of legislation pertaining to activities in the civil sector (such as terms of transactions, management of property, and so on), although it must be stressed that this has much to do with to the fact that legislation concerning the functioning of the state is very scarce in this code. The case in the Tang Code is almost the opposite. Much of this code is given over to regulating different areas of state, for example the function of the courts, the bureaucracy, and the security of the state, sovereign, or nation. Terms of transactions and so on are only sparsely dealt with.

The differences between the codes are striking when it comes to punishments, at least at first glance. The Tang Code mainly uses a small number of standard punishments: strokes with a lighter or heavier stick, penal servitude, exile, and death by strangulation or decapitation. The use of punishments in the Code of Hammurabi is less uniform, and includes blinding, cutting out the tongue or cutting off a hand, impaling, and burning, as well as other sanctions such as trial by ordeal (in this case, ordeal by water, known as the 'divine River Ordeal'), compensation, and so on.

This illustrates an essential methodological problem: some topics and punishments present in the Code of Hammurabi are not present or only rarely present in the Tang Code, and vice versa. This has the potential to cause problems whenever a system of classification is to be established. In other words, classifications created solely upon the basis of one of these codes would not really work when applied to the other. On the other hand, we cannot abandon the business of classification, only to return to it when we have been through all the codes to be studied.

Thus the challenge is to set up a clear system for comparative analysis that allows for real comparisons between all the codes to be studied. As we have already stressed, this means that the system should satisfy the demands of conceptual and classificatory coherence, methodological transparency, and interdisciplinarity. Secondly, the system needs to be flexible in order to permit the continuous reclassification of the observations whenever necessary, without jeopardizing the work that has already been done. In addition, in order to be manageable, such a reclassification system must be designed to be as timesaving as possible. In what follows we present the outline of just such a system, with examples drawn from the work we have already done with the Code of Hammurabi and the Tang Code.

A system for flexible comparativeness

In order to achieve both the precision and flexibility needed in comparative work, we have established a 'two-by-three' system of classification that springs from the two types of information we have identified in the codes – the types of human action that are regulated, and the prescribed punishments or other consequences stipulated in the codes – on three levels of abstraction in each case.[26] 'Level of abstraction' denotes the degree to which the categories are either rich in content or broad in scope.[27] In other words, the categories are extensive and general on the highest level of abstraction, whereas on the lowest level of abstraction the categories are narrow and specific (that is to say, rich in content). Regarding the types of human action that are regulated in the codes, property crimes or crimes of violence are found at the highest level of abstraction as they encompass a wide spectrum of events; on the middle level are robbery, forgery, and manslaughter; while the lowest level is reserved for short, specific summaries of the events in question. Similarly, when it comes to the classification of the punishments or consequences that the codes prescribe, broad categories such as punishment or agreement are found at the highest level of abstraction; categories such as the death penalty, penal servitude, or corporal punishment are on the middle level; and the lowest level contains even more precise descriptions of the punishments or consequences (for instance, two years of penal servitude or death by decapitation).

Thus in the classification of the types of regulated human action, each article is classified in a general mode (for example, as concerning property crimes or crimes of violence); classified in a more specific way (for example, as concerning theft or murder); and then summarized. The same principle – again with three levels of abstraction – is used in the classification of the punishments that the codes prescribe. For each article, the stipulated sentence is classified in a general way (for example, as being a punishment as opposed to some sort of agreement); classified in a more specific way (for example as penal servitude); and finally the exact extent of the sentence is noted (for example, two years of penal servitude). This two-by-three classification system enables us to obtain a general view of the law codes, to perform detailed statistical analyses of specific topics, and to compare different codes.

In order to meet the demand for classificatory coherence (the issues of interdisciplinarity and methodological transparency will be discussed below), we took great care in naming and defining the categories used in our analysis. For instance, the category for crimes of violence is defined as 'all forms of violence against human beings, regardless of intent and lethality, including attempt, incitement, and threat to commit such acts'.[28] One of its sub-categories, assault and battery, is further defined as 'to intentionally inflict bodily injury, illness, or pain upon another person or set the victim in a condition of powerlessness or similar'.[29] Reliance on explicit definitions such as these is important in order to avoid gradually and unconsciously distorting the meaning of the categories, but it also has other benefits. For instance, as only a certain number of named categories are included in our databases, both calculations and revisions are easy. However, as we address new law codes, we inevitably come across information that forces us to revise our categories and add new ones. Such revisions and additions are not external to our classification system; they are an essential and integral part of it. Let us spell out in detail how they are done.

Initially, as in all classificatory work, there are a number of articles that do not fit into any pre-defined category. Such articles are subsumed under the category *other/unspecified*. If more than one such article is found, we reconsider their status, and either change an existing category to include them or, if more appropriate, create a whole new category. Attempts or incitement to commit murder are a case in point. When we encountered such regulations, we changed our definition of the *murder* category to include these cases. The result became a definition of murder as 'the intentional killing of another human being, including conspiracy, attempts, incitement, and threats to perform such acts'. Another example, where the creation of a whole new category turned out to be necessary, concerns the category *causing public danger*. There are no regulations in the Code of Hammurabi dealing with such matters – or with anything similar, which is why we had to create a whole new category when we encountered such regulations in the Tang Code. The introduction of a new category is possible on either of the two higher levels of abstraction defined above. In other words, new items might be anticipated to fit into pre-existing, more abstract (level one) categories such as *sex crimes*. The only thing needed here is to insert a new, middle-level category (that is, a level two category). Thus when we encountered regulations concerning *procuring* in the Tang Code, we held it most appropriate to include them as a new category under the aforementioned middle-level category of *sex crimes*. In other cases, it has been necessary to introduce categories on both the highest and the middle levels. One example of the latter is the creation of the middle-level category, *regulations concerning civil administration*. Since, prior to our examination of other codes, there was only a single article regulating this in the Code of Hammurabi, we had categorized this article as *other/unspecified*. Proceeding to the Tang Code, we found it contained a larger number of regulations similar to this single example; since these regulations differed substantially from all the other categories in our system thus far, an entirely new middle-level category, with attendant sub-categories, was needed. Whether revising a pre-existing category or creating a new category, the place of the new categories in the system as a whole must be carefully considered, of which more anon. Lastly, we review all cases in the original category and all cases that might be included in a new or changed category, and make the necessary changes accordingly.

These revision procedures are neither especially time-consuming nor complicated thanks to the clear, simple construction of the classification system. This is essential if the system is to live up to our standards of being flexible and coherent at the same time. The technique is to effect these reclassifications by using the detailed information found on level three in our classification system – the most concretely descriptive level. Thus there is almost no need to go back to the sources themselves, and this saves a great deal of time. However, we recognize that there is room for improvement in this part of the system. Ideally, the actual text of the articles should also be included as a fourth level. There would never be any need to refer back to the original sources in such a system, and one could make all the revisions solely by consulting the database.

Although we wish our system to be as open as possible to time-saving classificatory revisions, obviously we want to minimize the need for such revisions. This was why we started out by surveying legal literature and encyclopaedias to get a sense of what we might find in the codes. When they have been compatible with our own objectives, we have sometimes used definitions from encyclopaedias or legal handbooks. These definitions have the advantage that they are the fruit of many people's minds, and are therefore effective and straightforward. Thus, aside from the nature of our basic questions, both legal literature and a close reading of the codes themselves have shaped of our classification system. For instance, the definition of *crimes of violence* is our own, while the definition of *assault and battery* is taken almost verbatim from the *Swedish National Encyclopaedia*.[30]

Any system of classification must both serve to keep its constituent categories apart (that is, to prevent them from overlapping) and assemble them in a systematic whole (that is, to indicate whether categories are 'related' or share common features). Definitions certainly go some way in positioning categories relative to one another. However, it is difficult to get a clear picture of the system as a whole and to evaluate its logic solely on the basis of a number of definitions, and instead we have supplemented the use of definitions with the creation of 'classificatory trees'.[31] In other words, in order to achieve a truly logical system and further check for overlapping categories we have pinpointed the connections between the various categories.

The first tree (Figure 1) shows the three major sectors of law identified thus far: the *public sector*, the *private sector*, and the *religious sector* (the left-hand shaded column). Since the two codes that we have examined both date from the distant past, other sectors must obviously be added to the tree when codes from later periods are studied. For instance, we expect that sectors such as international law, space law, and nature or animal conservation law will be added. From each of the three main sectors, the tree branches into more and more specific categories. Thus the ends of each branch (the right-hand shaded column) represent what are at present the most specific categories – which correspond to level two in the two-by-three system (level one, the most extensive and general category used in our classification system appears in the tree (the middle shaded column); level three, the summaries of different aspects of the regulations, does not). There are two categories in the classificatory tree that are more extensive than the most general categories used in our basic classification (one such level is the aforementioned sector-level). It would also be possible to distinguish levels between the levels one and two (the middle and right-hand columns). However, since we consider levels one and two to be the most relevant to our specific questions, we have focused on these two levels, and the results for these levels are thus routinely calculated for all the codes we process.

Regardless of which levels we focus upon in our analyses and presentations, all levels are important in order to maintain the coherence as well as the flexibility of the classification system. For instance, we have almost exclusively focused upon the most general of our basic classifications in the presentation of our results thus far (that is to say, level one, the middle shaded column in the tree).[32] However, this does not imply that level two might be redundant. In order to achieve a precise classification of regulations in more general categories, it is also necessary to decide which of the more specific categories these regulations belong to. With this methodology we thus obtain a clear picture of which specific cases make up the more general categories. To systematize the information in this way is also absolutely necessary for category revision, as described above, and even more so as the more general level has proven to be most interesting and relevant to us thus far, but this could change as new codes are included in the comparison. In passing, it should be pointed out that we also intend to 'tree' the punishments stipulated in the codes, which have been omitted here.

We have attempted to show how our particular method (that is to say, our definitions and classificatory trees) may bring a greater methodological coherence, precision, and flexibility to the field. In so doing, we have also laid the ground for the second pillar of our 'comparativist' mission: namely, to improve the methodological transparency and interdisciplinarity to which we have already alluded. From the start, we have sought to ensure that the methodology should be transparent, comprehensible, and of use to more than the primary investigators themselves. The classificatory trees are consequently not only methodological tools used in the creation of a smoothly working system; they are also didactic tools with which to introduce and explain our classificatory system, and to invite others to use it.

In order to improve the interdisciplinary qualities of the system, we have analysed the Code of Hammurabi independently of each other. We then compared and discussed our interpretations. However, at this stage such procedures should be seen as no more than explorative checks in need of further refinement. The basic problem with our way of conducting these interdisciplinary checks is that we did not clearly separate matters of definition from matters of interpretation. A more accurate, 'cleaner' way of checking would be to study the material with the categories already fixed. Any possible improvements to the categorization could then be contemplated separately and thus not be allowed to 'contaminate' the test of interdisciplinarity. It should be noted that not all the definitions of our categories had been formalized and written down when we ran these checks.

Despite the shortcomings, we still think that our interdisciplinarity test has helped us to substantially improve our system, and in practice it resulted in some revealing statistics. In an early analysis of the types of action regulated in the Code of Hammurabi, we differed in classification by slightly less than 9 per cent (that is to say, in 29 of the 326 articles, excluding cases where new categories were suggested). Another early test concerned the punishments and sanctions laid down in the same code: here we differed in approximately 13 per cent of articles. Following these tests, we examined the points where we differed and modified the system accordingly. For instance, we found that the majority of differences in categorization in our first test were due to misconceptions about categories that had not been set down in writing, clearly demonstrating the necessity of providing *all* categories with written definitions, even those that were seemingly uncomplicated. The main reason for the discrepancies in the other test was more particular; we found that it was sometimes difficult to establish whether a sum of money (or its equivalent) prescribed by the code was understood as a punitive fine or as compensation for loss or damage. We therefore created a new category – *fine/compensation* – for these specific cases in order to fine-tune the system by indicating that it was not possible to identify the reason for the payment.

What do we get?

What specific information do we get by applying our methodological instruments to the basic questions as we have presented them? We have gained information about both the absolute number of regulations,

Tree 1: Classificatory tree showing the categories in our system and some of the results of our investigations.

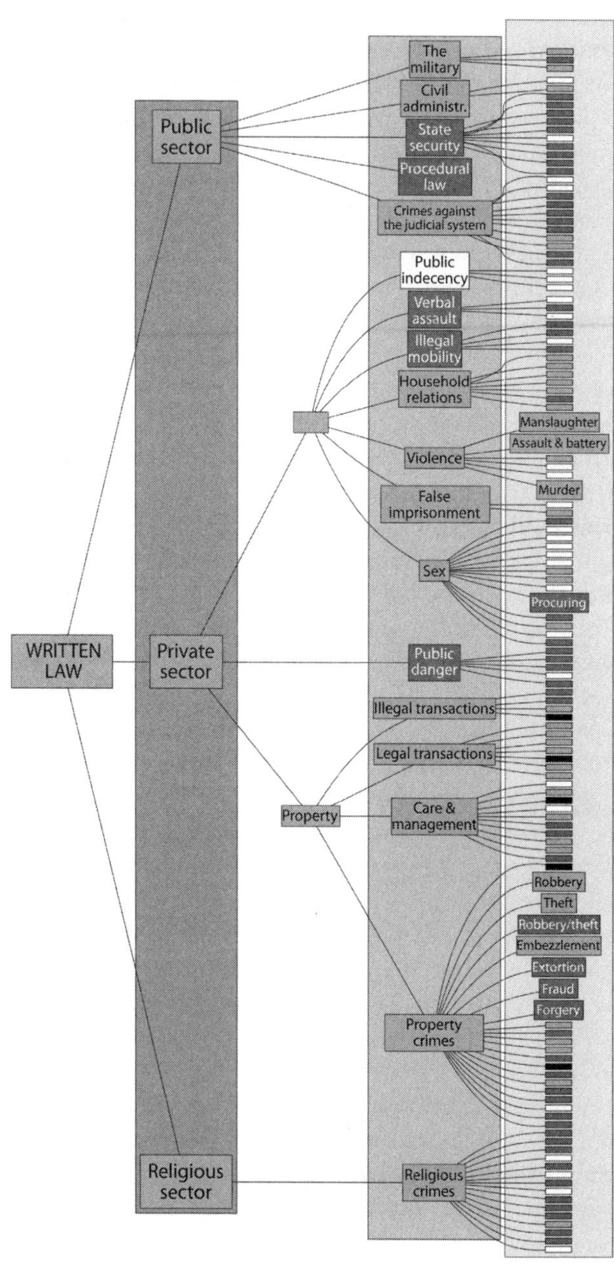

the relative scope given to different topics in the codes, and about the absolute and relative use of different punishments and sanctions. For instance, we can learn that 6.6 per cent of the regulations in the Tang Code concern relationships within the household, while the corresponding figure for the Code of Hammurabi is 12.2 per cent. Regarding the types of punishments applied, we learn that the legislators of the Tang Code resorted to capital punishment in 7 or 10 per cent of its articles, while Hammurabi does so in about 13 per cent of articles.[33] We can also determine which crimes were punishable by which punishments, and thus which crimes were considered more serious.

Moreover, we can also distinguish the types of crime and civil regulation represented *at all* in the codes. The classificatory trees are of great value here: they can be used both in the primary analysis (to make us aware of circumstances we might otherwise have overlooked) and to elucidate and present results; and they demonstrate the scope and peculiarities of the codes. The types of regulation that occur exclusively in the Tang Code are marked in dark grey in Figure 1, while those that only occur in the Code of Hammurabi are marked in black, and the ones present in both codes are marked in light grey. Since it is only based on two codes, this information might not amount to a comprehensive picture of the 'core' of legal codes, but its value will increase as the project progresses and comes to include information from a greater number of law codes.

Thus both differences and similarities between law codes from disparate cultures can be determined by this system, as can the development of legal codes over time. However, it will be necessary to expand our basic classificatory system as the investigation proceeds. Although it is unlikely, some categories may even be dropped and the information reallocated to other categories. Given that we have thus far only explored premodern and medieval law codes, it is interesting to consider how the categorization pattern of more modern legal codes might look. Given the workings of cultural dynamics in general, we expect some kind of growth over time. However, at this stage we can only hypothesize about how this development would look in detail. There are several interesting possibilities with which to reckoned, presented here in Figure 2. We have already noted that we suspect the number of sectors to be included in our classification system will increase (although at a slowing rate) as we investigate more recent codes: this is illustrated by the thick line. The various dashed lines denote possible scenarios

Graph 1: Hypotheses about the growth of legal codes over time

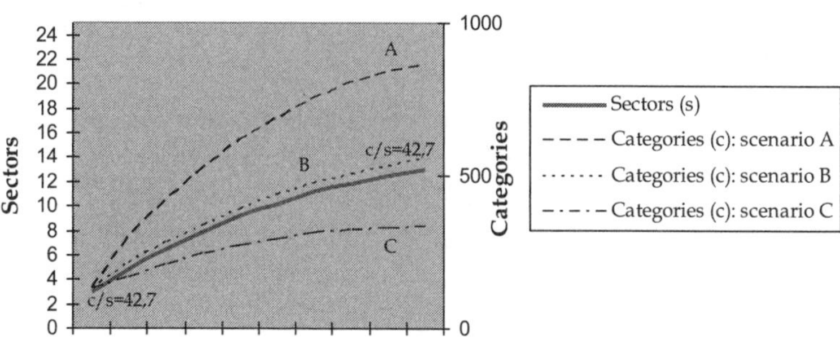

for the number of categories (in level two) relative to the number of sectors, all of which start with an average of 42.7 categories per sector (reflecting our present system of 128 specific categories in 3 sectors): in scenario A the growth in the number of sectors is accompanied by an even more pronounced growth in the number of categories; in scenario B the number of categories grows at roughly the same rate as the sectors, leaving the average number of categories per sector unchanged; while in scenario C, already alluded to in this chapter, the expansion in the sectors represented in the law codes is accompanied by a slower increase in the number of categories, resulting in a generalization of specific legal regulations.

To some degree, legal codes have developed as in this last scenario. For example, the regulations concerning such things as murder or battery are significantly more general in modern law than they were in premodern legislation. However, it is still not proven that instances such as these represent general trends over time; indeed, it is yet to be established empirically whether the development of legal codes as a whole follows any one path. The most striking characteristic will perhaps turn out to be that major sectors of law develop in different ways: generalization in one sector might be accompanied by particularization in another, for example. That being so, one important objective for further research will be to survey the interaction between the different sectors, and describe and discuss the processes that cause such change. And we are hopeful that we can come to grips with the general, long-term trajectories of law-making worldwide by applying the comparative tools we have presented in this chapter.

Notes

1 Magnus Enquist, Stefano Ghirlanda, Arne Jarrick & Carl-Adam Wachtmeister, 'Why Does Human Culture Increase Exponentially?', *Theoretical Population Biology*, 74 (2008).

2 See, for example, Robert L. Carneiro, *Evolutionism in Cultural Anthropology* (Boulder 2003) esp., pp. 161–163.

3 For a useful definition of complexity, see Joseph A. Tainter, *The Collapse of Complex Societies* (Cambridge 1988), p. 23.

4 This is at the heart of H. L. A. Hart, *The Concept of Law* (Oxford 1994 [1961]) ch. 4.

5 Cf. Colin Renfrew, *The Emergence of Civilization: The Cyclades and the Aegean in the Third Millennium BC* (London 1972), pp. 21, 486.

6 For examples, see Carrol Quigley, *The Evolution of Civilization: An Introduction to Historical Analysis* (Indianapolis 1979), pp. 101–115, who applies the concept of 'institutionalization' for such corrupting processes.

7 However, it is of crucial importance for the destiny of a society whether agreements are based upon written documents, which have a chance to survive their creators, or based upon oral agreements, which are irresistibly corrupted as they are transmitted down the generations. See Walter Ong, *Orality and Literacy: The Technologization of the Word* (London 1982) passim.

8 See John Searle, *The Construction of Social Reality* (London 1996) chs. 2, 4–5.

9 To some social scientists, laws are even considered the most profound of all institutions. See, for example, Bronislaw Malinowski, *A Scientific Theory of Culture and Other Essays* (Chapel Hill 1944), pp. 37, 142.

10 See John O'Manique, *The Origins of Justice: The Evolution of Morality, Human Rights, and Law* (Philadelphia 2003) ch. 3; Christine M. Korsgaard, *The Sources of Normativity* (Cambridge 1996) passim.

11 This has been pointed out many times before. See, for example, Joseph Strayer, 'The State and Religion: An Exploratory Comparison in Different Cultures: Greece and Rome, the West, Islam', *Comparative Studies in Society and History*, 1:1 (1958), p. 38. Cf. Hart (1994), pp. 44–45, 48, 51, 62.

12 See, for example, S. N. Eisenstadt, 'Internal Contradictions in Bureaucratic Polities', *Comparative Studies in Society and History*, 1:1 (1958), p. 64.

13 For a discussion, see Donald E. Brown, *Human Universals* (New York 1991).

14 This has been pointed out many times. See, for example, Clyde Kluckhohn, 'The Moral Order in the Expanding Society' in: Carl H. Kraeling & Robert M. Adams (eds.), *City Invincible* (Chicago 1960), pp. 394–395, 398; Max Rheinstein, 'Process and Change in the Cultural Spectrum Coincident with Expansion: Government and Law', ibid. pp. 416–417.

15 Compare with H. Moller, 'The Social Causation of the Courtly Love Complex', *Comparative Studies in Society and History*, 1:2 (1958), p. 140.

16 Starting with the first volume in year 1958, we first systematically analysed all articles from every tenth year and, second scanned the rest.

17 See, for example, S. Eisenstadt, *The Origins and Diversity of Axial Age Civilizations* (Albany 1986); C. Chase-Dunn & T. D. Hall, 'Cross-World-System Comparisons', in: S. K. Sanderson (ed.), *Civilizations and World Systems: Studying World-Historical*

Change (Walnut Creek 1995); Charles Tilly, *Big Structures, Large Processes, Huge Comparisons* (New York 1984).

18 Martha T. Roth, *Law Collections from Mesopotamia and Asia Minor* (Atlanta 1997), pp. 13–14, 23–24, 71–142.

19 See, for example, Marc Van De Mieroop, *King Hammurabi of Babylon: A Biography* (Malden, Oxford & Carlton 2005), pp. 38–39, 77–78; Marc Van De Mieroop, *A History of the Ancient Near East, ca. 3000–323 BC* (Malden, Oxford & Carlton 2004), pp. 39–118; Roth (1997), p. 71.

20 Mieroop (2005), pp. 99–100, 110.

21 See, for example, Roth (1997), pp. 71–142.

22 See, for example, A. F. P. Hulsewé, *Remnants of Han Law* (Leiden 1955); A. F. P. Hulsewé (trans.), *Remnants of Ch'in law: an annotated translation of the Ch'in legal and administrative rules of the 3rd century B.C. discovered in Yün-meng prefecture, Hu-pei province, in 1975* (Leiden 1985); John W. Head & Yanping Wang, *Law Codes in Dynastic China: A Synopsis of Chinese Legal History in the Thirty Centuries from Zhou to Qing* (Durham 2005) esp. pp. 15, 73–75, 91–93, 98, 105.

23 Wallace Johnson (trans.), *The Tang Code. 1: General Principles* (Princeton 1979), pp. 39–41, 45.

24 Johnson (1979) esp. pp. 41–43, 45; Johnson, Wallace (trans.), *The Tang Code. 2: Specific Articles* (Princeton 1997).

25 These statistics (and all statistics of the same kind referred to in the remainder of this text) are taken from our legal codes database, which has been created with information from English translations of these codes (the Code of Hammurabi: Roth (1997), pp. 76–142; the Tang Code: Johnson (1979); id. (1997)).

26 Until our database is complete the observations are registered in an Excel file.

27 On this distinction, see also Johan Asplund, *Sociala egenskapsrymder: En introduktion i formaliseringsteknik för sociologer* (Uppsala 1968), pp. 107–110.

28 In Swedish: 'alla former av våld mot människa, oavsett uppsåt eller huruvida det är dödligt eller inte, inklusive försök till, anstiftan till och hot om sådant'.

29 See also *Nationalencyklopedin* (Swedish National Encyclopaedia), s.v. 'misshandel', <http://www04.sub.su.se:2111/lang/misshandel> (accessed 10 November 2009).

30 Ibid.

31 On this, see Asplund (1968) passim.

32 Arne Jarrick, 'Mellan omsorg och brutalitet', in: Anders Björnsson & Bengt Wadensjö (eds.), *Det ansvarsfulla uppdraget: En vänbok till Mats Svegfors den 23 augusti 2008* (Stockholm 2008); Maria Wallenberg-Bondesson & Arne Jarrick, 'The Modelling of Legal Codes: Priorities, Punishments and Objectives in the Tang Code' (unpublished manuscript, 2010).

33 Two figures are given, since the Tang Code both prescribes 'normal' capital punishments and punishments that are graded up to the death penalty. The first figure only includes 'normal' capital punishments; the second includes these and the graded punishments that *could* reach up to the death penalty.

CHAPTER 10

Company Strategies and Sport

Christer Ericsson

The connection between sport and society is a growing field of interest among Swedish historians as well as historians in other countries. Several studies reveal that sport offers a major opportunity for social groups to consolidate and extend their values; this is something that has become increasingly important with the growing complexity of modern society.[1] Organized sport does not simply reflect developments in political and economic spheres; it also helps to shape society.[2]

The Australian historian Brian Stoddart has in several studies focused upon the British and their use of team sports, especially cricket, as a means of implementing British culture in the colonies. Stoddart's conclusion is that the game was not just a sporting code; it was also a political institution. The imperial authorities introduced cricket for reasons other than recreation. Cricket taught the middle and upper ruling classes in the colonies respect for authority, loyalty, honesty, courage, persistence, teamwork, and humility. 'The language of sport became a code, so that playing the game meant not so much to be involved in simply physical activity as to subscribe to the social conventions and beliefs that sport symbolized.'[3] The British historian James Anthony Mangan, in a study on the origins of sport in Asian society, has additionally shown that the establishment of British public schools in the colonies 'embraced a belief in the games field as a critical source of moral education.'[4] Playing games was an integral part of an educational philosophy. Morality was a product of play, and the sports field was essentially a place for moral education.[5] Sport was indeed an integral part of an educational philosophy among industrial leaders. My interest in this chapter is how organized sport was used in industrial companies in Sweden and Japan as a way of establishing cooperation.

Sport and business

Several studies from a variety of countries reinforce the conclusion that sport has been viewed as a means of achieving improved health and morals, and, above all, a sense of removing class barriers and deepening social solidarity. In the case of companies that used football (and sport in general) as part of their welfare schemes, it became a way of setting up social control. Various scholars have given explanations for why sports (and football above all) attracted support, suggesting that the leading lights strove for local prestige and identification with the local community and, in some cases, had a genuine interest in sport. Furthermore, sport was viewed as an arena that helped to legitimize the 'natural' hierarchy and maintain hegemony. There are also scholars who argue that sport was a site of class struggle and continuous debate, and that it provided the working classes with a voice to challenge the prevailing power relations in society.[6] In the history of sport in Britain, several scholars have touched upon the subject of company managements' relationship with sport (particularly football). Many of these works indicate that industrial companies had an instrumental view of sport and deliberately exploited it for their own interests.[7] Charles Korr notes in his study of the football club, West Ham United, that it was started by Arnold Hills, the owner of Thames Ironworks in London's East End. Hills's explicit wish was that it would strengthen the 'cooperation between workers and management.' Hills saw football as a way of 'raising the morale of his workers and the reputation of his firm.'[8] John Bale underlines the importance of tradition and rootedness to British football clubs: 'A tradition in British football is its localism – to support football was to become involved in a pattern of local loyalties; working class people could be helped to feel that they belonged to a community by the activities of the local football team and their attachment to that team.'[9]

The British historian Paul Gilchrist did an interesting study of the construction of a company myth referred to as the 'Herbert Spirit' by using the company magazine of the machine tool industry in Coventry: *Alfred Herbert Ltd (1888–1983)*.[10] The focus was a concern for 'modern patterns of life and leisure of the working classes.' In those days, rational recreation was important in order to 'ensure the lower classes were healthy, moral, and orderly.'[11] To this end, they provided companies and municipalities with new facilities for sport, leisure, and recreation; it was thought that improvements to the workers' physical state would lead to greater productivity. Patronage of sport and recreation at Alfred Herbert Ltd was important and, since the company provided modest facilities for its workers, sport became very popular. In fact, it became so popular that Sir Alfred and Lady Herbert chose to visit sport festivals and team matches in order to 'to be seen as a benevolent paternalist in action' and to 'play the role of aristocratic patrons by presenting cups, medals and prizes.'[12] Another British historian, Roger Munting, says that sport provision became a common aspect of a company's welfare capitalism from the second half of the nineteenth century. Munting argues that sport had a 'purpose beyond the immediate enjoyment; it was also important in extending a broader company culture.'[13] In the companies included in his investigation, the initiative was the employees' and the company provided the resources. The companies also stressed the virtue of games, fair play, 'a healthy mind in a healthy body, and so on', and working-class men and women were presented with sports facilities that would otherwise not have been available.[14] Munting concludes that the provision of such facilities was increasingly systemized by paternalistic corporate management in order to reduce labour turn-over and 'potential dissatisfaction in the work place.'[15] The American historian Gerald Gems showed in his study of the Pullman Company's manufacture of railway carriages in Chicago that the owner George Pullman (who had been influenced by Britain's industrial communities) came to the conclusion that 'wholesome leisure habits would deter employees from radical elements with magnificent facilities that allowed for any interest, sans a saloon in his effort to promote temperance.'[16] The owner founded the Pullman Athletic Association, which organized its first annual games in the spring of 1881. Employees were divided into teams to compete against other communities in baseball, cricket, football, and track and field. 'The comprehensive athletic programme enjoyed greater financial support than any other social agency, and sporting events and Pullman athletes won national recognition for the company and its owner.' It was Pullman's firm conviction that such programmes prevented strikes and unionization, created better relationships between labour and management, and increased loyalty to the company. Team sports taught competition as well as teamwork, 'self-sacrifice and obedience to authority in the form of a game official, team manager or captain.'[17] The Pullman Company was one of the larger manufacturers in and around Chicago in the 1920s and 1930s that organized leisure time for its employees in the same way.

In another American study, John Schleppi shows that in its efforts to attract and keep skilled and semi-skilled workers, the National Cash Register Company introduced sport and recreation.[18] The company manager, John Patterson, initiated several sports programmes during the early 1890s for the welfare of his employees. Physical fitness and health programmes became a part of the company's workers' lives. The company established an athletics club and a cycling club in 1897 and a baseball team in 1905, with factory and office staff as players. A large athletics field for baseball, tennis, and other sports was also opened. Why this interest in recreational programmes for staff? According to Patterson himself, 'There is no charity in anything we do. Isn't it just good business to lose three cents on a girl's lunch and get back five cents worth of work?' His motto was 'It pays'.[19]

An investigation of factory football undertaken by the Australian scholar Phil Mosley shows that between 1915 and 1929 (a period of considerable industrial strife) companies were in need of better industrial relations and that one of the means of achieving them was sport.[20] The British Tobacco Co. Ltd concluded in August 1932 that 'sport is a big and important item ... it has achieved all it was supposed to do – unite a huge force into one happy and contented family.' The management of Lewis Berger and Sons were similarly pleased that their employees' social and sporting associations had the effect of 'reducing strikes, go-slows, and any industrial disruptions.'[21]

Company owners such as Agnelli in Italy (Fiat) and Peugeot in France did not take an interest in football solely for sporting reasons. Football was initially regarded as a prolongation of the paternalism practised in industrial enterprises and operated by the likes of Agnelli and Peugeot. For example, Agnelli himself invited Fiat workers to watch matches – free of charge – in which Juventus' first team was playing. Through the *Gruppo Sportivo Fiat*, started in the 1920s, it encouraged its workers and employees to play football or other sports. The president of *Gruppo Sportivo* suggested that 'it was a question of a huge program of physical training, harmony, and fraternization between all the FIAT workers' families.'[22] Implicit in this was the intention to maintain social order and peace among employees through their sporting commitments. A similar objective was evident at Peugeot, where every effort was made to associate the club and its players with the 'wider Peugeot family'. The total integration of the football club into the Peugeot company strategy aimed to both modernize traditional paternalism and reinforce the sporting image of the firm.[23] Apart from their social role within these companies, the football teams also served to promote Fiat and Peugeot products.

Several studies have examined sport as a popular movement in Sweden.[24] A number of studies also deal specifically with football.[25] Despite this growing body of work, sport and industrial companies have not been well researched. Only three detailed studies are currently available,[26] all of which show that sport in general and football in particular was supported and became part of companies' paternalistic strategy in order to encourage the workers to view themselves as loyal 'family members'. My focus here is whether sport became a means of industrial strategy and an integral part of an educational philosophy among industrial leaders intent on establishing their hegemony over their companies in Japan and Sweden. It should be emphasized that the comparison draws on my own empirical studies of Swedish companies and studies of Japanese companies conducted by various scholars from different countries. A comparison between Sweden and Japan is not especially common among Swedish historians, but it is a revealing one, particularly in the light of the countries' different routes to becoming modern, democratic welfare states: Sweden's via popular movements, universal suffrage, democracy, and peace; Japan's via Bismarck-inspired authoritarian rule with a restricted franchise, an Imperial cult, imperialism, and war. My intention in this comparison is not simply to understand the similarities and differences between the objects of study and, based upon this, to be in a position to generalize; it is also to understand and explore their diverse and perhaps unique characteristics.

How then did management use sport as a means of strengthening the local community spirit in order to create a strong sense of social solidarity or 'togetherness'? How did they use sport, in theory and in practice, to create a consensus and strengthen their hegemony in order to encourage local patriotism and cooperation in their companies? How was it organized, and which institutional solutions were put in place? In theoretical terms, the concept of hegemony is mainly associated with Antonio Gramsci.

Hegemonic power is defined as the superior party – the hegemon – attempting to interpret reality in universal terms and, upon the strength of his hegemonic power, maintaining that there are no conflicts of interest in the interpretation. The Swedish sociologist Håkan Thörn defines hegemony thus: 'struggles for hegemony can be understood as a struggle about defining the world, and about symbols and concepts that constitute central elements of social unity in specific historical contexts.'[27] The important point here is that hegemonic power is not consensual; rather, it is a power relationship between parties with conflicting interests. Gramsci differentiated between hegemony and dominance.

Industrialization and company communities

Sweden was traditionally less developed than Continental Europe, and industrialization began after 1870. Sweden had been a major European exporter of iron, copper, and timber since the Middle Ages. However, improved transportation and communications, which the state supported, allowed it to utilize its natural resources from different parts of the country on a far larger scale, most notably timber and iron ore. This contributed to rapid industrialization: by the 1890s, the country had begun to develop an advanced manufacturing industry. A welfare state started to emerge in the 1930s.

Industrialization in Sweden began in rural areas in small communities of no more than a few thousand inhabitants. When we talk about 'foundry communities' in Sweden, we tend to imagine safe and well-organized communities with a strong sense of social fellowship or so-called *bruksandan* (foundry spirit). *Bruksandan,* in the form of an established local understanding, is also considered to have contributed to the Swedish *folkhemsmodel* (the Swedish welfare system model). The foundries were run along authoritarian, paternalistic lines, underpinned by a concern for much more than mere production. The managing director had personal relationships with his employees and provided for their needs from cradle to grave. Life at the foundry involved a strictly gendered division of labour, with the man working at the foundry and the woman looking after the home. The prerequisite for this type of paternalism was a connection between workers and management. The idea that there was a fundamental opposition between labour and capital belonged to the world-view of the twentieth century. However, the democratizing process and the growing trade union movement brought along a necessary renewal of paternalism. This new paternalism emphasized the importance of giving workers a greater understanding of the aims and resources of industry. Emotional bonds to the community and company replaced old personal ones, and it was this that characterized the new paternalism. The goal of the democratizing process was to reduce the differences between the classes.[28]

Another important means of achieving the goal of increased understanding between work and capital was for managing directors to teach employees about the conditions under which companies operated. The purpose was to foster an understanding and positive attitude among workers towards the company and their own work.[29] While paternalistic ideas and a clear social hierarchy still prevailed in this integration project, methods of exercising and legitimizing power within the foundry were changed. The previously authoritarian attitude of the 1920s and 1930s became an educational ethos. The authorities were to be teachers, tutors, and models for the people.[30] Thus the leadership of the foundry manager was to be based upon a change of strategy: from authority to didactics, from command to consensus. A new and more profound influence over the workers' world of ideas was required to establish the new paternalistic views and to maintain hegemonic power. The new times required socially responsible industrial managers who would voluntarily give workers insights into corporate affairs and create industrial democracy. However, this required cooperation and a new corporate mentality. Along with this didactic task, companies such as Sandviken Ironworks developed political solutions in the form of services that, in the long run, would tie workers and employees closer to the company. The company set up an office of internal affairs under the guidance of Sandviken's professional industrial manager, Karl Fredrik Göransson, to provide legal advice to workers relating to the formulating of contracts and the completing of income tax returns. It was also to handle health insurance and other insurance issues. There was also a nurse on hand to give advice and arrange medical help when needed, or to assist workers in the home if necessary. A well-functioning healthcare system was seen as vital for a cooperative approach. A periodical was also part of the overall staff planning, and published coverage of club activities, sports, and excursions, and biographies and photos of family celebrations. The publications were thought to promote a feeling of solidarity between the local community and the company.[31] This paternalistic, didactic strategy was common, pronounced even, among industrial leaders during the economic boom of the 1930s through to the 1970s, the period in Sweden's history that is now referred to as 'harvest time'.[32]

In Japanese society, meanwhile, the habits of industriousness are said by its historians to have deep roots. During the Tokugawa period

(1603–1868), there was a general interest in questions of productive efficiency both in the predominant agrarian sector and in the pre-industrial economy.[33] Textile production was widespread in pre-industrial Japan, and this development became the basis for the industrialization process. The population of Japan rose from approximately 20 million in 1600 to 30 million a century later, and Edo became the consumption centre.[34] The Meiji Restoration of 1868 replaced the highly conservative *baku-han* political system with an oligarchy of forward-looking reformers from the south-western periphery of the nation. New policies focused in particular upon industrialization since this was thought the key to a strong country. A Ministry of Industry was established as early as 1870, and in the early years the government often took the lead in establishing enterprises.[35] Henceforth, Japan was rapidly propelled into the ranks of the world's industrial powers, and traditional patterns were readily and fruitfully aligned with a new socio-economic order, although systematic learning from Western models was central to Japan's modern transformation.[36] It has been concluded that the government and the new group of entrepreneurial samurai powered Japan's industrialization.[37] However, it is important to emphasize that even in the 1920s and 1930s more than half of Japan's labour force continued to work in small enterprises or were self-employed.

Paternalistic practices have been seen as the hallmarks of a distinctively Japanese approach to managing industrial labour. It has almost been invariably assumed that this paternalistic tendency was a natural outcome of Japan's cultural heritage, 'reflecting a unique accommodation of traditional values to the impersonal dictates of modern industry.'[38] Paternalism formed the core of Japanese management practice both before and after the Second World War, and alternate paradigms of labour management floundered in Japan due to the culturally conditioned appeal of the paternalistic model. Other scholars argue that Japanese paternalism modelled itself on developing Western ideas of 'welfare capitalism'.[39] The important issue upon which most scholars agree is that management styles changed at the turn of the twentieth century from autocratic and arbitrary to an intensified paternalistic welfare strategy.

William Tsutsui's case-study of the Kanegafuchi Spinning Company (Kanebo) is instructive in this regard.[40] An elaborate range of paternalistic programmes was established between 1902 and 1907 under the leadership of Muto Sanji, who was one of Japan's first generation of professional industrial managers. Muto, with his impressive academic credentials and experience (or lack thereof) of the US, was similar in many ways to Karl Fredrik Göransson in Sandviken. Kanebo was a relatively small concern when Muto first joined the company; however, he rapidly transformed it into one of Japan's leading textile producers. Various concerns motivated this wave of reform; as was the case in Sandviken, the most compelling desire was to reduce labour turn-over by improving the living conditions of the Kanebo workers. Muto's paternalism aimed to provide all that the employees needed at work and in their private lives. Workers' housing was expanded and improved, especially the dormitories for unmarried workers. The meals service was upgraded and a company store was established selling at wholesale prices. Better relief for the sick and injured was also instituted. Company hospitals were established, as were systematic rules for compensation in the case of work-related accidents, and subsidized pension plans were expanded. The company sponsored sports, excursions, and hobby clubs. Schools were expanded for both male and female workers, technical training was made available for male workers, and female employees were taught practical domestic skills in preparation for marriage. The company also designed ways of encouraging 'sobriety, industrious character, and thrift' among its workers.[41] The company appointed 'sanitary inspectors' to investigate the housing conditions of employees not living in company facilities. The company also devised improved communications between workers and corporate management, with a company newsletter used to transmit managerial views to shop-floor employees and their families. In his paternalistic rhetoric, Muto emphasized Japan's 'beautiful customs' and expressed his view that Japan's family system could be extended to society as a whole 'by recreating the warmth that exists in the family between employers and employees, which will bring benefits to both sides.'[42]

One must remember that it is important to identify the differences between management rhetoric and practice when it comes to paternalism. However, there were important similarities in how the paternalistic corporate systems in Sandviken and Kanebo emerged and why they were implemented. One of the most important concerns was to increase understanding between work and capital by reducing labour turn-over. The social reforms that were implemented had obvious similarities. While the rhetoric was similar, there were clear cultural and historical differences. Karl Fredrik Göransson talked rhetorically of a renewal of a didactic paternalism, while Muto Sanji worked in his rhetoric on the supposition that there was an old, genuine, family tradition upon which to build. In contrast to Muto Sanji, Karl Fredrik Göransson never claimed that Sweden had a historical culture of 'beautiful customs'.

The origins of the Swedish sports movement

From the middle of the nineteenth century onwards, Swedish society was transformed by a rapid increase in population, mass migration, urbanization, and industrialization. Alongside these developments, new thoughts and ideas in the form of economic, political, and religious liberalism and socialism were established. Among other things, this transformation of Swedish society created a sense of rootlessness and thus a need for new forms of social relationships. Various organizations, which we refer to today as national movements, were formed; these sought political influence and reform within Swedish society.[43] The revivalist (Free Church), temperance, and labour movements were at the forefront of these organizations. Given the scope of their voluntary activities, ideological influence, and political significance, these three national movements occupy an important place in modern Swedish history. The 1880s saw the emergence of the revivalist and temperance movements, while the 1890s are considered to have seen the breakthrough of the labour movement.[44] It is estimated that national movements comprised roughly half a million people in Sweden at the turn of the twentieth century, with approximately 15 per cent of the population over the age of fifteen holding membership.

These were not the only national movements to grow and strengthen during the introductory decades of industrialization in Sweden. The sports movement, which would later become one of the largest and most comprehensive national movements, came into being during this revolutionary period. As in the other Scandinavian countries, the sports movement in Sweden historically took the form of voluntary associations or 'popular movements'.[45] Since participating in voluntary associations has long been regarded an important step in fostering democratic citizens, organizations are regarded as fundamental parts of the democratic system in Scandinavian countries. Voluntary organizations are open to anyone, regardless of age, sex, social status, ethnic origin, or place of residence. Ideologically speaking, British amateurism has had a crucial influence on the Scandinavian sports movement.[46]

The first breakthrough for sports came in the 1870s and 1880s, when a considerable number of associations in Sweden were formed. Those established then were primarily concerned with health promotion; competition was kept to a minimum. The competitive element became increasingly prominent during the 1890s in both older and newly formed organizations. In short, games, pastimes, and physical activities went through a process of *sportification* in which they became more organized and oriented towards performance, competition, and results.[47] There were 229 local sporting associations in Sweden in 1893 with approximately 20,000 members. The real upswing, however, did not come until after the turn of the century, and particularly in 1906–1908. The number of associations and members of sports associations had tripled by 1919, when there were 786 local sporting associations with 93,000 members. This increase continued, and by 1930 there were approximately 180,000 members distributed among some 2,300 associations: figures that more than doubled nine years later.[48] The Swedish Sports Confederation (Riksidrottsförbundet), which has governed all organized sports in Sweden since 1904, is an umbrella organization with the task of supporting its members' federations, representing the entire Swedish sports movement to the authorities, politicians, and so on. It defends the legitimacy of sport and argues for its value. Simply by being a member of one of the voluntary organizations under its aegis, one soon becomes involved in the democratic process.[49]

Some notable research has been undertaken on the connection between industrialization and modern sport in Sweden.[50] This illustrates that the development of sport in towns was closely linked to industrialization and urbanization. The sports movement was primarily a metropolitan phenomenon for a long time; however, sports associations outside the cities were also formed in sizeable communities, often in conjunction with the mining and sawmill industries. Some have also claimed that it was not until the introduction of the eight-hour working day in 1919 that the right conditions for sports were established in the lower, local hierarchy. Researchers are also of the opinion that sport and its organizations should be viewed in relation to changes in conditions of production and to social conflicts.[51]

From the outset, the higher echelons of the sports movement were recruited primarily from the middle and professional classes; these included company leaders, businessmen, and clerks. Although the working classes were not found on this level of the sports movement, they were visible in various sports associations on the district level. Public opinion about the sports movement was divided from the start. In politics, representatives of the rural areas and many Social Democrats adopted a negative outlook, whereas a majority of middle-class politicians in urban areas were positive. In general, the further people were located to the left of the political spectrum, the more negative they were towards the sports movement.[52] The scepticism of the labour movement stemmed not only from the class and professional background of those who administrated the sports movement; it also came from the perception that sport, with its emphasis upon performance, records, specialization and elitism, was 'useless'. However, the middle classes viewed the potential political and societal impact of sport as more important than any of its possible shortcomings. From the 1920s to the present, sport was and is seen as central to the creation of meaningful leisure time; its defenders emphasize the element of moral education in sport.

In contrast to other popular movements such as the Free Church and temperance movements, the sports movement has maintained a decidedly consensual perspective, despite its initial upper-class complexion. From the outset, unity across class barriers and fellowship between groups in the community were key objectives. Since the end of the nineteenth century, many in Sweden have said that sport is a phenomenon that transcends and eliminates class distinctions, and has the potential to unite classes and population groups.[53] Although democratically elected, the leading figures within the sports movement at the turn of the twentieth century (particularly on the national level) came almost exclusively from an aristocratic or middle-class background. The notion of sport as a consensual activity was one addressed to the working classes. This was possibly due to the fact that the middle-class people involved in the sports movement looked on it as a means of neutralizing the socio-political demands of the working classes: a mechanism to achieve consensus between the classes. The Swedish sports model is entirely dependent upon the voluntary support of local leaders as well as public funding, especially from local government.

The origins of the Japanese sports movement

In the 1870s at the dawn of Japanese modernization, modern sport was introduced by a variety of foreign countries and was soon enjoyed as recreation (for example, the origin of Japanese baseball was a by-product of the country's education policy).[54] Sport and physical education are closely related phenomena, especially in Japan, where sport is widely considered a sub-category of physical education. Understanding Japanese sports also means considering the development of physical education in the country. When Japan was modernized, an educational system similar to those of the US and Western Europe replaced the patchwork of local schools. Promulgating the Education Ordinance in 1872, the Meiji government institutionalized physical education in schools. Physical education, and above all gymnastics, was also deemed to be a necessary part of the curriculum for girls for no other reason than to prepare them for their future role as healthy mothers of boys destined to become defenders of the nation. However, this motivation ran counter to traditional notions of female modesty and beauty.[55] Schools focused on modern sports and played an important role in the development of sports in Japanese society. Baseball in particular and tennis were the most popular both before and after the Second World War. These sports were recreational activities that were originally enjoyed after school by Japanese students.[56] The British school system during the late-Victorian period also influenced Japan's educational system. The idea of Japanese school sports, germinated as student recreation, acquired cultural meaning through students' values. British sportsmanship inspired, instructed, and motivated Japanese youth 'physically, morally, and politically' – it was seen as the equivalent of the qualities of the old samurai culture or *Bushi*.[57] Different publications during the late nineteenth and early twentieth centuries stated that Japanese boys could learn moral qualities such as fair play, observance of rules, decision-making, self-reliance, compassion, decency, and loyalty from games. In short, the nature of British sportsmanship was not unlike the Japanese 'samurai spirit'. Both had the ambition of creating strong individuals for a strong state. Japan's growing imperialism was based upon Japanese sportsmanship; British sportsmanship was perceived as the source of British imperialism. If modern British sportsmanship had made Britain strong and brought it global pre-eminence, 'then Japan wanted both the means and the method'.[58]

Educational values then became associated with school sports, which society recognized; by 1935, school sports had become an established socio-cultural institution. Japanese sport creeds focused upon cultivation through sport that was linked to, and influenced by, Zen Buddhism, Confucianism, and Taoism.[59] Sport in Japan was not about playing games or having fun; it was an educational tool that taught children about obedience and hierarchy in an organization, as well how to withstand the pain of long training sessions. This made sport the ideal preparation for a working life spent in a Japanese company, in which the ability to work well in a group, accept a strict hierarchy, and tolerate punishing hours of work were all highly valued.[60] The promotion of sport through school education was very effective and, as Kotani put it, the government's promotion of sport through school education was 'very effective', although 'voluntary or citizen-led initiatives have not been fostered.'[61]

Sport culture was soon diffused all over Japan. According to Guttman and Thompson, some during the Taisho period (1912–1926) regarded sport as an end in itself to be pursued for its own intrinsic pleasure; any positive results accrued for the body and soul were extrinsic. Others viewed sport as a way of strengthening the nation by improving the physical condition and moral character of its people. The former view was probably the prevalent one. However, as the nation changed course and began its march towards war, this liberal and individualistic approach to sport was abandoned; a militaristic, collectivist, and instrumentalist view of sport became predominant. The Taisho period saw a rapid acceleration in the diffusion of modern sports during the 1920s.[62]

Traditional martial arts were banned during the Occupation with the exception of sumo, which was allowed to resume before the end of 1945. However, American advisors actively encouraged participation in baseball and other modern sports.[63] Sports were introduced into school curricula after the war, which meant that children from the lower classes could also experience sport. However, mass participation was ignored, as sport was regarded as something to watch rather than something in which ordinary people could take part.[64] The national middle-school baseball tournament was revived in January 1946; it was stressed that this would contribute to 'the development of democratic spirit and the reconstruction of Japan.'[65] As Guttman and Thompson conclude, 'Ideology changed: rhetoric did not: sport was for the good of the nation'.[66] Sport was still an amusement of the ruling classes at the beginning of the 1960s, and ordinary people were just spectators.

The post-war years saw the reconstitution of the industrial and commercial leagues that had offered pre-war Japanese an opportunity to continue to participate in sports after the end of their formal education. For most men and many women in the workforce, their company's sports programme provided the facilities for ball games and the martial arts. During the early 1960s and the rapid growth of the Japanese economy, industries began to advocate sport for their labour management. Uchiumi and Ozaki state that the main purpose of this was 'the enhancement of worker's physical fitness and health and the integration of young workers who had been influenced by socialism.'[67] Some have maintained that the special characteristic of Japanese sport has always been the role played by business enterprise.[68] The city of Koriyama is highlighted as an example of this situation in the first post-war decades. In 1962, 10,000 of the city's 138,000 inhabitants were members of sports clubs, mostly at school or at their place of employment. Not until the 1970s did sport policies 'for all' became a bigger interest in Japanese politics.[69]

Sweden and Japan compared

By comparing the development of the sports movement in Sweden and Japan, we can conclude that there are obvious differences. Although the sports movement in Sweden was initially inspired by British amateurism and organized by middle-class men, it was a voluntary and popular democratic movement that was open to everyone. The Swedish Sports Confederation organized voluntary organizations or clubs: it was autonomous in relation to the state, although the state did support it financially from the 1930s through the state-owned sport-gambling corporation. In this sense, the system is a corporate one. The idea of sport in Sweden has always been that it has the potential to unite classes and population groups in order to strengthen the political vision of the 'People's Home', as the welfare state is known. Conversely, sport was organized from above in Japan: as a political instrument of discipline, obedience, and hierarchy in order to prepare people for a life working in a Japanese company, which benefited Japan's economic development through 'effective' government-led projects such as school education. Sports in Japan have traditionally developed in school settings. 'Voluntary' or 'citizen-led' initiatives have not been fostered. In contrast to the Swedish model, membership of sports clubs correlates with social class, and clubs at the community level open to all were, and are, virtually non-existent. The highly educated and wealthy citizens were, and still are, more likely to be members of sports clubs and to participate in the clubs' activities.[70] Most sports and exercise programmes today in Japan are offered in four settings: schools, workplaces, private sport clubs, and community sport clubs. Once people graduate, the opportunities to continue regular participation in sport are limited.

Swedish company sports

I have chosen Sandviken Ironworks as a case-study, not for its success in Swedish sport, but because the company is quite simply a good example of a 'model industrial community' of the type common once the welfare concept of the 'People's Home' was established. Sandviken is situated in the county of Gästrikland, some 160 km north of Stockholm; it was founded in 1862 with the establishment of the ironworks. The cooperation that existed between the company and the local community in Sandviken, in sport as well in other local matters, was similar to that in other industrial communities in Sweden. In this sense, the study's findings have broader implications.

Several informal and formal meeting-places for personal contacts between the company and its employees were formed in Sandviken (especially during the 1920s) in order to counteract the general antagonism of labour and capital. The company's proprietors believed that hegemony would be secured via integration with the consent of the other classes in society. Integration and consensus would be achieved through education: the workers were to study economic and social questions and discuss the problems of trade and industry at discussion clubs. Hegemony could be established through local contacts, everyday conversations, and discussions in the neighbourhood about everyday problems. Karl Fredrik Göransson, the manager of Sandvikens Jernverks AB (Sandviken Ironworks Ltd), emphasized that an authoritarian style was no longer necessary and that the company could count on increased loyalty as long as it showed an interest in its workers. The message was that everybody at the foundry should be proud of working and living in the industrial community of Sandviken. The importance of building solidarity, unity, and consensus within the established system was emphasized for 'the common good'.[71] Sport (particularly football) was used in this project from the beginning of the 1920s. The company actively supported sport by giving land and financial support for the creation of sports fields. Jernvallen, Sandviken's stadium, was built in 1937 as a gift to company employees and the rest of the community. Göransson made prominent appearances at various sporting events in order to emphasize his interest in sport and shared 'love' for the ironwork's teams. He pointed to the health and moral benefits of participation in sport, stressing in particular the use of sport as an example of what the people of Sandviken could accomplish through cooperation. Sport, and particularly football, was viewed as a promoter of loyal cooperation among friends under the supervision of a competent management who understood the importance of team spirit.[72]

According to tradition, workers at the ironworks established the sports club Stjärnan (The Star) in 1901. The name was changed in 1907 to Sandvikens AIK (SAIK) when the club joined the Swedish Football Association. SAIK became the first worker-dominated football club in the country to establish a reputation for itself. Besides SAIK, the community also had Sandvikens IF, originally founded under the name of Kronan (The Crown) in 1903. There does not appear to have been any class differences between the teams. The ironwork's leader attempted to bring about a merger, in the belief that local identity and pride would most easily be formed if one powerful team represented the community. The fact that this merger never came about indicates that the company's power might have been great, but it was by no means absolute.[73] The clubs consisted mainly of local talent, and occasionally players signed from other clubs. These 'outside' players were offered good jobs at the ironworks.[74] The possibility of work also attracted many football players to Sandviken. From the 1930s to the end of 1950s, nine out of eleven regular players in Sandvikens IF worked at Sandviken's ironworks, of whom eight or nine were blue-collar workers.[75] Besides signing good players, the company was able to pay for good coaches and arrange for the players to train often and at reasonable hours. The clubs demanded that players behave appropriately; members of the clubs were excluded whenever they behaved 'improperly at club parties'.[76] They made it clear that members 'who behaved badly' were not welcome at parties that the club had arranged.[77] Applicants for club membership went through a vetting procedure. The clubs also emphasized the importance of the same moral characteristics as those of Göransson's didactic paternalism: steadiness, honour, a sense of justice, and consideration. Both the clubs and the trade unions demanded sobriety from their members.[78] As one sports journalist commented, one of the reasons behind Sandvikens IF's success was that 'Sandviken is dry, which contributes to the fact that its football stars are extremely steady.'[79]

One can easily identify the positive effects of the clubs' activities on the company; involvement in sport encouraged discipline and respect for the community and for authority. Members rejected alcohol and other demoralizing wastes of time such as gambling, and were fostered into collective and democratic ways of life through the culture of club meetings, where discipline and order were regular topics of discussion. The players of the various teams were also taught to obey the orders of the team captain without reservation. The recipe for success was hard work, dependability, discipline, and order. The company's interest in sport was not confined to the elite level either, since its proprietors felt that the spirit of Sandviken should be instilled in as many people as possible. Thus management made provision for a broad range of sports, especially football, that created a more widespread sense of solidarity between individuals at the ironworks and strengthened local community spirit (*Sandviksandan*).

In the same way, Åtvidaberg Industries (later Facit AB) dominated the community of Åtvidaberg, and here similar effects can be found. The management adopted an instrumental view, in which sport was seen as a way of eliminating class distinctions and creating solidarity.[80] There was a conscious strategy on the part of the management to use football to create a spirit of togetherness that would lead to greater solidarity between the community and the company. The image the management wanted to create was one of a harmonious society: a model society where the managing directors, Elof Ericsson (1922–1952) and then his son Gunnar Ericsson (1952–), considered the trade unions and the local Social Democrats to be their collaborative partners. Sport (especially football) served as a link between the management and the inhabitants of this model society. Facit's financial support was substantial, especially during the 1940s and 1960s.[81] Both father and son were very interested in sport, again especially football. Elof Ericsson was elected chairman of the Swedish FA in 1937 and regarded the local team, Åtvidabergs FF, as 'Elof's boys'. Football managed to communicate the image of Åtvidaberg as a model industrial society in which consensus and solidarity prevailed. Åtvidabergs FF won the Swedish football league championships in 1972 and 1973.

Japanese company sports

The 1920s were also the formative years for Japan's industrial leagues. Innumerable companies institutionalized their commitment to paternalistic capitalism by sponsoring baseball teams or encouraging their employees to establish them. Although the Yawata Iron and Steel Works, situated in northern Kyushu, was government-owned, its managers' attitudes to labour relations were essentially the same as those of a private enterprise. When Japanese industry was hit by a wave of strikes in the winter of 1920, Yawata Iron and Steel was not spared. In an effort to improve worker–management relations that were less than cordial, the company sponsored a baseball tournament. The plant's workers organized a representative team in 1924, which the company duly recognized in 1926. In 1927 the company team began to play against teams from other companies. Crowds of seven or eight thousand gathered to watch the games. At first, workers were expected to play baseball in their own time; the experiment in social control was so successful that members of the representative team were allowed to begin their daily practice at 1 p.m. The entire team was transferred to Yawata Iron and Steel's main office and given tasks that were considerably less strenuous than shovelling coal into a blast furnace. The company was of the opinion that this was a worthwhile use of resources. The management was persuaded that on-the-job productivity would increase and that sports would promote harmony between capitalists and workers. According to Guttman and Thompson, the management became enthusiastic and self-interested advocates of the ethos of fair play, good sportsmanship, teamwork, and adherence to the rules of the game – all qualities of an ideal worker. The companies who sponsored baseball teams were convinced that their sports programmes were beneficial to their employees as well as the firms themselves.[82]

The course of Japanese society was not entirely stable following the Second World War. Nakayama indicates that the Japanese government found it necessary to suppress both the radical political movement and the organized labour movement. Recreation in the workplace and corporate sport were developed as counter-measures to political and labour pressures. An enhanced corporate consciousness and a focus upon the welfare of employees were also emphasized. The Ministry of Education regarded the promotion of physical education in the workplace to be the responsibility of management. In cooperation with the Japan

Recreation Association, the Japan Federation of Employer's Association also launched a programme to support recreation in the workplace, which was increasingly encouraged throughout the 1960s. According to Nakayama, recreation in the workplace was a means of securing both young workers for a corporation and the social support needed by workers who had been exposed to industrialization and urbanization processes. Moreover, for the companies, the strong promotion of efficient production relied 'on the worker's will to work'.[83] Therefore, the Ministry of Education argued, the significance of sport and recreation in the workplace came to be highly regarded as maintaining the health of labourers. However, there would be an adjustment in the human relations between labourers and their superiors. Many employees of major corporations lived in company flats or houses in a company town, and received various company benefits needed to maintain their lifestyle. Besides the company corporate community, the large enterprises provided 'support extending to all aspects of regular workers lives'.[84] Many medium-sized businesses also set up sports clubs in addition to providing sporting – and living – facilities. The Ministry of Education conducted a survey, which revealed that large and medium-sized enterprises had particularly improved their facilities and organization of sport in the workplace; however, public facilities for sport were poorly equipped and the organization of sport in communities was underdeveloped. An 'enterprise-based welfare' that included recreation in the workplace was, and still is, an integral part of the Japanese style of management, and is regarded as an important factor in Japanese industrial development.[85] Human relations within the corporation extend to, and penetrate, the labourers' private lives; therefore, their life processes are completely assimilated into the dominant corporate system, and a kind of 'corporate community relations' is formed. The conflicts of interest between workers and management are absorbed into 'corporate cooperative systems' based upon this 'community feeling', neutralized by the reverence for the corporate consciousness. Corporate sport or recreation in the workplace was considered important for building and enhancing corporate community consciousness.

The special characteristic of Japanese sports has always been the role that business enterprises play. This is hardly unique, but it is certainly prevalent. The post-war years saw a reconstruction of the industrial and commercial leagues that had offered pre-war opportunities to those living in Japan to continue to participate in sport after the end of their formal education. For most men and many women in the workforce, it was the company's sports programme that provided the facilities for ball games and martial arts.[86] Company policy defined much of post-war Japanese life, and sport was no exception. Japan had no sport clubs for local community use and no teams representing local towns. Instead, football, volleyball, and basketball were all played in schools, colleges, and companies. Company players were full-time employees who usually spent the morning in the factory or at the office and then trained in the afternoon, and ate breakfast, lunch, and dinner together in the canteen. Sebastian Moffet says that, in contrast to professional or amateur Western sport, Japan's company sport resembled a capitalist version of the state-amateurism practised in Eastern Europe's Communist era. In order to improve their morale and help them identify with their employer, companies formed teams that played each other in a corporate league. Workers followed their company team's progress on the radio and in the newsreels. Companies also organized sports days, swimming excursions to the beach, and educational classes. Activities such as these helped to nurture a family corporate ethos – and enabled employers to manage workers' leisure time.[87]

Corporate sport began in the 1950s, as Japan began its post-war reconstruction. Textile companies set up the first big company sports teams. After 1965 and improved media coverage, corporate sport also became an interest that united employees; it then became more important for the company's name to be seen on television and in the newspapers.[88] The British introduced football in the Meiji in 1873 thanks to the efforts of a British naval commander; it then spread slowly via academic institutions, although it remained a marginal sport until the 1960s.[89] The Japan Football Association (JFA) was set up on 10 September 1921. Although most Western sports were introduced into Japan around the end of the nineteenth century, baseball quickly outstripped all the others; football was a minor affair. This changed in 1960 when a team from the electric wire manufacturer, the Furukawa Electric Company, became the first company team to win the Emperor's cup. An amateur football league, the JSL, which consisted of company club teams, was established in 1965.[90] Moffet describes a footballer's day at the company Yanmar Diesel: Takayoshi Yamano had a regular job at the company, but 'it wasn't really a job, and there wasn't anything for me to do'. The real day started in the afternoon, when he would train at the company football ground from two to five o'clock. He played matches against other companies at the weekends, which was his real value to the company because the results appeared in the paper along with the company's name.[91]

It was the trade union that initiated cultural and sports activities at the Toyota Motor Company until around 1950, and these activities were considered quite remarkable. Management first took a positive interest in cultural and sporting activities in around 1951, while the union was weakened by a recent major labour dispute. In this situation, the company constructed several different sports arenas for various sporting activities. The Toyota General Sports Meeting, which included ten companies allied to Toyota, was also held. The company constructed a general sports arena in 1957 and formed the Toyota Club, an integrated organization, in 1959. Most members in the sports section of the Toyota Club were clerks, engineers, and skilled factory workers, while representation from unskilled workers was low.[92] Around this time the company prioritized sports activities over cultural activities, and the promotion of sporting activities for all its employees over the development of sports clubs for athletes. In addition, sport and recreation, as well as the public relations magazine and the company communications system, were recognized to 'play a most important role in uniting the various groups within the company.'[93] The goal was to develop a 'Toyota Man' and create a Toyota spirit. Nakayama emphasizes that social studies and physical education are included as part of the life guidance provided for the trained worker. Teamwork is stressed and regarded as important in physical education. Morale, human nature, and trust in the corporation are informed by the spirit of cooperation, and this cooperative consciousness is produced by teamwork. The teamwork that develops through physical education soon leads to a sense of being a Toyota team member. The organization for skilled workers also has a committee for physical education that organizes sports teams at every company location and runs the training and internal company matches.[94] The role of sport in the workplace has been to develop employees' enthusiasm for work, to bring them into a harmonious relationship, and to cultivate a feeling of solidarity and corporate awareness. In 1960, Toyota City had a population of about 47,000, of which approximately 14,000 were employees of the Toyota Motor Company. Toyota City's governing sports body (Taiiku-Kyokai) consisted of 22 sports associations, many members of which were employees of the Toyota Motor Company or associated corporations.

Conclusion

If we briefly compare company sports in the two countries, we can conclude, from the examples offered by the different companies, that in Sweden sports were frequently used in the integration project from the beginning of the 1920s, both in theory and in practice. The companies actively supported sport by building sports grounds and providing financial support for the clubs. In their educational philosophy, the management of the companies pointed to the health and moral benefits of participation in sport, in particular emphasizing the use of sport as an example of what the management and employees and their families could accomplish thorough cooperation. Sport was viewed as a promoter of loyal cooperation among friends under the supervision of a competent management. In Japan, sport was also supported by companies from the beginning of the 1920s in an effort to improve relations between employer and employee. The management philosophy was that sports would promote harmony between capitalists and workers and that production figures would increase. Like fair play, good sportsmanship, and teamwork, sports ethos was an important concept. After the Second World War the support of corporate sport was intensified as a counter-measure to political and labour pressures, egged on by the Ministry of Education, which considered physical education in the workplace a management responsibility. Corporate sport was considered important for the creation and improvement of a corporate company community consciousness: a harmonious relationship.

We can conclude from this study that the attempt to nurture responsible and loyal co-workers could be optimized if a paternalistic strategy was used across the board and employees were encouraged to pursue activities that would strengthen the ties between companies and their employees. These areas can be considered no-man's-land in the struggle between labour and capital. The social integration project created a need for new and more efficient forms of socialization. In the 1920s and on in both Sweden and Japan, sport was one of the new elements in the integration project; an arena in which hegemony over the workers was established and the possibility of conflict minimized. Spare time was identified as an opportunity to nurture and encourage the workers through the playing of new, organized, codified, and rule-bound sports and learning to accept and respect authority figures. In Sweden, football was singled out as a particularly valuable tool for achieving these ends, and the management of various companies felt that by founding and supporting a football club they could create common ground with their workers and hence achieve hegemony through consensus. In Japan, in response to workers' radicalization and in order to prevent such influence, companies have made strong attempts to compete for their employees' leisure time, considering such efforts to be a part of management strategy. Companies have organized and supported sporting and cultural events in numerous ways – and with copious amounts of money. The main difference between the countries is how sport was organized and modelled. In Sweden it was regarded as a popular democratic movement that Swedish company managers understood how to use, whereas in Japan company managers organized sports as a means of establishing cooperation. As the Swedish historian Torbjörn Andersson has pointed out, in Sweden companies prevented their clubs from going professional because the consensus regarding amateurism was too strong.[95] In Japan, the support from the government began to decline in the 1980s, and commercially-based sports clubs increased dramatically.[96] In order to be effective producers, the companies clearly needed physically fit and disciplined workers, and both in Sweden and Japan sport was viewed as an important way of ensuring an effective workforce. This was clearly an important factor in the companies' support for sporting activities. However, the role of sport and the sports movement as an institution that taught moral virtues, sportsmanship, and respect for authority, and inculcated a sense of fair play, was also important, as these were qualities that would be beneficial to the companies. The argument presented in this chapter is that sport was important in creating a consensus between employer and employee, for it was a way of reaching stability and, ultimately, hegemony within the confines of the companies. The conclusion of this study is that although there are obvious historical and cultural differences between companies in Britain, the US, Australia, Italy, Sweden and Japan – differences in both the industrialization and modernization of these countries, and in how sport was introduced and how it was shaped – there are similarities in its use in company strategy as an integral part of an educational philosophy. One explanation for this is that it was business enterprise that created these similarities. Companies saw sport as a way of strengthening company spirit and company harmony.

Notes

1 Brian Stoddart (ed.), *Sport, Culture and History: Region, Nation and Globe* (London 2008).

2 Stoddart (2008), p. 45.

3 Stoddart (2008), p. 73.

4 James Anthony Mangan, 'Imperial Origins – Beginnings', in: J. A. Mangan & Fan Hong (eds.), *Sport in Asian Society: Past and Present* (London 2003).

5 Mangan (2003), p. 37.

6 See, for example, Stephen G. Jones, *Sport, Politics and the Working Class: Organised Labour and Sport in Inter-war Britain* (Manchester 1998).

7 See, for example, Charles Korr, *West Ham United: The Making of a Football Club* (London 1986); John Bale, *Sport and Place: A Geography of Sport in England, Scotland and Wales* (London 1989); John Hargreaves, *Sport, Power and Culture: A Social and Historical Analysis of Popular Sports in Britain* (New York 1986).

8 Korr (1986), pp. 3–4.

9 Bale (1989), pp. 28–29.

10 Paul Gilchrist, 'Sport Under the Shadow of Industry: Paternalism at Alfred Herbert Ltd' (2008), p. 1–4, <http://brighton.academia.edu/PaulGilchrist/Papers/119284/Sport_under_the_shadow_of_industry_paternalism_at_Alfred_Herbert_Ltd> (accessed 18 June 2011).

11 Ibid. p. 3.

12 Ibid. pp. 16, 18.

13 Roger Munting, 'The Games in Ethic and Industrial Capitalism Before 1914', *Sport and History*, 23:1 (2003) p. 50.

14 Ibid. pp. 53, 56.

15 Ibid. p. 63.

16 Gerald Gems, 'Welfare Capitalism and Blue-Collar Sport: The Legacy of Labour Unrest', *Rethinking History*, 5:1 (2001), pp. 43–44.

17 Ibid. pp. 43, 47.

18 John R. Schleppi, 'It Pays: John H. Patterson and Industrial Recreation at The National Cash Register Company', *Journal of Sport History*, 6:3 (1979), p. 20.

19 Ibid. pp. 22, 24, 26.

20 Phil Mosely, 'Factory Football: Paternalism and Profits', *Sporting Traditions: The Journal of the Australian Society for Sports History*, 2:1 (1985), p. 25, <http://www.la84foundation.org/SportsLibrary/SportingTraditions/1985/st0201/st0201d.pdf> (accessed 18 June 2011).

21 Ibid. p. 31.

22 Paul Dietschy & Antoine Mourat, 'The Motor Car and Football Industries from the Early 1920s to the Late 1940s: The Cases of FC Sochaux and Juventus', in: Jonathan Magee, Alan Bairner & Alan Tomilson (eds.), *The Bountiful Game? Football Identities and Finances* (Aachen 2005), p. 52.

23 Ibid. pp. 52, 57.

24 See the works of historian Jan Lindroth.

25 Rolf Pålbrant, *Arbetarrörelsen och idrotten 1919–1939* (Uppsala 1977); Tomas Peterson, *Leken som blev allvar: Halmstads bollklubb mellan folkrörelse, stat och marknad* (Lund 1989); Bill Sund, *Fotbollens maktfält: Svensk fotbollshistoria i ett internationellt perspektiv* (Uppsala 1997); Torbjörn Andersson, *Kung Fot-*

boll: Den svenska fotbollens kulturhistoria från 1800-talets slut till 1950 (Eslöv 2002).

26 Bo Andersson & Thommy Svensson (eds.), *Samhälle och idrott i Jonsered 1830–1980* (Alingsås 1985); Christer Ericsson (2002); id., *Fotboll, bandy och makt: Idrott i brukssamhället* (Stockholm 2004); Torbjörn Andersson, 'Fotbollen i Finspång', in: Lars Lagergren & Anette Thörnquist (eds.), *Finspång en bit av folkhemmet: Sju uppsatser om ett industrisamhälle under 1900-talet* (Bjärnum 2006), pp. 65–93.

27 Håkan Thörn, *Rörelser i det moderna: Politik, modernitet och kollektiv identitet i Europa 1789–1989* (Stockholm 1997), p. 32.

28 Karl Molin, *Den moderne patriarken: Om arbetsledarna och samhällsomvandlingen 1905–1935* (Stockholm 1998), pp. 102–103; Christer Ericsson, *Vi är alla delar av samma familj: Patron, makten och folket* (Stockholm 1997).

29 Molin (1998), pp. 115–120.

30 Ericsson (1997).

31 Karl Fredrik Göransson, *Hur man sköter sitt folk: Samförstånd mellan företagare och arbetare* (Stockholm 1927), p. 44.

32 Christer Ericsson, *Kapitalets politik och politikens kapital* (Stockholm 2008).

33 William M. Tsutsui, *Manufacturing Ideology: Scientific Management in Twentieth-century Japan* (Princeton 2001), p. 14; Masayuki Tanimoto (ed.), *The Role of Tradition in Japan's Industrialization: Another Path to Industrialization* (Oxford 2006).

34 David Flath, *The Japanese Economy* (Oxford 2003), pp. 40–41.

35 Curtis Andressen, *A Short History of Japan: From Samurai to Sony* (Sydney 2002), pp. 88–91.

36 Tsutsui (2001), p. 15; Flath (2003), p. 41.

37 Andressen (2002), p. 90.

38 William M. Tsutsui, 'Rethinking the Paternalist Paradigm in Japanese Industrial Management', *Business and Economic History*, 26:2 (1997).

39 See, for example, Tsutsui (1997), pp. 561–562.

40 Ibid. pp. 566–569.

41 Quotation from ibid. p. 567.

42 Quotation from ibid. p. 568.

43 Sven Lundkvist, *Folkrörelserna i det svenska samhället 1850–1920* (Uppsala 1977), pp. 190–191.

44 Jan Lindroth & K. Arne Blom, *Idrottens historia: Från antika arenor till modern massrörelse* (Farsta 1995) p. 190.

45 Bo Öhngren, *Folk i rörelse: Samhällsutveckling, flyttningsmönster och folkrörelser i Eskilstuna 1870–1900* (Uppsala 1974), p. 11.

46 Tomas Peterson, 'The Professionalization of Sport in the Scandinavian Countries', Idrottsforum.org, 20 February 2008, <http://www.idrottsforum.org/articles/peterson/peterson080220.pdf> (accessed 18 June 2011).

47 Ibid.

48 See Leif Yttergren, *Täflan är lifvet: Idrottens organisering och sportifiering i Stockholm 1860–1898* (Stockholm 1996). For a discussion of sportification see, for example, Eric Dunning and colleagues: Eric Dunning, *Sport Matters: Sociological Studies of Sport, Violence and Civilisation* (London 1999).

49 See Jan Lindroth, *Idrottens väg till folkrörelse: Studier i svensk idrottsrörelse till 1915* (Uppsala 1974), pp. 82–84.

50 Further, see Paul Sjöblom, 'En svensk idrottsmodell i marknadstappning: Värderingar,

normer och strategier i kommuner och föreningar 1970–1999', Idrottsforum.org, 15 March 2006, <http://www.idrottsforum.org/articles/sjoblom/sjoblom060315.pdf>.
51 Lars Göran Tedebrand, 'Idrott och etablissemang', *Historisk tidskrift*, 95 (1975); Pålbrant (1977).
52 See, for example, Pålbrant (1977).
53 Jan Lindroth, *Gymnastik med lek och idrott: För och mot fria kroppsövningar i det svenska läroverket 1878–1928* (Stockholm 1993), p. 45.
54 Johnny Wijk, *Idrott, krig och nationell gemenskap: Om riksmarscher, fältsport och Gunder Hägg-feber* (Eslöv 2005).
55 Yuko Kusaka, 'The Emergence and Development of Japanese School Sport', in: Joseph Maguire & Masayoshi Nakayama (eds.), *Japan, Sport and Society: Tradition and Change in a Globalizing World* (London & New York 2005), pp. 19–23; Kanji Kotani, 'Sustainable Sport and Environmental Problems', in: ibid. p. 92.
56 Allen Guttman & Lee Thompson, *Japanese Sports: A History* (Honolulu 2001), pp. 90–93.
57 Kusaka (2005), pp. 19–22.
58 Ikuo Abe & J. A. Mangan, "Sportsmanship' – English Inspiration and Japanese Response: F. W. Strange and Chiyosaburo Takeda', in: James Anthony Mangan & Fan Hong (eds.), *Sport in Asian Society: Past and Present* (Portland 2003), p. 102.
59 Ibid. pp. 102, 104, 109, quote at, p. 111.
60 Kusaka (2005), pp. 33–34.
61 Sebastian Moffet, *Japanese Rules: Japan and the Beatiful Game* (London 2002), p. 92.
62 Kotani (2005), p. 92.
63 Guttman & Thompson (2001), p. 129.
64 Ibid. p. 163.
65 Kazuo Uchiumi & Masataka Ozaki, 'History of Sport Policy and Sport Industry in Japan Since 1945', *Hitotsubashi Journal of Arts and Sciences*, 34 (1993), p. 104.
66 Quote from Guttman & Thompson (2001), p. 164.
67 Ibid. p. 164.
68 Uchiumi & Ozaki (1993), pp. 106–107.
69 Guttman & Thompson (2001), p. 166, referring to Sugimoto Atsuo.
70 Uchiumi & Ozaki (1993), p. 108.
71 Masaru Ikeda, Yasuo Yamaguchi & Makoto Chogahara, *Sport for All in Japan* (Tokyo 2001).
72 Göransson (1927), pp. 3, 8–9.
73 Karl Fredrik Göransson, Family archive, vol. 52, Riksarkivet (Swedish National Archives), Stockholm.
74 Saik archive, meeting records 1907, Sandviken's Municipality Archive (SKA).
75 Bill Sund, 'Fotboll och makt', in: Eva Blomberg, Björn Horgby & Lars Kvarnström (eds.), *Makt och moral: En vänbok till och med Klas Åmark* (Linköping 1998).
76 *Idrottstidningen* 1933; *Rekordmagasinet* 1956.
77 For an example, see SIF meeting records, 29 March 1925, SAK.
78 SAIK meeting records, 21 March 1925, SKA.
79 For example Svenska Metallarbetare förbundet, avd. 135, Sandviken, meeting records, 12 March 1928, SKA.
80 *Idrottstidningen*, 27 September 1933.

81 R. Andersson, 'Elofs grabbar: Fotboll, industri och samhälle i brukssamhället Åtvidaberg', diss., Linköpings University 1997; Tom Petersson, 'Fotboll som företagar- och varumärkesstrategi: Åtvidabergs FF, Åtvidabergs Industrier/Facit och familjen Ericsson', *Idrott, Historia, Samhälle: Svenska idrottshistoriska föreningens årsskrift* (2006), pp. 51–72; Ericsson (2004).
82 Petersson (2006), p. 60.
83 Guttman & Thompson (2001), p. 132.
84 Masayoshi Nakayama, 'Economic Development and the Value of Sport', in: Maguire & Nakayama, (2005) p. 62.
85 Nakayama (2005), p. 63.
86 Nakayama (2005), p. 63.
87 Guttman & Thompson (2002), p. 166.
88 Moffet (2002) pp. 7, 9.
89 Moffet (2002) pp. 8–10.
90 Guttman & Thompson (2001), p. 216; Moffet (2002) p. 8.
91 Guttman & Thompson (2001), p. 216. Hitoshi Ebishima & Rieko Yamashita, 'FIFA 2002 World Cup in Japan: The Japanese Football Phenomenon in Cultural Contexts', in: Maguire & Nakayama (2005), p. 125.
92 Moffet (2002), p. 7.
93 Nakayama (2005), p. 64.
94 Ibid. p. 64, citing Nihon Jinbun Kagaku-Kai.
95 Ibid. p. 64.
96 T. Andersson (2006).
97 Takayuki Yamashita, 'The Changing Field of Japanese Sport', in: Maguire & Nakayama (2005), p. 161.

PART III

INSTITUTIONAL CHANGE

CHAPTER 11

Productivity in Swedish Merchant Shipping, 1470–1820

Johan Söderberg

There are few issues on which economic historians tend to disagree as much as the conditions of the emergence of the modern world market. One important aspect of this is the long-term trend in sea freight rates and the productivity of merchant shipping. Some prominent researchers argue that freight rates were substantially reduced only after the introduction of steamship in trans-oceanic trade after 1820. Kevin O'Rourke and Jeffrey Williamson place this issue into a wider context as they maintain that this transition also marks the beginning of globalization. Only with this transport revolution could commodity prices converge worldwide. Prior to this, long-distance trade was limited to expensive goods such as silk, silver, and exotic spices, which could bear high transport costs. In that world, trans-oceanic trade had an impact only on the living standards of the very rich who could afford such luxuries. With the steamship, regional markets with different prices melted together into a world market. As international freight rates collapsed, trade volumes increased, particularly in cheap and bulky goods.

According to these authors, globalization is a very modern phenomenon. Moreover, the 'big bang' of globalization (to use O'Rourke and Williamson's expression) can be dated to a short and decisive period: the 1820s.[1] Other scholars have arrived at quite different conclusions from the available evidence. Douglass North has argued that freight rates in Atlantic shipping declined from about 1600 due to improved organization combined with the decline in piracy and privateering, allowing ships to reduce the cost of manpower and armaments. Better security was the key to cheaper freight.[2] Charles Knick Harley has questioned North's analysis and dates the start of the long-term decline in transatlantic freight rates to about 1850 (that is to say, to an even later date than O'Rourke and Williamson). According to Harley, the decisive factor was that the advances of the Industrial Revolution were applied to shipping with the introduction of metal hulls and steam propulsion. Harley interprets these results as affirming the primacy of mechanical invention.[3]

Some researchers observe an increased efficiency in shipping already during the medieval period. Peter Spufford notes that new types of ship were developed during the fourteenth century, such as the Hanseatic cog and the carrack in the Mediterranean, which saved on crews compared to previous types of vessel. The sailing ships of Venice, Genoa, and Barcelona grew in size and became cheaper to run. As a result, freight rates for grain and other bulk cargoes dropped. This made it possible to trade in bulk goods between the Mediterranean and north-western Europe.[4]

The cost of sea freights can also be related to the question whether or not there was any general tendency towards a relative price decline for knowledge-intensive goods in Europe in the medieval or early modern era. If prices of knowledge-intensive goods declined, this should have been to Europe's advantage in gaining world economic dominance; it may also have been part of creating the prerequisites of the Industrial Revolution. For instance, Hoffman (2006) reports that preliminary data from Britain, France, and Germany show that the relative price of artillery, handguns, and gunpowder declined between the fourteenth and the eighteenth century. Price data thus suggest a potential explanation for why the West developed a comparative advantage in violence over the rest of the world.[5]

The price of long-distance sea freight is of great interest in this context as it depended upon developments in shipbuilding, access to information about supply and demand of various goods, and the organization of trade at a high level. Seen from this perspective, the relative price of sea freight can be classified into a broader group of goods (that is to say, iron, paper, and books), the production of which required comparatively large amounts of knowledge and capital.[6]

The seemingly innocent question of shipping productivity thus turns out to have a bearing on at least three big research issues:

- The view that long-term economic growth took off during the nineteenth-century Industrial Revolution or resulted from a much longer process that may have started as early as the Middle Ages.

- The evolution of relative prices of knowledge-intensive goods and services, and their role in the emergence of European economic dominance.
- The prerequisites and timing of globalization.

These issues are obviously important for our understanding of the economic history of the world. However, all of them cannot be addressed in this chapter. Instead, here the focus will be upon the evolution of labour productivity in the long term from about 1470 to 1820.[7] Two data sets are used. The first and largest one is based on merchant shipping data from Stockholm, while the second derives from the Swedish East India Company in the period 1732–1803.

A few years ago, I came across some sparse data suggesting that the cost of sea freight fell during the late medieval period in Sweden. I was curious to know if this could be explained by the use of larger ships. I asked Jan Glete for his opinion. He answered promptly, as always, in an email of 12 January 2006, giving the following information:

> I have not seen any research that can give any good clue as to the role of the evolution of ship sizes for transport costs in Swedish foreign trade. What we know is that cargo ships were built increasingly larger during the late Middle Ages, and that the technological development of the rig made this possible. However, technological progress improved smaller ships as well, and it is evident in a long-term perspective that scale advantages in shipping were of rather limited importance until the breakthrough of steamships. Small vessels continued to be competitive, partly because they were more flexible and could bring small cargoes to shallow ports, but partly because the advantages of scale were limited with sailing-ships.
>
> Timber and equipment cost about as much for large and small ships, calculated per tonne of cargo. The crew also must be approximately in proportion to the size of the ship, since the handling of sails and anchors was done with muscle power. Some overhead costs could be reduced with a larger cargo, but I find it difficult to see any dramatic difference.
>
> One reason why bigger ships could be cheaper was that they were less expensive to protect: a large crew was, by itself, a factor that served to discourage plundering, whereas smaller ships needed a larger crew (or sailing in convoys) to get protection. If heavy weap-

> ons were taken aboard for protection larger ships had a considerable cost advantage relative to smaller vessels. Very small vessels, with little space below deck and with no room for superstructures, cannot have been well suited to long, uninterrupted voyages. The somewhat larger ships, on which the crew could sleep below deck or in a closed superstructure, had a considerable advantage here since they could sail continuously. However, a carrying capacity of a few hundred tonnes was sufficient to accomplish that, and the major part of long-distance trade in Northern and Western Europe was probably carried out with such ships. In the Mediterranean, very large ships (carracks) were built, but they were probably primarily designed to provide protection by means of hulls and large crews.
>
> These are just a few thoughts on the matter. Much remains to be done here. (Author's translation)

Jan had an unusual ability to develop an independent point of view in a compact yet lucid manner. His historical vision inspires this chapter. It summarizes the evidence on the scale advantages in shipping in Sweden prior to the advent of the steamship, and presents new results on the evolution of labour productivity in shipping in the Stockholm trade as well as in the East Indian trade.

Ship size and cargo up to the mid sixteenth century

The documentary evidence for Swedish merchant shipping during the medieval period is scanty. Most of the available information refers to cargoes rather than to the maximum carrying capacity of the ships. However, comparisons of actual loads may be quite as interesting from an economic point of view as data on ship measurements. Carrying capacity and actual loads were expressed in lasts. The composition of cargo is not usually reported in the sources used for this study. A weighted average of three different lasts has been constructed: the iron/copper last, the salt last, and the grain last. This average composite last comprises 1.8 tonnes for the period 1470–1664 and 2.0 tonnes for the period 1665–1820 (see Appendix for details).

The Gdańsk toll books are among the best available sources for the extent and composition of Swedish foreign trade in the late fifteenth century. A total of fifty-seven ships arrived at Gdańsk from Stockholm in the three years 1474–6.[8] Their average cargo can be estimated at 10 tonnes per ship, or 11 tonnes if vessels without any cargo are excluded.[9] These figures do not inform us about carrying capacity, yet they do provide a strong indication that small vessels dominated this trade route. A few years later, similar information is available for ships leaving Gdańsk for Stockholm: a total of twenty-seven ships for the years 1490–2. The average cargo was then higher: 17 tonnes.[10] We do not know whether the increase since the mid 1470s was due to different mixes of Swedish ships versus presumably larger Hanseatic ships, to a real growth in cargo sizes during the late fifteenth century, or if it can be explained by other factors. At any rate, it seems clear that the average cargo was rather small, not exceeding 20 tonnes.[11] Other pieces of information point in the same direction. In a letter from 1507, the Mayor and Council of Stockholm reported that a ship of five lasts had arrived from Lübeck with a cargo of stone and sand. Four boatswains were aboard.[12] Assuming that these men were the crew, this corresponds to the very low tonne-per-man ratio of 2.25. In 1508, a clergyman in Finland reported that his ship of six lasts (11 tonnes) had been taken from him off Tallinn; it was carrying a cargo of half a last of train oil and two lasts of rye.[13] Even though this was a small ship, it did not carry a full cargo.

The sources become much more detailed a few decades later. In 1536, twenty-one ships arrived at Stockholm from Gdańsk with an average cargo of approximately 35 tonnes. The average cargo of Swedish ships leaving Stockholm was about 60 tonnes in 1549 and again in 1560 (in the latter year, ships making for Gdańsk carried an average cargo of 78 tonnes).[14] These are much higher figures than those we have noted for the Stockholm–Gdańsk trade in the late fifteenth century, and suggest a strong increase in actual cargoes since that date. If we accept the average cargo of 11 tonnes per ship in the mid 1470s and the 1549 figure of 57 tonnes, annual growth amounts to an impressive 2.3 per cent. Similar comparisons can be made for other points in time. As summarized in Table 1, the average growth rate between the late fifteenth and the late sixteenth centuries varies between 1.2 and 1.6 per cent per year. This appears to have been an extremely dynamic period in the history of merchant shipping in Sweden.

The growth of cargoes was certainly linked to the construction of larger ships. In 1536, the biggest domestic ships in the Stockholm trade carried a cargo of 75 tonnes. This fell far short of the largest ships arriving at Stockholm from Hamburg and Gdańsk, of which at least eight carried cargoes: from about 90 up to 180 tonnes in the same year. By 1549, the situation was already quite different. The two largest domestic ships in the Stockholm trade now held cargoes of 575 and 285 tonnes, respectively, and there were several others exceeding 100 tonnes.[15] The ability to build large domestic ships had much improved, partly thanks to the recruitment of skilled shipwrights from abroad. In a few years in the mid sixteenth century, seven or eight large carriers of approximately 300 to 600 tonnes, most of them defensively armed merchantmen, were built at various shipyards in the country. Sweden also purchased ships from Lübeck and the Netherlands, and they could of course be copied.[16]

The development of shipbuilding capacity in Sweden is in turn related to the emerging consolidation of state power. Jan Glete has characterized King Gustav Vasa (1523–1560) as 'an innovative fiscal-military entrepreneur'.[17] He had a keen interest in strengthening the navy as well as the merchant fleet. It was during his reign that the Baltic was cleared of pirates for the first time; the Swedish and Danish navies, competing with each other, managed to uphold a maritime monopoly on violence. In Jan Glete's formulation, this pacification meant that the Scandinavian kings were selling protection to shipping in the Baltic in return for customs duties. The Danish king officially raised the Sound Toll on the grounds that it financed his protection of foreign shipping. The Swedish leadership also wanted to bring about more competition among merchants, which would lead to lower import prices.[18]

Kjell Kumlien has estimated the average size of cargo on ships leaving Stockholm for Gdańsk to have been 43 tonnes (24 lasts) for some years in the 1580s, whereas shiploads on the Stockholm–Lübeck route were larger at an average of 63 tonnes. Kumlien adds important information, as he states that the average crew was six men on both routes.[19] This makes it possible to calculate tonne-per-man ratios, which turn out to be 7.2 on the Gdańsk route and 10.5 on the ships headed for Lübeck. In an international perspective, these are high figures for the period. Labour productivity was clearly higher in the Stockholm trade than in the English merchant fleet, where it was only about 5 in the 1580s, similar to the ships of German Hanseatic towns around 1600.[20]

The relationship between average cargo sizes and maximum carrying capacity is not known. For the mid sixteenth century, however, the geographer Nils Friberg has carried out a thorough study of shipping in Stockholm. He assumes that cargo comprised 80 per cent of the carrying capacity of ships in domestic trade arriving at Stockholm from northern Sweden or Finland. He argues that, in sailing from the Finnish province of Österbotten to Stockholm, peasant-traders commonly used a traditional ship type that required a crew of five men when crossing the Gulf of Bothnia and had a capacity of 11–16 tonnes.[21] The average cargo at the time was 9–13 tonnes. Based upon carrying capacity, the tonne-per-man ratio would have been in the range of 2.2 to 3.2.

If we accept these calculations, the average cargo carried by the peasant-trader ships in the Österbotten–Stockholm trade in the sixteenth century was about the same as the average shipload in the Stockholm–Gdańsk trade around 1475. Due to the probably more frequent use of ship types that were more advanced than those the Österbotten peasant-traders used, although not that different from what we have seen in the Österbotten–Stockholm trade around 1550, it seems reasonable to expect labour productivity for the latter route to be somewhat higher. Allowing for some guesswork, a tonne-per-man ratio in the range 3.0–3.5 is a realistic estimate of the average labour productivity of the Stockholm–Gdańsk trade in 1475.

Based upon these ratios, an estimate of the growth of labour productivity of 1.1 to 1.3 per cent a year is obtained for the period from 1475 to the late 1580s. We may note that, in their broad overview of shipping productivity in Europe, Lucassen and Unger find no case of tonne-per-man ratios reaching 5 prior to the mid sixteenth century. Even a somewhat lower tonne-per-man ratio of 4–5 was quite high by international standards of the day.[22]

Labour productivity in the Stockholm trade, 1580–1820

There are plenty of archival sources available that allow researchers to further explore the evolution of ship and crew sizes in Sweden in the early modern period.[23] Starting in the late seventeenth century and continuing up to 1841, captains of ships departing Stockholm had to report to the city's Board of Trade (*Handelskollegium*), their name and residence, the name of the ship and its home port, as well as details of the crew. These lists are called ship records (*skeppsprotokoll*) up to 1741.[24] Each crewman was listed by name along with his age, residence, and pay. For many years (though not for most of the first half of the eighteenth century), the size of the ship (in lasts) is also given. There is often information on the type of ship (galleon, brigantine, and so on). Some volumes of ship records also detail the owners of the ship as

Table 1: Average annual growth of cargo ships in the Stockholm trade, 1470s to 1580s

Start year	*Route*	*Average cargo, tonnes*	*End year*	*Route*	*Average cargo, tonnes*	*Growth rate, %*
1474/76	Stockholm–Danzig	11	1549	Swedish ships leaving Stockholm	57	2.3
1474/76	Stockholm–Danzig	11	1560	Swedish ships leaving Stockholm	62	2.1
1490/92	Danzig–Stockholm	17	1536	Danzig–Stockholm	35	1.6
1490/92	Danzig–Stockholm	17	1549	Swedish ships leaving Stockholm	57	2.1
1474/76	Stockholm–Danzig	11	1560	Stockholm–Danzig	78	2.3
1474/76	Stockholm–Danzig	11	1586/88	Stockholm–Danzig	43	1.2
1474/76	Stockholm–Danzig	11	1586/88	Stockholm–Lübeck	63	1.6
1536	Danzig–Stockholm	35	1586/88	Stockholm–Danzig	43	0.4

Sources: Lauffer (1893), pp. 16, 31; Forssell (1875), pp. 40–42; Kumlien (1953), p. 290.

well as the names of the charterers who paid the freight. This is a rich source that could be useful for many research purposes; only data on ship size, crew size, and home port (except in 1692) are used for this study. Basic statistics are presented in Table 2 for four cross-sections at 1692, 1750, 1780, and 1820, along with similar data for the 1580s. Very few steamships were in use by 1820, and they are not included in the material used here.[25]

As seen in Table 2, the mean size of ships departing from Stockholm in 1692 was 142 tonnes. The median was considerably lower at 100 tonnes. This difference was due to a small number of large ships influencing the mean, yet not the median; the biggest ships were rated at 300 lasts (600 tonnes). Thus the average size was twice that of the ships on the Stockholm–Lübeck route in the 1580s, and nearly three

Table 2: Average size and tonnage per man of ships leaving Stockholm in the 1580s, 1692, 1750, 1780, and 1820

Variable	**1580s**	**1692**	**1750**	**1780**	**1820**
Carrying capacity, metric tonnes	66	142	129	125	130
Size of crew	6.0	9.4	7.9	7.3	7.1
Tonnage per man on board	11.0	13.4	14.8	15.4	16.7
Tonnage per man on board, Swedish ships			14.4	14.6	16.1
Tonnage per man on board, non-Swedish ships			15.6	18.1	19.5
N, all ships		230	437	550	462
N, Swedish ships			241	429	380
N, non-Swedish ships			171	121	82
Swedish ships, %			42	78	83

Source: Kumlien (1953), pp. 290, 298; Handelskollegiet, Sjöfolkskontrollen, Skeppsprotokoll (1692) and Skeppsinlagor/manlistor (1750, 1780, and 1820), Stockholms stadsarkiv.

Note: Ships with Swedish homeports (including Finnish ports) are classified as Swedish; all others are considered non-Swedish. The carrying capacity of the 1580s is based upon the assumption of a relationship of cargo to carrying capacity of 80 per cent.

times that of ships going to Gdańsk during the same period. In other words, a sizeable increase in the size of Stockholm merchant ships had taken place between the late sixteenth and the late seventeenth century. Domestic carvel-built and mounted ships paid lower customs dues, since the government wanted them to be used as a naval reserve.[26] The trend towards larger ships was therefore partly driven by the merging of merchant shipping and the early modern military–industrial complex.

The maximum size of Stockholm ships had probably already been reached by the mid seventeenth century, when the average amounted to 274 tonnes.[27] Aksel Christensen presents this finding, noting that Sweden by that time had succeeded in establishing a modern mercantile fleet that could compete with the Dutch traders in the Baltic region. However, this does not necessarily mean that the Swedish merchant ships were built to an optimal size in economic terms. During the latter part of the seventeenth century and the early part of the eighteenth, the average ship size tended to decline.[28] Thereafter the average tonnage of ships did not change much between the late seventeenth and the early nineteenth century; it declined slightly from 142 tonnes in 1692 to 125 tonnes in 1780, after which there was a slight increase.[29]

Labour productivity increased over time, measured as the ratio of the size of the ship to the size of the crew. The average tonne-per-man ratio grew steadily from 13.4 in 1692 to about 15 in 1750 and 1780, and on to 16.7 in 1820.[30] This indicates a high productivity for Stockholm shipping as compared to results from several other studies. For instance, Christopher French finds a tonne-per-man ratio of about 11 in the London–Jamaica trade and 12 in the London–Virginia trade in the mid eighteenth century.[31] North reports much lower figures for ships entering New York, for which the tonne-per-man ratio was no more than 4.4 during the years 1715–1719, increasing to 6.9 tonnes in 1763–1764.[32]

As Table 2 shows, productivity growth was stronger among non-Swedish than among Swedish ships. Non-Swedish ships increased their labour productivity from 15.6 to 19.5 tonnes between 1750 and 1820. Swedish ships exhibited weaker growth – from 14.4 to 16.1 tonnes per man during the same period. The average growth rates amounted to 0.32 and 0.16 per cent per year, respectively. Several Dutch, British, and American ships appear to have had high labour productivity. Thus non-Swedish ships exhibited twice the productivity growth of Swedish ships in the period 1750–1820. This difference in productivity growth can be partly explained by the fact that Swedish ships were declining in average tonnage, from 147 tonnes in 1750 to 124 tonnes in 1820, while non-Swedish ships showed the opposite trend, increasing from 107 to 160 tonnes.

At the same time, Swedish ships became more dominant in terms of total shipping to Stockholm, increasing their share from 55 to 82 per cent between 1750 and 1820. Stockholm shipping, then, gives the impression of increasingly being divided into two. By the end of the period, relatively small Swedish ships dominated one segment. They were probably sailing shorter distances than the larger, non-Swedish ships of the other segment, which was oriented towards freight to the Western European market.

Labour productivity in Stockholm shipping also increased prior to the mid eighteenth century. The average growth in productivity during the period studied is reported in Table 3. For the period from the 1580s to 1820, annual growth amounted to 0.18 per cent.[33] For this reason it is important to note that rising labour productivity was not produced by taking larger ships into use, but by saving on manpower. Average crew size declined from 9.4 in 1692 to 7.9 in 1750, and further to 7.3 and 7.1 in 1780 and 1820, respectively. Labour productivity var-

Table 3: Average annual growth of labour productivity of ships leaving Stockholm, 1580s to 1820

Period	Growth rate, % all ships	Swedish ships	Non-Swedish ships
1580s–1692	0.08		
1692–1750	0.17		
1750–1780	0.12	0.05	0.50
1780–1820	0.20	0.24	0.19
1580s–1820	0.13		

Sources: Table 1 and Kumlien (1953), pp. 290, 298.

ied systematically according to the size of the ship. There was a strong correlation between the size of the ship and the tonne-per-man ratio for all years under consideration (Figures 1 to 4). However, we can also discern a tendency towards a levelling out of productivity among larger ships. Among ships of approximately 150–200 tonnes or more, labour productivity did not increase much with increasing size.

The graphs also reveal interesting differences between the four cross-sections. The most notable is that ships with a very low labour productivity disappeared with time. In 1692, there were numerous ships with a labour productivity of less than 10 tonnes per man aboard, whereas only a few such ships existed in 1820. This, of course, contributed to a higher average level of productivity. The distribution of ship sizes in 1820 was clearly more compressed compared to that of 1692. It is remarkable that the productivity changes were largely taking place at the low end of the scale, not the high end.

Labour productivity in the Swedish East India trade, 1732–1803

The outlier on the far right of Figure 2 demands comment. This ship, the *Prins Carl*, belonged to the Swedish East India Company and weighed 930 tonnes. Built in Stockholm in 1750, it left the capital for Gothenburg, which was the usual port of departure for voyages to China. The ship had a crew of 104 men, which was much more than other large merchant ships at the time, and consequently a low tonne-per-man ratio. The *Prins Carl* was designed for an even larger crew of

Figure 1: Ship size and tonnage per man in 1692

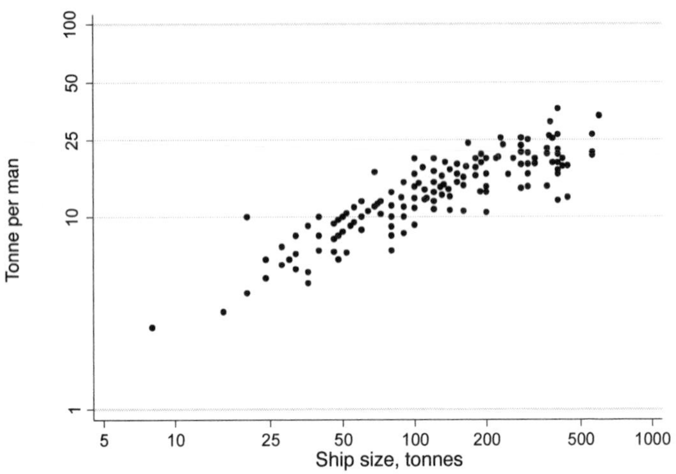

Figure 2: Ship size and tonnage per man in 1750

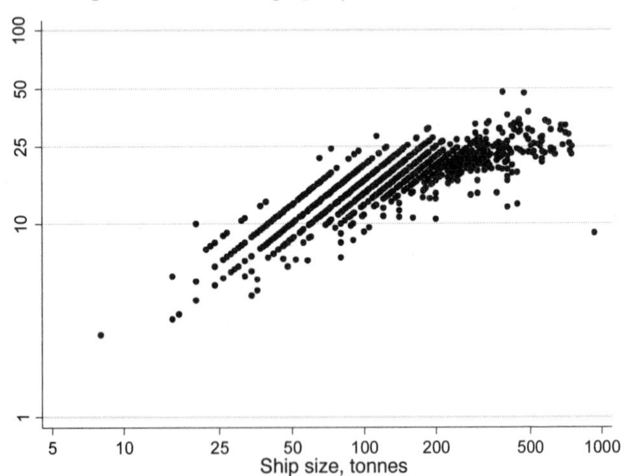

140 men when sailing to the East Indies, which would bring down the tonnage per man even further. It also carried thirty cannons, which was normal for Swedish East India Company ships by the mid eighteenth century.[34] This low tonne-per-man ratio was a typical feature of the ships of the Swedish East India Company. A heavily armed ship and large crews were considered essential to ensure security during the long journey, and the high value of the cargo brought home was calculated

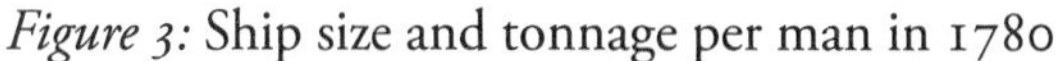

Figure 3: Ship size and tonnage per man in 1780

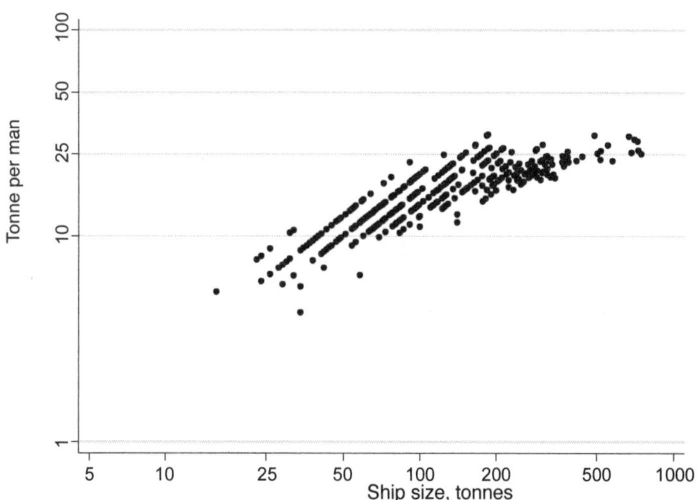

Figure 4: Ship size and tonnage per man in 1820

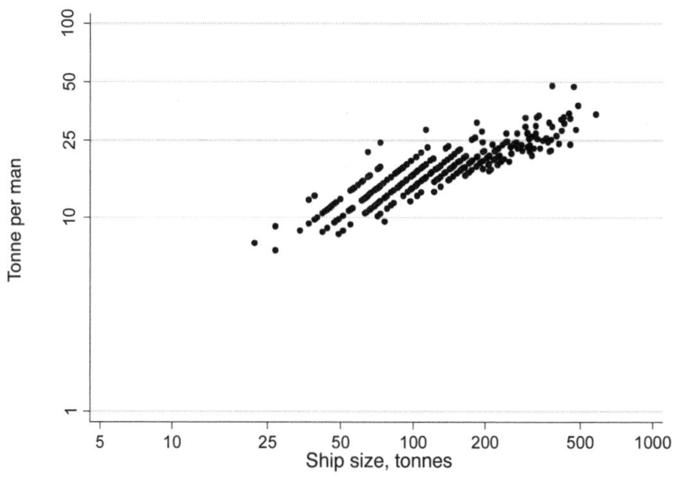

to pay for the cost of protection.[35] The *Prins Carl* made a handsome profit of 40 per cent on its first voyage. Profits of the order of 30 to 40 per cent were common among the ships of the Swedish East India Company by the mid eighteenth century.[36]

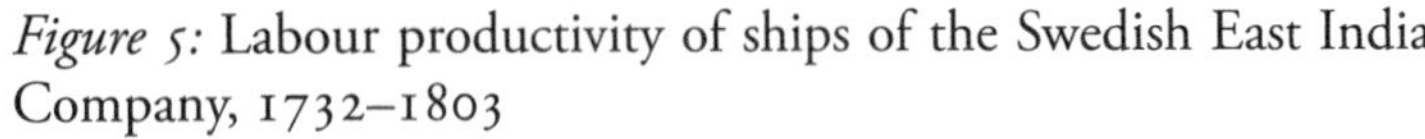

Figure 5: Labour productivity of ships of the Swedish East India Company, 1732–1803

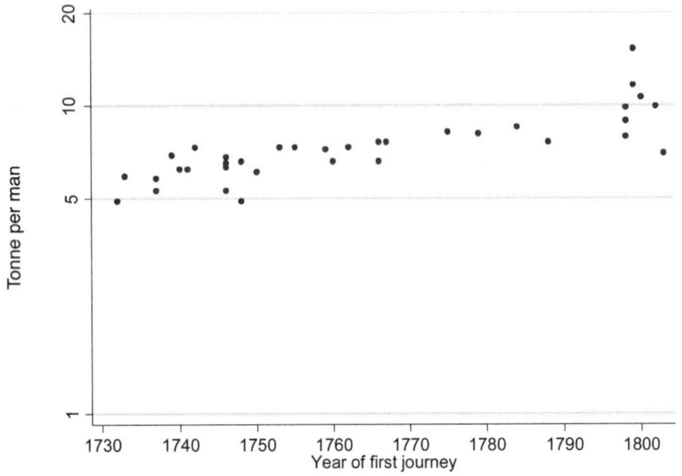

The different risks on the trade routes are reflected in marine insurance premiums. These were quite low in the mid eighteenth century for ships from Stockholm to destinations in the Baltic or the North Sea (1 per cent of the value of the cargo to Lübeck, 2 per cent to London); higher for Mediterranean destinations (5 per cent to Alicante and Marseilles); and even higher for the ships to China (11 per cent for the two-year voyage Cadiz–Canton–Gothenburg).[37] These were peacetime premiums. The cost of insurance increased dramatically during wartime. This was the case after the outbreak of the Russo-Swedish War in 1788, when, according to the directors, insurance against capture could not be acquired even for premiums of 70 to 80 per cent of the cargo.[38]

There was, however, room for considerable productivity growth among the Swedish East India Company ships. The first of the Company ships began its journey in 1732. Over time, their tonnage increased, average crew sizes remained fairly constant at about 125 men, and the number of cannons was reduced. It seems that none of the cannons on any of the ships were ever fired in anger, although they were made ready in a few threatening situations.[39] This experience may have facilitated the transition towards more lightly armed ships. As a consequence of these changes, the tonne-per-man ratio gradually inched up (as shown in Figure 5). It approximately doubled, from not more than 5 at the start of the series to 10 in around 1800. The average productivity growth in the period 1732–1803 was 0.8 per cent per year.[40] This is a much higher rate than that reported in the previous section for ships departing from Stockholm, and accords with Douglass North's observation that tonne-per-man ratios were consistently lower on routes where there was a threat from pirates (such as the East Indies) than on routes that had been pacified (the Baltic, Northern Europe, and the North Atlantic).[41] As the perceived risk of piracy diminished, substantial productivity growth could be achieved by investing less in defence measures.

Despite this productivity growth, East India voyages became unprofitable towards the end of the eighteenth century. Most of the profits of the Swedish East India Company came from the tea trade to Britain and the Netherlands. These markets were to all intents and purposes closed to the Swedish East India Company during the 1780s and 1790s due to changing toll and import regulations. Meanwhile, American ships began to sail to the East Indies, successfully cornering much of the market. The directors of the Swedish East India Company maintained that American shipping benefited by several circumstances, such as a more favourable geographical location, low-cost shipbuilding, and cheap access to silver from Spanish America.[42]

Concluding discussion

This study has shown that the labour productivity of merchant shipping in Stockholm grew in the late medieval and early modern periods. Initially, this was primarily an effect of increasing size of ships; later, from the late seventeenth century onwards, productivity gains stemmed from falling crew sizes. As a result, the average tonne-per-man ratio rose from approximately 11 in the 1580s to 13.4 in 1692, and again to 16.7 in 1820.

Why then did ship sizes not increase after the mid seventeenth century? Research on Dutch shipping has shown that the ships employed on the Baltic route were increasingly confined to a standard range of tonnages. Even though the Dutch could build large ships of up to 800 tonnes in the early seventeenth century, these were not used in the Baltic trade. Following a period of experimentation with various types and sizes of ships, the range of tonnages narrowed; vessels of 200–240 tonnes had become dominant by the 1630s, and this seems to have been the optimal size for this route.[43] The use of larger ships apparently had its disadvantages, such as long waiting periods before a ship could acquire a full cargo.

The Stockholm data examined here encompass a variety of routes, and we should certainly not expect to find any strong tendency towards a single, optimal ship size. Yet, it is worth noting that the choice of ship size was the subject of considerable controversy in Sweden. An interesting debate took place in the early 1720s, shortly after the end of the Great Northern War,[44] when some of the leading Stockholm merchants argued that, in order to press down freight prices, ships should be of a minimum 150 lasts (300 tonnes). Only the large ships were capable of carrying Swedish goods to distant countries and returning home to Sweden with those countries' products – especially salt, which was regarded as the most essential import.

The Stockholm merchants were strongly divided on the issue, however. The majority spoke up in favour of small and medium-sized ships: they were easier to charter, quicker to load and unload, and able to sail faster, while swift, small ships (frigates) stood a better chance of avoiding pirates in the Mediterranean trade.[45] Not all foreign ports could accommodate large ships or were interested in cargoes of up to 1,000 tonnes of iron. Other arguments were that European industrial imports did not require a large tonnage, and that big ships suffered from overcapacity when visiting medium-sized or small ports. The majority conceded that the small ships were proportionately more expensive to fit out, yet argued that no one would use big or small ships for their own sake; rather, it would be because they were suited to the particular purpose of the trade. Meanwhile, the Board of Trade (*Kommerskollegium*) recommended lower toll fees (*helfrihet*) for all carvel-built ships of at least 50 lasts (100 tonnes) that had been constructed in Sweden, as well as for all ships that sailed beyond the Channel, regardless of size – a proposal the government accepted. In other words, the advocates of small and medium-sized ships emerged victorious from the debate. This was in contrast to the policies pursued before and during the Great Northern War, when large ships had been favoured.[46] The notion that it always made economic sense to use as large a ship as possible was questioned; there were growing doubts as to whether large ships were the optimum in the late seventeenth and early eighteenth centuries.

To a certain extent, these results parallel North's in his study of Atlantic shipping, which concluded that average ship sizes increased very slowly, if at all, until 1800.[47] Yet labour productivity increased substantially due to declining crew sizes. More efficient manning was thus the key to rising labour productivity in Atlantic shipping. This seems to also have been true of Stockholm shipping during the late seventeenth and eighteenth centuries. The results, however, diverge in another respect. The average size of ships in the Stockholm trade increased substantially before the mid seventeenth century. A transition from small- to middle-sized ships was taking place between the late medieval period and the late sixteenth century. North disregards productivity advances prior to 1600, whereas this study underscores them. The key period came between 1475 and the mid sixteenth century, during which time average cargoes grew by about 2 per cent a year.

There was a tendency towards weaker productivity growth in the Stockholm sea trade during the eighteenth century. However, this did not apply to all Swedish shipping. The Swedish East India Company offers an example of a relatively strong growth of labour productivity of approximately 0.8 per cent per year during the period of 1732–1803. This clearly outdistanced the merchant ships in the Stockholm trade, where the corresponding figure was not more than 0.1–0.2 per cent during the same period.

The sources of productivity advances thus varied according to the period and the type of shipping. The major gains in the phase of dramatic growth in the Stockholm trade (*c.* 1475–1560) seem to have been in terms of the size of cargo per ship, which was connected to the use of larger ships. The trend was very different after the late seventeenth century, when crews were substantially reduced while ships declined somewhat in tonnage. Yet another trend appeared in the East India trade as ships grew in tonnage over time; crew sizes, however, did not decline. Lower protection costs seem to have been decisive in the productivity growth on the East India route. This bears out North's emphasis on the importance of protection costs in productivity change. The results also highlight the versatility of productivity advances in shipping: if one road forward was blocked, another could be found and exploited.

Two different methods have been used here for estimating productivity growth: the first, employed for the period up to the 1580s, is based upon comparisons of actual shiploads carried; the second, used for the period from the 1580s to 1820, relies upon data on the ratio between carrying capacity and crew size, and does not take actual loads into account. Using certain assumptions, the results for the two periods can be linked in order to obtain an estimate of long-term productivity growth. Disregarding the pitfalls, labour productivity growth was estimated at 1.1 to 1.3 per cent per year for the period from the mid 1470s to the 1580s. This is a much stronger growth than that for the period from the 1580s up to 1820, when it was only about 0.2 per cent per year. For the entire period in question, which stretches from the 1470s to 1820, labour productivity growth can be estimated at approximately 0.5 per cent a year.[48]

Three main results emerge from this study of Swedish shipping. The first is that productivity growth shows a long continuity, covering several centuries. While the transition from sail to steam certainly was a breakthrough, the long evolution of the technology and the shipping economics were also of great significance; it laid the groundwork for the transformation of the nineteenth century. The second main result is that the major phases of growth came quite early in the process: from the 1470s up to the seventeenth century. Jan Glete was correct in emphasizing the importance of improved safety for the expansion of seaborne trade in the Baltic after approximately 1570.[49] However, there was also an earlier phase of remarkable growth with regard to the size of ships and cargoes from approximately 1475 up to the mid sixteenth century. This growth cannot have been the result of pacification of the Baltic, which had not occurred by this point. Apparently, ship sizes and labour productivity could grow despite the existence of piracy, privateering, and war. Two factors may have been of particular importance here. The first was the advent of the Dutch in the Baltic trade, offering low-cost competition with the Hanse. Late medieval Swedish rulers strived for increased trade with the Dutch, noting that their presence in the Baltic served to reduce prices. One result of this was increased salt imports from Amsterdam to Stockholm.[50] Another factor, as Jan pointed out in his email quoted above, was that larger ships could be more heavily armed, and that, along with the size of the crew, should have deterred pirates. In other words, poor safety encouraged the construction and use of larger ships.

The third result was that an average annual labour productivity growth of 0.5 per cent was seen over a period of 350 years. This is an impressive achievement for a pre-industrial economy. Though such a growth rate may seem low by modern standards, it clearly surpasses any evidence of most economic activities prior to the Industrial Revolution. For example, real income per capita in Holland is likely to have grown by approximately 0.1 per cent per year during the same period. Had per capita growth in the Netherlands been 0.5 per cent rather than 0.1 per cent during the period of 1475–1820, real income by 1820 would have been more than four times as high than was the case.[51]

In contrast to O'Rourke and Williamson's assertion, long-distance trade prior to the introduction of the steamship was not always limited to luxuries such as silk and exotic spices, which only affected the living standards of the very rich. Trade in cheap and bulky goods (meaning grain and timber) was possible in the Baltic centuries prior to the early nineteenth century; this was also true for similar trade between the Baltic and north-western Europe, and contributed to price convergence between markets that were separated by quite substantial distances. Globalization is not a very modern phenomenon after all. Neither are productivity advances in shipping.

So was Jan on the right track when he conjectured about the nature of pre-industrial shipping? Was his scepticism regarding the advantages of scale well founded? In the very long run, scale did indeed have an impact: the smallest vessel in the 1820 cross-section of Stockholm shipping was 22 tonnes, which may well have exceeded the average ship size of the 1470s. There is no doubt that larger ships generally saved on labour. Nevertheless, the cost of labour was only one component in the total cost. The early modern Stockholm trade offers a complexity that brings to mind Jan's discussion of the interplay between technological progress, flexibility, and size. The very small ships that were common in the late seventeenth century were unable to survive over time. Meanwhile, it is clear that average ship sizes did not grow during the period 1692–1820, imposing an upper limit on advantages of scale, just as Jan suspected. Not only middle-sized ships continued to be competitive; many small vessels were as well.

The advantages of scale are more evident in the Swedish trade with the East Indies. This long-distance trade used increasingly large ships, which saved on labour. As fewer and fewer cannon were carried as the eighteenth century progressed, the China trade also benefited from reduced costs of protection. Nevertheless, these ships were unable to compete with American ships towards the end of the century. Once again, advantages of scale did exist; however, they are not necessarily the key to understanding the problem.

Jan thought that the history of Swedish shipping in the pre-industrial period has not received the attention that it deserves. This is likely to remain the case for some time. However, potential researchers will always be able to find inspiration in Jan's fascinating writings in the field of maritime history.

Appendix: weights and measures

Prior to 1726, when the 'last' was standardized at 2.448 tonnes, there were several different lasts in use in Sweden. A mathematics textbook from 1693 distinguishes between a small last of 12 barrels, a medium last of 18 barrels, and a large last of 24 barrels.[52] In addition, the size of the last varied for different goods. The weight of the fifteenth-century grain last in Stockholm can be estimated to have been about 2⅓ tonne due to the fact that its relation to the Lübeck grain measure (the *Schepel*) is known.[53] The iron last was lighter than the grain last: it is thought to have corresponded to 12 shippounds, or 133 kg in Stockholm from the mid sixteenth century to 1634 and 136 kg thereafter.[54] This meant a 12-barrel iron last was 1.596 tonnes up to 1634 and 1.632 tonnes thereafter. The salt last varied in size. There are examples of a last of 12 barrels, and also of 16 and 18 barrels. The Stockholm authorities decided in 1478 that imported salt should weigh 15 lispounds (*lispund*), excluding the weight of the barrel itself.[55] If we assume that one lispound is 6.65 kg and a weight of the empty barrel was 1 lispound, then a barrel of salt would have been 106.4 kg; thus a 16-barrel salt last came to 1.702 tonnes. This weight is assumed here to have applied for the period up to 1600. To further complicate matters, the weight of the lispound increased over time. For the period from 1665 to the mid nineteenth century, it is assumed to have been 8.5 kg.[56] The weight of the 16 lispound barrel of salt would then have been 136.0 kg, corresponding to a 16-barrel salt last of 2.176 tonnes. A weighted average of the various lasts has been constructed based upon these data. Iron and salt were more important than grain in the Stockholm trade. If the iron and salt lasts are reckoned at twice the weight of grain, the average composite last is 1.8 tonnes for the period of 1470–1664 and 2.0 tonnes for the period 1665–1820.

Notes

1 Kevin H. O'Rourke & Jeffrey G. Williamson, 'When Did Globalization Begin?', *European Review of Economic History*, 6 (2002), pp. 23–50.

2 Douglass C. North, 'Sources of Productivity Change in Ocean Shipping, 1600–1850', *Journal of Political Economy*, 76:5 (1968), pp. 959–960.

3 C. Knick Harley, 'Ocean Freight Rates and Productivity, 1740–1913: The Primacy of Mechanical Invention Reaffirmed', *Journal of Economic History*, 48:4 (1988), pp. 851–876.

4 Peter Spufford, 'Trade in Fourteenth-Century Europe', in: *The New Cambridge Medieval History: c. 1300–c. 1415*, ed. Michael Jones (Cambridge 2000) p. 185.

5 Philip T. Hoffman, 'Why Is It That Europeans Ended Up Conquering the Rest of the Globe? Prices, the Military Revolution, and Western Europe's Comparative Advantage in Violence' (2005), <http://gpih.ucdavis.edu/files/Hoffman.pdf>, (accessed 27 May 2011).

6 Peter Lindert et al., 'Preliminary Global Price Comparisons, 1500–1870' (2004), <http://www.iisg.nl/hpw/papers/lindert.pdf>, (accessed 27 May 2011).

7 Here, as in many other studies, labour productivity is measured as the tonne per man ratio. This is not an ideal indicator for several reasons, since it does not take the distance travelled into account and attributes the construction of larger ships, an increasingly capital-intensive activity, to labour only. (For a discussion of various productivity measures, see Gary M. Walton, 'Productivity Change in Ocean Shipping after 1870: A Comment', *Journal of Economic History*, 30:2 (1970), pp. 435–441.)

8 Victor Lauffer, *Danzigs Schiffs- und Waarenverkehr am Ende des XV. Jahrhunderts* (Danzig 1893), p. 16.

9 For an earlier estimate for the year 1474, see Kjell Kumlien, *Sverige och hanseaterna* (Stockholm 1953), p. 275.

10 Lauffer (1893), p. 31.

11 Even though much larger vessels were used in the Baltic trade, it is clear that they were far from dominating the Stockholm–Danzig route. The ships in the salt trade on Tallinn, for instance, were almost invariably larger than 50 tonnes during the fifteenth century: Thomas Wolf, *Tragfähigkeiten, Ladungen und Masse im Schiffsverkehr der Hanse: Vornehmlich im Spiegel Revaler Quellen* (Cologne 1986), p. 157; Mikko Meronen, 'Skutor från 1400-talets början i skriftliga källor', *Bottnisk kontakt*, 12 (2005), p. 112.

12 Svenskt Diplomatariums huvudkartotek över medeltidsbreven (SDhk), <http://www.riksarkivet.se/default.aspx?id=2453&refid=8005>, 35928 (accessed 29 May 2011). A messenger also was on board; however, he is not reckoned as part of the crew in this calculation.

13 Diplomatarium Fennicum, <http://vesta.narc.fi/cgi-bin/db2www/fmu/haku?language=swe>, 5336 (accessed 29 May 2011).

14 Hans Forssell, *Sveriges inre historia från Gustav Vasa*, 2 (Stockholm 1875), pp. 40–42. The cargos reported here take into account that the tonne measure used by Forssell corresponds to 0.884 metric tonnes. His data on average cargos refer to Swedish ships only. Since foreign ships were often larger than domestic vessels, this results in an underestimate of the average cargo in the trade on Stockholm taken as a whole.

15 Forssell (1875), p. 40–41.

16 Jan Glete, *Navies and Nations: Warships, Navies and State Building in Europe and America, 1500–1860*, 1 (Stockholm 1993), pp. 135–137; id., *Warfare at Sea, 1500–1650: Maritime Conflicts and the Transformation of Europe* (London 2000), pp. 116–123; id., *Swedish Naval Administration, 1521–1721: Resource Flows and Organisational Capabilities* (Leiden 2010), pp. 332–346.

17 Glete (2010), p. 74.

18 Glete (1993), pp. 112–114, 133–139. See also Leos Müller's chapter in this volume.
19 Kumlien (1953), pp. 290, 298.
20 Jan Lucassen & Richard W. Unger, 'Labour productivity in ocean shipping, 1450–1875', *International Journal of Maritime History*, 12:2 (2000), pp. 130–131.
21 Nils Friberg, *Stockholm i bottniska farvatten: Stockholms bottniska kontaktfält och handelsfält under senmedeltiden och Gustav Vasa – en historisk-geografisk studie* (Stockholm 1983), p. 154.
22 Lucassen & Unger (2000), p. 130.
23 For a brief overview, see Hans Christian Johansen, 'Scandinavian shipping in the late eighteenth century', *Economic History Review*, 45:3 (1993).
24 In 1742, the ship protocols were replaced by a new series labelled *Skeppsinlagor/manlistor*, which provides similar information.
25 On the beginnings of steamship traffic in Stockholm, see Georg A. Gustavsson & Erik Hägg, *Stockholms ångbåtssjöfart: Ångfartygs-befälhavare-sällskapets minnesskrift 1857–1932* (Stockholm 1932).
26 Carvel-built ships had planks placed edge to edge; unlike traditional clinker-built ships with their overlapping planks. The carvel building technique made for stronger hulls and allowed heavier armament on the decks (Glete (2000), p. 29). In discussions on naval policy in Sweden during the late seventeenth century, carvel-built ships were thought to have twice the lifetime of clinker-built vessels (Sven Gerentz, *Kommerskollegium och näringslivet* (Stockholm 1951), pp. 166–172).
27 Data for 1648 in Aksel E. Christensen, *Dutch Trade to the Baltic about 1600: Studies in the Sound Toll Register and Dutch Shipping Records* (Copenhagen 1941), p. 98. By that time, Dutch vessels dominated Stockholm shipping. However, with an average of 270 tonnes, these were practically the same size as the Swedish ships in Stockholm.
28 Another high figure was reached in 1667 with an average of 238 tonnes; it was of a temporary nature, as a number of Dutch merchant ships were sold to Sweden during the Second Anglo–Dutch war. In 1670, the average size had already declined to 180 tonnes: Birger Fahlborg, 'Ett blad ur den svenska handelsflottans historia', *Historisk tidskrift*, 63 (1923), pp. 240, 246, 254, 274 n 1.
29 Similarly, the average tonnage of the Finnish ships employed in foreign trade did not grow during most of the eighteenth century: Yrjö Kaukiainen, *A History of Finnish Shipping* (London & New York 1993), p. 49.
30 These tonne-per-man ratios are seemingly lower yet they are, in fact, quite consistent with those reported by Leos Müller, *Consuls, Corsairs, and Commerce:. The Swedish Consular Service and Long-Distance Shipping, 1720-1815* (Uppsala 2004), p. 157 for Swedish ships entering Cadiz. Müller estimates this ratio at between 20 and 23 tonnes per man for three years during the last quarter of the eighteenth century. With an average tonnage of just above 300 tonnes, these ships were more than twice as large as the average ship engaged in the Stockholm trade. Ships of 300 tonnes in the Stockholm trade also display a labour productivity slightly above 20 tonnes per man (see Figure 3 for the situation in 1780).
31 Christopher J. French, 'Productivity in the Atlantic Shipping Industry: A Quantitative Study', *Journal of Interdisciplinary History*, 17:3 (1987), pp. 630–631. See also Lucassen & Unger (2000), p. 130, and Müller (2004), pp. 157–158, for other comparisons indicating the comparatively high productivity of Swedish ships.

32 North (1968), p. 959.

33 The tonne-per-man ratio for the 1580s is calculated as the average of 7.2 and 10.5 on the Danzig and Lübeck routes, respectively.

34 Sven T. Kjellberg, *Svenska ostindiska compagnierna 1731–1813: kryddor, te, porslin, siden* (Malmö 1974), pp. 177–184.

35 This applies to the East India trade of other European nations as well. Jan Glete notes that only the large East Indiamen still carried heavy armaments towards the end of the eighteenth century, when piracy in European and American waters had been largely suppressed. Armed ships with large crews were feasible from an economic point of view due to the high value of their cargo: Glete (1993) p. 53.

36 Johan Fredrik Nyström, *De svenska ostindiska kompanierna: Historisk-statistisk framställning* (Gothenburg 1883), pp. 36, 154–157; Kjellberg (1974), p. 314.

37 Leos Müller, *The Merchant Houses of Stockholm, c.1640–1800. A Comparative Study of Early-modern entreprenurial behaviour* (Uppsala 1998), p. 208.

38 Kjellberg (1974), p. 153.

39 Ibid. p. 171.

40 The results reported here are based upon a total of 35 ships. Koninckx has calculated the number of crew per tonne and year on the East Indiamen for the period of 1732–1765 that, as to be expected, gives a significant downward trend: Christian Koninckx, *The First and Second Charters of the Swedish East India Company (1731–1766)* (Kortrijk 1980), pp. 304, 472.

41 North (1968), p. 960. Jan Luiten van Zanden and Milja van Tielhof make the same point with regard to Dutch shipping, where the routes to Norway and the Baltic used small crews compared to the heavily manned voyages to the Mediterranean and Asia: Jan Luiten van Zanden & Milja van Tielhof, 'Roots of Growth and Productivity in Dutch Shipping Industry, 1500–1800', *Explorations in Economic History*, 46 (2009), p. 391.

42 Kjellberg (1974), p. 154.

43 A functionary in Estonia, Paul Casseburg, stated in 1684 that the grain trade with the Dutch was unprofitable with small ships of approximately 30 lasts. Only ships of 150–200 lasts (300 to 400 tonnes) could profit by this trade: Arnold Soom, *Der baltische Getreidehandel im 17. Jahrhundert* (Stockholm 1961), p. 227. This is a higher figure than the optimal size of the 1630s referred to here; however, Casseburg was taking the low Dutch grain prices of the time into account.

44 Eli F. Heckscher, *Ekonomi och historia* (Stockholm 1922), pp. 171–175; Bertil Boëthius, *Magistraten och borgerskapet 1719–1815* (Stockholm 1943), pp. 97–99; Gerentz (1951), pp. 166–172.

45 On the contrast between frigates and the heavy warships with hundreds of men on board, see Violet Barber, 'Dutch and English Merchant Shipping in the Seventeenth Century', *Economic History Review*, 2:2 (1930), p. 261 n. 1.

46 Boëthius (1943), pp. 97–99. The Board of Commerce was already critical of the large ships in 1663, and regarded them as difficult to navigate. The Board feared that the Dutch, using cheaper and lighter ships, would outstrip the Swedes: Fahlborg (1923), p. 216. In another debate around 1680, many Stockholm merchants regarded the smaller ships to be advantageous since their building or purchase did not require foreign loans at a high interest: Gerentz (1951), p. 131.

47 North (1968), p. 958 n. 8.

48 Above, the tonne-per-man ratio in 1475 was assumed to be in the range 3.0 to 3.5. This gives a growth rate of 0.5 percent a year for the period 1475–1820, regardless of whether the calculation is based on the lower or upper point in this interval.

49 Glete (2000), pp. 125–126; see also Leos Müller's chapter in this volume.

50 Johan Söderberg, 'Prices and Economic Change in Medieval Sweden', *Scandinavian Economic History Review*, 55:2 (2007), p. 142.

51 Calculated from data in Stephen Broadberry et al., 'British Economic Growth, 1270–1870: Some Preliminary Estimates', working paper, University of Warwick, 18 March 2010, p. 60.

52 Anders Anderson, 'Om svensk skeppsmätning i äldre tid', *Sjöhistorisk årsbok* (1945–1946), p. 60.

53 Sam Owen Jansson, 'Om läst och lästetal', *Sjöhistorisk årsbok* (1945–1946), pp. 38–40.

54 Mats Morell, *Om mått- och viktsystemens utveckling i Sverige sedan 1500-talet* (Uppsala 1988), pp. 10–11, 30.

55 *Stockholms stads tänkeböcker 1474–1483*, ed. Emil Hildebrand (Stockholm 1917), p. 182.

56 Morell (1988), p. 30.

CHAPTER 12

The Swedish Convoy Office and Shipping Protection Costs

Leos Müller

The role of trade in Europe's economic development since 1500 has drawn much attention in recent years. It seems difficult, even for sceptical scholars, to dismiss the dynamism of the European trade after that date. This early modern commercial dynamism is partly related to the 'discoveries' of transatlantic routes to the Americas and the sea-route to Asia. However, at least regarding Asia, this trade exchange was not new. In comparison with the previously land-based trade, the novelty of the post-1500 European trade boom was the role of ocean-going sailing ships, which made transport much cheaper and which provided Europeans with long-term strategic advantages. The introduction of such ships is one of the crucial explanations for the causes of the early modern European trade boom, and ultimately the causes of European economic and military world dominance since the early modern period.

There are historians who doubt this, and stress the fact that agriculture dominated economies prior to 1800. Trade does not matter much in their story of Malthusian stagnation, and transport mattered even less. In such a perspective, shipping was not very interesting; it was a small, slow sector with barely noticeable changes in efficiency between 1500 and the mid nineteenth century. There was no 'transport revolution' before the introduction of steam and steel to shipping in the course of the nineteenth century, and this late change was causally connected to industrialization. If there was a trade boom before 1800, its origins were to be sought anywhere than the shipping industry.

Undoubtedly, the shift from sail to steam in the nineteenth century amounted to a revolution in transport technology. The fall in shipping costs in the nineteenth century was dramatic, and was a crucial factor in the world trade boom after 1850 and the wave of globalization between 1850 and 1914. However, two points that play down the 'revolutionary' character of the steam-and-steel revolution must be made. First, the revolution was very slow, since the cost benefits of steam compared to sail were very different depending on the routes and trade sectors. Moreover, the spread of steam technology was directly related to the efficiency of the steam engine. Steam engines were still very inefficient mid century. This explains why Sweden's first steamboat, *Amfitrite*, could be launched in 1818, but sailing ships still dominated Sweden's merchant fleet in the 1890s. Only in 1899 did Sweden's steam tonnage exceed that of sail.[1] Secondly, the focus on technological innovation, so typical of the perception of modern economic growth, might conceal the fundamental role of institutional and organizational changes in the post-1500 European trade boom and, indeed, the role of institutional change in the nineteenth century. The organization of trade improved significantly between 1500 and 1800. Waiting times in ports were reduced. Information flows became 'better, faster and cheaper'.[2] Insurance premiums fell, reflecting lower capital costs in the advanced economies as well as improved shipping safety. The long-term development of shipping must therefore be understood in the context of the different factors that affected it – not only technological change and not only industrialization.

The improvements in shipping safety – the protection cost factor – are directly related to the issue of the rise of fiscal-military states in Western Europe. A very important part of this transformation was the build-up of navies, the most obvious examples being Britain, the Dutch Republic, and France. The Baltic also saw a similar build-up, first in Denmark and Sweden, and in Russia post-1700. The naval competition between Denmark and Sweden in the sixteenth century improved shipping safety; by the 1580s, this made the Baltic trade one of the most dynamic economic sectors in the European economy. Jan Glete characterized the process, particularly the difference between wider Europe and the Baltic, in the following terms:

> The pacification of the Baltic was very important … The Dutch used the opportunity to develop peaceful shipping and trade in the Baltic. They began to make large-scale investments in this trade and in the Nordic countries (especially Swedish industry), and Dutch

> shipping interest began to develop cheap cargo-carriers, the *fluits*, specialized for the non-violent Baltic trade … By the 1570s and 1580s, the Baltic became a unique haven for seaborne trade in a Europe where civil wars, piracy, loosely controlled privateering, and unpredictable royal actions causing high protection costs for shipping were the norm.[3]

The post-1500 trade expansion, both global and Baltic, can also be related to institutional and organizational changes across Europe. The concept of protection costs, the focus of this chapter and a source of great interest to Glete, is one possible way of approaching this development. The aim of this chapter is to specifically study one particular institution in Sweden that was established to reduce and externalize the protection costs of Swedish shipping in the eighteenth century. *Konvojkommissariatet*, the Swedish Convoy Office, was founded in 1724 to organize the convoying of Swedish ships sailing to Southern Europe. Yet its major task became maintaining peaceful relations with the Barbary states of North Africa (Algiers, Tunis, Tripoli, and Morocco). These states were engaged in a *guerre de course* against all Christian ships, making shipping in Southern European waters and further afield insecure and costly. Signing a peace treaty, including a gift exchange and a semi-diplomatic recognition of the Barbary states (the appointment of a consul), were accepted ways of making the shipping in Southern Europe more secure. The Convoy Office may also be perceived as an institution that significantly increased the security of Swedish ships in Southern Europe and reduced their protection costs.

Since other shipping nations were less successful in maintaining peaceful relations with North Africa, Swedish ships enjoyed a comparative advantage. This partly explains the long-term increase in Swedish shipping activities in Southern Europe. The Swedish Convoy Office is a revealing example of an institution that reduced the protection costs of trade. I will also argue that, due to Sweden's importance in the tramp trade in Southern Europe, the Convoy Office did indeed improve the general functioning of European trade during the volatile decades of the late eighteenth century. I will specifically look at the motives of Sweden's commercial policy towards Southern Europe after 1700 and the role of the Convoy Office in the institutional shipping package that Swedish authorities created in the 1720s. Moreover, I will outline the development of Swedish trade and shipping activities in Southern Europe and compare this with the outlays of the Convoy Office. Lastly, I will provide a tentative picture of costs and benefits of Sweden's commercial policy towards Southern Europe.

Transport costs and economic development

The development of trade – both short-distance and long-distance seaborne trade – is closely related to the issue of transport costs. There are generally only two mechanisms that determine whether trade will expand: supply-side production costs and productivity; and transport costs and productivity. In an economy in which transport costs constitute a very large share of the final commodity price, even small productivity improvements in transport have a significant impact upon the volume of trade. The early modern economy between 1500 and 1800 was one in which transport costs were prohibitively high, and therefore even small changes in transport costs had an impact.

There is an ongoing debate on the characteristics of economic growth prior to nineteenth-century industrialization and the role of trade in this development. The literature on this subject is rapidly expanding. An important part of the debate concerns the role of early modern shipping and transport costs. Authors who are generally sceptical about the economic development before 1800 tend to be fairly doubtful about the role of trade and transport costs prior to the steam-and-steel revolution.[4] In recent decades, the pessimists have appeared to dominate regarding transport costs. Charles Knick Harley reopened the debate on the transport costs issue in an article from 1988 on the development of British freight rates between 1740 and 1913. He asked if there was a significant decline in freight rates before the introduction of steam and iron in shipbuilding. In the article, Harley challenged an older view, represented by Douglass North, that stressed the role of organizational and institutional changes before steam and steel. Harley's data mainly concern British and American freight rates, yet give clear evidence of a sharp decline in freight rates between the mid nineteenth century and the First World War.[5] Harley does not address the issue of shipping productivity prior to his starting-point of 1740; however, he dismisses the role of organizational and institutional changes before 1800. Productivity change in the shipping industry was a technical issue.

In 1991, the historian of early modern America, Russell Menard, addressed the question of the transport revolution between 1300 and

1800. He found few signs of declining freight rates between the Middle Ages and 1800:

> Freight rates in the mid eighteenth century were only slightly lower than in the best years of the High Middle Ages; productivity gains in transport were not impressive compared to advances in agriculture and manufacturing.[6]

As Menard states, shipping was not a dynamic sector in the early modern economy; any increase in trade volumes had to depend either upon cheaper goods on the supply side or upon changes in demand. Yet Menard does not dismiss the role of organizational and institutional changes in the development of shipping. With the help of freight rate data, Jeffrey Williamson, Kevin O'Rourke, and Saif Shah Mohammed have recently argued for a rapid decline in transport costs as a major factor in globalization between 1850 and 1914. They also state, agreeing with Menard and Harley, that there was no significant productivity change in shipping before 1800. However, they are primarily interested in the process of the globalization of trade after 1850.[7] The issue of productivity in shipping before 1800 is mainly addressed in Williamson and O'Rourke's two articles from 2002. On the one hand, these authors are not so sceptical about trade development; they see significant trade growth before 1800 – 1.1 per cent per annum in the period 1500–1800. This can be compared to Maddison's figures for the growth of GDP per capita, which has been estimated at 0.2 per cent per annum for Western Europe and 0.1 per cent per annum for Europe and Latin America as a whole.[8] On the other hand, the authors argue that all such trade growth can be explained by changes in the interplay of supply and demand. There was no sign of price convergence among the globally traded commodities, which means that the share of transport costs in the final commodity price was the same in 1800 as in 1500.

These authors rely heavily upon price and freight rate data in their work. The great advantage of such data is the detailed and long-term characteristics of the series; the problem is the specific characteristics of the data series. Usually, the freight rate data concern one commodity on one route, often in one country, while the countries covered are usually Britain, the US, and the Dutch Republic. Looking at the variation and volatility of the shipping industry, it is tricky to draw wide-ranging conclusions from such a series.

A more robust indicator of the long-term and general changes in the shipping industry is probably the tonne-per-man ratio on board, expressing the labour productivity in shipping.[9] There are general data on the total tonnages of European merchant fleets, numbers of ships, average tonnages, and crews. Naturally, even such data pose a large number of problems, from measurement of tonnages to the quality of ship registers, to estimates of crew sizes.[10] The Canadian historian Richard Unger has collated such statistics, drawing various conclusions regarding shipping. His view of the shipping sector before 1800 is the opposite to that of Menard, Williamson, and O'Rourke. Unger stressed in a survey of 2006: 'Shipping was almost certainly an engine for economic change in Europe in the sixteenth and seventeenth centuries ... Shipping was the modern, novel and innovative sector, enjoying rapid technical advances.'[11] He sees the shipping sector between 1500 and 1800 as the most dynamic sector in economy. This dynamism was related to more general improvements in shipping: technical as well as organizational. One indicator of the rapid development is the increase in European tonnage from about 0.65–1 million tonnes by 1600 to 3–3.37 million tonnes by 1780, or by between 0.6 per cent and 1 per cent per annum.[12] Such rate of growth in tonnage is consistent with the overall growth in trade and was much higher than the growth of the European economy as a whole. Thus when looking at the total growth in European tonnage, there is no doubt that shipping was one of the most dynamic sectors of the early modern economy and that growth was surely related to the expanding seaborne trade. In spite of the transatlantic trade and the discovery of the sea-route to India, the major boom occurred in closer waters: in the North Sea and the Baltic. However, was this growth related to improvements in labour productivity?

Unger and the Dutch historian Jan Lucassen attempted to calculate labour productivity in European shipping using estimates of tonnages and numbers of men employed. Such estimates met staggering problems, however, due to the lack of comparable data for different merchant fleets and the use of ships on a variety of routes. The Dutch and British datasets that Lucassen and Unger collected indicate growth in the labour productivity of shipping. Regarding Dutch shipping, there was significant growth in tonne-per-man ratio in the seventeenth century, from about 8 tonne-per-man to 18 tonne-per-man; this was followed by a decline to 9–10 tonne per man after 1700. Regarding British shipping, there was a more continuous improvement between the sixteenth and eighteenth centuries, from an average of about 5 tonne-per-man by the 1580s to about 10 tonne-per-man by the 1770s.[13] French and Scandinavian data also show an increase in productivity in the eighteenth century.

Behind such averages, however, there are big differences according to the period (and impact of political events), the sizes of the ships, and the routes plyed. For example, the decline in an average Dutch tonne-per-man ratio in the eighteenth century might be explained by the stagnation of Dutch shipping in the Baltic and by the shift of shipping activities towards the more lucrative yet more dangerous Dutch East India and Atlantic routes that required larger crews. The most labour-efficient shipping routes – those to the Baltic and Norway – still showed improved labour productivity during the eighteenth century. However, this had no noticeable impact upon the Dutch totals.[14]

In a recent article, the Dutch historians Jan Luiten van Zanden and Milja van Tielhof provide a more detailed picture of productivity changes in the Dutch shipping industry between 1500 and 1800.[15] They first calculated the volume of Dutch shipping between 1503 and 1790 in tonne-km and found a long-term average increase of almost 1 per cent per annum. This figure is consistent with Unger's average for the development of European tonnage as a whole (a rate of 0.6–1.0 per cent per annum). An even closer look at the analysed routes and periods shows large differences. From a Swedish point of view, the most significant information concerns the decline in Dutch Baltic shipping between 1650 and 1750, as well as the decline in Dutch shipping in the Mediterranean. These were the two markets in which Swedish shipping expanded. This decline of the Dutch shipping in the Baltic and Mediterranean was partly explained by the expansion of the Dutch shipping to the East Indies and by Atlantic shipping after 1750.[16] Van Zanden and van Tielhof's estimate of labour productivity between 1503 and 1780 is consistent with Unger and Janssen's Dutch data. They found a modest increase during the sixteenth and early seventeenth centuries, a rapid increase (of 75 per cent) between 1636 and 1694, and stagnation (modest decline) in the eighteenth century.[17]

Van Zanden and van Tielhof do not provide any simple answers to the question of whether the development was driven by a change in technology or by a change in organization and institutions. They do, however, stress the connection between peace, small crews, and low armament costs, for example. They also point out the role of *voorbij-*

landvaert, direct passage, that bypassed the Dutch Republic as a way of increasing the efficiency of shipping.[18] The organizational and institutional changes also played a significant role.

Finally, the analysis presented here also demonstrates that it is almost impossible to separate political and commercial factors from technological ones when explaining productivity changes. The story of the fluyt, a new type of ocean-going vessel prompted by the imposition of the *pax Hollandica*, which was in turn was linked to the specific political economy of Holland, illustrates how political and technological factors were intertwined. The fluyt was also the result of the strong expansion of the shipping sector and industry in the 1550–1620 period, which made increased specialization possible in the shape of different ship designs for different routes. Productivity growth was therefore based upon changes in commerce, politics, and technology that largely occurred at much the same time.[19]

Jan Glete would most probably have described the new situation as *pax Baltica*. A detailed summary of Unger, van Zanden, and van Tielhof's work is motivated by the role of Dutch shipping in Sweden. For a long time, the Dutch were the leading carriers of Swedish exports and the major competitors to the Swedish shipping industry. The reduction of the Dutch carrying trade to and from Sweden had been one of the major motives for Sweden's mercantilist policy. The package of shipping policy institutions of the 1720s, including the Swedish Navigation Act (*Produktplakatet*), was introduced to reduce the Dutch import trade to Sweden. Meanwhile, the Swedes copied the Dutch shipping organizations and institutions in many ways. Sweden's policy in the Mediterranean is a good example of this emulation strategy.

Recent work on the efficiency of early modern shipping, based upon labour productivity and total-factor productivity, points to the difficulty in separating the technological aspects from the organizational and institutional aspects of the development of shipping. It often seems that politics, organizational change, and new institutions enabled technological change. Another conclusion we may draw is the overall complexity and volatility of the whole shipping industry. There were vast differences between labour productivity in coal shipping between Newcastle and London and in East India Company shipping in the Indian Ocean. The same kind of differences between the Dutch/Baltic shipping in the early seventeenth century and the Dutch/Asia and transatlantic shipping in the eighteenth century explains the relative decline of Dutch efficiency after 1700. The average size of a ship does not say much about its economy. Size must be compared with the commodities transported, loading and unloading times, the vessel's speed and crew, and so on. All of these aspects must be considered when we are looking at the competitiveness of Swedish shipping in Southern Europe. This business was in many ways different to the business in the Baltic and North Sea; it is also important to stress that the Swedish shipping in Southern Europe differed significantly from Dutch, English, French, and Danish shipping in the area.

The Convoy Office and shipping in Southern Europe

The major reason for Sweden's commercial engagement in Southern Europe after 1720 was its reliance upon Mediterranean and Portuguese salt. During the course of the seventeenth century, Swedes became accustomed to salt from Portugal and the Mediterranean and they did not want to buy salt from other sources. The Southern European salt was initially carried in Dutch bottoms; however, with introduction of Swedish mercantilism in 1650, it was increasingly carried by Swedish vessels. Salt supplies were disrupted during the Great Northern War (1700–1721), and Sweden once again became dependent upon the Dutch shippers. This dependency became a political problem after the war. High transport costs, high salt prices, problems with balance of trade, and the volatility of the salt supply were all problems that in Sweden were associated with Dutch shipping. The solution was the Swedish Navigation Act, designed to exclude all foreigners from the import trade to Sweden, with exception of producing countries. The Dutch ships were the targets. The Act was passed in 1724 by the Swedish Diet, and soon Dutch ships almost disappeared from Swedish ports.[20] Even if salt was the most important strategic issue in the debate in 1720–1724, the Navigation Act's objectives were also to promote Swedish exports – mainly bar iron, tar, and pitch – to Southern Europe and to build up the Swedish merchant fleet. Looking at the trade statistics and registered shipping tonnage, the Navigation Act was a success. Supplies of salt increased, as did Swedish iron exports to Southern Europe.[21] Another commodity, sawn timber, grew in importance over the course of the century, while the volumes of Swedish exports and imports from Southern Europe also developed satisfactorily.

Unfortunately, however, little is known about the profitability of the commodity exchange with Southern Europe. Sweden's commercial policy toward Southern Europe had been questioned by politicians as well as by small merchants who found the costs of shipping high and the possibility of building up their own tonnage limited.[22] This criticism appears justified if we look at the composition of Swedish trade with Southern Europe. Salt was a cheap commodity, which made its transport costly; as a result, the salt trade most probably unprofitable. There were certainly more valuable and profitable imports such as wine, fruit, silk, and so on; however, these were limited. The major export item was bar iron. However, Swedish iron exporters were faced with competitive markets for iron in Portugal, Spain, and Italy, and complained that Dutch ships were also carrying iron – as ballast. This meant the iron carried on Dutch ships was cheaper (transport cost-free) than iron carried on Swedish ships.[23] In addition, a rising share of Sweden's trade to Southern Europe consisted of sawn timber: a bulky and very cheap cargo. In relation to the large distances between the Baltic Sea and the Mediterranean, the limited sailing season, and the composition of Swedish cargoes, the conditions for Swedish shipping to Southern Europe were not very good. Why then did the Swedes continue to send their ships to the Mediterranean?

One factor that spoke in favour of Swedish competitiveness was the high labour productivity (tonne-per-man) in shipping to Southern Europe. Swedish ships were larger on average than their competitors'; naturally, as they were carrying bulky goods. However, they required small and relatively cheap crews. Average Swedish ships in Southern Europe had a tonnage of 90–100 lasts (*c.*220–250 metric tonnes) and labour productivity over 20 metric tonnes per man.[24] This can be compared to the aforementioned Dutch and English figures. A contemporary treatise from 1768 and another that compares crew wages also indicate that Swedish crewmen were cheaper that those of other competing marines.[25] The high labour productivity and low crew costs were undoubtedly important in the success of Swedish shipping in Southern Europe. The variety of ships employed in this trade was also large, which indicates the considerable flexibility of the Swedish shipping industry. On the other hand, shipbuilding costs did not appear to have played a big role.

Swedish tramp shipping in Southern Europe was most probably a decisive factor in the viability of Swedish trade in the area. Many Swedish-flagged ships carried cargoes between foreign ports before they returned to Sweden, and this kind of freight business improved the economy of the trade as a whole. Ship-owners and merchants were often one and the same. Tramp shipping, however, was an option only if Swedish vessels and trade were safe.

After the end of the Great Northern War, the major threat to Swedish ships in Southern Europe were Barbary corsairs who captured foreign ships and sold their crews into slavery or exchanged them for ransom. Swedish shipmasters and seamen had already encountered the Barbary corsairs by the late seventeenth century; there were Swedish slaves in Algiers and Tunis by 1690. The Swedish authorities raised the means to buy the Swedish seamen free. The new shipping policy after 1721 required a more sustainable solution. The establishment of the Convoy Office and peace treaties with the Barbary states were the most important steps in this direction.

The necessity of reorganizing the convoying system became apparent in about 1720, when corsair activity increased. Yet convoying was not only a matter of protecting Swedish ships from the Barbary corsairs; it was also intended to protect them from belligerents in the North Sea and the Atlantic. The new convoying system was discussed at the 1723 Diet at the same session that debated the Navigation Act. A new duty, *extra licenten*, to finance the convoys was enacted, payable on all exports and imports – unsurprisingly, a move that was not welcomed by merchants and ship-owners not involved in long-distance trade requiring convoying. The duty was collected by the Convoy Fund (*Konvojkassan*) and was supposed to cover convoy costs, the release of enslaved seamen, and peace treaties with the Barbary states.

Gothenburg became the first seat of the Convoy Office. Convoying was traditionally organized jointly by the Admiralty and the Board of Trade (*Kommerskollegium*), and the Convoy Office steering committee included representatives from the navy and the Swedish merchant community, and its president was chosen from among the admirals. According to its instructions, the Convoy Office was supposed to organize at least two convoys a year, with two naval ships of at least 50 guns apiece. The merchant ships were collected in Gothenburg and convoyed to Cadiz in Spain; there was no convoying of Swedish ships beyond Gibraltar. Such a system was costly and very slow. Many shipmasters refused to follow the slow convoys and instead sailed alone on their own risk.

Another duty of the Convoy Office became increasingly important:

peace treaties with the Barbary states. In 1726, Sweden opened negotiations with Algiers, the most important Barbary state, and a peace and trade treaty was signed in 1729. Sweden's negotiator, the Scottish merchant George Logie, was appointed the first Swedish consul to Algiers. A system of Algerian passports – identity documents for Swedish ships sailing in Southern Europe – was established in imitation of the systems used by other states. The peace treaty with Algiers also ushered in an era of costly gift exchanges between Sweden and the Barbary states. Even this exchange was an already well-established practice by which European powers bought peace with the corsairs. Swedish gifts consisted mostly of arms, gunpowder, naval stores, and other goods. The official exchanges, including the dispatch of naval vessels, gift exchanges, and the appointment of the consul, were organized and paid for by the Convoy Office. In time these duties became the most important part of the Office's work. The same George Logie signed peace treaties with Tunis and Tripoli in 1736 and 1741. A treaty with Morocco was signed almost thirty years later in 1763, and proved to be the most expensive. Morocco was the only really independent state in North Africa. Algiers, Tunis, and Tripoli were semi-independent principalities under formal Ottoman rule.

The signing of peace treaties with the four North African states meant Swedish ships were safe. This reduced their insurance premiums and increased the demand for Swedish shipping services. Sweden's peaceful relations with the Barbary states, in combination with her neutrality in the Anglo-French wars, paved the way for the boom in Swedish shipping in the second half of the century. Looking at the series of Algerian passports issued (the best source for studying Swedish shipping in Southern Europe), there was an increase in shipping activities during the Seven Years War (1756–63) from about 150 to 200 voyages.[26] Yet the major shift came during the American War of Independence (1778–83), when the number of passports issued doubled from 220 to over 400, and once again during the French Revolutionary Wars. According to the Algerian passport registers, there were 624 voyages beyond Cape Finisterre in northern Spain in 1800. In comparison to Sweden's total shipping activities, the significance of the trade in Southern Europe increased substantially. Approximately 30–40 per cent of Swedish-flagged tonnage was destined for Southern Europe.[27] This boom was also reflected in the trade in commodities. Salt imports in particular rose in the second half of the century from about 150,000 barrels mid century to 300,000 barrels by the 1790s.[28] Unlike the trade in commodities, for which the statistics are well preserved, there are no good data on the invisible freight incomes from Swedish tramp shipping. According to a rough estimate drawn up by the clerks of the Board of Trade for 1769, 1770, and 1771, the income was 150,000 *riksdaler* per annum. In comparison, the same three years' imports of salt were valued at 142,000, 109,000, and 200,000 *riksdaler*.[29] Regarding the freight incomes, the figure is questionable at best.

What were the costs of Sweden's shipping policy in Southern Europe? The Convoy Office, which could be said to roughly equate to the state's protection for shipping in the area, has left detailed accounts.[30] Here, I use the summaries drawn up by Johan Henrik Kreüger in his work on Sweden's relations with the Barbary states and the history of the Swedish Convoy Office. Kreüger's data provide us with a good overview of the different entries in the accounts and the changes in the situation of the Convoy Office over the years.[31] Table 1 covers the period 1728 to 1801. First, the annual figures indicate the extreme variation in outlays, which was related to the unpredictability of the situation in North Africa. Secondly, the overall level of the outlays was low until the 1750s –below 30,000 *riksdaler* annually. The situation changed with

Figure 1: Annual outlays of the Swedish Convoy Office, 1728–1801 (riksdaler specie).

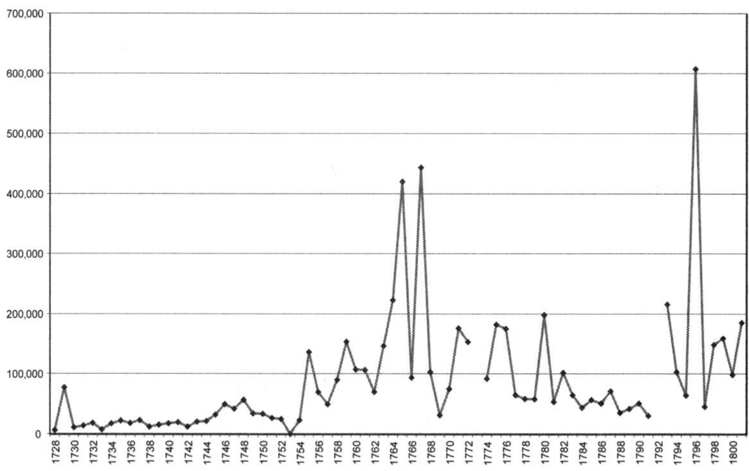

Source: Johan Henrik Kreüger, Sveriges förhållanden till Barbareskstaterna i Afrika. (Stockholm: Norstedt, 1856), Appendices.

the costly peace treaty with Morocco in 1761, and the Office's outlays were well over 100,000 *riksdaler* per annum for the remaining decades of the century; indeed, average annual costs exceeded 150,000 *riksdaler* in the most expensive decades (1761–70 and 1791–1801). These were very substantial sums, although they must be related to the total value of Sweden's shipping and trade in Southern Europe.

When we look at the account detail, the costs of gift exchange appear to dominate. However, there were large differences between the Barbary states, which reflected their relative importance as regional powers. Morocco, the strongest state, was the most costly, closely followed by Algiers. On the other hand, the peace treaties with Tunis and Tripoli were relatively cheap, bar a few exceptional years. Consular services in North Africa (a consul's salary and the costs of his office) were actually almost as expensive as the gift exchanges. The Convoy Office was also responsible for Sweden's diplomatic and consular representation

Table 1 Swedish Convoy Office annual outlays, 1728–1801 (in '000 *riksdaler*)

Period	1728–1740	1741–1750	1751–1760	1761–1770	1771–1780	1781–1790	1791–1801
	13 years	10 years	10 years	10 years	10 years	10 years	11 years
Morocco				394	198	85	132
Algiers	115	87	96	149	145	51	699
Tunis	14	0	19	78	17	27	119
Tripoli	12	17	27	7	65	3	106
Consular service *	50	81	102	166	187	110	59
Constantinople †	18	64	116	185	154	136	42
Convoy office ‡	12	9	14	29	13	11	10
Capital costs, interest	5	43	83	300	190	2	128
Convoying §	26	16	234	454	182	96	351
Sum above	252	317	691	1 762	1 151	521	1 646

Sources: Johan Henrik Kreüger, *Sveriges förhållanden till Barbareskstaterna i Afrika* (Stockholm, 1856), Appendices, Lit K, 34–35.
Note: The data for total outlays in each period of ten years or more are rounded to the nearest digit. The outlays for Morocco, Algiers, Tunis, and Tripoli are the costs of gift exchange.
* includes the costs of the consular service in North Africa, including consuls' salaries.
† includes the costs of the diplomatic mission to Constantinople and the Smyrna consul.
‡ includes the costs of the office in Sweden (salaries, housing, etc.)
§ includes the costs for naval ships employed by the Convoy Office (the low total figure for 1781–1790 is most likely Kreüger's error).

in the Ottoman Empire, and this again was a major cost. Meanwhile, in some years the convoying itself was a major cost.

Duties on Swedish trade were supposed to cover the substantial outlays of the Convoy Office. However, *extra licenten* was never enough to meet the Office's costs, and it frequently balanced its accounts with loans or the state's financial help. During the course of the century, the Office's debts were frequently written off, and the authorities tried to find other ways to fund its activities. As already noted, the Convoy Office was also perceived as a controversial institution because it served only the interests of merchants and ship-owners engaged in long-distance trade. In 1790, following another period of insolvency, the Convoy Office was abolished and its duties were transferred to the Royal State Office (*statskontoret*). This new system did not work either, and after only seven years the Convoy Office was re-established in 1797 with essentially the same organization as before.

Due to the high cost of peace with Tripoli, the Convoy Office's finances were once again in a disastrous state by 1800. The hole in its accounts had to be filled by the state yet again. Moreover, the question of the viability of Swedish shipping in Southern Europe was once again raised. Was it worth the costs? The Convoy Office consulted leading merchant associations and ship-owners in Sweden in the spring of 1801. The Office's final written report concluded that, in spite its very large outlays, it was a necessary institution and that Sweden needed both the commodities trade with Southern Europe and the tonnage and tramp shipping that made this trade profitable.[32] The following passage from the report summarizes the logic of eighteenth-century Swedish trade in Southern Europe, although as an in-house report it naturally cannot be seen as an independent and unbiased evaluation. It essentially expresses the concerns of the people engaged in the long-distance shipping business:

> That without our own shipping there would be no profit to be had by the export of our bulky commodities; that exports alone would not sustain Sweden's shipping if it were not for the substantial contribution from tramp shipping and the import of essentials, especially salt; that tramping would not be possible if the Swedish flag were not respected; that if salt alone was imported into the realm by foreign ships, the realm would be the poorer by at least one million *riksdaler* annually; that if the tramp trade could not be

> pursued by Swedish mariners other than in the North Sea, barely one-third of the merchant fleet would find employ; that the Mediterranean tramp trade employed a tonnage of 12 to 15,000 lasts in weight; that if the Mediterranean trade ceased, 15,000 people who are employed in shipping, partly as seamen, partly other as employees in the industry, would lose their jobs.[33]

The Convoy Office survived the Napoleonic Wars: it became a joint institution for Swedish and Norwegian shipping interests in 1814. Nevertheless, the importance of the Mediterranean trade declined after 1815. The advantage of Sweden's neutrality disappeared in a world dominated by *pax Britannica*; salt lost its strategic significance; and the market for iron was transformed by the British Industrial Revolution. France occupied Algiers in 1830, which ended the hundred-year period of Swedish gift exchanges with Algiers, Tunis, and Tripoli. Another fifteen years later, the Office ceased to send ships to Morocco when the two countries signed a new treaty in 1845, which finished the habit of gift exchanges. Consular representation in North Africa continued to serve Swedish and Norwegian shipping interests. The Convoy Office survived until 1867, but its tasks changed; its money was used in many different ways, from the funding of Sweden-Norway's consular sections to supporting expeditions to Australia and the Pacific in order to support seamen. The Convoy Fund (*Handels- och sjöfartsfonden*) was used in 1851 to purchase the freedom of 519 slaves in Saint Barthélemy, the only Swedish colony in the West Indies.[34] It is historical irony that a fund once used to purchase the freedom of enslaved Swedish seamen in North Africa was used 150 years later to free African slaves in the Swedish West Indies.

Conclusion

Sweden's eighteenth-century carrying trade in Southern Europe was a unique phenomenon. Records of foreign ships in large Southern European ports such as Marseilles, Livorno, Cadiz, and Lisbon reveal that Sweden was one of the largest carriers, on par with the Danes. By the late eighteenth century, the two Nordic merchant fleets together were bigger than the Dutch.[35] According to a French consular report from the mid 1780s, Sweden's merchant fleet reached approximately 170,000 tonnes, which made it the fifth largest in Europe and probably the world.[36] According to the same report, Sweden's merchant fleet was bigger than that of Spain, Portugal, and the Kingdom of Two Sicilies.

However, Sweden, unlike Spain, Portugal, and even the Dutch Republic and Denmark, had no colonies. The Swedish East India Company trade – the only sector of Swedish trade comparable with the colonial trade – employed usually between two and four vessels annually. There were some Swedish-flagged ships employed in the transatlantic trade and in the Indian Ocean, but they were few and far between, and their activities were limited to wartime (especially the American War of Independence). Accordingly, the bulk of Swedish vessels sailed in European waters: in the Baltic and North Seas, the Mediterranean, and along the Atlantic coasts of Spain, Portugal, and France. Notably, over the course of the century Swedish vessels had partially replaced the Dutch in both Northern and Southern Europe. As Dutch research underlines, the Dutch ships were moving on to new, more profitable markets in the transatlantic and East Indies trade.

The package of policies adopted in the 1720s and 1730s was of great significance for opening up the trade with Southern Europe. The primary motive was the supply of salt; however, the policy also aimed to find new markets for Sweden's staple commodities – iron, tar, pitch, and sawn timber – as well to find a substitute for Dutch carriers in Sweden's trade. The policy was successful if one looks at the indicators of trade volumes, salt prices, and the decline of Dutch shipping in Sweden. Yet these motives are not sufficient to explain the boom in Swedish shipping and trade that came fully fifty years after the passing of the Swedish Navigation Act.

The policy of promoting Swedish trade and shipping in Southern Europe came at a price. The costs of convoying and the consular service in North Africa were high. Critics of the regime argued that only the small mercantile elite of Stockholm merchants and ship-owners profited from the policy, while the state and the public carried the costs. The commodity exchange with the Barbary states was insignificant. However, the eighteenth-century critics of these shipping policies were not alert to the ramifications of the alternative, especially when it came to the role of Sweden's tramp shipping in Southern Europe.

The market for shipping services in the Mediterranean was remarkably open in comparison to the regulated regimes in Britain, Denmark, and Sweden, and Swedes were well placed to take advantage of this openness. However, shipping capacity or high labour productivity cannot be seen as the primary Swedish advantage, even if the figures are impressive, for the large carrying capacity, high average tonnage per ship, and the consequent high tonnes-per-man ratio were all the outcome of the awkward composition of Swedish foreign trade that required vast carrying capacity. Instead, I would argue that the key advantage of Swedish ships was their low protection costs. First, Sweden had peaceful relations with the Barbary states from 1729, which reduced risks and protection costs for Swedish-flagged ships and made them more attractive to charter. As the Convoy Office balance sheets show, the costs could be extremely volatile, yet if we look at the whole period spanning from 1730 to 1800, the annual average costs were not unreasonable when compared with the total value of Sweden's trade and freight income in Southern Europe. The solution of a formal Convoy Office also appears more efficient than if individual ship-owners had organized protection. Second, there was Sweden's neutrality, an accidental consequence of her decline as a great power after 1721, not a conscious foreign policy. Although Sweden found it difficult to accommodate to the new situation – she long nursed great-power ambitions and fought a number of unsuccessful wars against Russia, Denmark, and Prussia – crucially it meant that she was not drawn into the Anglo-French wars at sea. This neutrality was of particular value in Southern Europe where Sweden had no political ambitions and was perceived as a small, benevolently disposed, and distant state.

Jan Glete argued that the Baltic became a unique haven of peaceful trade in the sixteenth and seventeenth centuries thanks to the naval presence of the Swedish and Danish fiscal-military states. True, Dutch carriers had to pay Sound tolls, but they could reduce their protection costs and employ slow, capacious, and cheap vessels such as fluyts in the safe waters of the Baltic. In the eighteenth century, Sweden's age as a European great power was past. Instead of territorial expansion eastwards, the Swedish state promoted a policy of economic development, part of which was a boom in Swedish shipping and trade westwards and in Southern Europe. Swedes could enjoy the same low protection costs here as the Dutch had a century before in the Baltic. This time, low protection costs were ensured by peace treaties with the Barbary states and by Sweden's neutrality in the Anglo-French wars. Low protection costs undoubtedly gave Sweden the competitive edge in Southern Europe, and having once been an important provider of protection in the Baltic Sea in an earlier period, Sweden became a carrier that could utilize the protection that other nations provided.

More research is needed to show how Swedish protection costs changed over the course of the eighteenth century. However, we may conclude that this advantage made the Swedish maritime sector highly dynamic and innovative. In the second part of the century, Sweden's maritime sector, including shipping, fishing, and shipbuilding, was one of the most dynamic sectors of the kingdom's economy.

Notes

1 Berit Larsson, *Svenska varor på svenska kölar: Staten, industrialiseringen och linjesjöfartens framväxt i Sverige 1890–1925* (Gothenburg 2000), pp. 24–26.

2 John J. McCusker, 'The Demise of Distance: The Business Press and the Origins of the Information Revolution in the Early Modern Atlantic World', *American Historical Review* 110:2 (2005), pp. 295–321; Leos Müller & Jari Ojala (eds.), *Information Flows, New Approaches in the Historical Study of Business Information* (Helsinki 2007) p. 15.

3 Jan Glete, *Warfare at Sea 1500–1650: Maritime Conflicts and the Transformation of Europe* (London 2000), pp. 125–126.

4 For an extremely pessimistic view of the period before 1800, see Gregory Clark, *A Farewell to Alms: A Brief Economic History of the World* (Princeton 2007).

5 C. Knick Harley, 'Ocean Freight Rates and Productivity 1740–1913: The Primacy of Mechanical Invention Reaffirmed', *Journal of Economic History*, 48 (1988), pp. 851–876.

6 Russell R. Menard, 'Transport Costs and Long-range Trade, 1300–1800: Was There a European 'Transport Revolution' in the Early Modern Era?' in: James D. Tracy (ed.), *The Political Economy of Merchant Empires* (Cambridge 1991), p. 274.

7 Kevin H. O'Rourke & Jeffrey G. Williamson, *Globalization and History: The Evolution of a Nineteenth-Century Atlantic Economy* (Cambridge, Mass., 1999); id., 'When Did Globalization Begin?', *European Review of Economic History*, 6 (2002), pp. 23–50; id., 'After Columbus: Explaining Europe's Overseas Trade Boom, 1500–1800', *Journal of Economic History*, 62 (2002), pp. 417–456; id., 'Once More: When Did Globalization Begin?', *European Review of Economic History*, 8 (2004), pp. 109–117; Saif I. Shah Mohammed & Jeffrey G. Williamson, 'Freight Rates and Productivity Gains in British Tramp Shipping 1869–1950', National Bureau of Economic Research (NBER), Working Paper 9531 (2003) <http://www.nber.org/papers/w9531>, (accessed 1 June 2011).

8 Angus Maddison, *The World Economy: A Millennial Perspective* (Paris 2001), p. 244. Maddison's figures have been criticized. Jan Luiten van Zanden chooses another way to estimate GDP growth by looking at three measures of economic maturity: levels of urbanization, tonnages of merchant fleet – reflecting the trade volumes – and iron production. Jan Luiten van Zanden, 'Early Modern Economic Growth: A Survey of the European Economy, 1500–1800', in: Maarten Prak (ed.), *Early Modern Capitalism: Economic and Social Change in Europe 1400–1800* (London 2001). See also Jan Luiten van Zanden, *The Long Road to the Industrial Revolution: The European Economy in a Global Perspective, 1000–1800* (Leiden 2009), pp. 239–243.

9 Johan Söderberg uses the same method for measuring shipping productivity in this volume.
10 Jan Lucassen & Richard W. Unger, 'Labour Productivity in Ocean Shipping, 1450–1875', *International Journal of Maritime History*, 12 (2000), pp. 127–141; John J. McCusker, 'The Tonnage of Ships Engaged in British Colonial Trade During the Eighteenth Century', in: *Essays in the Economic History of the Atlantic World* (London & New York 1997), pp. 43–75.
11 Richard W. Unger, 'Shipping and Western European Economic Growth in the Late Renaissance: Potential Connections', *International Journal of Maritime History*, 18 (2006) p. 88.
12 Unger (2006), pp. 89–90.
13 Lucassen & Unger (2000) p. 130.
14 Ibid. p. 137
15 Milja van Tielhof & Jan Luiten van Zanden, 'Roots of Growth and Productivity Change in Dutch Shipping Industry, 1500–1800', *Explorations in Economic History*, 46 (2009), pp. 389–403.
16 Ibid. pp. 392–393.
17 Ibid. p. 394.
18 Ibid. p. 400. In the period of increasing *voorbijlandvaert* (1550–1650) the share of ballast declined from 40 to 20 per cent! After 1650 the trading networks failed to organize *voorbijlandvaert* and productivity declined even more.
19 Ibid. p. 402.
20 Leos Müller, *Consuls, Corsairs, and Commerce: The Swedish Consular Service and Long-distance Shipping, 1720–1815* (Uppsala 2004), p. 62.
21 Staffan Högberg, *Utrikeshandel och sjöfart på 1700-talet: Stapelvaror i svensk export och import 1738–1808* (Stockholm 1969).
22 See especially Eli F. Heckscher, 'Produktplakatet: Den gamla svenska sjöfartspolitikens grundlag', in: *Ekonomi och historia* (Stockholm 1922).
23 Müller (2004), p. 72.
24 Ibid. p. 155. Calculation of tonne-per-man ratio is based upon a limited sample of Swedish ships in Cadiz; however, the result is consistent with other data (ibid. p. 157, table 5.10). 1 heavy last=18 shippounds=2.448 metric tonnes. The unified measure procedure was introduced as late as in 1726.
25 Johan Westerman, 'Om Sveriges fördelar och svårigheter i sjöfarten, i jämförelse emot andra riken', in: *Kongl. Vetenskaps Academiens handlingar för år 1768* (Stockholm 1768).
26 The issuing of passports was strictly regulated and controlled. Thus, the surviving registers of passports issued are both rich and reliable sources that provide a detailed picture of Swedish shipping in Southern Europe. According to the regulation for Algerian passports (also called Turkish passports), all Swedish-flagged vessels sailing beyond Cape Finisterre in northern Spain had to have such passports. This means that the registers also include all passports for the China trade (Swedish East India Company) and ships plying the Atlantic. These numbers were insignificant. See Müller (2004) ch. 5.
27 Eli F. Heckscher, *Den svenska handelssjöfartens ekonomiska historia sedan Gustaf Vasa* (Uppsala 1940) p. 24.
28 *Historisk statistik för Sverige: Utrikeshandeln 1732–1970*, 3 (Örebro 1972), pp.

122–123. Much of the increase in demand for salt was related to the fishing boom on the west coast (salt herring).

29 Ibid. p. 158.

30 Johan Henrik Kreüger, *Sveriges förhållanden till Barbareskstaterna i Afrika* (Stockholm 1856).

31 Kreüger's tables are based upon the Convoy Office account books. Kreüger converted all figures to *riksdaler specie* to make his data comparable, yet it is important to be aware of the complicated and volatile monetary situation in Sweden, with three different kinds of accounting money, which all had different rates. See *Historisk statistik för Sverige: Utrikeshandeln 1732–1970*, 3 (1972), p. 62.

32 See Kreüger (1856), pp. 30–31, and Bengt Carlson, 'Sverige handel och sjöfart på Medelhavet 1797–1803', in: Åke Holmberg (ed.), *Handel och sjöfart under gustaviansk tid* (Gothenburg 1971), pp. 1–25.

33 'Att utom egen sjöfart vinst icke vore att vänta på våra voluminösa export-varor; att blotta exporten icke skulle underhålla Sveriges betydliga sjöfart, om icke frakthandeln och importen af egna behofver, synnerligen af salt, uti betydlig del dertill bidrogo; att frakt ej kunde erhållas, om icke Svenska flagga respekterades; att om importen endast af artikeln salt till riket skulle förrättas med främmande fartyg, riket derigenom skulle förlora minst en million Riksdaler årligen; att om icke frakthandeln kunde af Svenska sjöfarande begagnas annat än på Nordsjön, knappt en tredjedel av handelsflottan skulle dermed kunna syslosättas; att enskildta Medelhafs-frakter syslosatte 12 à 15,000 lästers drägt; att om farten på Medelhafvet upphörde 15,000 personer, dels sjöfolk, dels andra industriidkare, som i och för sjöfarten äro syslosatte, skulle blifva utan arbete.' Report quoted in Kreüger (1856), p. 31.

34 Kreüger (1856) p. 40.

35 For entries of different flags in Marseilles, see Charles Carrière, *Négociants marseillais au XVIIIe siècle* (Marseilles 1973), p. 1061; see also Dan H. Andersen & Hans-Joachim Voth, 'The Grapes of War: Neutrality and Mediterranean Shipping Under the Danish Flag, 1747–1807', *Scandinavian Economic History Review*, 48 (2000), pp. 6–7.

36 Ruggiero Romano, 'Per una valutazione della flotta mercantile europea alla fine del secolo XVIII', in: *Studi in onore Amintore Fanfani*, 5: *Evi moderno e contemporaneo* (Milan 1962), pp. 573–591.

CHAPTER 13

A Real Challenge from the South

The Southern Cone of Latin America in the new global food order

Ulf Jonsson

In contemporary debate, observers have increasingly focused upon recent changes in the global agro-food system. A number of countries in the global South have challenged the prominence of the Western powers. The Southern Cone of Latin America – Argentina, Paraguay, Uruguay, and Chile – is emerging as a new centre of gravity in the global agro-food system, moving away from a heavy dependence upon simple commodity exports.[1] A number of South East Asian countries, such as Thailand, have also succeeded in widening their agro-food export baskets. The flow of high value foodstuffs among countries in the South has also increased. Some countries in the South, most notably Brazil, are also making heavy inroads into the poorest import-dependent countries (that is to say, Africa south of Sahara, which North American and European sources used exclusively to supply). The imports cover the small high-value goods that these countries can afford, primarily, meat, poultry, and dairy products. However, food imports are more significant in terms of both quantity and value in so-called emerging economies (for example, China, India, Russia, and East Asian countries such as South Korea). Temperate foodstuff exporters in the developed world face increasingly tough competition from Latin America.

Do these changes add up to a power shift, a kind of new geopolitics of food? To paraphrase a recent article in the business magazine *Fortune*, to what extent has Brazil out-farmed the American farmer?[2] These questions evidently cannot be grasped by focusing upon relations between nation states in an international system – the classical domain of the discipline of international relations. To a large extent, it is a well-known fact that the present agro-food system is the playground of huge transnational companies that not only influence trade and food-processing, but also exercise a tremendous influence on how the rules of the game are formed in bodies such as the World Trade Organization.[3]

However, the main focus in this chapter is the extent to which the recent expansion constitutes the rise of new agro-food powers in the Southern Cone, particularly Brazil, or whether it can be written off as just another wave of commodity booms. The region has certainly known a number of successive commodity booms. In the late nineteenth century, Argentina's rather archaic pastoral economy (where jerked meat, hides, and wool made up the lion's share of a modest export sector) changed to a frontier economy that supplied the world market with wheat, maize, and high-quality beef. On the eve of the First World War, Argentina was the leading wheat exporter in the New World, with Canada a strong second with 2,000 million tonnes. Argentina was also the number one maize exporter during the same period.[4] Coffee was certainly the most important commodity boom in Brazil during the second half of the nineteenth century. By 1850 Brazil was already producing over 50 per cent of the world's coffee, and by 1906 Brazilian production was five times more than that of the rest of world combined.[5]

In spite of these periods of rapid expansion and increasing incomes, the Southern Cone has not thus far challenged the dominant Western powers in the global food system. The region has remained dependent upon rather unsophisticated commodity exports. Booms and busts succeeded one another; scarcely solid foundations for sustained long-term growth and more robust development.

The new political economy of agriculture and food has inspired my analytical framework to a considerable degree. This is not a single comprehensive school of thought; rather, it is a congregation of scholars who have taken a critical stance on central tendencies in the contemporary agro-food system.[6] In spite of the diversity of approaches, we can delineate a number of common themes in critical agro-food studies. A central concern is a deeper understanding of how the stratification of countries in the international division of agro-food labour is constituted and governed. The idea of international agro-food regimes developed by Harriet Friedmann and Philip McMichael can be highly useful in this context.[7] For me, the idea of international food regimes does not constitute a fully-fledged theory; rather, it is a set of interrelated concepts that can be very fruitful.

Friedmann and McMichael originally identified two fully developed agro-food regimes and a third that was emerging. The first is a British-centred regime (1870–1914) that initially involved a global exchange of manufactured goods and a flow of agro-food products from the settler economies (the United States, Canada, Australia, and Argentina) to the European (particularly the British) market. The flows of tropical goods such as coffee, tea, and cocoa also increased considerably. In fact, this regime manifested itself in the periphery as successive waves of commodity export booms. Core countries played a preponderant role. A pattern of expansions and contractions could be observed among commodity-exporting countries. The relationship between Western core countries changed considerably with the emergence of a second international agro-food regime under US hegemony after the Second World War; however, commodity-exporting countries in the periphery continued under very much under the same conditions as in the earlier regime. Booms and busts were very much part of the everyday experience, as was Western dominance.

Many scholars today argue we are seeing the emergence of a new international food regime under the hegemony of transnational agro-food companies rather than states, as well as a certain shift in the power balance between countries. The hot spots of the new international agro-food regime are increasingly found in the middle-income countries of the South. The extent to which these hot spots are under the dominance of transnational agro-food companies or whether we are seeing new important actors from the South are both matters of controversy.

The idea of an emerging new third international food regime contains many valuable insights. However, I think there is an overemphasis on corporate dominance. States have not ceded control of the arena completely. The neo-liberal offensive is more of a process of re-regulation than deregulation of the agro-food sector, as is more often the case. With some remarkable exceptions, there is a tendency in the international agro-food regime discussion to overemphasize the structural component at the expense of the actors.[8] The influence of the hegemonic centre is also overstated. The roll of conflict and challenges from different actors must be brought into the picture. This is the reason why I prefer the concept of a 'food order', which nods at the greater diversity in the way global food production and consumption is governed.

Consequently, it is highly pertinent to ask to what extent the rise of the Southern Cone in the present-day global food order represents something new: a challenge to established power relations or just a continuation of old patterns of Western dominance? At first glance, the theme developed in this chapter may seem to be far from Jan Glete's main research preoccupations. However, I think that the focus on changing power relations connects quite well with his work and interests as a business historian.

The Southern Cone and a new global food order

The changes in Brazil and the Southern Cone countries have been regarded as the result of dramatic transformations in the global food order over the past three decades. One of the most striking features is an increase in the extent and intensity of trade from these countries, as well as a shift in the composition of agro-food exports. The impressive expansion of the soybean sector in Argentina and Brazil, and the increase of livestock production and exports from Brazil, both exemplify this. The value of agro-food exports has grown considerably since the early 1960s: five times in the case of Brazil. Argentina's growth rate is somewhat less impressive; however, it is still substantial.[9] In fact, the figures reflect two distinct phases: with the introduction of soybeans, growing export earnings were generated in a classical commodity boom from the early 1960s to 1980, while the sustained growth up to the present day is a bit more complex, as I will discuss.

Behind these figures is a dramatic change in the agro-food export baskets of Brazil (in particular) and Argentina (to a somewhat lesser degree). The structure of Argentinian and Brazilian agro-food exports in the early 1960s had the same characteristics as they did in the heyday of the commodity boom of the late nineteenth and early twentieth centuries. Meat, wool, and cereals made up the bulk of Argentina's participation on the world market in the 1960s, as they had done in the first decades of the twentieth century[10]. Coffee and other tropical goods constituted almost 90 per cent of Brazilian agro-food exports. With a growing meat and wheat production in Europe, the post-war international agro-food regime severely hit the Argentinian economy. The country had to compete on the world market with highly subsidised European and North American goods. Nevertheless, the structure of exports remained very much the same in spite of worsening conditions. Brazil had to face highly volatile prices on the global market, which checked the country's long-term economic development.

There has also been a significant change in the composition of trading partners. In the simple commodity-export phase, the Southern Cone was stuck in a North–South exchange very much of the same order as other commodity exporters. The South–South flow is currently growing, and steadily. Emerging markets in Asia, the Middle East, and the former Soviet bloc have primarily increased in importance. However, Brazil and Argentina are also making serious inroads into the markets of poor net food-importing countries in Sub-Saharan Africa. These markets were once the home turf of the European Union and the US.

To what extent do these changes constitute a radical break with past patterns of dependent commodity exports? This is a problem best addressed by considering the soybean sector in Brazil and Argentina. Due to the fact that the soybean sector constitutes such an important share of the agro-food export basket, it is reasonable to ask whether this is not just another agro-food commodity boom, where more extensively utilized resources have been previously put to more productive use. Is it an export boom of the same kind as the expansion of coffee and wheat exports before the First World War? Given that soybeans and processed soybean products now constitute more than 50 per cent of Argentina's agro-food exports and approximately 40 per cent of Brazil's, the soybean expansion seems to be exactly that.[11] This is particularly true for Brazil, at least on the surface. The soybean 'frontier' has rapidly conquered large tracts of the Midwest bush savannah (*cerrado*) and is now moving into the Amazon, all sparsely populated and very extensively cultivated regions.[12] Imprecise estimates indicate that the potential land available for field cultivation amounts to 57 and 170 million hectares, respectively. There are over 160 million hectares of pasture in and immediately adjoining the bush savannah region, which now harbours the world's biggest beef herd. A substantial part of this land could relatively easily be switched to soybean production.[13]

Thus the soybean expansion of the last forty years displays many features of classical commodity expansion. In fact, Brazil's soybean exports now show a heavier concentration upon raw beans than was the case in the 1970s and 1980s. A combination of internal and external factors has contributed to this a seemingly reverse pattern of development. Heavier export taxes levied on raw beans initially stimulated the processing of soybeans into oil and meals. The result was an early development of processing (crushing) capacity in the pioneering regions in the south of the country. The infrastructure was less developed on the new soybean frontier. Consequently, crushers were less interested in investing in this region, far from harbours and the livestock industry.

The situation in Argentina is very different. Tax incentives are still used to stimulate processing. However, what has been more important for the development of soybean processing is that a large part of the soybean-producing region is within a radius of 300–350 km from a complex of deep-water ports in the state of Santa Fe (in the greater Rosario area). The world's biggest soybean processing zone is located in this region. Heavy investments in the last ten years have succeeded in making Argentina a low-cost soybean processor. This region also processes a substantial part of the Paraguayan-grown crop. Thus Argentina has moved on from the first stage of simple commodity exports in the soybean sector. Thus far, however, very little of the soybean meal and oil is transformed into more complex products. The distinguished Argentinian scholar Graciella Gutman and her co-authors classify Argentina as primarily a commodity exporter.[14] I think that it is a reasonable point of view to certain extent. The soybean processing industry in the Santa Fe region has few forward linkages to the Argentinian agro-food processing industry outside the soybean sector. Only 3 per cent of production is consumed in-country. Soybean products are not used to any significant degree as an input in the food- and the feed-processing industry. Argentinian livestock industries have traditionally depended upon grass-feeding. Cattle breeders and dairy farmers have increasingly substituted alfalfa pastures for maize due to increasing competition between soybeans and pastureland on the humid pampas. In beef production, the North American approach with feedlots has expanded considerably. Thus far, soybeans have not been used extensively as cattle feed.[15] Processed soybean goods have a fairly standardized character. Value is certainly added to the product compared to raw soybeans; however, the really high-value parts of the extended global soybean chain are located elsewhere.

In contrast to the grain or coffee chains of the early twentieth century, the leading companies play a much more assertive role in the contemporary soybean chain. The soybean complex constitutes an example of a relatively hierarchical global commodity chain. The leading firms – Cargill, Bunge, Archer Daniels Midland, and Louis Dreyfus – exercise a dominant influence over the different stages, with a high degree of control over the technological development in all parts of the production process.[16] An illustrative example is the world's largest soybean processing zone, located in Puerto General San Martin, some 30 km north of Rosario in the Santa Fe province in Argentina. The industry in this region uses the state-of-the-art technology. Transnational giants Cargill, Bunge, and Dreyfus have a combined pressing capacity of almost 30,000 tonnes of soybeans a day.[17] These companies are not normally involved in farming. However, through their control of upstream activities they are in a strong position when it comes to matters such as seeds, pesticides, and fertilizers.[18] They also have a major interest in the downstream beef, poultry, and pork industries that are heavy users of soybean products as a concentrated protein feedstuff.

There are considerable economies of scale in storage and transport to be had, particularly in long-distance trans-oceanic trade. Consequently, it is the leading transnational oilseed companies that decide the geographical location of processing. They pursue a global sourcing strategy, reacting to the incentives created in interaction with national and regional power-holders. Brazil is currently more interesting as a supplier of raw materials than as a processing location. However, states and other national actors are not completely powerless; for example, the size of different market counts.

China's position in the global soybean chain can serve as illustration. In the last ten years, the Chinese appetite for soybeans and soybean derivatives has fuelled a spectacular growth in the soybean-exporting countries. China's scale has a tremendous impact. Most of the soybeans that China imports are destined for the livestock industry, primarily pork and poultry.[19] The Chinese state and private actors are actively pursuing a policy of domestic processing, relying upon joint ventures with the big oilseed transnationals to get access to the cutting-edge technology.[20] The enormous size of the Chinese market makes it an attractive location for direct investment, sourcing raw soybeans from Brazil, the US, and, to a lesser extent, Argentina. In fact, China has been Brazil's single largest soybean client since the early 2000s. The dramatically increased importance of China for Brazilian soybean exports is demonstrated in Figure 1.

Similar processes are underway in a number of smaller, yet rapidly growing, Asian and other middle-income countries. To a large extent, the demand in these cases is also derived from an expanding livestock industry, most importantly poultry and pork. Western Europe remains the biggest market for soybean meals and cakes; however, the Asian share is constantly rising. In 2005, the European Union took over 56

Figure 1. Brazilian soybean exports 1996–2004, millions US dollars (semi-logarithmic scale)

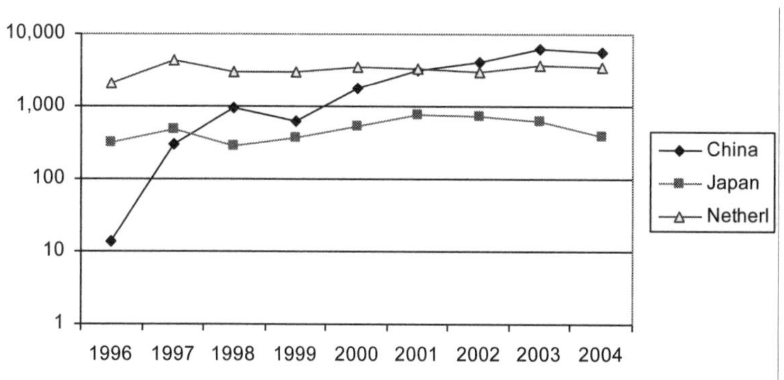

Source: Comtrade.

per cent of Argentinian soybean cake exports. The Asian share was 21 per cent. The most important Asian importers were the Philippines, Malaysia, and Thailand, all countries that have seen the rapid expansion of their poultry and pork production.[21] These markets are too small to be worth investing in local crushing capacity. Consequently, sourcing soybean cakes directly from Argentina is an attractive option for the big players in the global soybean market. Western Europe has a considerable crushing capacity; however, the demand from feedstock outpaces the supply.

Market size also matters when we consider the further processing of cakes, meal, and oil into final consumer products or more sophisticated input. As mentioned, domestic consumption of soybeans constitutes only 3 per cent of Argentinian production, while the same proportion in Brazil has been approximately 25 per cent in recent decades. If we take a closer look into the relationship between export and domestic consumption, the pattern reveals an increasing domestic use of soybean meal in Brazil: almost 44 per cent of soybean meal production went to the domestic market in 2005–6. Of a total production of 22 million tonnes, 10 million tonnes was absorbed by the home market: most was consumed in the booming poultry and pork industries.[22] In 2004, Brazilian poultry exports surpassed those of the earlier world leader, the US.[23]

The Brazilian poultry industry increasingly must supply demanding markets (such as Japan, the biggest client in value terms) with more elaborated, high–value cuts and processed products rather than standardized whole chickens; this is the case even if whole chickens are an important item for the Middle Eastern markets. Thus the soybean chain in Brazil has served as a lever to develop high-value agro-food exports to the expanding markets in Asia and the Middle East.[24] The market leaders in the Brazilian poultry and pork industry are dominated by domestic enterprises (currently, at least).[25] Brazilian meat processors are currently involved in a rapid series of mergers and consolidation. The two biggest pork and poultry firms, Sadia and Perdigaão, have recently concluded a merger to form the biggest pork and poultry processor in the world: Brazil Foods. The company is expected to become the third largest Brazilian exporter behind the state-owned oil company, Petrobras, and the steel and mining giant, Vale.[26] Recent investment plans of almost a billion US dollars will increase the slaughtering capacity to 145 million chickens and 2.5 million hogs a year. The operation will also include a feed factory with an annual production of 1.2 tonnes consuming 67.5 million bags of soybeans. The demanded quantity corresponds to 1.35 million hectares, thus absorbing 20 per cent of the Mato Gross soybean crop. In response to the industrial investments, local poultry and pig producers are expected to invest a further 200 million dollars.[27] Brazil Foods is reinforcing its position as a major player on the global market by adopting a highly integrated operation; the company has recently opened production facilities abroad.[28] Thus Brazil Foods has a number of core-like characteristics. In the beef industry, JBS Friboi has taken over the US company Swift & Co and created the world's largest beef producer in terms of animals slaughtered, surpassing the former leaders, the US-based company Tyson Foods.[29] Brazilian firms are using the Mercosur market to pursue an aggressive acquisition policy in the neighbouring countries of Argentina and Uruguay. The meat-packing company, Mafrig, is a leading player in this context. The same company has also acquired the European group, OSI.[30]

The leading Brazilian-owned companies are becoming transnationals, thus challenging the giants in Europe and the US. Many business analysts see a strengthening of the Brazilian competitive advantage in emerging markets. A market analyst at GIRA (a leading firm of consultants in the agro-food sector) described the comparative advantage of Brazil in industrialized hog production: 'Brazil will be able to provide lower feed grain prices because it has the capacity for arable expansion and it has *no problem with manure disposal* – a problem that has hindered the growth of the European industry because of environmental concerns.'[31] In other words, the weak position of environmental interests is a significant element in Brazil's competitive advantage. This 'export' of environmentally doubtful production out of the immediate sight of consumers and the media serves to hide the public mistrust of large-scale industrial types of animal production (as in the Western World, and in Europe in particular).

Brazil also consumes an even larger share of the soybean oil produced; in past years this has been approximately 60 per cent. Consequently, the big players in the global soybean chain are more interested in developing advanced forms of oil-processing in Brazil, where there is a substantial domestic demand that can supplement the more risky export markets. For example, Solae, a subsidiary of Bunge, in partnership with Du Pont specializes in tailor-made proteins for food-processing industries worldwide. Headquartered in Saint Louis, the company has recently established a production and research centre in Brazil.[32] Thus far, Argentina is stuck in its commodity-exporter pattern. The large transnational companies more thoroughly condition the development of the Argentinian soybean chain. The country is an interesting option as the primary processor of standardized soybean input.

Speculation, in more ways than one

There have been substantial problems with the environmental and social sustainability of the soybean chain. The industry has had a much more dynamic impact upon the Brazilian agro-food sector than in Argentina. The size of the domestic market is an important factor in this. The potential demand and the huge resource base give Brazilian actors an advantage when dealing with the big transnational actors, for Brazil is not just any old sourcing zone that can easily be substituted. However, this is certainly not the only factor, or even the most decisive one, as Brazilian policies vis-à-vis the agro-food sector have been more consistently and consciously directed at strengthening global competitiveness than have the policies in Argentina.[33]

The development of a global, competitive agro-food sector in Brazil has resulted in structural changes in all parts of the agro-food chain that go far beyond the soybean and meat industries. Nevertheless, the Brazilian rise to pre-eminence in the global agro-food system took place firmly within the framework of modern, high-input agriculture and standardized, capital-intensive food processing. Consequently, a large number of small farmers and landless rural workers have been excluded. The soybean chain is an obvious example of these weaknesses. Soybean cultivation is highly capital intensive, and generates little employment; the same is true of soybean processing, which, like all modern process industries, does not create much employment. Modern meat-packing is also highly capital intensive. The 900-million-dollar investment by Brazil Foods is expected to generate 6,000 new jobs.[34] The question of an increasingly unequal division of income becomes vital in a situation where long-term, stable employment in the urban sector does not expand at a rate sufficient to absorb the labour force that is pushed out of agriculture.

Nevertheless, compared to the Argentinian reliance on commodity exports, Brazilian development shows greater potential. Brazil has reached a more advanced stage as a global agro-food power. This is certainly a development that is firmly anchored in the paradigm of the productivist agro-food system, which is coming under increasing pressure in the developed world. State-financed research and promotion has played a fundamental role in this process. State-controlled agricultural agencies have mobilized a great deal of research money in order to open up the interior bush savannah.[35] The familiar story of North–South patterns of dependency must be nuanced. Brazil's emergence as a global agro-food power is not entirely conditioned by outside forces, for while there are most definitely still strong elements of the old story of dependence upon powerful economic interests in the North, there is much less of this in Brazil.

The emerging markets in middle-income countries (and in China in particular) are also very much a new feature. The dependence upon markets in Europe and the US has been significantly weakened. The expanding Asian and Middle Eastern economies will probably fuel agro-food exports for a considerable time to come. Brazilian governments, from Cardoso to Lula da Silva, have pursued policies intended to strengthen Brazil's geopolitical role. This ambition certainly involves much more than the agro-food sector. In fact, the most striking aspect of the development of the Brazilian overseas trade in the last three decades is the rise of manufactures and semi-manufactures in the export basket, so that by 2004 agro-food products answered for only slightly over 30 per cent of the total.[36] However, Brazil remains an important and growing agro-food power. Agro-food exports are still a very important source of foreign exchange, although not the only one. A competitive agro-food sector remains a strategic tool to achieve a new geopolitical role. Important questions for future research will include a critical analysis of attempts to use Mercosur and general Latin American integration as instruments to strengthen Brazil's – and the region's – position in the global agro-food system.[37]

In the short and middle term, Brazil and the other Southern Cone countries have a good chance of extending their influence as suppliers of standardized high value products such as meat and diary goods; it is possible that the European market will also constitute a valuable addition to the meat market, in particular that of pork and poultry. Large-scale animal production in Europe is facing increasing resistance from affluent, well-educated consumers. As the analysts from GIRA noted, the environmental concerns about waste disposal from concentrated animal feeding operations (CAFO) is halting further expansion in Europe (see p. 15). Europe could increasingly decrease its industrial animal production and redirect more of its efforts to artisan production; this would be compatible with decoupled subsidies within the framework of the multi-functionality of agriculture. Mass production for poorer consumers in the developed world under environmentally doubtful conditions can be sourced from the South. However, we are not yet at this point; the lobbies of mass production are still strong.

In a somewhat unintended and paradoxical way, the movement highly critical of the present agro-food order may still contribute to the formation of a division of agro-food labour where mass production will be concentrated in a number of hot spots or powerhouses in the South. This would also be a development path compatible with the present overall dominance of corporate giants. These companies can easily co-exist with artisan production with an ecological or gastronomic emphasis. Developments in the new agro-food powerhouses are certainly riddled with contradictions that can be captured in the three overarching questions that Douglas Constance identified as guidelines in critical agri-food scholarship: the agrarian question, the environmental question, and the food question.[38]

The socio-economic impact of soybean production is well documented. It is a highly capital-intensive activity; it encourages a considerable degree of land concentration. When replacing more labour-intensive forms of cultivation, it often brings a significant reduction in the rural population. This is largely the case in Argentina and Paraguay.[39]

However, the situation is somewhat different in Brazil. The population was very sparse before the agricultural expansion started in the new soybean Brazilian frontier zone in the *cerrado* (in states such as Mato Grosso, Goiás and Western Bahia). The area harvested for soybeans in Mato Grosso grew from 0.79 million hectares in crop in 1985–1986 to almost 6 million hectares in 2005–2006.[40] The region experienced population growth during the initial stages, but, nevertheless, soybeans do not create much employment after the land-clearing phase. Production units (often around 20–30,000 hectares) in the *cerrado* do not employ more than one permanent worker per 160–200 hectares.[41] Land grabbing and irregular land transfers in the frontier conditions of the *cerrado* region have been frequent, contributing to social polarization. The jobs created in the service sector by sales of pesticides, fertilizer, and farm machinery, repair and maintenance, and banking mostly employ highly qualified people from outside the region rather than dispossessed small farmers and the rural landless. A modern high-tech soybean farm in the Southern Cone does not differ much from its counterpart in the North American Midwest. The farms usually have substantially larger acreage.[42] The polarizing and labour-displacing effects have been even more pronounced in Argentina, where the soybean expansion has largely occurred on lands occupied by middling farmers who practise a relatively varied form of agriculture. The rapid introduction of genetically modified seeds and no-tillage cultivation has meant a radical reduction in labour demand. As documented in a survey conducted in a significant portion of the pampas, there was a 31 per cent drop in the number of farms between 1992 and 1997. By renting several thousands of hectares and subcontracting the actual cultivation to specialized firms, networks (or sowing pools) often organize soybean cultivation today. This is a kind of faceless agriculture where finance and the pooling of financial resources are the priority. In many senses, this is the archetype of neo-liberal agriculture.[43]

Meanwhile, dairy production for example in the states of Santa Fe and Cordoba, the milk belt of Argentina, has met with increasing difficulties in the battle for acreage. It is not only dairying; other traditional forms of agriculture that produce a variety of crops and meat sense the competition from soybeans as well.[44] The regional Consortia of Agriculture predicts that Argentina will be a net importer of beef by the year 2012, noting that farmers are increasingly turning to soybeans in order to profit from high international prices.[45]

The disappearance of small and medium farmers has always accompanied agricultural modernization. This was very much the story in the developed world in the heyday of agricultural transformation in the post-war period. In the early 1950s, much of the agrarian workforce transferred to industry and other urban occupations – the normal course of economic modernization. This process coincided with a rapid growth in formal employment in the North. Relatively unskilled labourers released from the countryside could find gainful employment. Modern industry is now much less labour-absorbent than it was in the immediate post-war period. This is very much the case in soybean processing; it is a modern, high-tech processing industry. Industrial animal production and modern meat-packing industries are not heavy users of labour. The enormous investments at Brazil Foods will not generate more than 6,000 direct jobs. The indirect employment effect in the expanding CAFO sector is not very impressive either. For example, one of the future suppliers of Brazil Foods' new operation, the Fazenda Mano Julio, employs 25 permanent workers to produce 146,000 pigs yearly.[46] There is obviously much truth in the MST/Via Campesina critique of weak job-creation in industrial agriculture.

The environmental consequences of large-scale industrial agriculture are well documented. Questions regarding the long-term sustainability of this model have long been on the agenda in public debate in Europe. This is not only the concern of the ecologically minded; the mainstream farming organizations are also discussing and experimenting with production methods that consume fewer chemicals and less fossil fuel.[47] Of course, it is very much a conversion under pressure. The price of this energy-intensive input is sharply increasing. Nevertheless, there is a growing consciousness that we have reached the end of the road of the conventional productionist model. The big players on the soybean market are loudly voicing their adherence to the principles of sustainability. Bunge has issued a very elaborate report on its efforts to promote sustainability in Brazilian agriculture.[48] At the same time, a large number of scholars have pointed out the serious effects upon the production models that Bunge and the other giants in the soybean industry promote. The objections cover issues such as the loss of biodiversity, adverse effects on local communities caused by the heavy application of pesticides, and the long-term loss of soil fertility.[49] The geographer Christian Brannstrom and the resource rights specialist Corina Steward have shown how difficult it is to enforce even the timid environmental regulations that apply on the soybean frontier.[50] An Argentinian NGO, Grupo de Reflexión Rural, has produced a well-documented review of pesticide use and its consequences for surrounding local communities.[51] Although this is a partisan statement, it is impossible to ignore the facts presented. Thus when the industrial agro-food model is exported to the South, the difficult features that we have experienced in the North are often even more pronounced. In the land-abundant frontier conditions of Brazil, it may be a considerable time before the long-term consequences are felt.

The industrial agro-food model promotes the production of highly standardized foodstuffs for mass markets. This does not exclude product differentiation, as the Brazilian poultry industry has demonstrated by producing high-value cuts for the Japanese and whole chickens for Middle Eastern consumers. However, the growing interest in alternative food with an ecological or gastronomic emphasis among well-off consumers in the North has been ignored: in the shorter term, the demand for meat in a large number of middle-income countries will be enough to fuel a continued expansion in the Southern Cone, and it may be some time before the kind of criticism of mass production heard in Europe today reaches the middle-income countries. The main priority is still quantity – an adequate supply of products at a reasonable price. This is even truer of poor, net food-importing countries, which are increasingly dependent upon cheap food imports from Latin America.[52]

Soybeans and soybean derivatives will continue to play an important role in the mass production of pork and poultry, expanding rapidly in many middle-income countries. Supplying low-income consumers will most probably continue to be important in the North. While trading input for large-scale animal production, CAFO will be supplemented with imports of soybean-bred pork and poultry. The clout of the Southern Cone in the global food system will continue to grow. To describe the region as the new rising global food power is not without foundation.

Nonetheless, the industrial agricultural and agro-food model in the region is highly contested in all three respects: agriculture, the environment, and food issues. In Brazil, attention has centred on the agrarian question as a result of the actions of the Movement of Landless Rural Labourers (MST). Environmental concerns are increasingly integrated into the general socio-economic critique. Argentinian critics in academic circles and NGOs have focused more upon food security and food safety issues. The loss of Argentinian food sovereignty and growing food insecurity is a recurring theme.[53] One could say that the order of the questions' importance is reversed: agriculture, environment, and food in Brazil; food, environment, and agriculture in Argentina. There are clear historical reasons for this divergence. Argentinians are used to enjoying a varied diet containing a great deal of red meat at reasonable prices: meat price hikes are potentially destabilizing. In a highly urbanized society such as Argentina, it is easier to mobilize consumer interest.

Even so, the two centre-left governments in Brazil and Argentina are squeezed between agro-industrial special pleading and the popular electoral base. An economic policy favouring agro-food exports is crucial in pleasing global investors and financial institutions. The recent conflict between the Argentinian government and agricultural special interest groups is an illuminating example; it was not small family farmers that invaded the streets. The government conceded. For the time being, the agro-industrial export combine has triumphed. The situation in Brazil is different. Through a number of programmes aimed to increase the status of the farmers as independent food producers, the present government has tried to please the small farmers as well. However, the main effort has been to increase the global competitiveness of industrial agro-food production.[54] To a greater extent than Argentina, Brazil has the resources stand on its own two feet. The pressing question is the extent to which it is possible to balance global competitiveness with social inclusion and ecologically sustainable production. To put it bluntly, what is the room to manoeuvre in the present global food order given that giant corporations play such an immense role? This intriguing question must be treated case by case. For me, it seems reasonable to assume that a large country such as Brazil could constitute a possible arena in which to countervail the dominance of global corporate forces, especially in a context of regional integration. In the end, this is also a question of political and social mobilization.

Concluding remarks

To what extent is the rise of the Southern Cone a new phenomenon in the global food order, implying new geopolitical relationships in which North American and European dominance is significantly reduced? Are these changes part of a growing third international agro-food regime, a genuinely new global food order? Or are we witnessing a repetition of the same old story of Western dominance that has characterized commodity booms in the past?

The soybean sector has many features in common with past patterns. Four large transnational companies – Cargill, Bunge, Archer and Daniel Midlands, and Dreyfus – dominate trade and processing. This is true for the all-important soybean exporters: the US as well the Latin American countries. The same companies have a very strong position in up-stream activities and fertilizers, and through joint ventures in pesticides, seeds, and biotechnology as well.[55] These companies also have a strong presence in downstream activities dependent on soybean products such as the meat-packing industry. The conditions under which soybeans are produced, traded, and processed are determined in a limited number of boardrooms. In this sense, the dominance of large transnational companies is markedly stronger than in the commodity boom of the late nineteenth and early twentieth centuries.

However, there are also a number of new dimensions. There are a number of Brazilian-owned groups in the new corporate-dominated food order that are expanding globally and are acquiring or merging with companies in the North. This is also true in other rapidly expanding agro-food sectors, such as sugar and ethanol. Brazil is not just another junior partner; the sheer quantity of its resources makes the country indispensable as a sourcing zone. The scope for action for national players is larger than in Argentina, not to mention Paraguay, Bolivia, and Uruguay, the even smaller newcomers on the soybean scene. The Brazilian state has power enough not to concede at every turn to outside pressure.

The pattern of international agro-food exports is showing a new trend: the importance of South–South flows is increasing. This is not a story of a wholly harmonious relationship. Only recently, Vietnamese farmers complained about low-price competition from Brazil on the poultry market.[56] Poor African farmers watch as their potential income from small-scale poultry production disappears; they have even greater reason to worry. We can expect a continuous growth of South–South agro-food flows in the present context of WTO-induced liberalization. Southern Cone exporters will increasingly out-compete traditional suppliers in these markets in the US and Europe; they will also constitute a formidable competitor to local farmers and food industries. This is emphatically not the same old story of outright North–South dependency. The smaller countries in the Southern Cone region (including

Argentina) have a smaller margin for error than resource-rich Brazil does. Brazilian actors in the meat industry are very much an independent force of considerable importance.

These developments are taking place within the framework of a corporate-dominated global food order, in which the power is still predominately located in the North – in the US, Europe, and Japan. Thus far, the distribution of the profits of the agro-food sector has unequal in the extreme; however, not all the gains are captured by economic interests in North. Under Lula's presidency, a cautious yet determined redistribution of income in favour of the poor has thus far resulted a fair amount of social stability despite of the social struggle organized by movements such as Via Campesina/MST.

Brazil is now a leading global agro-power in its own right. The contours of a new global agro-food order are increasingly visible. A new pattern in the geopolitics of food is forming, eroding the influence of the old centres of power. The long-term prospects and future development of this new food power is extremely difficult to predict; it is a huge understatement to say that the present global food order is uncontested. However, there is considerable room for expansion in a resource-rich country such as Brazil in both the short and middle term. Furthermore, even if the contemporary agro-food model is substantially modified, the region will continue to play an important role in feeding the world. The food power of the Southern Cone is here to stay for the foreseeable future.

Notes

1 *The Economist* featured the development in the bush savannah, the *cerrado*, in Brazil under the title, 'The Miracle of the Cerrado: Brazil Has Revolutionized Its Own Farms? Can It Do the Same For Others?', *The Economist*, 27 August 2010.

2 Susan B. Hecht & Charles C. Mann, 'How Brazil Outfarmed the American Farmer', *Fortune*, 151:1 (2008).

3 On the role of transnational companies in the formation of global food politics, see Philip McMichael, 'The Power of Food', *Agriculture and Human Values*, 17:1 (2000).

4 For a broad picture of Argentina's rise as a leading cereal exporter, see James Scobie, *Revolution on the Pampas: A Social History of Argentine Wheat* (Austin 1967); Jeremy Adelman, *Frontier Development: Land, Labour, and Capital on the Wheatlands of Argentina and Canada 1890–1914* (Oxford 1994). The figures are from, p. van Hissenhofen, *Le Mouvement des Grains dans le Monde* (Brussels 1938).

5 Steven Topik & Mario Sampar, 'The Latin American Coffee Commodity Chain:

Brazil and Costa Rica', in: Steven Topik, Carlos Marichal & Zephyr Frank (eds.), *From Silver to Cocaine: Latin American Commodity Chain and the Building of the World Economy* (Durham 2006) p. 124.

6 For an early example of the views put forward by the *New Political Economy of Agriculture* scholars, see Alessandro Bonano et al. (eds.), *From Columbus to ConAgra: The Globalization of Agriculture and Food* (Kansas 1994), pp. 15–25.

7 Harriet Friedmann & Philip McMichael, 'Agriculture and the State System: The Rise and Decline of National Agriculture', *Sociologica Ruralis*, 19:2 (2002). For an interesting development of this approach, see Harriet Friedmann, 'From Colonialism to Green Capitalism: Social Movement and the Emergence of Food Regimes', *Research in Rural Sociology and Development*, 11 (2005).

8 Harriet Friedmann, 'What on Earth is the Modern World-System? Foodgetting and Territory in the Modern Era and Beyond', *Journal of World System Research*, 6:2 (2000) constitutes an example of an interesting movement out of an too a strict structural model.

9 FAO, Key statistics of food and agriculture external trade 1961–2004.

10 For an overview of Argentina's agro-food exports in the first four decades of the twentieth century, see Lois B. Bacon & Friedrich C. Schloemer, *World Trade in Agricultural Products: Its Growth; Its Crisis; And the New Trade Policies* (Rome 1940), pp. 1014–1017.

11 The soybean complex answered for more than 50 per cent of Argentinean and close to 40 per cent of Brazilian agro-food exports 2004; FAO Key statistics of food and agriculture external trade (2004).

12 Susan B. Hecht, 'Soybeans, Development and Conservation on the Amazon Frontier', *Development and Change*, 36:2 (2006).

13 Peter Goldsmith & Rudolfo Hirsch, 'The Brazilian Soybean Complex', *Choices: The Magazine on Food, Farm and Resources*, 21:2 (2006).

14 Graciella Gutman et al., 'Les mutation agricoles: et agroalimentaires argentines des années 90: Liberalisation, changement technologique, firmes multinationales', *Région et Développement*, 23 (2006).

15 Carlos Steiger, 'Modern Beef Production in Brazil and Argentina', *Choices: The Magazine on food, farm and resources*, 21:2 (2006).

16 For an overview of the rate of concentration in the oilseed business, see William Hefferman, 'Consolidation in the Food and Agriculture System', *Report to the Nation Farmers Union* (1999). The same companies dominating the global oilseed sector are also the leading grain traders and are involved in a number of different agro-food markets, for example coffee, cocoa, and fruit and juices.

17 <www.bungeargentina.com>; <www.cargill.com.ar> (accessed 7 December 2009).

18 Bunge is the biggest fertilizer producer in Latin America. Recently Bunge agreed a joint venture with the Moroccan state-owned phosphates-mining company to supply raw materials and intermediate goods for Bunge's fertilizer business in Brazil and Argentina (ICIS, *Chemical Business*, 2007).

19 China today consumes more than 54 kilos of meat per inhabitant compared to less than 5 kilos in the 1960s (FAO).

20 *Chemical Market Reporter*, 18–24 July 2005: *Oils, Fats & Waxes*, 30 April 2005.

21 Comtrade 2007.

22 Soya Tech: <www.soyatech.com/oilseeds_statistcs> (accessed 29 August 2007).

23 UN Statistical Division Comtrade.

24 Brazil is also increasingly supplying the African market, out-competing European producers; USDA Foreign Agricultural Report Gain Report BR7606 (2007).

25 Among the eleven companies answering for 85 per cent of exports in 2005, only two were transnationals: SEARA, a subsidiary of Cargill, and Frangosul, owned by Doux, the French giant in the global poultry industry. Together these two companies had an export share of 24 per cent; USDA Foreign Agricultural Report, Gain report BR5620 (2005). Since then the Brazilian meat processor Mafrig has bought SEARA from Cargill.

26 *Business Latin America*, 8 June 2009.

27 <www.brazilintl.com> (accessed 15 August 2008).

28 *Emerging Markets*, January 2008.

29 <http://reuters.com> (accessed 9 June 2008).

30 <http://english.fleichwirtschaft.de> (accessed 27 January 2010).

31 <www.thepigsite.com> (accessed 16 June 2008).

32 Soya Tech, <htpp://72.32.142.180/news_story> (accessed 19 September 2007).

33 Fabio R. Chaddad & Marcos S. Jank, 'The Evolution of Agricultural Policies and Agribusiness Development in Brazil', *Choices: The Magazine on food, farm and resources*, 21:2 (2006).

34 <www.brazilintl.com> (accessed 16 August 2008).

35 Chaddad & Jank (2008).

36 Pablo Fonseca dos Santos, *External Trade in Brazil: Recent Developments* (Paris 2004); *The Economist* intelligence unit 2007, *Country report: Brazil.*

37 The Brazilian president Lula da Silva expressed ideas along these lines in an interview in the Argentine paper *Clarin*, focusing on the geopolitical role that the Mercosur region could play in Africa by reinforcing regional integration; see <www.servicios.clarin.com/notas/jsp/clarin/v8/imprimir.jsp?pagid=1755208> (accessed 24 September 2008).

38 Douglas Constance, 'The Emancipatory Question: The Next Step in the Sociology of Agrifood Systems?', *Agriculture and Human Values*, 25:2 (2008).

39 Albert Berry, 'When Do Agricultural Exports Help the Rural Poor? A Political Economy Approach', *Oxford Development Studies*, 29:2 (2001).

40 <www.soyatech.com/info.php?url_text=oilseed_statistics&err=1> (accessed 7 June 2008).

41 Ulrike Bickel & Jan Maarten Dros, *The Impacts of Soybean Cultivation on Brazilian Ecosystem: Three Case Studies*, WAFT Forest Conversion Initiative (2003).

42 In fact, the frontier conditions of the *cerrado* region have attracted a number of US farmers who have invested in land and started soybean operations in recent years; see also the radio station NPR 2006, <www.npr.org/templates/story/story.php?storyId=5125718> (accessed 30 September 2008).

43 For an overview, see Martine Guibert, 'La Nouvelle Agriculture Argentine: Entre innovations et incertitudes', *Déméter* (2010).

44 Miguel Teubal, 'Genetically Modified Soybeans and the Crisis of Argentina's Agriculture Model', in: Gerardo Otero (ed.), *Foods for the Few: Neoliberal Globalism and Biotechnology in Latin America* (Austin 2008), pp. 206–214.

45 <http://www.thebeefsite.com/news/24555/argentina-may-import-beef-by-2012> (accessed 18 June 2011).

46 <www.manojulio.com.br/conteudo/atividades-suinocultura.asp#call> (accessed 3 September 2008).

47 The mainstream French agro-food think tank Club Demeter devoted a large part of its yearbook 2006 to questions of sustainability and how to increase sustainability in large-scale, conventional agriculture; see Alain Capillon, (coordinator), 'Introduction au dossier: La nécessaire evolution des pratiques agricoles pour le développement durable', *Déméter* 2006: *Economies et stratégies agricoles* (Paris 2006), pp. 61–72.

48 <www.bunge.com/about-bunge/agriculture_in_brazil.html, 2008-09-03>.

49 See, for example, Philip M. Fearnside, 'Soybean Cultivation As a Threat to the Environment in Brazil', *Environmental Conservation*, 28:1(2001).

50 Christian Brannstrom, 'Environment Policy Reform on North-eastern Brazil's Agricultural Frontier', *Geoforum*, 36 (2005); Corina Steward, 'From Colonization to 'environmental soy': A Case Study of Environmental and Socio-economic Valuation in the Amazon Soy Frontier', *Agriculture and Human Values*, 24 (2007).

51 Lilian Joensen, 'The Crop-sprayed Villages of Argentina', in: Javiera Rulli (coordinator), *United Soya Republics: The Truth About Soya Production in South America*, available at <http://lasojamata.iskra.net/en/node/91> (accessed 18 June 2011).

52 A number of net food-importing countries in West Africa have been more and more dependent on Brazilian chicken imports, hurting local, small-scale, rural producers, see Ulf Jonsson & Erik Green, 'Africa and the Liberalisation of Global Agri-business Markets Moving Beyond Presumed Patterns of Trade', paper presented at the Swedish Economic History Meeting, Stockholm 2007.

53 For arguments along these lines, see Walter H. Pengue, 'Production agroexportadora e (in) seguridad alimentaria: El caso de la soja en Argentina', *Revista Iberoamericana de Economia Ecológica*, 1 (2004); Lilian Joense & Stella Semino, 'Argentina's torrid love affair with the soya bean', *Seedling* (October 2004) <http://www.grain.org/seedling_files/seed-04-10-2.pdf> (accessed 18 June 2011).

54 For an overview of Brazilian agricultural polices in the last forty years, see Frank R. Chaddad, 'The Evolution of Agricultural Policies and Agribusiness Development in Brazil', *Choices: The Magazine of Food, Farm and Resource Issues*, 21:2 (2006).

55 See Hefferman (1999), pp. 4–10.

56 <www.poultrysite.com/poultrynews/farme-struggle-against-low-meat> (accessed 3 October 2008).

CHAPTER 14

Fixed versus Floating Capital in the Medieval Iron Trade, 1385–1504

Bo Franzén

Swedish industry springs from many wells, and one of them goes all the way back to medieval iron production. During and after the Middle Ages, there was a prevalence of both large-scale iron production in furnaces and smaller scale production of bloom iron in the wood-fuelled, smaller bloomeries that were set up on the nearest dry slope. The latter, simpler method used limonite, or bog ore, and probably dates back to the start of the actual Iron Age in Sweden (from around 500 BC), although medieval bloom iron was not necessarily of lower quality than osmund, iron made by the eponymous furnace process. Some have claimed that the furnace technology used was imported to Sweden during the Middle Ages; however, more recent results indicate that it was already in use prior to AD 1000. These sensational archaeological findings were made during an ongoing multidisciplinary project under the aegis of Jernkontoret (the Swedish Ironmasters' Association) in which this author has participated as an economic historian. The project, 'Iron Production and State Formation in Sweden, 1150–1350', aims to clarify the origins and early history of iron. 'The Atlas Project', a recent extensive inventory and survey of mines and smelting-houses, was the inspiration for the project, as was the sensational discovery in 2000 of the remains of a previously unknown smelting-house close to Hyttehamn (lit. smelting-house harbour) on the shores of Lake Vättern. This chapter on the economy of late medieval iron production is a progress report from the Jernkontoret project.

Substantial research has been done on the medieval iron trade; however, there are several compelling reasons to continue investigating the earliest iron industries on Swedish soil. First of all, it is clear that forgeable iron and forged products (weapons) were exported as early as the High Middle Ages – well before 1350 – and that this trade played an active part in bringing Sweden into contact with international markets. Secondly, this international demand fuelled technological innovations in Sweden. Another way of saying this is that for several centuries the iron trade paved the way for a comparatively 'backward medieval community' to adopt and progressively utilize various innovations.

My purpose here is to shed some light on the division between floating and fixed capital during the Middle Ages in Sweden. Fixed capital refers to property, which was popularly referred to as *fastighet*, *äga*, or *jord* (property, holdings, or land), and in this context is synonymous with the medieval term *hytta* (smelting-house): that is to say, the property where the furnace was located, along with other associated buildings such as coal sheds and smithies. It is difficult to draw a hard line between fixed and floating capital; however, floating capital includes the many goods and services required for iron production. It would seem unlikely that this production would have ever reached any significant magnitude in the absence of secure, long-term credit or advances. The floating expenses mainly consisted of wages for the smelting-house labourers, and the costs of ore, firewood (for roasting the ore), charcoal, and the significant amount of heavy transport involved in all of these stages, including transporting the finished osmunds to market.

Iron was likely traded in pre-Christian times; however, as one would expect, there are no written records from the real economy to afford us any insight into this trade. Swedish pricing data mainly date to the later Middle Ages (1350–1527). In the present case, the main focus is upon the years between 1385 and 1504. Medieval primary sources are notoriously terse and difficult to interpret; yet this does not mean that intensive source-critical analysis cannot discover certain patterns. It was the historian Fernand Braudel who claimed that the floating portion of pre-industrial capital was much larger than the fixed portion.[1] During one of my last visits to Jan Glete before he passed on, I told him of my idea for a paper. His immediate response was to tell me that he believed the floating portion of capital – the system of advances – was dominant during the Swedish Middle Ages. The conclusions drawn in this chapter indicate that Jan was right about this matter, as he was about so much else.

An institutional approach

My approach here is inspired by ideas presented in the classic work, *The Rise of the Western World: A New Economic History*, by Douglass North and Robert Thomas, published in 1973. They advance in this work a model of analysis for the pre-industrial economy of the years 900–1700. This model is not offered as an alternative to classical economic theory; its foundation is still that an economy involves the free exchange of goods and services – utilities, in a single word – for other goods and services. This is obviously a definition similar to that of Adam Smith; however, it is important to note that the market is not taken for granted as a phenomenon in this *institutional extension*. In other words, the question is rather which of the social institutions benefit or impede the free trade in utilities. These institutions can be both formal and informal in nature, yet they should not be confused with organizations or government agencies. Two examples of such medieval institutions are the liquidation of property by pledging it as collateral, and the right to offer personal property for sale in the market squares of the trading towns. *Riksrådet* (the council of the realm) and the convent of St Klara are examples of institutions in the other, organizational sense.

Scepticism regarding the market during the Middle Ages may seem unwarranted; we have good reason to believe that trade in what was to become Sweden long predates the Middle Ages. However, it would be wise not to overlook the question of the extent to which consumption and production were actually based upon commerce rather than other institutions such as self-subsistence or coercion, slavery or serfdom (there were thralls and serfs in medieval Sweden, and slavery was only made illegal in the fourteenth century). It is irrefutable that technological advances were made during the five centuries of the Swedish Middle Ages, although this modernization also seems to have seen its share of setbacks and regressions. Medieval smelting-houses naturally have many points of contact with these enlarged financial practices. We often hear that more advanced technology drives economic growth; however, that approach is not applicable here. In institutional economics, the use of better technology is considered to be part of the actual growth, rather than its cause.[2]

What then are the implications of an institutional interpretation of the Middle Ages in Swedish economic history? In my opinion it can be summarized thus: a backward, primitive society that was progressively modernized by means of increasing commerce. This medieval commercialization occurred both in the towns and in rural areas, fuelled by demand both within the realm and abroad. There are clear indications that individual liberties (including trade) were on the rise during late thirteenth century, if not before. They can be summarized as the transition from a coercive basis of labour to a free working class; expanded markets for land and credit; a large number of new trading towns; and the increasing participation of women in the public sphere.[3]

The iron trade is properly regarded in the light of this progressive commercialization of medieval Sweden. Despite the fact that the technology used in the furnaces had been available for centuries, the fact that Swedish osmund came into its own as a serious bulk commodity some time around the year 1400 holds no contradictions, in my opinion. Foreign demand is justifiably considered to have played an important role in this, at least in providing producers with the necessary long-term credit or advances.[4] However, the financial institutions required for the unimpeded trade of goods and services had nothing to do with the primitive, coercive institutions of the High Middle Ages such as slavery and serfdom.

Fragmentary sources

This investigation primarily builds on previous research in the field of economic history and on information gathered from medieval primary sources. There are several kinds of manuscript evidence involved, such as charters, verdicts, wills, and so on. The most useful for our purposes are deeds of purchase from the region of Bergslagen. These medieval Swedish letters are compiled in a database, commonly known as Huvudkartoteket (SDhk), managed and continuously updated by the Svenskt Diplomatarium department at Riksarkivet (the National Archives of Sweden). The main catalogue of Diplomatarium Suecanum contains 40,000 entries, which summarize an equal number of letters and charters. Some entries also contain the wordings of the documents in a digital format, although this mainly applies to those dated prior to 1370 and for the years 1401–1420.

Huvudkartoteket is a most valuable resource for researchers, despite its shortcomings. There are five centuries of material, admittedly unevenly distributed, two-thirds of which is dated later than 1400. This means that the further one progresses through the Middle Ages, the more sources there are. (I refer readers to my work *Emancipation and Urbanization in What Was to Become Sweden, circa 1200 to 1527* for a closer look at the structure and contents of Huvudkartoteket.[5]) Here I have mainly used Huvudkartoteket's 'Innehåll' (contents) category, which contains summaries of the contents of the documents in modern Swedish. It is these summaries or regests that I have searched for instances of *masugn* (blast furnace) and *hytta* (smelting-house). It should be mentioned that the regests are not entirely consistent when it concerns the type of information they include from the original sources.[6] This means that more instances of smelting-house prices may be discovered in the material than have been identified thus far. Since the authors of the regest entries do not always include the prices mentioned in the originals, the pricing data to which we actually have access are mostly from the published versions in the *Diplomatarium Dalekarlicum*. They often simply mention that a purchase was made. A complete table of all the regests that relate to smelting-houses can be found at the end of this chapter (Table 2). The following example of how a smelting-house changed hands half a millennium ago serves to illustrate a typical scenario:

> [18 January 1488] Peter Skrivare, judge of a hundred court in Dalarna, certifies that burgher Jap Djäkne [indicating his literacy] of Västerås, at the sessions in Skedvi parish [in Dalarna] made over ownership and sold one-half of a smelting-house to Jon Olsson for three lasts of iron.[7]

Before I discuss how this price can be utilized, I would like to emphasize that a smelting-house of the type referred to here should not to be confused with a furnace. Admittedly, in order to deserve the name of *hytta*, a smelting-house would most often house a furnace. However, sources reveal that a smelting-house would often have land, buildings, tools, and so on attached – it may also be considered part of a farmstead – and is thus a broader concept than 'furnace'. Furthermore, we have reason to assume that some of the smelting-houses in the sources were primarily used to produce copper rather than iron. However, this should be of little consequence as the furnaces used for producing the two metals were constructed in a similar fashion. It is even conceivable that these furnaces could be used for producing either metal.

If we return to the price of the smelting-house, it should be emphasized that the price of iron (measured in weight of silver) displays a general downward trend, albeit a slow one. Thus the cost of iron became ever lower as the Reformation drew closer. As with other utilities, osmund was subject to price fluctuations due to shifts in supply and demand; however, these price movements never seem to have been particularly violent.

The quote concerns a half-share of a smelting-house. For comparative purposes, the price of three lasts of iron must thus be doubled to six lasts of iron. A natural question at this point would be to ask what exactly was the value of six lasts of iron more than half a millennium ago? We have a document dated 1489, preserved from the trading town of Arboga, that indicates that one last was worth 34 marks or *mark penningar* (lit. marks in pennies).[8] This would give a price of 204 marks for the purchase of the entire smelting-house in the example above. According to the economic history index published by my colleague Rodney Edvinsson at <www.historia.se>, this price would equate to 173,817 Swedish kronor in 2009 terms. Attempting to make conversions of this accuracy across the centuries has not been a common practice in Swedish historical research in the past. A large number of source-critical reservations spring to mind, many of which are raised at Edvinsson's website. Other conversions of this and other medieval prices will be made in future, but my intention in highlighting this rather low comparative value of a medieval property here is that the numbers verify what we already knew: medieval society was a very poor society by our standards.

Table 2 in the appendix notes where the source refers to an unspecified share in a smelting-house; where no price is given; or where the price is unavailable at present. However, a selection of thirteen good-quality price records can be made, drawn unevenly from the years 1385–1504 (Table 1). Empirically speaking, this is evidently a fragile base; however, it may be more useful than expected considering the fact that these are observations that date back to the Middle Ages. For comparative purposes, they have been converted to their equivalent value in weighed silver (grams of silver or g Ag). The practice of converting prices based upon a selected standard is known as *deflating*; the purpose of this is to facilitate the comparison of prices over time. Silver has become the most commonly used standard among researchers, even though theoretically almost any repository of value could be used as a deflator. Although the relative price of silver (like any article of trade) is subject to market fluctuations, the price volatility of silver in the medieval period seems to have been minor, while the use of a silver deflator vastly simplifies international comparisons. I have used the Swedish silver mark of 210.616 grams of silver (which was nine-tenths of a Cologne Mark, the widely used unit of weight).

Table 1: Thirteen selected Swedish smelting house prices from 1385–1504

Year	*Production unit*	*Production unit price*	*Equivalent' in g Ag*
1385	One-third of the Västgötahyttan smelting-house near Norberg, for 51 marks	153 marks	5,371
1392	Iron smelting-house etc. in Klingsbo, Dalarna	24 shippounds of copper	17,376
1402	Farm and smelting-house [Garpenberg? Finnhyttan?]	16 shippounds of copper	14,752
1412	The southern farm (=one-half) in Främby with 'house, land, fields, meadows, stream, and smelting-house'	12 shippounds of copper ('Västerås measure') or 7 barrels of iron per shippound copper	6,552
1417	House, land, two smelting-houses, smithy in Nedansjö, and one-half of the property in Västerås	4 lasts and 3 barrels of iron	4,214
1427	Smelting-house and farm at Kopparberget	2 shippounds and 5 lispounds of copper	900
1430	One-half of a smelting-house in Kvarnaboda with tools, one-half of a mine in Bråfall in Gesberg and Betsberg as 'brukspant' (a collateral pledge including the right to use the property pledged) 'without reduction of the main total' for 4 shippounds of copper and 3 barrels of iron	8 shippounds of copper and 6 barrels of iron	3,588
1434	House, meadows, and smelting-house by Kopparberget	15 lispounds of copper (1 lispound is ¾ of a shippound)	300

1481	Smelting-house in Gruvriset near Kopparberget	5 shippounds of copper and 6 ells of broadcloth from Leiden	1,291
1481	Smelting-house at Vikeberg with house, land, field, and meadow (in Dalarna)	2 shippounds of copper	506
1487	Knutshyttan smelting-house in Stora Tuna parish in Dalarna	130 marks in Stockholm coinage	2,489
1488	One-half of a smelting-house for 3 lasts of iron	6 lasts of iron	3,558
1504	Asphyttan smelting-house for 50 Danish marks (=40 Swedish marks)	40 marks in Swedish pennies	674
	Total		61,571
	Average		4,736
	Coefficient of Variation		114 %

Source: Table 2.

Table 1 invites three fairly obvious observations. First of all, smelting-house *prices vary substantially*, which is only to be expected given previous research concerning fixed property during the Middle Ages in Sweden.[9] This evidently has to do with the condition of the facilities, access to water for the furnace's water-wheel, and other aspects of location such as proximity to raw materials, markets, and so on. Secondly, the units of value involved are surprising, as fully ten of the thirteen *prices are given in kind*; only three are given in cash terms. The surprise here is that in the late Middle Ages the value of fixed property was more commonly given in monetary terms. However, this should by no means be taken to indicate that the purchase was, in fact, paid for in cash. Instead, a common practice was to use intermediary goods (that is to say, goods valued in terms of currency and then used as such). Third, strikingly, it would seem that the *pricing trend was negative* – the units for the mass production of metals such as iron and copper became progressively cheaper for people to build. By plotting the information presented in Table 1 against the silver prices, the relevant values from the CPI (the consumer price index that my colleagues Johan Söderberg and Rodney Edvinsson have compiled) can be seen (see Figure 1).

The two methods for converting prices in cash or kind into units

Chart 1: Selected prices for Swedish smelting-houses deflated into gram silver, 1385–1504

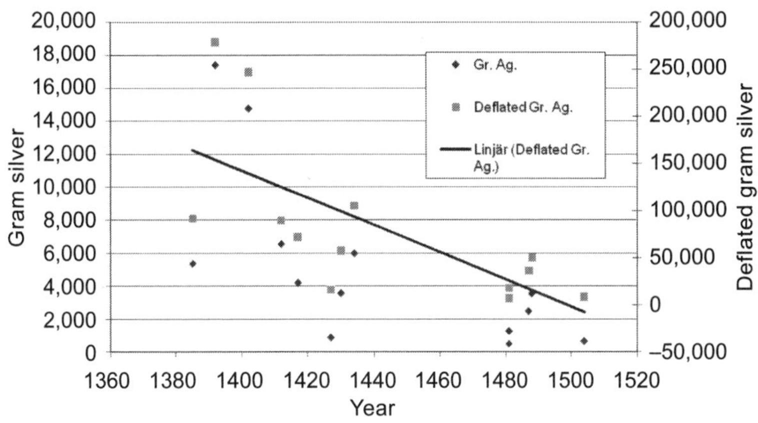

Source: Table 1 and the Consumer Price Index available at <www.historia.se>. (The CPI is a price converter of which Jan Glete thought very highly.)

more suitable for comparison do not differ significantly from each other, although it should be stressed that they are not entirely independent of each other either. However, both price conversions indicate a significant downward trend in the prices of smelting-houses in the fifteenth century. This would also seem to be an indication of falling iron and copper prices during the same period. The price of iron and copper in Sweden has been discussed in the literature, and recently Johan Söderberg has done a great deal to broaden and systematize our understanding of existing sources, situating price trends in a comparative international context. This analysis also includes the staple grain (barley), which staple (or its substitute) must display a negative pricing trend in order for sustainable economic growth to occur.

Figure 1 confirms previous research: the relative prices of iron and copper were in steady decline throughout the Middle Ages. This observation would seem to imply a development in the late Middle Ages where these metals became ever cheaper, to the benefit of all mankind. This indicates a transition. Furnace-based production prior to the fifteenth century was an exclusive, expensive business that later increased in importance, eventually becoming our earliest form of mass production. This had an impact upon everyday life, as cheaper pots made of

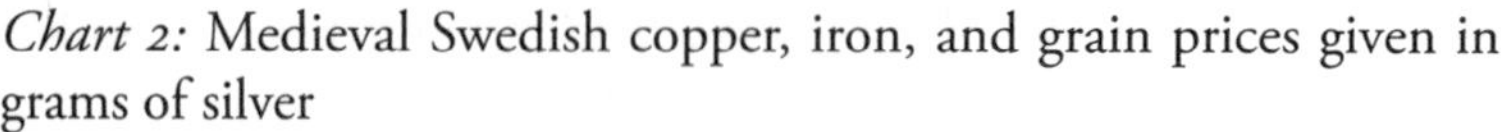

Chart 2: Medieval Swedish copper, iron, and grain prices given in grams of silver

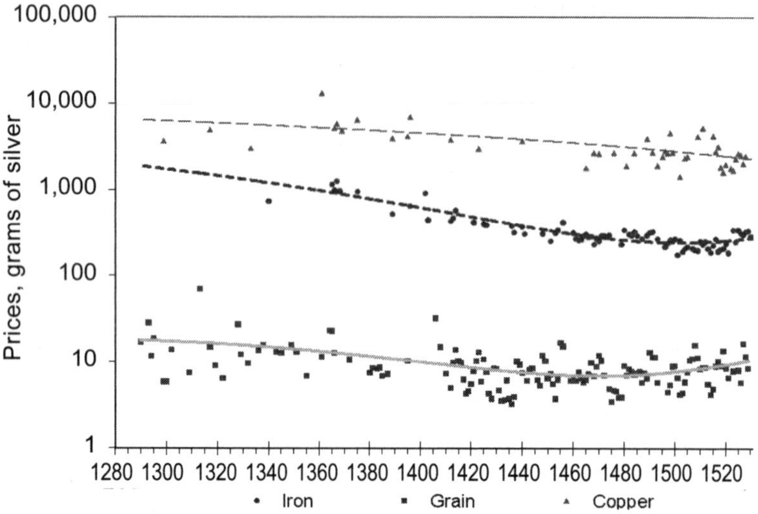

Source: Johan Söderberg, 'Prices and Economic Change in Medieval Sweden', *Scandinavian Economic History Review*, 55:2 (2007) Figure 2, p. 133.

iron and copper became affordable to a larger number of consumers from the lower social strata. The fact that grain (the most important commodity of all) never saw any lasting price reduction indicates that the real leap in standard of living was still centuries away. The trend curve in the logarithmic price chart confirms this fact: the trend would look a lot more dramatic in a chart based on analogue values. The lack of mobility in grain prices throughout the medieval and early modern period was a severe bottleneck, holding back all attempts to achieve lasting improvements in people's welfare.[10]

Moving on to the actual production of iron, the work performed in a smelting-house was typically an occupation taken by the rural population. As opposed to its older contemporary the bloomery, a furnace required water-wheel-propelled mechanical power for its bellows, which were used day and night to maintain a high and even temperature. Any lengthy interruption to this fragile, proto-industrial process could be disastrous. So great was the need for water power that water would normally be stored in reservoirs and channelled in along a small wooden aqueduct during actual production. When successful, the furnace produced pig iron, which would subsequently be refined into osmund – pieces of iron weighing approximately 300 grams, cut in such a way as to indicate the quality of the iron and to facilitate working it in smithies.

Access to water was one of the limiting factors that determined how long a smelting-house could be in production. Under ordinary circumstances, a *blasting*, the period when the furnace was in operation, would last two or three weeks. However, the blasting was only one stage of the process, and was preceded by work such as the mining of ore, wood-cutting, roasting and breaking up the ore, charcoal-burning, and the extensive haulage all of these activities required. In absolute terms, compared to the bloomery the blast furnace was very demanding in terms of labour and raw materials; however, in terms of productivity, the blast furnace yielded far more than a bloomery: per unit, osmund was simply cheaper to produce than bloom iron was. Alternative occupations were sometimes unavailable in rural areas, which may explain why bloomeries were found alongside furnaces throughout the Middle Ages and into the early modern era.

The question of how much labour was required for medieval iron production has no simple answer, despite the fact that a blasting is performed every year as an archaeological experiment at the Nya Lapphyttan smelting-house in Norberg in an attempt to reclaim knowledge that has been lost over time. The initial estimate by archaeologists Ing-Marie Pettersson Jensen and Catarina Karlsson covers the entire course of production, from mine to harbour, and is based on an example route of Lindesberg–Arboga–Stockholm. Their assumption is that the smelting-house was ordinarily operated in two shifts, with each team working half of a twenty-four-hour period; thus one working day represented twelve hours of labour. To this we must add the days of labour required before the actual blasting and the haulage required to get the product to market. Pettersson Jensen and Karlsson's tentative conclusion is that one blasting required 500 days' labour, as well as 80 days' child labour, to yield one last (or 12 barrels) of osmund, which they estimate to have equalled 1.8 tonnes of iron. When the work is divided into pre- and post-blasting sessions, the total days' labour comes to 240 and 220, respectively (the child labour was limited to the actual blasting).[11] I must again underline the fact that these figures are speculative and that research into these matters is ongoing. Indeed, I suspect that future investigations may support the conclusion that a typical medieval blasting could very well have produced far more than one last of iron – perhaps even as much as two to four times that amount.

What, then, was the value of 500–600 days' labour during the Middle Ages? This too is an extremely difficult question to answer, mainly due to the lack of contemporary data. Johan Söderberg's extensive pricing database holds some salary data for medieval labourers, but from cities that bear no relation to the rural region of Bergslagen. Although some assumptions regarding the wages paid for 500 days' labour could be made, the uncertainties involved are sufficient to dissuade me from the attempt for the time being. Thus the hypothetical number of days' labour is merely intended to illustrate the large amount of unskilled and skilled labour required to produce iron. Along with market towns, it was the chain of production from mine to finished iron that would come to symbolize the increasing liberties that followed the fall of the Carolingian state in around AD 1000. The far more decentralized and commercialized system that ensued is what we now call feudalism.

Was the labour system in Sweden's medieval mining industry non-coercive? I believe there is good reason to assume that this was the case; however, it would have necessitated advance payments of significant value to the workers, which in turn would have required the availability of long-term and long-distance credit or a *debenture system*. Such advances, which were usually paid for in kind, required interest. The return on fixed property (land), which can be employed as a standard for medieval long-term interest rates, seems to have been in the vicinity of 5 per cent for the fourteenth century on.[12] In other words, a piece of real estate was expected to yield a return equal to its own value over twenty years (as long as we disregard the complications of compound interest).

My main concern here is the proportion of fixed and floating capital. The fragmentary sources we have concerning the iron trade's fixed capital (smelting-house prices) indicate falling prices as well as great statistical dispersion. If we were to select a typical case, 6 lasts of iron for a half-share in a smelting-house in 1488 seems a suitable choice. The price is not too far from the average, and seems to indicate a value of six blastings' worth of production in fixed capital. Thus a smelting-house that was used once or twice a year would be worth three to six years of iron production. This is a lot more than the 5 per cent that seems to have been the average for other kinds of property. This further underlines the sheer quantity of floating capital required in this first system of large-scale mass production.

Summary

Is it then possible to determine the proportions of fixed and floating capital in Swedish medieval iron production? The prices of the osmund production facilities – that is to say, smelting-houses – are central to my investigation. A remarkably fragmented array of Swedish sources offers thirteen such prices from the late Middle Ages. The conversions and approximations involved pose extensive challenges to the sources, yet the upshot is that it is clear there was a significant fall in smelting-house prices during the fifteenth century. This is no way incompatible with Johan Söderberg's latest findings, which indicate that the price levels of iron and copper (which was also produced in furnaces) displayed negative trends during the period in question.

According to tentative estimates, the cost of the 500–600 days' work required in the course of one blasting would have yielded slightly less than two tonnes of quality iron. However, the uncertainties are too great to yield reliable estimates. In my opinion, future research may well reveal that a typical blasting could yield two to four times the present approximation of two tonnes of iron. However, the significant amounts of labour required should be seen in light of the fact that the return on investments in a smelting-house seems to have been much higher than for other types of fixed property. This is not to say that smelting-houses were by definition more profitable than farms. What it does underline, however, is that there was considerable need for floating capital or credit; what would come to be referred to as *förlag* (advances) in the iron production industry. The calculations here imply that advances made up a comparatively large proportion of capital in medieval Sweden.

Appendix

Table 2: Foundries in the circulation of valuables: 1385–1508

Source	*Year*	*Property*	*Full unit price*	*Price convert to gram of silver*
RPB 2092	1385	One-third of the Västgötahyttan smelting-house near Norberg for 51 marks	153 marks	5,37
SDhk 11318	1392	Iron smelting-house etc. in Klingsbo, Dalarna	24 shippounds of copper	17,37
SDhk 15897	1402	Farm and smelting-house [Garpenberg? / Finnhyttan?]	16 shippounds of copper	14,75
SDhk 17453	1410	Share of smelting-house in Östergötland	10 marks	
SDhk 17770 SD 1524	1412	The southern farm in Främby with 'house, land, fields, meadows, stream, and smelting-house'	12 shippounds of copper ('Västeråsvikt') or 7 barrels of iron per shippound[16]	6,55
SDhk 18842 SD 1524	1417	House, land, two smelting-houses, smithy in Nedansjö, and one-half of property in Västerås	4 lasts 3 barrels of iron=51×3=153 marks	4,21
SDhk 20797 DD 863	1427	Smelting-house and farm at Kopparberget	2 shippounds and 5 lispound of copper[19]	90
SDhk 21385 DD 970	1430	One-half of a smelting-house in Kvarnaboda, with tools, one-half of a mine in Bråfall in Gesberg and Betsberg as 'brukspant' (a collateral pledge including the right to use the property pledged) 'without reduction of the main total' for 4 shippounds of copper and 3 barrels of iron	8 shippounds of copper and 6 barrels of iron	3,58
SDhk 22071 DD 865[22]	1434	House, meadows, and smelting-house by Kopparberget	15 lis pounds of copper (1 lispound is 3/4 of a shippound)	30
SDhk 23440 DD 869[24]	1440	Share of a smelting-house at Hosjön lake	14 lispund of copper for 1 last of barley in Mora[25]	33
SDhk 27290[27]	1458	Svenhyttan smelting-house at Lekeberg		

)hk 28726 B 16 fol. 3v, no. 137, RA 02 (see hardcopy of 16 texts, DK)[28]	1467	Two shares of smelting-house in Värmland		
)hk 29868) 938	1475	Share of 'Hyttgärde' (smelting-house with land) [in Dalarna?]	3 barrels of iron 4 ells of broadcloth ½ mark in pennies[29]	
hk 30891 DD 132	1481	Smelting-house in Gruvriset near Kopparberget	5 shippounds of copper and 6 ells of broadcloth from Leiden	1,291[30]
hk 30994) 881	1481	Smelting-house at Vikeberg with house, land, field, and meadow in Dalarna	2 shippounds of copper[31]	506[32]
hk 31876) 307	1487	Knutshyttan smelting-house in Stora Tuna parish in Dalarna	130 marks in Stockholm coins	2,489[33]
hk 31997	1488	One-half of a smelting-house for 3 lasts of iron	6 lasts of iron[34]	3,558[35]
hk 32206) 274	1489	Two shares of Betsbergshytta smelting-house	250 marks[36]	
hk 32378) 275	1490	One-half of a smelting-house in Skedvi parish	Dispute with verdict – no price	
hk 33360) 911	1496	Smelting-house including a house, a mill, and mine in Silverberget in Tuna parish, bishopric of Västerås	Deed of gift with no price	
hk 33367) 278	1496	A smelting-house and mill near Falene (Falun?)	Deed of purchase, no price present	
hk 34905 A. mqvist, Bergslagen rd och bild, no. 20 l of 1954), p. 2	1504	Asphyttan smelting-house for 50 Danish marks (=40 Swedish marks)	40 marks in Swedish pennies	674[37]
hk 35654 Bergskoli archive D VI: 4, 53 r (Tilas collecn No 4), RA	1507	Donation of the Gjutarehyttan smelting-house, and so on to the Huseby abbey		
hk 36062) 211	1508	Permanent gift and interest for giver of religious service there of half a mark's interest in Dormsö with smelting-house and mill	Will, no price present	

te on sources: DD – *Diplomatarium Dalekarlicum*, 1–3: 1248–1552 (Stockholm 1842–1853); RPB – *nska Riks-archivets pergamentsbref*, 1–2: 1351–1400 (Stockholm 1866, 1868); SD – *Svenskt Diplomaium från och med 1401*, 1–3: 1401–1420 (Stockholm 1875–1904); SDhk – *De svenska medeltidsbreven i nskt Diplomatariums huvudkartotek*, CD-ROM version 2, Swedish National Archives (Stockholm 2001).

Notes

1 Fernand Braudel, *Civilisationer och kapitalism 1400–1800*, 2: *Marknadens spel* (Stockholm 1986), pp. 222–223, 228.

2 Douglass C. North & Robert Paul Thomas, *The Rise of the Western World: A New Economic History* (Cambridge 1973), p. 2.

3 Bo Franzén, *Folkungatidens monetära system: Penningen mellan pest och patriarkat 1254–1370* (Stockholm 2006), pp. 13–14; id. *Emancipation och urbanisering i medeltidens Sverige: Trender mot ett mer fritt och rörligt feodalt samhälle cirka 1200–1527* (Stockholm 2009), pp. 5–6.

4 Sven Ljung, *Arboga stads historia*, 1: *Tiden intill 1551* (Stockholm 1949), p. 243; Bo Franzén, *Sturetidens monetära system: Pant eller penningar som information i köpstaden Arboga* (Stockholm 1998), pp. 26–27.

5 Franzén (2009), pp. 19–23. Just over a third of the letters that were undoubtedly written in Sweden seem to have been written for purely financial purposes. It may be no surprise that around a third of the letters seem to have been written for more or less commercial purposes; perhaps it is more noteworthy that this figure remained constant throughout the period of 1087–1527; Franzén (2009), p. 23 and table 6:1, p. 63.

6 Franzén (2009), pp. 21–22.

7 Based on *De svenska medeltidsbreven i Svenskt Diplomatariums huvudkartotek* (SDhk), CD-ROM version 2, Swedish National Archives (Stockholm 2001) 31997.

8 Atb: *Arboga stads tänkebok*, 1–4, ed. Erik Noreen & Torsten Wennström (Uppsala 1935–1950) 2, p. 351; Bo Franzén, *Sturetidens monetära system: Pant eller penningar som information i köpstaden Arboga* (Stockholm 1998) p. 259.

9 The average price of a smelting-house of 5,175 g Ag from table 1 can be compared to the average price of sold land (per *markland* unit) or farm in 1277–1370 of approximately 3 kg ag. and 1131 g Ag for sold and pledged courtyard in Arboga 1453–1520. (Sources: relational databases created by the author for Franzén (2006), and Franzén (1998).) For average prices and price distribution for farms/*markland* units and other land area units for the years 1278–1370, see Franzén (2006), p. 154.

10 Johan Söderberg, 'Prices and Economic Change in Medieval Sweden', *Scandinavian Economic History Review*, 55:2 (2007), p. 148.

11 Ing-Marie Pettersson Jensen & Catarina Karlsson, 'Ett skepp kommer lastat! Från Bergslagen till Skeppsbron', unpublished memorandum from the Jernkontoret project 'Järnet och riksbildningen' ('Iron production and State Formation in Sweden 1150–1350') (2009), pp. 12–13. The authors summarize their calculations thus on, p. 13: 'Approximately 493 days of and 80 days of child labour at 12 hours each, for the production of 1.8 tonnes of osmond iron. That is the equivalent of a little more than 16 months of labour for one man, as well as two and a half months for a child, without any days off.'

12 Franzén (2006), pp. 138–140.

13 Based upon a market price of 6 marks in pennies per mark silver 153/6=25.5 mark silver=5,371 g Ag.

14 Average of 1388 and 1395 records for shippounds copper (that is to say, 526+922/2=724 g Ag per shippound copper).

15 According to 1395 record of 922 g Ag per shippound copper.

16 Price is only given in the original text.
17 According to 1412 record of 78 g Ag per barrel of iron: 7×12×78=6,552 g Ag.
18 Average of 1413 and 1420 records of 1,148 + 835/2=991.5 g Ag per last of iron: 4.25×991.5=4,214 g Ag.
19 Price not given in SDhk; however, it is given in DD (*Diplomatarium Dalekarlicum*).
20 According to 1422 record of 400 g Ag per shippound copper: 2.25×400=900 g Ag.
21 According to 1422 record of 400 g Ag per shippound copper and 388 g Ag. For a half last of iron according to record from 1425: (8×400)+388=3,588 g Ag.
22 Price not given in SDhk; however, it is given in DD.
23 According to 1422 record of 400 g Ag per shippound copper (1 shippound=20 lispund).
24 Price not given in SDhk; however, it is given in DD.
25 Price not given in SDhk; however, it is given in DD.
26 According to record of 337 g Ag per last of grain from year of 1440: 0.7 (14 lispund) of a shippound copper (that is to say, 481.4 g Ag per shippound copper).
27 Or perg. RA 0101 (defective); Pär Hansson, *Örebro kyrka och stad* (Örebro 1994), p. 15.
28 Illegible photocopy.
29 Price not given in SDhk; however, it is given in DD.
30 According to record from 1480 of 253 g Ag per shippound copper and 2 öre in pennies per ell from Arboga in 1490. Considering the silver price in the same year and town, and considering that 12 marks in pennies per mark silver (Atb 2:377 and 2:366) converts to 1/96 mark silver per öre in pennies, which, based on an Ag mark weight of 210.616 g Ag, converts to 21.19 g Ag per öre in pennies. Twelve times this weight in silver is 26.3 g Ag: (5×253)+26.3=appr. 1,291 g Ag.
31 Price not given in SDhk; however, it is given in DD.
32 According to record from 1480 of 253 g Ag per shippound of copper.
33 Based upon 11 marks in pennies per mark ag. at 210.616 gr.
34 34 marks per last according to credit adjustment from Arboga, 1489 (Atb 2:351).
35 Based upon an iron price of 593 g Ag per last of iron from the same year.
36 Price not given in SDhk; however, it is given in DD.
37 Based upon a market price of 12.5 marks in pennies per mark silver 40/12.5=3.2 mark silver=674 g Ag.

CHAPTER 15

Command and Control during Sweden's Last War

The introduction of divisions and army-corps to the Swedish Army, 1813–1814

Gunnar Åselius

The 2001 US Army field manual defines a major military operation as 'a series of tactical actions ... conducted by various combat forces of single or several services, coordinated in time and place, to accomplish operational and sometimes strategic objectives in an operational area'.[1] If this definition is accepted at face value, military operations were rare before the Napoleonic Wars. As long as armies were comparatively small and military force difficult to project over large distances, there was little need for coordination. Moreover, temporal and geographical coordination requires that your troops have access to accurate clocks and maps and are sufficiently mobile to adapt to new directives. Only with the French Revolution and the creation of conscript mass armies did the resources for the large-scale projection of military force become available. About the same time, pocket-watches came into widespread use and were sufficiently accurate (although they had existed in Europe since the sixteenth century). Moreover, Europe (west of Russia) had been mapped out at least at a scale of 1:100,000 at the turn of the nineteenth century, while the technique of printing colour-sheets had become sophisticated enough to allow for entire armies to be equipped with topographical maps.[2] Finally, following the Agricultural Revolution in Western Europe in the latter half of the eighteenth century, armies had also become sufficiently mobile to be moved around without time-consuming logistical preparations (at least west of the Elbe and north of the Pyrenees).[3]

Institutions such as the division and the army-corps came to embody the new operational art of warfare. Marshal de Broglie introduced the divisional system in France in 1759, which was then further refined by Lazare Carnot during the French Revolutionary Wars in the 1790s. An army division was a large military unit, in which regiments from a certain geographical region were brought together for training and manoeuvres in peacetime, and for fighting as a self-contained tactical formation in war. Each division consisted of two to four brigades, each brigade of two to four regiments (the French revolutionaries labelled a regiment a *demi-brigade*), and each regiment of two to four battalions. A division was made up of some 5,000–10,000 men, represented all arms and was controlled through a well-defined chain of command, with the divisional general and his staff at the top. Napoleon's contribution to this development was to create homogenous infantry and cavalry divisions with supporting artillery, and to put two or three infantry divisions and one cavalry division together into one army-corps. Additional artillery and cavalry were then added at the army-corps level, as were special troops such as engineers and baggage train. In this way, the unwieldy mass armies that had been inherited from revolutionary France could be divided into more functional parts, which were stronger than divisions (the army-corps counted some 30,000–35,000 men); units that were capable of independently solving a wide range of missions, yet were sufficiently mobile.[4]

One of the great merits of the divisional and army-corps system was that it overcame the 'control span problem': the limitations of the human brain in simultaneously handing a multitude of variables. With each corps consisting of two to four divisions; each division of two to four brigades; each brigade of two to four regiments; and each regiment of two to four battalions, no commander on any organizational level had to communicate with more than two to four sub-commanders at any given time: something that greatly enhanced efficiency.[5] Moreover, with the Emperor's own headquarters at the top, the creation of a proper HQ on each level resulted in more standardized routines for communication within the command system and to the emergence of templates for written orders, reports, and briefings. As a consequence, steps were taken in many countries after the Napoleonic Wars to give staff officers a more formalized training. To this end, the Kriegsakademie in Berlin was reorganized in 1816, and specialized staff colleges were founded in Paris and St Petersburg in 1818–1819.[6]

The adoption of the divisional and army-corps system by Napoleon's opponents eventually undermined French military superiority, ultimately contributing to Napoleon's defeat. Under the command of the newly elected Crown Prince Karl Johan (former French marshal Jean Baptiste Bernadotte), the Swedish army went to war for the last time in 1813–1814; it also began organizing its larger units according to this model. This last campaign culminated in Napoleon's defeat at the Battle of Leipzig in October 1813 and his subsequent surrender at Fontainebleau in April the following year. Karl Johan and his Swedish staff officers led one of the three allied armies: the Army of the North. The participating Swedish force (a total of 23,000 men organized in three divisions) constituted an independent army-corps, which finally halted its advance in southern Belgium in early 1814. Once these troops had been shipped back to Sweden in the summer, Karl Johan invaded the former Danish provinces in Norway and fought a two-week-long campaign, which led to the founding of the Swedish–Norwegian Union (a political constellation that lasted until 1905). During the Norwegian campaign, the Swedish army was organized into two army-corps consisting of three divisions each. The two army-corps proved able to coordinate their movements successfully and to operate in cooperation with the Swedish navy.

An extensive literature exists on Sweden's military campaigns in Germany and Norway in 1813–1814, most of which was written in the nineteenth and early twentieth centuries. It discusses issues such as Karl Johan's loyalty to his allies in the coalition, how effectively the Army of the North contributed to Napoleon's defeat, and whether the Norwegians were really militarily defeated in the summer of 1814 or whether the country just agreed to an armistice after their demands for political autonomy had been met.[7] The aim of the present chapter is not to contribute further to these discussions; rather, it is merely to study the introduction of the division and army-corps in the Swedish army at the time. How was the new command system established? What were the incentives for institutional change, and what were the main obstacles for implementing the new order?

Gustaf Wilhelm af Tibell and the 1805 staff service regulations

To the question of how military innovations reached Sweden from France in the early nineteenth century, the literature usually emphasizes the role of Gustaf Wilhelm af Tibell (1772–1831). Tibell was one of the founders of the Swedish Royal Academy of War Sciences and served as a staff officer in the French army in Italy in the campaigns of 1798–1801. He prepared a draft version of the Swedish army's staff service regulations, which King Gustav IV approved in the autumn of 1805. Tibell's biographer, General Lars Tingsten, regarded this document to be Tibell's 'most important work in the military sciences', as it regulated the working procedures of Swedish military HQs during Sweden's participation in the Napoleonic Wars (1805–1814).[8] However, there are important differences between Tibell's text and the regulations as they were approved. By studying these differences, it is possible to obtain a more balanced picture of French influence on the Swedish army.

According to Tibell's draft, the army should always be divided into divisions when it marched off to war. Each division, consisting of approximately 4,000 men, should contain troops from all branches and be able to operate independently of other divisions. Tibell also discusses how different types of terrain in the theatre of operations will influence the proportion of infantry, cavalry, and artillery within the division.[9] Meanwhile, the authorized regulations make no mention of the division as the basic all-arms unit in the Swedish army; instead, this role falls to the brigade. Neither is the strength and composition of the brigade specified; it simply states that each brigade should contain all branches according to 'a certain established standard', and that all brigades should be of roughly equal strength. According to the authorized regulations, several brigades may be also temporarily joined together under one commander, in units such as 'lines', 'wings', or divisions.[10] The term 'wing' was apparently the ordinary designation for a large detachment of the main force. Terms such as 'line' (*linje*) and 'wing' (*flygel*) described how these detachments were positioned relative to one another in the centre or on the flanks when the army deployed for battle.

Tibell's proposal states that the army should have a general HQ and that every division should have a divisional HQ. Tibell also makes room for the HQ of a future corps by stating that where several divisions are temporarily combined they should have an army HQ and a commander of their own.[11] The authorized regulations concludes that a commander of a 'line' or 'wing' should not have an organized HQ (except for a few personal adjutants): he should do nothing else but relay correspondence to and from the brigades under his command, adding any personal comments he might have. However, a number of brigades brought together in a division should have a permanent HQ of their own, organized in a way that was similar to the main army HQ. The divisional HQ was always to transmit orders and instructions from the army commander in their entirety to subordinate brigade HQs, as well as pass on reports to the army HQ from the brigade level.[12] Consequently, the divisional HQ is portrayed as a level of command of secondary importance.

Thus the authorized regulations are much briefer than Tibell's proposal and give no detailed instructions. The regulations also point to differences between HQs on different organizational levels. The most striking difference is that Tibell speaks of the division as the basic all-arms formation, while the regulations see the brigade in that role. One should perhaps not exaggerate the importance of this, as Tibell's small-sized division (4,000 men) might as well be labelled a brigade. The authorized regulations do not accord any major significance to the division level; they also mention 'the wing' and 'the line' when describing large temporary formations under a unified command. These are concepts that are entirely missing in Tibell's text.

What might explain the differences between Tibell's proposal and the final version of the staff service regulations? We may assume that Tibell had limited experience of writing service regulations in Swedish and that his text required some editing before it could be given official endorsement. However, it is also clear that Tibell's proposal had to be adjusted to existing organizational structures and practices in the Swedish army. What were these organizational structures and practices, and how had large all-arms units such as the division originally become part of the Swedish military organization?

Large all-arms units in the Swedish Army until 1813–1814

The usual Swedish term for an army division was *fördelning,* which translates as a 'distribution' or an 'allocation'. Previous research confirms that the *fördelning* existed in the Swedish army as early as the eighteenth century, although these divisions were not independent tactical units combining different arms. The first unit of that kind appeared only in the 1770s in the shape of the Savolax Brigade in Finland. Mixed brigades and even divisions became more common during the wars against France, Russia, and Denmark in 1805–1809. The army-corps finally appeared as a large-scale mixed unit during the campaigns of 1813–1814.[13]

The Swedish General Staff wrote the history of its own organization in the early 1920s. At the time, Sweden's soldier-king Charles XII (1682–1718) was highly admired. Therefore, it was natural for the General Staff historians to see him as the introducer of the divisional system. A royal ordinance issued on 20 November 1717 on organizing the Swedish army into large formations called *tilldelningar* provided the basis for this interpretation.[14] Although there is no doubt that King Charles wanted to create permanent bodies that would be much larger than regiments, his *tilldelning* formations differed from the divisions in France at the end of that century, for they were not intended to serve as tactical units on the battlefield. For example, they were not to include troops from different branches. The entire army was to be made up of eight infantry and eight cavalry divisions, and there was to be only one mixed division. The latter force consisted of infantry, cavalry, artillery, and fortification troops. The reason for its creation was not the wish to have at least one combined-arms unit in the Swedish army; rather, it was to ensure that a few selected regiments of high lineage and rank – infantry as well as cavalry regiments would only have to fight alongside each other – without having to mix with any of the newly organized, low-status, wartime regiments (the so-called *tremänning* and *femmänning* regiments). Charles XII had no tactical ambitions with the *tilldelning*; the formulations in his ordinance state that regardless of whether 'the number of regiments increase or decrease [in future], the divisions will always remain fixed'. If any more regiments were to be established, 'new divisions will not be organized from them, but they will be dispersed among the divisions already existing'.[15]

Charles XII's *tilldelning* reform never had any practical consequences; however, a divisional organization was indeed introduced into the Swedish army some thirty years later, in the reign of King Fredrik I. The term *fördelning* then appeared for the first time. This ordinance, which was issued in May 1747, refers to Charles XII's ordinance and the need to improve discipline, financial control, drill, and training.

The divisional commander's duties were to inspect exercises in the regiments that belonged to his division, supervise the division's regimental commanders, and watch over its ammunition supplies. (The Swedish army had gone to war against Russia a few years earlier, in 1741; the Swedes were terribly ill-prepared and as a result had suffered a catastrophic defeat. The divisional reform may well have been inspired by that experience.) The ordinance also specifies the composition of each of the four divisions: the 1st Division was to consist of the Foot and Horse Guards, the Army Artillery, the Uppland, Södermanland, Närke, Västmanland, Östgöta, and Helsinge regiments; the 2nd Division of the regiments in southern Sweden; the 3rd Division of the regiments in northern Sweden (including the province of Dalarna's regiment); and the 4th Division of the regiments in western Sweden.[16] The garrisons in exposed border areas of Finland and Pomerania were not included in the divisional organization, probably because their preparedness was deemed to be already under satisfactorily control.

The 1747 ordinance does not suggest that the division should constitute a distinct command level in wartime. An HQ was organized around the commander-in-chief ten years later, when Sweden entered the Seven Years War and dispatched an expeditionary force to Pomerania, yet it was not on the divisional level. The divisional organization only determined the billeting areas of the Swedish regiments.[17] Sweden's war against Russia in 1788–1790 started without proper preparation. King Gustav III was on the front most of the time, commanding from upon plans that his closest advisors had drafted in great secrecy. There was fairly limited scope for a proper HQ even on the highest level. The tactical formation of the Swedish army in 1788–1790 was the brigade, although two or more brigades frequently manoeuvred together in temporary formations. The Savolax Brigade was the only brigade in the Swedish army that was mixed: it was composed of light infantry, dragoons, and artillery, and specialized in fighting in difficult terrain. In reality, neither the Savolax Brigade nor any other unit in the Swedish army had received much tactical training above company level before the war. [18]

After King Gustav III had been assassinated and his brother Charles had become regent, the number of divisions in the Swedish army doubled from four to eight in May 1792. The troops in Finland and Pomerania were now included in the divisional organization, forming the Finnish Division and the Pomeranian Division. The other six divisions were the Life Division (the Guards units and the regiments in the Stockholm region); the Skåne Division (the regiments and artillery units in the province of Skåne); the Småland Division (the regiments and artillery units in the province of Småland); the Västgöta Division (the regiments and artillery units in the provinces of Västergötland, Dalsland, and Bohuslän, including the Gothenburg Squadron of the Archipelago Fleet); the Western Division (the regiments and artillery units in the provinces that constituted West-Central Sweden before the loss of the Finnish part of the realm in 1809, viz. Uppland, Närke, Värmland, Södermanland, and Västmanland); and the Northern Division (the regiments and artillery units in the provinces of Dalarna, Hälsingland, Jämtland, and Västerbotten).[19]

By the early 1800s, certain peacetime administrative structures labelled 'divisions' had thus existed in the Swedish army for more than half a century. However, there was not yet any larger tactical formation than the brigade, which was singled out as the basic tactical unit in the 1805 staff service regulations. When the Swedish army went to fight against the French in Pomerania in 1805–1807, the expeditionary force was organized into brigades (four infantry, one cavalry, and one artillery). In reality, these brigades were mixed units. The term 'division' (*fördelning*) was occasionally used during the campaigns in Pomerania in order to designate temporary formations made up of many battalions. However, there were no organized HQs below the force HQ; the number of regimental officers (officers holding the rank of major, lieutenant-colonel, or colonel) was no more than five per brigade.[20] The divisional level of command became more important in 1808–1809 during the campaigns in Finland and along the Norwegian border. However, the term 'army' was often used instead of division when the divisional commanders acted as regional commanders – of the Western, Finnish, Skåne, or Southern Armies.[21]

Under Bernadotte, a former French marshal and newly elected crown prince, the divisional organization was further refined following the conclusion of peace treaties with France, Denmark, and Russia in 1809–1810. There were advanced plans in September 1812 to invade the Danish island of Zealand, according to which four Swedish divisions would operate as self-contained tactical units. While negotiations were going on with Russia, Britain, and Prussia about joining the coalition against Napoleon at the beginning of 1813, there was still no sign of the Swedish army preparing to introduce the army-corps as an additional level of command. Since Sweden's crown prince could not read Swedish, Major-General Carl Johan Adlercreutz delivered an organizational proposal in French on 30 January. The proposal was for 'une Armée de 30 000 hommes' that would be shipped over to Germany while an 'Armée de l'Ouest' would protect the border against Norway. However, the term *Corps d'Armée* was not yet in use.[22]

Swedish troop transports to Germany were well in hand when a new royal ordinance appeared in April 1813 that revised the existing divisional organization. In what seems to have been an adjustment to reflect Sweden's new international role in the coalition against Napoleon, the ordinance consistently used the French term *division* instead of the Swedish *fördelning* – although when the war was over in 1815, the Swedish army would again change its vocabulary, abandoning the term *division*, and eventually bringing back the term *fördelning* for large all-arms tactical units. (The term 'division' only reappeared at the cost of *fördelning* in the early 2000s, indicating that the Swedish armed forces had yet again shifted emphasis from national defence to overseas expeditionary warfare.) The 1813 organization also reflected Sweden's recent territorial losses, for it was based on five instead of eight divisions. The Finnish and Pomeranian divisions had been scrapped and the units of the former Western Division (minus the Värmland Infantry) merged into the Life Division. What remained were the 2nd Eastern Division (the former Småland Division); the 3rd Southern Division (the former Skåne Division); the 4th Western Division (the former Västgöta Division plus the Värmland Infantry); and the 5th Northern Division, which retained its composition from the 1792 organization.[23]

Karl Johan joined the Swedish troops in Pomerania in mid May, and met with the allies to draw up the coalition's campaign plan at the castle of Trachenberg in Silesia in early July. The allies agreed that the Swedish crown prince would command one of the three coalition armies: the Army of the North, composed of two Russian and one Prussian army-corps (under Wintzingerode, Vorontsov, and Bülow, respectively). There was also the option of occasionally using another Prussian army-corps (Tauentzien). Moreover, the Army of the North would consist of a Prussian and a Russian light infantry detachment (Tettenborn and Chernyshev, respectively) and the Swedish expeditionary force (von Stedingk).[24] Only then, when the Swedish army was assigned a role as a sub-element within a larger entity, did the concept of army-corps find its way into Swedish military parlance. Prior to the end of July 1813, the term *Corps d'Armée* appears in official documents to describe the Swedish troops in Germany.[25]

It soon proved impossible to use the Swedish army's peacetime divisional structure to set up the wartime organization. The 1st Division of the Swedish Army-Corps was originally set up around a core of regiments from the Life Division, and the 3rd Division was based upon the units of the 2nd Eastern Division. However, none of the five divisional areas were large enough to supply all of the necessary components. The 2nd Division, which was formed around units from the 3rd Western Division, had to borrow some light cavalry from the Skåne Hussars of the 4th Southern Division District. Since the training of horse artillery in the Swedish army had been centralized to the Wende Artillery Regiment in the southern-Swedish garrison of Kristianstad, all divisions had to be supplied with light artillery from the 4th Southern Division. When an artillery-corps reserve was organized later in the summer and Swedish troops had to reinforce General Wallmoden-Gimborn's combined allied army-corps outside Hamburg, it became necessary to dissolve the 3rd Division and distribute its units between the 1st and 2nd divisions and Wallmoden-Gimborn's force. Further to the Napoleonic model, Karl Johan adapted the Swedish army-corps in September by concentrating all cavalry into a special cavalry division, making the 1st and 2nd divisions pure infantry/artillery units.[26]

Swedish troops were withdrawn from Wallmoden-Gimborn's combined allied army-corps in January 1814; the former 3rd Division of the Swedish expeditionary force was reconstituted. Thus the Swedish army-corps now consisted of three infantry divisions and one cavalry division. The army-corps was temporarily reorganized in March as four infantry divisions and one cavalry division (the 4th Infantry Division that consisted of one Swedish brigade and one brigade from the Duchy of Mecklenburg). The former structure of three infantry divisions and one cavalry division was reinstated before the army-corps returned to Sweden in the summer. When the Swedish troops had been shipped back from the Continent in June–July 1814, they were concentrated in and around Gothenburg. The 1st and 3rd Infantry divisions and the Cavalry Division became the I Army-Corps (supported by special detachments of corps artillery and corps engineers). The 2nd Infantry Division along with the 4th and 5th Infantry divisions (supported by a cavalry brigade and a special detachment of corps engineers) formed the II Army-Corps. The newly formed 4th and 5th Infantry divisions were also assembled without regard to the peacetime divisional organization; each division comprised units from the Life Division as well as from the 4th Western and 5th Northern divisions.[27]

Command and control in the Swedish Army, 1813–1814

The Army of the North's HQ comprised a large number of 'camp-followers' during the campaign in Germany (1813–1814). There was a total of approximately 600 people: Karl Johan's political chancellery, the ambassadors and military attachés of Sweden's allies, the crown prince's own entourage and personal servants, 78 attendants at the disposal of HQ personnel, 350 Swedish guardsmen and their officers, 60 hussars and Cossacks in Karl Johan's Russian Guard of Honour, 33 Prussian gendarmes, and orderlies. The situation in Norway in 1814 is less clear, although the number of those not in military service was considerably smaller.[28]

There were fewer than 60 officers engaged in 'proper' staff work in the Army of the North's HQ – or less than one-tenth of the total. Although historians' assessments may vary on certain points, they generally agree that the Swedish staff officers performed poorly and lacked proper training. While there had been staff officers in the Swedish army since Gustavus Adolphus (1611–1632), Gustav III (1771–1792) had been the first to establish a permanent 'Adjutant-General's Office' (*generaladjutantexpeditionen*). Officers from the Adjutant-General's Office were to participate in the army's summer exercises, thus assisting the commanders of the various divisions. However, these officers were not stationed together: they normally served with their home regiments. Not until 1806 did King Gustav IV (1796–1809) issue formal instructions for staff officers, according to which officers who had proven to be 'diligent and thrifty in service' with 'excellent capabilities in all fields of the science of war' could be appointed as 'His Majesty's adjutants'. These officers would be assigned to staff duty at time of war along with officers from the Field Surveying Corps, an army unit that had been formed in 1805 to handle reconnaissance, cartography, and the recording of Sweden's military history. A proper General Staff did not come into being until 1816. Educational requirements for officers admitted to the General Staff were only standardized after 1833, when a degree from the Marieberg Artillery College became mandatory.[29]

In light of how the Napoleonic Wars transformed officer training in most Western countries, one might assume that the Swedish army was not unique in its educational shortcomings.[30] However, foreign officers who served in the Army of the North HQ in the autumn of 1813 (such as Russia's Colonel Pozzo di Borgo and Britain's General Sir Charles Stewart) maintained in their reports home that the Swedish staff officers' performance fell far below international standards because of their lack of training and experience.[31]

According to Berndt Brehmer, theorist in the field of command and control science, there are at least three functions that could be described as timeless and that all command and control systems must perform: collecting data; comprehending the meaning of these data (a process Brehmer terms sense-making); and understanding how to plan for future activities based upon this. In the military context, this latter phase results in orders being issued to units to take action from which a new situation evolves, whereupon new data must be collected, which again must be made sense of, leading to further planning, new orders, and on in a continuous cycle.[32] However, one must note that Brehmer's model of the military decision-making process shows the imprint of the twenty-first century – the age of information technology and 'network-centric warfare' – when a strict delimitation between these different functions may be easier to maintain than was the case in the Napoleonic age.

The most thorough evaluation of the Army of the North's command and control functions can be found in Colonel Karl Vitzthum von Eckstädt's supplementary volume to the Prussian General Staff history series on the 'Wars of National Liberation'.[33] However, Vitzthum von Eckstädt, whose study appeared in 1910, tends to measure the performance of the army HQs of the Leipzig campaign by the military standards of Wilhelmine Germany, duly ignoring their proper historical context. How then to reach a fair evaluation of the efficiency of Swedish military staff during the campaigns of 1813–1814? One way is to study supposedly more advanced armies in the same campaigns in order to determine the extent to which the functions that Brehmer mentions were allowed to shape their command and control systems.

Napoleon's HQ (*la Maison*) was divided into three autonomous parts: the *Petit quartier général* (the Emperor's personal HQ); the *Quartier général du major général* (the General Staff of the Grande Armée); and the *Quartier général de l'intendant* (the Administrative-Economic Staff).

Two different sections in Napoleon's staff system answered for data collection: the Topographical Bureau (divided between the *Petit quartier général* and the *Quartier général du major général*) supplied geographical data, and the Statistical Bureau (*Petit quartier général*) supplied data on the enemy. In addition, cavalry reconnaissance directed by the various corps commanders supplied *la Maison* with a steady stream of situation reports from the field. However, the functions of sense-making and planning were less discernible in the Napoleonic organization. In fact, the Emperor himself did most of that work; his chief of staff, Alexander Berthier, elaborated upon his drafts afterwards, transforming them into intelligible orders. Berthier also handled routine decisions and issued orders that were deemed too insignificant to bother the Emperor with. Additionally, there were special staff sections for artillery, engineering, and training in the *Quartier général du major général* to support the planners with their technical expertise.[34]

The other two allied armies in Germany in 1813 consisted of the Austrian-led main army under Field Marshal Prince Karl Zu Schwarzenberg (known as 'the Bohemian Army') and the Prussian-led 'Silesian army' under the control of General Gebhardt von Blücher. There were distinct organizational bodies in these HQs that handled data collection: the first of the four chancelleries in the Bohemian Army's HQ – *Geheime Kanzlei des Fürsten* – and the *Nachrichtenbureau* in the General Staff of the Silesian Army. The sense-making and planning functions were also visible in the organizational set-up of these two HQs. One of the four chancelleries in the Bohemian Army was named the *Operationzkanzlei* and charged with operational planning. In support, it had the *Armee-Generalkommando* – another of the four chancelleries – that contained an *Artilleriedirektion* and a *Feldgeniedirektion* (field engineering board) staffed by technical experts. The Silesian Army HQ contained a special *Generalstabsbureau,* where a number of junior officers were occupied with routine calculations and march preparations while a major-general was responsible for technical advice on artillery and engineering.[35]

The Army of the North's HQ had a special section for intelligence collection, led by a Prussian lieutenant-colonel named Count Kalkreuth. Since they were campaigning on German soil, it was probably sensible to appoint a native German to this position. However, these functions were less visible when it concerned sense-making and planning, much as in Napoleon's HQ. Vitzthum von Eckstädt points out that Karl Johan made all the important decisions on his own; in typical Napoleonic fashion, he did not involve any of his staff officers. He also notes that Karl Johan had a marvellous memory for detail: the orders he wrote were less bold and ingenuous than Napoleon's, yet they were written in the same clear and simple manner. Vitzthum von Eckstädt also states that the Army of the North kept its records and correspondence in much better order than did the two other allied armies, as it moved more slowly and engaged the enemy less often.[36] However, the Army of the North's HQ lacked special sections for artillery and engineering, and of all the army HQs in the 1813–1814 campaign it was probably the weakest when it came to planning. Karl Johan's education in Napoleon's army may have been the reason why certain command and control functions in the Army of the North's HQ were less developed than those in the two other allied armies.

Count Charles de Suremain, who had fled to Sweden from revolutionary France in the 1790s, served as chief of artillery in the Swedish army-corps during the 1813 – 1814 campaign. Suremain later claimed that the Army of the North's chief of staff, Adlercreutz, was unhappy with two things in particular: Karl Johan's cautious advance; and the fact that, in fighting France, Sweden found herself on the same side as her arch-enemy, Russia. According to Suremain, Adlercreutz knew little of modern warfare and foreign languages. He was of the opinion that Adlercreutz was ill suited to command the staff of a multinational military force in which the working language was French. While Adlercreutz should have led the Swedish Army-Corps instead, Suremain thought a better choice as chief of staff would have been Major-General Count Gustaf Löwenhielm. Löwenhielm had served as adjutant-general (chief of staff) in Finland in the campaign of 1808 (where he was taken prisoner). He was fluent in French, experienced in diplomacy, and had personally drafted the final version of the allied campaign plan during the Conference of Trachenberg. Löwenhielm was also responsible for organizing the Army of the North's HQ and would have been the natural choice to lead it. For political reasons, however, it was impossible to replace Adlercreutz with Löwenhielm. Adlercreutz had been one of the leading revolutionaries in the 1809 *coup d'état* that had opened the door for Bernadotte to ascend the Swedish throne; Löwenhielm was a well-known supporter of the previous Gustavian dynasty.[37]

The 1805 Swedish staff service regulations state that one of the adjutant-generals in an army HQ should be assigned the position of 'office adjutant-general' (*generaladjutant av expeditionen*) with responsibility for internal affairs. Another adjutant-general should be appointed 'adjutant-general on duty' or 'adjutant-general of the day' (*generaladjutant av dagen*); he was expected to take care of day-to-day matters, always accompany the commander-in-chief, and keep registers of general correspondence and any intelligence received from secret sources.[38] In effect Löwenhielm held this latter position at the Army of the North HQ, and therefore probably exercised considerable influence anyway. According to Vitzthum von Eckstädt, neither Löwenhielm nor the office adjutant-general (Major-General Tawast) was allowed to offer advice to Karl Johan, as proper staff officers should. Even Adlercreutz was more Karl Johan's personal secretary than his chief of staff. As Vitzthum von Eckstädt underlines, the Swedish army did not distinguish between staff officers and mere adjutants.[39] However, other armies did not make this distinction either – and with good reason.

According to current military practice (as per the US Army field manual), staff officers can be characterized either as coordinating officers, special officers or personal staff officers. Coordinating officers are responsible for general functions at HQ such as personnel, intelligence, operations, supplies, communications, and so on. Special staff officers serve as the force commander's assistants in their special area of technical expertise (fire support, engineering, and so on). Personal staff officers serve directly under the force commander as his expert advisors in positions such as chaplain, chief surgeon, judge-advocate, and so on. (They differ from the other two categories of staff officer, who are subordinate to the chief of staff).[40]

The organizational charts from the 1813–1814 campaigns reveal that, in the light of this categorization, one can easily identify a number of special and personal staff officers in equivalent positions: chiefs of artillery, fieldwork, cavalry, and military mail, chaplains, chief surgeons, judge-advocates, and so on. As a rule, the heads of some of the coordinating functions can also be identified (the equivalent of today's intelligence and operational sections for instance), and a couple of junior officers are named as their assistants; however, the great mass of staff officers is not earmarked for any special branch at all. Instead, one finds a large number of divisional generals in Napoleon's *Petit quartier général* who were assigned as the 'Emperor's adjutants'. A number of colonels in the *Quartier général du major général* are assigned a similar role under the Chief of the General Staff. The third chancellery in the Bohemian Army HQ (the *Detailkanzlei*) had a number of colonels and lieutenant-colonels who were listed as general-adjutants. In the Army of the North, Karl Johan had at his disposal one adjutant-general (General von Carlheim-Gyllenskiöld), thirteen senior adjutants (ranging in rank from captain to lieutenant-colonel), and one Russian and five Prussian adjutants (who were actually liaison officers from the subordinate corps). Chief of Staff Adlercreutz commanded another six senior adjutants. The HQ of the Prussian-led Silesian Army was the exception to the rule: its *Adjutantur* employed but a handful of unassigned officers.[41]

Why were army HQs in the Napoleonic age crowded with staff officers without specific assignments? The military historian Martin van Creveld has suggested that since reports usually becomes increasingly blurred when they move up the military hierarchy, a commander always needs 'a kind of directed telescope ... which he can direct, at will, to any part of the enemy's forces, the terrain, or his own army in order to bring in information'. This is information that the ordinary reporting system indicates would be of crucial importance but is unable to supply in sufficient detail. The Emperor's adjutants in Napoleon's army often played the role of the 'directed telescope'. These were men who had personal command experience that enabled them to understand what was happening, as well as the diplomatic tact to admonish officers of senior rank, and sufficient physical endurance to stay in the saddle all day.[42]

In a similar spirit, the Swedish army staff service regulations of 1805 state that staff officers who were not assigned to be adjutant-general on duty should be prepared to take on special missions such as commanding rearguard detachments, forward detachments, or reconnaissance patrols.[43] The initial stages of the Swedish invasion of Norway in July 1814 offer a telling example in the shape of Lieutenant-General von Vegesack's temporary command of the forward element of the II Army-Corps – which, at the time, was also the avant-garde of the entire army. This force of three Jäger battalions from the Jämtland and Dalarna infantry regiments would have been too insignificant to be led by a lieutenant-general under normal circumstances. However, by placing Vegesack in command of the avant-garde, Karl Johan secured some control over the II Army-Corps, which was not under his direct command. Vegesack was later given the command of the force that laid siege to the strategically important fortress at Fredriksten: a mere four battalions. However, the mission was also deemed vital to the outcome of the campaign.[44]

By not assigning all of his staff officers specific positions within his HQ, a military commander of the early nineteenth century could keep a pool of qualified observers at his disposal. He could then dispatch these troops to the battlefield whenever there was a need to gather critical information or handle an evolving crisis. Modern commanders depend to an even higher degree upon sensors and advanced technology for information gathering; their planning preparations are more detailed and rigorous. They also expect their subordinates to show greater initiative and independent judgement than their Napoleonic predecessors. Moreover, modern means of communication – such as mobile phones or helicopters – offer the modern commander the opportunity to intervene personally over long distances; his forerunners did not have such luxuries two hundred years ago. For this reason, the value of Napoleon's 'directed telescope' may seem less obvious today.

Brehmer's model does not say that the three basic command and control functions (data collection, sense-making, and planning) must be kept apart organizationally; however, in an ideal world, a certain mutual autonomy is surely to be preferred. The data collection function should report facts – even if they contradict any earlier assumptions that have been made. The sense-making function should have the integrity to reinterpret a situation it finds unavoidable, and the planning function should ask for the data and directives it deems necessary, not simply those that happen to be at hand. The delimitations between data collection, sense-making, and planning were less clear-cut in Napoleon's day than they may seem today. Since mounted couriers were then the fastest means of communication, information seldom travelled faster than six miles an hour across the battlefield; therefore, no level of the command and control system could acquire anything more than a fragmented picture of events.[45] As we have seen, both Napoleon and Karl Johan performed at least two of the three functions simultaneously. Their adjutants-general were engaged in all three functions: they rode off to a certain corner of the battlefield, analysed the situation there, proposed the orders they thought necessary to the commander on the spot, and then penned a report afterwards informing HQ what had happened.

We find a number of unassigned staff officers in the Army of the North in 1813–1814 who could have served as 'directed telescopes' in von Stedingk's Swedish Army-Corps HQ. Apart from the chief of staff (Lagerbring), there were three senior adjutants (*överadjutanter*; one colonel and two majors) and seven staff adjutants (*stabsadjutanter*; three captains and four lieutenants). There was also a field secretary, the chiefs of artillery, and engineers (the latter being responsible for construction work as well as surveying and collecting geographical intelligence). Additionally, there was a chaplain, a chief-commissary for supplies, a quartermaster general, a judge-advocate, the chief surgeon, a chief wagon-master, a field postmaster, and a field printer. This amounts to a total of 21 positions. However, the divisional HQs in the Swedish Army-Corps had far fewer personnel: the divisional commander, two to three senior adjutants, and one to two staff adjutants, while there were only a brigade commander and one or two staff adjutants in the six brigade HQs.[46]

The following positions made up the II Army-Corps HQ in the Norwegian campaign in the summer of 1814: a corps commander (von Essen), a chief of staff, an adjutant-general of external affairs, chiefs of artillery and cavalry (with three adjutants each), a chief army surgeon, an army chaplain, a chief supervisor of field bakeries, ten senior adjutants (two of them liaison officers from the navy), six staff adjutants, three field secretaries, three general clerks, two engineer officers for surveying, a hospital doctor, two senior pharmacists, a field pharmacist, four assistant physicians, a hospital clerk, a janitor, an HQ commandant, a placemajor (the commendant's chief of staff), a senior wagon-master, two police constables, a horse vet, a military prosecutor, a judicial clerk, and a head of the military mail service and his secretary. This amounts to a total of 57 positions. However, only 20 or so of these were military officers. The growth of the corps HQ had occurred mainly through the addition of various civilian experts and officials; this was especially true in the medical services. All other logistical functions had been allocated to the main Army HQ, and, since Karl Johan was both commander-in-chief and commander of the I Army-Corps, this was located with the I Army-Corps HQ. The General Army HQ encompassed the following positions: a chief of staff (Adlercreutz), chiefs of artillery, cavalry, engineers and field hospitals, a chief commissary for supplies, a judge-advocate, and a field printer. Divisional HQs were kept small during the Norwegian campaign, just as they had been during the campaign in Germany. Apart from the divisional commander, there was only a senior adjutant or chief of staff, a couple of staff adjutants, an engineer officer for surveying, a field surgeon, and a judge-advocate. Brigade HQs were limited to the brigade commander, the brigade adjutant, and an engineer officer.[47] The resources for staff work and planning in the Swedish army of 1813–1814 were truly scarce below army-corps level.

Conclusion

This chapter has examined the introduction of the division and the army-corps in the Swedish army during the final stages of the Napoleonic Wars. Earlier literature has emphasized the role of Gustaf Wilhelm af Tibell in introducing the new 'French way of war' to Sweden, especially through his proposal for new staff service regulations, which he prepared after his return from French military service and published in the spring of 1805. There were actually important differences between Tibell's proposal and the official version of the staff service regulations that King Gustav IV later approved. In the Swedish army it was the brigade that was the basic tactical all-arms unit. Although divisions had existed since the 1740s, they were primarily peacetime administrative structures. Tibell's proposal had to be adjusted to reflect these existing practices.

The breakthrough of the division as a tactical unit and the introduction of the army-corps only occurred in the spring of 1813, when Karl Johan was on the point of commanding the allied Army of the North in the coalition against Napoleon; there was a need to harmonize the Swedish command and control system with international standards. Moreover, it became clear that the Swedish army's established, peacetime divisional districts were too small to support its wartime divisions.

The predominant view among historians on the 1813–1814 campaign in Germany is that the Swedish staff officers of the Army of the North performed rather poorly. What seems undisputable is that, as a former French marshal, Karl Johan did indeed command in the centralized fashion that he had learned in Napoleon's armies. There were few trained staff officers in European countries – and particularly in Sweden, where there were no one who could rival Karl Johan's solid experience, so his was probably a sensible solution. The shortage of suitable personnel meant that the capacity for staff work and planning came to be concentrated at the army-corps level and above. The Swedish divisional and brigade commanders in 1813–1814 had only a handful of officers to assist them in their HQs.

The problems that centralization in the Napoleonic command system created were balanced by the 'directed telescope': the practice of dispatching trusted adjutants to distant corners of the battlefield to gather the necessary information, analyse the situation, and even act on the commander's behalf. Modern command and control science sees data collection, sense-making, and planning as different functions in the command and control system. Such distinctions were hard to maintain in the Napoleonic Age. For this reason alone it is unwise to assess the Swedish command and control system of 1813–1814 according to military standards of later periods.

The organizational hierarchy that evolved out of the Napoleonic Wars comprised eight levels of tactical command between the corps commander and the squad leader at the bottom; this would remain relatively unscathed in modern armies until the end of the twentieth century. Only developments in the post-Cold War era (such as the march of information technology, the down-sizing of military forces, and the growing role of multinational operations) provoked the leading powers to reform their command and control systems, which had dominated army organizations for the last two centuries.[48] The Gulf War in January 1991 may well have been the last occasion in history when two army-corps were seen lining up on a national border, waiting to advance across it, just as the Swedish army did in July 1814, when it went to war for the very last time by invading Norway.

Jan Glete described organizational innovation as new combinations of resources and new institutions. He also emphasized that established informal networks are important for people's willingness to put trust in formalized networks (as in the case of the early modern state). Thus he saw the relationship between premodern traditional 'informality' and modern bureaucratized 'formality' as dynamic and inclusive rather than competitive and exclusive.[49]

In this perspective, the operational art of warfare could be described as an innovation. Resources released by the European Agricultural Revolution (which demographically and logistically broadened the basis for mass armies) were combined with new military institutions from France (in the form of the division and the army-corps). The creation of large, self-sustained, independent units not only lowered the transaction costs of coordinating the movements of hundreds of thousands of soldiers in a theatre of operations. As a rule, those tactical systems that have been the most effective in exploiting the division of labour between different branches have also been the most successful throughout military history. The army division and army-corps, which offered organizational frameworks for the large-scale use of combined arms, proved highly competitive on the battlefield.

The incentives for institutional change in the Swedish army came from Sweden's role in the international coalition against Napoleon. However, the introduction of general conscription in 1812 also increased the availability of new resources. A limited number of Swedish conscripts had already served in Germany in 1813–1814; almost 40 per cent of the 45,000 Swedish soldiers in Norway in 1814 were conscripts.[50] The main obstacle to implementing the new system in Sweden, as well as in many other countries, was the lack of trained officers rather than resistance from groups intent on defending the old order. The competence deficit was remedied in two distinct ways: the centralization of vital command functions at the army-corps level and above, and through the use of 'directed telescopes'. In a sense, this is an illustration of Glete's point about the symbiotic relationship between informal and formalized networks. Select officers who enjoyed the commander's trust were sent onto the battlefield to manage critical situations and collect vital information, regardless of their rank or formal training. These officers were not given any specific HQ assignments; rather, they were a part of the commander's personal entourage.

Informal networks remained important when the military educational institutions were reorganized in post-Napoleonic Europe in order to produce properly trained staff officers in sufficient numbers. In the 1830s, when the Marieberg Artillery College in Stockholm formalized the teaching of operational art and military history, the students used a textbook written by Johan Petter Lefrén (1784–1862), and listened to lectures given by Johan August Hazelius (1797–1871). Lefrén, who was a major in 1814, had served as senior adjutant in the II Swedish Army-Corps HQ during the campaign in Norway, while Hazelius had held the rank of second lieutenant and served as one of Lefrén's adjutants. Lefrén was the one who had secured Hazelius' appointment as teacher at the artillery college.[51] Lefrén and Hazelius knew and trusted each other, and they had shared memories of working in a modern military staff where officers were inadequately trained. This left them firm believers in the stricter regulation of military education.

Notes

1 US Army, Field Manual FM 3-0, 'Operations', Washington DC, 14 June 2001, 2-5, <www.globalsecurity.org>; cf. the current Swedish military doctrine, Försvarsmakten, *Doktrin för gemensamma operationer 2005* (Stockholm 2005), pp. 25–28.

2 There is a good discussion of these problems in Edward Hagerman, 'Union Generalship, Political Leadership and Total War Strategy', in: Stig Förster & Jörg Nagler (eds.), *On the Road to Total War: The American Civil War and the German Wars of Unification, 1861–1871* (Cambridge 2001), pp. 146–147; see also Martin van Creveld, *Command in War* (Cambridge, Mass. & London 1985), pp. 60, 290 n. 6.

3 See William H. McNeill, *The Pursuit of Power: Technology, Armed Force and Society Since 1000 A.D.* (Chicago 1984), pp. 187–206; Eric J. Hobsbawm, *Revolutionens tidsålder* (Stockholm 1979), p. 128; Martin van Creveld, *Supplying War: Logistics from Wallenstein to Patton* (Cambridge 1977), pp. 47–55.

4 Trevor N. Dupuy, *The Evolution of Weapons and Warfare* (New York 1984), p. 160; Creveld (1985), pp. 60–61, 72–73; David Chandler, *The Campaigns of Napoleon* (London 1988 [1966]), pp. 185–186; John R. Elting, *Swords Around a Throne: Napoleon's Grande Armée* (London 1997 [1988]), pp. 49, 57–59; Claus Telp, *The Evolution of Operational Art, 1740–1813: From Frederick the Great to Napoleon* (London 2005), pp. 35–58.

5 Berndt Brehmer, 'Understanding the Functions of C2 is the Key to Progress', *International C 2 Journal*, 1:1 (2007), pp. 211–232.

6 Martin van Creveld, *The Training of Officers: From Military Professionalism to Irrelevance* (New York & London 1990), pp. 22–24; Brian Bond, *The Victorian Army and the Staff College 1854–1914* (London 1972), pp. 42–43; Carl van Dyke, *Russian Imperial Military Doctrine and Education, 1832–1914* (New York 1990), pp. 1–6.

7 A selection of the Swedish Crown Prince's orders and correspondence during the campaign of 1813 is published in *Receuil de ordres de movement, proclamations et bulletins de S A R le prince royal de Suéde: commandant en chef de l' armée combinée du Nord de l'Allemagne 1813 et 1814* (Stockholm 1838) (Swedish edition: *Samling af bref, ordres, proklamationer och bulletiner utfärdade av HKH kronprinsen af Sverige, högste befälhavare öfver den förenade norra tyska armén åren 1813 och 1814* (Stockholm 1841). The tendency to criticize Karl Johan's conduct as commander of the Army of the North had already been strong among contemporary observers and remained so when the Grosse Generalstab in Berlin began studying events based upon archival material. See, for example, Barthold von Quistorp, *Geschichte der Nord-Armee im Jahre 1813* (Berlin 1894); Rudolf Friederich, *Der Herbstfeldzug 1813*, 1–3 (Berlin 1903–1906); Qusitorp's work, highly critical of Karl Johan, appeared in an early version as a series of articles in the *Militärwochenblatt* during the 1860s. An attempt to defend the Swedish Crown Prince against his German critics is Georg Swederus, *Sveriges krig och politik 1808–1814* (Stockholm 1864); similar apologetic ambitions can be found in Gustaf Lagerhjelm, *Napoleon och Carl Johan under kriget i Tyskland 1813: Krigshistoriska betraktelser* (Stockholm 1891), and Lars Tingsten's trilogy on Sweden's wars and foreign policy during the period 1809–1814, *Huvuddragen av Sveriges yttre politik, krigsförberedelser m.m.: Från och med fredssluten 1809–1810 till mitten av juli 1813*; *Huvuddragen av Sveriges krig och yttre politik: Augusti 1813–janu-*

ari 1814; *Huvuddragen av Sveriges krig och yttre politik: Februari–augusti 1814 (från Kiel till Moss)*, (Stockholm 1923–1925); for comparatively balanced assessments, see Ernst Wiehr, *Napoleon und Bernadotte im Herbstfeldzuge 1813* (Berlin 1893); Torvald T:son Höjer, *Carl Johan i den stora koalitionen mot Napoleon: Från landstigningen i Stralsund till stilleståndet i Rendsborg* (Uppsala 1943). The most thorough studies of the Swedish army during the campaign in Norway in 1814 can be found in Gustaf Björlin, *Kriget i Norge 1814: Efter samtida vittnesbörd framställt* (Stockholm 1893); and C. W. Kleen, *Detaljer ur fälttåget i Norge 1814* (Stockholm 1915). Björlin's book was written in response to Julius Mankell's revisionist interpretation in *Fälttåget i Norge 1814: Kritisk belysning* (Stockholm 1887).

8 Tingsten (1924), pp. 12–13; Lars Ericson Wolke, *Krigets idéer: Svenska tankar om krigföring 1320–1720* (Stockholm 2007), pp. 236–238.

9 Gustaf Wilhelm af Tibell, *Försök till reglemente för arméns general-stab* (Stockholm 1805) §§ 1–5.

10 *Tjenste-föreskrift för arméns generalstab 1805* (Stockholm 1805) §§ 1, 5.

11 Tibell (1805) §§ 8–9.

12 *Tjenste-föreskrift* (1805), §§ 5–6.

13 Ericson Wolke (2007), pp. 226–228; Gunnar Artéus, 'Swedish Army Organisation, 1780–1820', in: Johan Engström & Fred Sandstedt (eds.), *Between the Imperial Eagles: Sweden's Armed Forces During the Revolutionary and Napoleonic Wars*, Meddelanden från Armémuseum, 58–59, 1998–1999 (Stockholm 2000); Carl Herlitz, 'Units of the Swedish Army 1788–1820', ibid.; Lars Tingsten, *Gustaf Wilhelm af Tibell: Huvuddragen av hans liv, hans verksamhet såsom generaladjutant för armén och hans avskedande tillika. En studie i svensk krigföring år 1808* (Stockholm 1924), pp. 1–7.

14 *Generalstaben 1873–1923: En minnesskrift* (Stockholm 1923), pp. 3–4.

15 'Förordning om tilldelningarnas inrättande', issued in Lund, 20 November 1717, published by Sigfrid L. Gahm Persson in: *Kongl. stadgar, förordningar, bref och resolutioner angående Swea rikes landt-milice till häst og fot*, 4: *Från och med år 1695 till och med år 1718* (Stockholm 1814), pp. 1604–1606, quotation from § 3.

16 Royal ordinance, 6 May 1747, Krigsexpeditionen, Registratur 1719–1824, B I a, vol. 39, Swedish National Archives, Stockholm.

17 M. M. Klinckowström, *Historiska uppgifter rörande svenska generalstabens organisation* (Stockholm 1849), pp. 9–11. Cf. Teofron Säve, *Sveriges deltagande i sjuårskriget åren 1757–1762* (Stockholm 1915).

18 Ericson Wolke (2007), pp. 180–183; Lars Ericson, 'Kriget till lands 1788–1790', in: Gunnar Artéus (ed.), *Gustav III:s ryska krig* (Stockholm 1992), pp. 87–88. On the lack of training in larger units before the 1788–1790 war, see Nils-Göran Nilsson, 'Den gustavianska armén', ibid. pp. 54–56; Klinckowström (1849), pp. 12–13.

19 Circular to all regimental commanders and provincial governors on the disposition of the army, 10 May 1792; instruction to the division generals same date, Krigsexpeditionen, Registratur 1719–1824, B I a, vol 97, Swedish National Archives, Stockholm.

20 The infantry brigades comprised three infantry battalions, two cavalry squadrons, and a light battery; the cavalry brigade held six squadrons and a horse battery; the artillery brigade consisted of one howitzer battery and the entire artillery train. See Gustaf Björlin, *Sveriges krig i Tyskland 1805–1807* (Stockholm 1882), pp. 81–82, 201, 228–229.

21 See the various volumes of the official history Generalstaben, *Sveriges krig 1808–1809*, 1–9 (Stockholm 1890–1922).
22 Adlercreutz, 30 January 1813, Kriget i Tyskland 1813–1814, Nordarméns högkvarter. Koncept, förslag, vol 9, Swedish Military Archives, Stockholm. The refinement of the divisional organization can be studied in Krigsrustningshandlingar 1811–1812, Diverse handlingar, vol. 3, Swedish Military Archives; cf. Tingsten (1923), pp. 118–126, 131.
23 Adlercreutz, 5 April 1813, 'Underdånigst project till Arméens indelande i 5 divisioner', Militaria, M 77, Swedish National Archives; 'Om arméns fördelning i divisioner och brigader m.m.', 6 April 1813, Krigsexpeditionen, registratur 1719–1824, B I a, vol 154, Swedish National Archives; cf. Tingsten (1923), pp. 99–100.
24 Karl Johan to Adlercreutz, 5 July 1813, Kriget i Tyskland, Nordarmén, Högkvarteret, vol. 57, Swedish Military Archives; Höjer (1943), pp. 172; Tingsten (1923), pp. 195–200.
25 See, for example, 'Förslag öfver Svenska Arméen i Tyskland för från och med den 1 juli till och med den 15 juli 1813', Kriget i Tyskland, Nordarmén; Högkvarteret, vol. 34, Swedish Military Archives.
26 Tingsten (1924) p. 67.
27 Ibid. pp. 333–334; Tingsten (1925), pp. 54–55, 178, 212, 276–277.
28 Karl Vitzthum von Eckstädt, *Die Hauptquartiere im herbstfeldzuge 1813 auf dem deutschen Kriegsschauplatze* (Berlin 1910), pp. 94–95; Siriacy (no date), 'Escorte Russe à la Suite de S. A. R. le Prince Royal de la Suède', Swedish Military Archives, Kriget i Tyskland, Nordarmén, Högkvarteret, vol. 27; Siriacy, 27 October 1813, 'Liste über die beim Hauptquartier S:e Könglichen Hoheit des Kronprinzen von Schweden befindliche Gendarmen und Königl. Preussiche Ordonansen'; ibid. on the HQ organization in Norway, see Björlin (1893), pp. 332–340.
29 Klinckowström (1849), pp. 1, 12–13; *Generalstaben* (1923), pp. 5–9.
30 Creveld (1985), p. 73.
31 Höjer (1943), pp. 214–216.
32 Brehmer (2007).
33 Vitzthum von Eckstädt (1910).
34 Creveld (1985), pp. 66–69; Vitzthum von Eckstädt (1910), pp. 98–101.
35 Vitzthum von Eckstädt (1910), pp. 92–93, 96–97.
36 Ibid. pp. 26, 30–33, 38.
37 Charles Jean Baptiste de Suremain, *Sverige på franska republikens och kejsardömets tid: Generallöjtnant de Suremains minnen från anställning i svensk tjänst 1794–1815* (Stockholm 1902), pp. 273–274. The French original version was published in the same year in Paris by G. de Suremain as *Mémoires du lieutenant général de Suremain: (1794–1815), publiés par un de ses petits-neveux*; Löwenhielm's biography, according to Nils F. Holm, 'Gustaf Carl Fredrik Löwenhielm', *Svenskt biografiskt lexikon*, 24 (Stockholm 1982–1984).
38 *Tjenste-föreskrift* (1805), §§ 8–10.
39 Vitzthum von Eckstädt (1910), pp. 24, 30.
40 FM 101-5, 2-2, 4-9–4-32 (see note 1).
41 Vitzthum von Eckstädt (1910), pp. 92–101.
42 Creveld (1985) p. 75.
43 *Tjenste-föreskrift* (1805) § 8.

44 Björlin (1893), pp. 92–97; Tingsten (1925), pp. 217–218.

45 Creveld (1985), p. 87.

46 'Förslag öfver Svenska Arméen i Tyskland för från och med den 1 juli till och med den 15 juli 1813', Kriget i Tyskland, Nordarmén, Högkvarteret, vol. 34, Swedish Military Archives.

47 Björlin (1893), pp. 24, 332–340.

48 On the reformation of command structures after the Cold War, see Jonathan M. House, *Combined Arms Warfare in the Twentieth Century* (Lawrence 2001), pp. 261–267, 276–286.

49 See, for example, Jan Glete, *War and the State in Early Modern Europe: Spain, the Dutch Republic and Sweden as Fiscal-Military States, 1500–1660* (London & New York 2002), pp. 2–9, 213–217.

50 Lars Ericson Wolke, *Svensk militärmakt: Strategi och operationer i svensk militärhistoria under 1500 år* (Stockholm 2009) p. 162.

51 Gunnar Åselius, 'Historien som vägvisare till framtidens segrar: Om krigshistoriens plats i svensk officersutbildning', in: *Inte bara krig: Nio föreläsningar i Krigsarkivet*, Meddelanden från Krigsarkivet, 28, (Stockholm 2006), pp. 47–50; Björlin (1893), pp. 332–343.

CHAPTER 16

The Wage-earners' Paradise?

A century of the Norwegian and Swedish welfare states

Klas Åmark

Much of the international and comparative research on welfare states in recent decades has dealt with the kinds of different welfare state regimes, how they should be explained, and what their consequences have been. The Danish sociologist Gösta Esping-Andersen's seminal work *Three Worlds of Welfare Capitalism* (1990) has been a pioneer in this discussion. He identifies three ideal types of welfare state regime, which he gives ideological labels: conservative, liberal, and social-democratic. The different regimes are defined by the way in which they relate to the fundamental problem of social policy or how the social security systems handle the wage-earners' market dependence and their ability to maintain their standard of living when the market fails. Sweden, Denmark, Norway, Finland, and the Netherlands are all countries that chose a social-democratic welfare state regime.[1]

When explaining the causes of the development of the different welfare state regimes, Esping-Andersen argues that 'politics matters'. Statistical analyses show a co-variation between the choices of a welfare state regime and the political power balance within each country. We also find the social-democratic regime type in countries with a strong social-democratic movement. However, this is not only the result of political strength. The capability of the social-democratic parties to organize political alliances and class coalitions was also crucial. Social Democrats cooperated with farmers in the 1930s and with white-collar workers in the 1950s and 1960s.[2] However, statistical methods have their shortcomings. Esping-Andersen notes the following questions about the importance of political power structures:

> What such linear models cannot accomplish is what, in the end, must be answered: namely, is political power a decisive or only a spurious historical variable? When we identify the singular influence or working class mobilization on, say decommodification or universalism, to what extent are socialist parties mediating forces? Are there alternative historical influences, which pre-determine a particular outcome of the welfare state? Answers to these kinds of questions must await new breakthroughs in the statistical analysis of welfare state development.[3]

There are other scholarly methods that could be used to answer these questions other than advanced statistical analyses; one such method is the historical case-study. Questions about alternative influences and how causal factors are connected to one another in detail are well suited for such studies.[4]

There are important and well-known differences between the social security policy of the social-democratic parties in the 1930s and the much more advanced and costly programmes that these parties developed and promoted from the 1950s onwards. Esping-Andersen interprets these changes as changes in the degree of decommodification and as results of a gradual and general social democratization of the welfare state.[5]

Swedish sociologists Walter Korpi and Joakim Palme offer a more sophisticated analysis of the individual social security systems and their constructions. In analysing the Scandinavian social-democratic experience, they distinguish between a basic security model and an encompassing model that is characterized by universalism and income security. These more precise definitions permit an analysis of the decisive steps in the development of the modern social-democratic welfare state regimes during the 1950s and 1960s. According to Korpi and Palme, there are only three countries that developed the encompassing model, namely Sweden (with its path-breaking reforms in the 1950s), Norway, and Finland. The causal issues seem readily understood: there is a strong correlation between social-democratic power and the encompassing model.[6]

However, recent historical and social science research, which has considered Swedish and Norwegian developments in detail, shows the relevance of the methodological questions that Esping-Andersen asks. In Sweden, we meet a major political struggle within the labour movement between Gustav Möller, the powerful Social Democrat Minister of Social Affairs (1932 and 1951), Landsorganisationen (the Swedish Trade Union Confederation), and representatives of the voluntary health insurance funds and unemployment funds.[7] This type of political battle over major principles within the political blocs and within one social class becomes problematic for the power resource theory that Esping-Andersen and Korpi and Palme advocate. They assume that the political struggles over welfare politics and welfare state regimes are fought between representatives of the main social classes and the most important power blocs in each country: conservative, liberal, and social democrat. This kind of thinking registers the differences and contradictions within the power blocs.[8] However, this theory does not assist in explaining and interpreting these contradictions.

A system of social insurance is not only what it appears to be; it is not only about economic redistribution, social rights and social security, and relations between social classes: it also contains hidden texts or messages. Those messages deal with what Max Weber called a 'legitimate order'.[9] We have reason to ask what kind of order institutions of social insurance promote or favour. New solutions to the problem of social security change the existing legitimate order. For some actors, these changes result from conscious actions. Yet while for some they might be the most important political goal, other actors might completely neglect this problem.

From stringent theory to contextuality

In the words of the German historian Jürgen Kocka, 'To render historical science more stringent and analytically more powerful and at the same time to increase its scale and relevance, it should be more comparative.'[10] This is his challenge to the many historians who prefer to study one case at the time, often from their own country. The British historian Jane Lewis is more sceptical about the use of comparisons. She says: 'Comparative research all too often tends to work with aggregate country-specific data and, in so doing, loses sight of the nature of the contextual complexities, which alone render differences explicable'.[11] Kocka is also well aware of the fact that many historians would prefer to use historical comparisons to strengthen the individuality of the cases compared or to highlight the specific characteristics of the main object being studied, rather than to look systematically for similarities between different cases or countries. It is easier to understand the peculiarities of the history of one's own country if it is compared to the histories of other countries. However, Kocka also recognizes the tension – or should we say contradiction – between comparison and contextuality, which is something of a trademark for historians.[12] Lewis's criticism is primarily directed at the typically comparativist social scientist, while Kocka wants to persuade traditional historians to work more comparatively – and to be more theoretical. Both recognize the problem: the tension between context and comparison. However, how should this tension be handled? How should historians organize their comparative work without falling in the social science trap?

Social scientists prefer to compare numerous countries. This is part of their methodology, their idea that they are testing theories. In doing so, the more cases they can compare, the better. When one compares many countries, it is almost necessary to work with quantitative methods in order to measure dependent and independent variables and to look for statistical co-variations between them. Since historians usually prefer depth over breadth, they also prefer comparisons between few cases. Studies of two countries are common, such as comparisons between the US and Germany, Germany and France, France and Britain, and sometimes between Britain and Sweden. All these are more usual than a comparison between two Nordic countries, although the possibilities for such studies are good. Broader historical comparisons of several countries, of the kind that Jan Glete successfully conducted, are rather unusual.

Two-country studies give the historian the possibility to do thorough and solid studies of both countries. However, these studies raise a major problem for the historian – the question *two of what kind*? This is crucial question, since the organization of both the historical investigation and the text is strongly dependent upon what the researcher thinks he or she is comparing. A comparison is not directed by an idea about what types of system are being compared; therefore, is quite difficult to conduct. The historian will, in his or her own way, meet a wide range of facts and factors in the sources and literature involved in the investigation, all of which demand to be taken into consideration. However, how should we choose our data? One answer is to use some kind of theory. This alternative is evidently the one that Jürgen Kocka favours. However, it could also be very useful to have a typology to hand that suggested which type each country belongs to. And social scientists have been eager to provide these kinds of typologies, at least in the field of welfare state research. If we accept such typologies, then we know what we are comparing. For example, France and Germany are said to number among the conservative welfare regime states, while Britain belongs among the liberal welfare regime states. When comparing France and Germany, we can expect to find essential similarities in the way their welfare systems are constructed; when we compare Britain with France or Germany, we can expect to find essential differences. The typology will act as a counterweight to the historian's natural inclination to look for differences. The typology gives us clues about what we should look for, how we should organize our investigation, and how to frame our text.

So why compare Norway and Sweden? Scholarly comparisons often function most efficiently when two similar countries are compared.[13] There are especially good possibilities of finding common explanations and fruitful ways to characterize each individual country. Norway and Sweden are similar countries in many ways. Developments in both countries since the nineteenth century are closely analogous: falling mortality rates, population growth, emigration to the US, democratization, women's suffrage, the popular movements, and the growth of the labour movement. It is striking how similar the grand national narratives are.[14] The comparison between Norway and Sweden is about two similar cases – not only when it comes to their welfare states but in many other respects. The fact that the similarities are important does not mean that the differences are not worthy of our attention. The differences tell us important things about the conditions of the political life. This is why I chose to compare the development of the social insurance systems in Norway and Sweden in a Swedish monograph, summarized in this chapter.[15]

Roots of the Norwegian and Swedish social insurance systems

In reality, the discussions about a new type of social insurance started in both Norway and Sweden as early as the 1880s.[16] These discussions were part of a general European development at the time. However, the two countries did not follow the German chancellor, Otto von Bismarck, and the conservative solution he introduced in Germany of social insurance directly addressed to the industrial working class. Instead, it was a typical, liberal, 'help to self-help' policy that played a dominant role until the 1930s in both Norway and Sweden. The aim of this policy was not to help the poorest people. Instead, they had to accept the care offered by the poor relief system, if society was prepared to support them at all.

New solutions began to emerge at the end of the nineteenth century, and were initially directed at normal, respectable wage-earners. The new social insurance was meant for those who were doing their social duty by taking responsibility for both themselves and their family. Meanwhile, the insurances excluded those who had sufficient economic resources to be expected to cope on their own, without the help of the state.

State-organized obligatory health insurance was established in Norway in 1909, when it comprised three elements: health care compensation with broad coverage; a sick leave benefit for respectable wage-earners; and a voluntary, complementary insurance for those who did not have the right to sick leave. During the inter-war years about half of the cost of the Norwegian health insurance went on health care expenses. Meanwhile, health care paid less than 10 per cent of the costs for health insurance in Sweden. This cost allocation means that any comparisons between the Norwegian health insurance and those of other countries can be tricky, and has led to Norwegian researchers overestimating the cover provided by Norwegian sickness benefits. They appear to interpret it as being more universal than it actually was. As historian Anne Lise Seip put it, Norwegian health insurance became the backbone of Norwegian social insurance.[17] When it was being developed, it was easy to connect other insurances to the already existing administration and regulatory systems; this was the case with work accident insurance, unemployment insurance, and maternal insurance. Path dependence was more important for Norwegian social insurance than it was for the Swedish system.

State support was first introduced in Sweden in the 1890s with voluntarily organized sickness funds; the system existed until 1955. This kind of voluntary fund support still exists for unemployment funds in Sweden. An important state pension reform was introduced in 1913 consisting of two different measures: one was a broad, old-age pension financed by contributions; the other a means-tested pension for those who could not support themselves by gainful employment.[18]

Social Democrats in power

The differences between the two countries were still sizeable in the 1930s in both the reform processes and the choice of solutions. As a result of the Social Democrat's accession to power in 1932 in Sweden and in 1935 in Norway, along with the resulting bout of reform, the similarities became more important in both respects. This was especially true of the state pensions, which were now introduced in Norway, and unemployment policies. The two countries had very different experiences in the Second World War: Norway was occupied by Nazi Germany; Sweden remained neutral and independent. As a result, different courses of action emerged in the 1950s. The five-year occupation of Norway by Germany resulted in cross-party collaboration and a sense of the Norwegians pulling together. The very successful emergency administration that evolved in Sweden during the War taught the Swedish Social Democrats how much politicians actually could do to change society by political means.[19]

Conflicts both within the social-democratic movement and between the political parties became much more wide-ranging in Sweden than they did in Norway, especially during the 1950s. The political alternatives were hotly contested, both in parliament and in the contest for voters in the electoral arena. The Swedish Landsorganisationen became an important force for reform in both economic and social policies; this was a role that the weaker Norwegian Landsorganisationen did not even try to play.

In the reform process, Sweden was ahead of Norway the entire time. Much this was due to the fact that Sweden had fared much better during the Second World War so that mobilizing economic resources for social security purposes was easier. As a result, the Swedish solutions (especially the reform of the old-age pension in the 1950s) became a part of the Norwegian context within which the Norwegian political struggle was fought. Swedish developments had made supplementary pensions and fully established income security a tempting alternative in Norwegian politics as well.[20]

Earlier research has shown that it is remarkably difficult to decide whether income security or flat-rate benefits would be the most consistent with social-democratic ideology. Some researchers argue that income security is an expression of bourgeois values, and is the result of Social Democrats carrying through a policy that had been already institutionalized during the liberal period of social politics. Other researchers argue that universal income security is the result of a typically social-democratic welfare state policy. My own conclusion is that one cannot argue that either social policy unequivocally corresponds with specific class interests. Interests are seldom unambiguous and distinct. A self-minded actor is often necessary to decide which interests are most important and should be defended in the name of the social class. That was also the case with the social insurance in Norway and Sweden.[21]

Income security and flat-rate benefits were two principal alternatives that had adherents in both labour movements. The ultimate solutions were determined after extended debate, especially in Sweden. Landsorganisationen in Sweden finally pushed through the income security principle in most kinds of social insurance. We find here what I call term 'productive justice', to borrow a formulation from Landsorganisationen itself – the opinion that there were fair differences in the wage systems between workers with varying competences, which should be reflected in the social insurance systems. Skilled workers had the right to earn higher wages and have better working conditions than did unskilled workers; men had the right to higher wages than women; and adults had the right to be paid higher wages than the young. The ideology of productive justice can also be found in the collective agreements and the trade unions' own dues and benefits. This ideology dominated the regulatory systems for both the labour market and social insurance.

The most distinct expression of this way of thinking can be found in the income-related benefit systems, which were first introduced in Sweden in the 1950s. Alongside a number of other major reforms, the labour movement institutionalized productive justice as a legitimate social order. The demand for justice became a powerful incentive in the reforming process, especially between blue-collar workers, who had to fight for their rights, and white-collar workers, whose employers granted them privileges. This class perspective in the formative period following the Second World War can be easily underestimated.[22]

Universalism

We often meet the notion in the literature that the social-democratic welfare state is universal; that social rights are founded upon citizenship and are the same for all citizens. This social-democratic model is then contrasted to other models, which are not universal: for example, the targeted model in which the poorest are given the public's support on the basis of income or needs tests, or the occupation-based models in conservative countries in Europe, where rights are guaranteed according to the individual's occupation.[23] However, detailed historical studies of who should be allowed to participate in social insurance paint a slightly different picture. A seldom observed feature in both the Swedish and the Norwegian social insurance systems was that the insurance, which protected recipients from loss of income during their active working life, was directed at employees, while self-employed and independent workers were long excluded from the insurance system or were treated differently. Modern, respectable, controllable, responsible wage-earners were the ones the state prioritized; it was their needs that were taken care of first. Marginalized groups were offered weaker rights or were completely excluded from the system. Even Social Democrats were suspicious of groups that were difficult to control such as the seasonally employed, family members working in family businesses, the self-employed, domestic staff, and the like. A long time passed before they were included in the social insurance system.[24]

For quite a time, many of those who were involved in the labour movements in both countries believed that it was offensive for the state to support 'rich people'. Social rights were also restricted by society's ability to control them. Groups that were difficult to control were often kept out of the system. The labour movements in both countries were building a wage-earners' paradise (especially in the 1940s) rather than the solidaristic, universal welfare state for all citizens, which social scientists thought they had found.

The boundaries of social insurance, and thus of social rights, were gradually pushed back during the prolonged reform process. Different groups of actors were active in this process. The bourgeois parties were sometimes most active; at other times, the Social Democrats were. The expansion was part of a general modernization process. As Walter Korpi has argued, social rights are never self-evident or guaranteed for long: they are not only always challenged, they are always tested and renegotiated.[25]

Politics as choice

Regardless of whether or not they were in power, the social-democratic labour movements have played a central role in both Norway and Sweden – especially since the 1930s. This provides an excellent opportunity to compare two political movements of the same kind and understand how strong political parties have functioned as historical actors. If either of the labour movements had been rational actors that acted according to their class interests and social-democratic ideology (as many social scientists have assumed), there would have been two important consequences: there would have been a general consensus within the movements about what to do; and the labour movements in the two countries would have sought similar solutions for like problems. Their policies would have been very much the same.

Historical facts tell us a slightly different story. The Swedish and Norwegian labour movements have not systematically moved towards well-defined goals in their social politics. They have both tested different solutions for how the growing welfare state should be modelled. I have found four different social-democratic alternatives for social insurance systems that were current in the period following the Second World War. The powerful minister of social affairs in Sweden, Gustav Möller, wanted to introduce a social insurance system with flat-rate benefits – offering the same amount to all regardless of income. However, he lost out to Landsorganisationen, which wanted to see a system in which social insurance would protect against loss of income and guarantee recipients' living standards when they could not work. This is the system that still exists today in Sweden, with the possible exception of the new old-age pension system that was introduced in the 1990s.

The Norwegian minister of social affairs was Sven Oftedal (a doctor and German concentration camp survivor). He wanted to introduce a system that differentiated between flat-rate old-age pensions and income-related benefits. By negotiating with the employers' association, the Norwegian Landsorganisationen tried for an alternative with collective agreements instead. The labour market organizations had organized and financed health insurance and supplementary pensions for those who these agreements affected. The Norwegian labour movement finally abandoned both of these alternatives in the 1960s in favour of a model that was inspired by the solution that the Swedish Landsorganisationen had successfully implemented. By following different paths, both countries ended up with similar systems.[26]

One reason why the paths taken were different was that political actors cannot do exactly as they please. Social insurance consists of complicated systems of rules; they cannot be introduced and changed at will. A series of moral and technical questions must be solved along the way. In the typical reform process in countries such as Norway and Sweden, consideration must be paid to a number of different areas: existing rules, expert opinion, special interest groups, the findings of public inquiries, other political parties, the administrative reach of public systems, and the future behaviour of the electorate. Those involved attempt to find the windows of opportunity and avoid hidden obstacles in a political environment that is beset with restrictions and limiting factors. They test alternatives; they try different routes; and they cast about for new alternatives. Sometimes doors open unexpectedly; at other times, they surprisingly slam shut. For a long time, the Norwegian Labour Party and Landsorganisationen were opposed to contributory unemployment insurance; then in the 1930s Labour suddenly did an about face and accepted a compromise with the liberal Left Party (Venstre) in order to implement a solution (in spite of the opposition of the lower ranks of the party). The Norwegian Landsorganisationen first pursued collective agreements for both supplementary pensions and health insurance; however, Gustav Möller later accepted and demanded state-organized solutions, to the extent of convincing both the Social Democratic Party and the Swedish parliament to accept his solution for health insurance; however, the party leadership postponed the reform until the idea was overturned.

When the Swedish reform of supplementary pensions (ATP) was formalized in 1959, the Swedish Employers Association and many large companies rounded on the Conservative Party – much to the Conservatives' surprise – for being firmly opposed to the reform. When Sweden's Liberal Party (Folkpartiet) failed to win both the voters' support and a parliament majority in the thick of ATP reform in 1957, the party did a U-turn and began to consider new, more 'wage-earner friendly' alternatives. The liberals lost again in the next parliamentary election. The theory of rational actors goes only so far in explaining such behaviour. Politics is not about will, as the Social Democratic prime minister and party leader Olof Palme tried to convince Swedes; it is about making choices. Politicians are forced to choose between existing alternatives.[27]

According to institutional theory, it is now well known that existing institutions and rules make it difficult for political actors to change direction or to introduce completely new solutions.[28] However, existing institutions also influence the reform process by offering the actors a simple alternative: institutional continuity. This means that reforms gradually develop step-by-step, and in terms of the exercise of power are much easier to implement than radical reforms are. Norwegian policies in the 1950s provide good examples of how leading reforming politicians preferred institutional continuity: they treated reforms as though they were purely technical problems that had to be accommodated to the modernization process at large. However, this also meant that the politicians gave pundits and labour market organizations real power to shape the rules. The gain was political consensus and the absence of bitter political struggles. The price paid by the governing political party was that it could not instil its own norms into the institutions.

Gender order

Gender order is also a part of the legitimate social order, as it speaks to how men and women's work should be distributed in society. Earlier research has convincingly shown that there was a distinct difference between the gender contracts in Norway and in Sweden, especially after 1945. The housewife ideal was stronger and survived far longer in Norway than it did in Sweden. This difference can be seen in married women's rights to gainful employment; the development of state childcare; the attitude towards care or cash benefits for mothers in Sweden who stayed at home with their children. The nuclear family has also been stronger in Norway than it has in Sweden. This can be seen in variables such as the joint custody of children born out of wedlock and the legal rights of people living together without being married; these situations occurred much more frequently in Sweden than they did in Norway. Moreover, the number of divorces is comparatively lower in Norway.[29]

According to the literature, we have reason to expect clear differences in the normative messages sent out by the social insurance systems since there is a stronger emphasis upon the role of the housewife and the nuclear family in Norway than in Sweden. However, the general development shows important parallels instead. The debates in the 1930s about the population crisis, family politics, and the social rights of men and women resulted in a number of changes to social insurance as well. Universal child benefit and family supplements to income security insurance were adopted in both countries in the 1940s (somewhat faster in Norway than they were in Sweden). The old-age pensions were also similar, with the same recognition that women had the same right to a pension as men.

The process of change was also similar. Trade union demands for higher benefit levels and supplementary pensions made family supplements to social insurance (which favoured families with housewives) both superfluous and impossible. Therefore they were abolished. This was not the primary motive for the changes, but rather an unintended effect of the growing demands upon income security. One difference between the countries can be seen in the pace of reform: the reforms were introduced earlier and went further in Sweden than they did in Norway. Thus social insurance became an incentive for women to find waged work earlier in Sweden than it did in Norway.[30]

In some respects there were distinct differences between the countries. Housewives in Sweden were favoured when they had children (for example, with maternity benefits, and later with the right to health insurance even if they were not in paid work). The complicated Swedish reform process for maternity insurance resulted in parental insurance in 1974, which extended to fathers. There was no equivalent in Norway; maternity insurance automatically tracked the changes in health insurance. Meanwhile, Norway's particular solutions were directed at single mothers. Radical reforms in the 1910s aimed to strengthen their position. The lively Norwegian debates about a 'mother's wage' referred to this group. Maternity benefits were introduced in Norway in 1964, and they had no equivalent in Sweden: they applied to unmarried mothers and gave them the possibility to stay at home and take care of their own children while their children were young. From an international perspective, Norwegian maternity insurance was definitely restrictive. The systems were different in some respects, and the differences all pointed in the same direction: institutionalized rules favoured housewives in Sweden, while unmarried mothers received stronger support in Norway. The norms that characterized social insurance did not reflect, either directly or simply, the existing gender contract and other observed differences in either country.

There is the argument that the equality of men and women in the Nordic countries was the result of their participation in the labour market. This observation chimes with my results. The implementation of income security for wage-earners became one of several incentives that saw more women choose waged work over staying at home. Social rights embraced women's roles as wage-earners. Meanwhile, the labour market has retained a strong element of gender inequality.[31] The strong labour market dependence upon equality was not only a force for change; it also brought restrictions and obstacles that impeded the implementation of equality. The social insurance systems in Norway and Sweden formally hold men and women to be equal; however, the corrective measures demanded to counteract the differences in the labour market are noticeably absent.

Conclusion

It was very much social-democratic policy in the 1930s that social insurance and social security were part of citizenship rights. All citizens should have the right to a decent living without needs tests controlled by powerful bureaucrats. As Esping-Andersen has argued, the ambition to establish social rights was a much more important motive for the actors than the ambition to decommodify the labour force.[32]

The more developed income security policy that was introduced in Sweden in the 1950s is more complicated to interpret in terms of social rights. The most important motive for the Swedish Landsorganisationen was the demand for justice and equality between blue-collar and white-collar workers (between the working class and the middle class). Income security was to be a social right, encompassing all wage-earners, regardless of their employers' ambitions and actions. However, the character of this social right was dependent upon the social order created in the labour market. The state guarantees social rights; however, they are realized through the mediation of political parties, special interest organizations, and volunteer organizations. Social rights are realized through the workings of civil society and its organizations. Voluntary health insurance funds and unemployment funds influenced the rules – and implementation – of state social insurance. The labour market actors set up their own schemes, which in turn strongly influenced the power of the state to choose its own solutions. Evidently, we can talk of the 'relative autonomy of the civil society'.

Social norms were institutionalized as organizations that belonged to civil society. These became the precondition for how individuals were to be categorized and divided into social classes: according to income and productive capability in the labour market. In this way, a strong and legitimate order was created, with its own rules and its own mouthpieces. This institutionalization was strong in Sweden, and weaker in Norway. The historical record shows that this process had started long before the heyday of the state-organized social insurance systems, and that this kind of institutionalization arises not only through state policy; it is also inherent to civil society.

The concept of 'politics matters' is not sufficient to explain the conflicts over principles within the political blocs, nor does it clarify the fact that representatives from different political camps can advocate the same political solutions. One reason for this is that class interests – which are interpreted through institutionalized social norms and discourses – do not give a clear indication of which principle should be preferred. The institutionalized and legitimate order for how workers should be categorized became an insuperable obstacle to the introduction of flat-rate benefits in both Sweden and Norway. Thus the analysis should be broadened to include studies of institutionalized social norms and discourses in order to explain the decisive choices in the welfare policies of democratic states.

Notes

1 Gösta Esping-Andersen, *Three Worlds of Welfare Capitalism* (Cambridge 1990) ch. 2.

2 Esping-Andersen (1990), pp. 29–32; id., 'The Making of Social Democratic Welfare State', in: Klaus Misgeld, Karl Molin & Klas Åmark (eds.), *Creating Social Democracy: A Century of the Social Democratic Labor Party in Sweden* (Pennsylvania 1993) esp., pp. 63–64.

3 Esping-Andersen (1990), p. 138.

4 Peter Baldwin, *The Politics of Social Solidarity: Class Bases of the European Welfare State 1875–1975* (Cambridge 1990) ch. 1.

5 Esping-Andersen (1990), pp. 108–111.

6 Walter Korpi & Joakim Palme 'The Paradox of Redistribution and Strategies of Equality: Welfare State Institutions, Inequality and Poverty in the Western Countries', *American Sociological Review*, 63 (1998).

7 See, for example, Torsten Svensson, *Socialdemokratins dominans: En studie av den svenska socialdemokratins partistrategi* (Uppsala 1994); Per Gunnar Edebalk, *Välfärdsstaten träder fram: Svensk socialförsäkring 1884–1955* (Lund 1996).

8 See, for example, Esping-Andersen (1990), pp. 65 ff; Korpi (2001).

9 Max Weber, *Economy and Society: An Outline of Interpretive Sociology, 1* (Berkeley 1978) chs. 1,5, 6–7.

10 Jürgen Kocka, 'The Uses of Comparative History', in: Ragnar Björk & Karl Molin, *Societies Made Up of History* (Stockholm 1996).

11 Jane Lewis, 'Introduction: Women, Work, Family and Social Policies in Europe', in id., (ed.) *Women and Social Policies in Europe* (Aldershot 1993) p. 3.

12 Kocka (1996), pp. 198, 206–207.

13 Klas Åmark & Joakim Palme, 'Historia, samhällsvetenskap och välfärdsstat i brytningstid', *Sociologisk forskning*, Supplement (1999).
14 Klas Åmark 'Att skriva Norges – och Sveriges – historia', *Historisk tidskrift*, 121 (2001).
15 The book was written as part of the research programme 'The Welfare State at the Crossroads'.
16 See, for example, Urban Lundberg & Klas Åmark 'Social Rights and Social Security: The Swedish Welfare State 1900–2000', *Scandinavian Journal of History*, 26 (2001); Åmark (2005) ch. 2.
17 Anne-Lise Seip, *Veiene til velferdsstaten: Norsk sosialpolitkk 1920–1975* (Oslo 1994), pp. 198–199.
18 Lundberg & Åmark (2001).
19 Åmark (2005) ch. 3.
20 Ibid. ch. 6.
21 Ibid. pp. 196–200.
22 Ibid. ch. 4.
23 See, for example, Esping-Andersen (1990); Korpi & Palme (1998).
24 Åmark (2005) ch. 4.
25 Walter Korpi, 'Contentious Institutions: An Augmented Rational-action Analysis of the Origins and Path Dependency of Welfare State Institutions in the Western Countries', *Rationality and Society*, 13 (2001).
26 Åmark (2005) ch. 6.
27 For Palme, see esp. Henrik Berggren, *Underbara dagar framför oss: En biografi över Olof Palme* (Stockholm 2010).
28 Paul Pierson, *Dismantling the Welfare State? Reagan, Thatcher, and the Politics of Retrenchment* (Cambridge 1994).
29 Åmark (2005) ch. 9.
30 Åmark (2005) ch. 9; id., 'Women's Labour Force Participation in the Nordic Countries During the 20th Century', in: Niels Finn Christiansen, Nils Edling, Per Haave & Klaus Petersen (eds.) *The Nordic Model of Welfare: A Historical Reappraisal* (Copenhagen 2006).
31 See esp. Walter Korpi, 'Faces of Inequality: Gender, Class and Patterns of Inequalities in Different Types of Welfare States', *Social Politics: International Studies in Gender, State and Society*, 7 (2000).
32 Esping-Andersen (1990).

PART IV

JAN GLETE'S WORKS

Jan Glete's published books, articles, reviews and edited works, 1975–2011

Compiled by Jonas Nordin

1975

1. *Kreugerkoncernen och Boliden*, Kreugerkoncernen på svensk och internationell kapitalmarknad [Summary: 'The Kreuger Group and Boliden'], (Stockholm: Liber, 1975) 394 pp.
— Doctoral thesis, Department of History, Stockholm University.

2a–u. *Svenskt biografiskt lexikon*, 21, 23–26, 28–33 (Stockholm: Svenskt biografiskt lexikon, 1975–2008).
— Volume 21: 'Ivar Kreuger' (together with Björn Gäfvert & Anders Hiller), pp. 543–550. Volume 23: 'Erik David Lindblom', pp. 295–296; 'Arthur Waldemar Lindén', pp. 377–380; 'Edvin Mauritz Lindgren', pp. 430–431; 'Karl Arvid Lindström', pp. 626–628; 'Karl Johan (Jonas, John) Henning Lindström', pp. 646–647. Volume 24: 'Gunnar Fredrik Magnuson', pp. 692–693. Volume 25: 'Karl Gunnar L:son Mothander', pp. 752–753. Volume 26: 'Carl Ludvig Arnold Munthe', pp. 46–48. Volume 28: 'William Olof Olsson', pp. 343–345. Volume 29: 'Gustaf von Psilander', pp. 510–512. Volume 30: 'Axel Bernhard Roos', pp. 324–327. Volume 31: 'Johan Oscar Ehrenfried Rydbeck', pp. 12–19. Volume 32: 'Sheldon', pp. 109–110; 'Francis Sheldon', pp. 110–112; 'Charles Sheldon', pp. 112–114; 'Gilbert Sheldon', pp. 114–117; 'Francis af Sheldon', pp. 118–120; 'William Smith', pp. 569–571; 'Harald Sohlberg', pp. 622–624. Volume 33: 'Edvard Hugo Stenbeck' (together with Andreas Tjerneld), pp. 217–222.

1976

3. 'Svenska örlogsfartyg, 1521–1560: flottans grundläggning under ett tekniskt brytningsskede', *Forum navale*, 30 (1976), pp. 5–74.

4. Review of *Kungl. Artilleriet: medeltid och äldre vasatid*, by Jonas Hedberg, *Historisk tidskrift*, 96 (1976), pp. 250–253.

1977

5. 'Svenska örlogsfartyg, 1521–1560: flottans grundläggning under ett tekniskt brytningsskede', *Forum navale*, 31 (1977), pp. 23–119.

1978

6. 'The Kreuger Group and the Crisis on the Swedish Stock Market', *Scandinavian Journal of History*, 3 (1978), pp. 251–272.

7. 'Rationaliseringsrörelsen i Sverige', review of *Rationaliseringsrörelsen i Sverige:*

effektivitetsidéer och socialt ansvar under mellankrigstiden, by Hans De Geer, *Historisk tidskrift*, 98 (1978), pp. 350–356.
— Thesis review; faculty examination conducted by Jan Glete.

1979

8. 'Två Kreugeravhandlingar', review of *Ivar Kreugers tändsticksmonopol, 1925–1930*, by Ulla Wikander, *Historisk tidskrift*, 99 (1979), pp. 333–339.
— Thesis review; faculty examination conducted by Jan Glete.

1980

9. 'Teknikhistoria – viktigt i ekonomisk och historisk forskning', *Daedalus*, 49 (1980), pp. 55–65.

1981

10. *Kreugerkoncernen och krisen på svensk aktiemarknad: studier om svenskt och internationellt riskkapital under mellankrigstiden*, Stockholm Studies in History, 28 [Summary: 'The Kreuger Group and the Crisis on the Swedish Stock Market'], (Stockholm: Almqvist & Wiksell, 1981) 673 pp.
11. 'SSU i Stockholm 1917–1960', in: Jan Glete & Gunnar Söderholm, *Boken om sta'n: SSU i Stockholm 1917–1981* (Stockholm: Stockholms socialdemokratiska ungdomsdistrikt, 1981), pp. 9–107.
12. 'STAB på den internationella marknaden', review of *Corporate Growth: the Swedish Match Industry in its Global Setting*, by Håkan Lindgren, *Historisk tidskrift*, 101 (1981), pp. 360–364.

1982

13. 'Tungt och lätt eller konsten att gå på två ben i starkströmsindustrin: några reflektioner från en studie om ASEAs historia', *Daedalus*, 51 (1982), pp. 73–87.

1983

14. *ASEA under hundra år, 1883–1983: en studie i ett storföretags organisatoriska, tekniska och ekonomiska utveckling* (Västerås: Asea, 1983) 367 pp.
15. Review of *Sjøfartshistoriske artikler gjennom 20 år*, by Roald Morcken, *Historisk tidskrift*, 103 (1983), p. 490.

1984

16. *Storföretag i starkström: ett svenskt industriföretags omvärldsrelationer – en sammanfattning baserad på 'ASEA under hundra år'* (Västerås: Asea, 1984) 84 pp.
17. 'Varför har svensk starkströmsindustri blivit högteknologisk? Några synpunkter på starkströmsindustri och industriellt företagande i Sverige under hundra år', *Daedalus*, 53 (1984), pp. 39–57.
18. 'Erfarenheter av forskning och utveckling i svensk industri: några synpunkter ur ett ekonomiskt–historiskt perspektiv', supplement to *Bioteknik: förutsättningar för ökat nationellt samarbete*, Forskningsrådsnämnden, Rapport 84:5 (Stockholm: FRN, 1984) 14 pp.
19. '1500-talets Kalmar: köpstad och kronostad', review of *Kalmar under Gustav Vasa och hans söner*, by Sven Lilja, *Historisk tidskrift*, 104 (1984), pp. 82–87
— Thesis review; faculty examination conducted by Jan Glete.
20. 'Maktspel kring handelspolitiken', review of *Staat, Wirtschaft und Handelspolitik:*

Schweden und Deutschland, 1918–1921, by Olof Åhlander, *Historisk tidskrift*, 104 (1984), pp. 108–112.
— Thesis review; faculty examination conducted by Jan Glete.

1985

21. *Kustförsvar i omvandling: teknik, doktriner och organisation inom svenskt kustförsvar 1850–1880* (Stockholm: Militärhistoriska förlaget, 1985) 110 pp.
22. 'De statliga örlogsflottornas expansion: kapprustningen till sjöss i Väst- och Nordeuropa, 1650–1680', in: Robert Sandberg (ed.), *Studier i äldre historia tillägnade Herman Schück 5/4 1985* (Stockholm: Historiska institutionen, 1985), pp. 257–271.
23. 'Sails and Oars: Warships and Navies in the Baltic During the 18th Century (1700–1815)', in: Martine Acerra, José Merino & Jean Meyer (eds.), *Les marines de guerre européennes XVII–XVIIIe siècles* (Paris: Presses de l'Université de Paris-Sorbonne, 1985), pp. 369–401.
— Also published in French, see no. 95.
24. Review of *Redare i Roslagen: segelfartygsrederier och deras verksamhet i gamla Väta socken*, by Kerstin G:son Berg, and *Öländska segel*, by Anders Nilson, *Historisk tidskrift*, 105 (1985), pp. 114–115.
25. 'Arbetsgivarehistoria', review of *Fred eller fejd: personliga minnen och anteckningar*, by Bertil Kugelberg et al., *Personhistorisk tidskrift*, 81 (1985), pp. 62–65.

1986

26. '"Demand pull" och "Technology push": doktriner och ny teknik i svenskt sjöförsvar, 1850–1880', *Daedalus*, 55 (1986), pp. 135–145.
27. Review of *Navis Oneraria: the Cargo Carrier of Late Antiquity: Studies in Ancient Ship Carpentry*, by Christoffer H. Ericsson, *Historisk tidskrift*, 106 (1986) p. 131.
28. Review of *The North Sea: a Highway of Economic and Cultural Exchange: Character – History*, by Arne Bang-Andersen et al., *Scandinavian Journal of History*, 11 (1986), pp. 189–190.
29. 'Emil Lundqvist', review of *En man för sig: Emil Lundqvist och Stora Kopparberg under mellankrigstiden*, by Sven Rydberg, *Personhistorisk tidskrift*, 82 (1986), pp. 156–157.

1987

30. *Ägande och industriell omvandling: ägargrupper, skogsindustri och verkstadsindustri, 1850–1880* (Stockholm: SNS, 1987; 2nd edn. 1995) 333 pp.
31. 'Demand Pull or Technology Push? Pre-Conditions for the Development of the Swedish Heavy Electrical Industry', in: Fabienne Cardot (ed.), *1880–1980: un siècle d'électricité dans le Monde, Actes du Premier colloque international d'histoire de l'électricité, organisé par l'Association pour l'historie de l'électricité en France, Paris 15–17 avril 1986* (Paris: Presses universitaires de France, 1987), pp. 243–251.
32. 'Svenska Arbetsgivareföreningen', review of *SAF i förhandlingar: Svenska Arbetsgivareföreningen och dess förhandlingsrelationer med LO och tjänstemannaorganisationerna 1930–1970*, by Hans De Geer, *Personhistorisk tidskrift*, 83 (1987), pp. 170–171.
33. Review of *Glory and Failure: the Difference Engines of Johann Müller, Charles*

Babbage and Georg and Edvard Scheutz, by Michael Lindgren, *Lychnos* 1987, pp. 238–240.
— Thesis review; faculty examination conducted by Jan Glete.

1988

34. 'Teknikhistoriska synpunkter på några äldre fartygsmodeller', *Sjöhistoriska museet 50 år*, Sjöhistorisk årsbok 1988–1989 (Stockholm: Föreningen Sveriges sjöfartsmuseum i Stockholm, 1988), pp. 66–77.
35. 'Delen och helheten: något om möjligheterna att förena historiens makro- och mikroperspektiv', in: Ingrid Hammarström (ed.), *Lokalt, regionalt, centralt: analysnivåer i historisk forskning: åtta provföreläsningar för professuren i historia, särskilt stads- och kommunhistoria vid universitet i Stockholm 10–11 maj 1988*, Studier i stads- och kommunhistoria, 3 (Stockholm: Stadshistoriska institutet, 1988), pp. 101–111.
36. 'Ship Lists and Source Material (Locations)', *Warship: a Quarterly Journal of Warship History*, 45 (1988), pp. 53–57.
37. *Ägandets historia: företagsägandet som tema i svensk historisk forskning*, SNS Occasional Paper, 6 (Stockholm: SNS, 1988) 41 pp.
38. *Long-term Firm Growth and Ownership Organization: a Study of Business Histories*, Ägandeprogrammet, Occasional Paper, 8 (Stockholm: SNS, 1988) 27 pp.
— See also nos. 39, 41 and 69.
39. 'Long-term Firm Growth and Ownership Organization: a Study of Business Histories', in: *Industrial Institute for Economic and Social Research*, Working Paper, 212 (Stockhom: IUI, 1988) 27 pp.
— See also nos. 38, 41 and 69.

1989

40. 'Ägande och skogsindustriell omvandling i Norrland 1850–1950', *Thule* (1989), pp. 95–104.
41. 'Long-term Firm Growth and Ownership Organization: a Study of Business Histories', *Journal of Economic Behavior and Organization*, 12 (1989), pp. 329–351.
— Revised version of nos. 38–39. See also no. 69.
42. 'Fartygsmodeller till nytta och nöje', in: Gunnar Nordlinder (ed.), *En utställning av modeller: Sjöhistoriska museet 28 april–29 oktober 1989* (Stockholm: Sjöhistoriska museet, 1989), pp. 5–19.
43. 'Amphion', *Nationalencyklopedien*, i: *A–Asa* (Höganäs: Bra böcker, 1989), p. 307.

1990

44. 'Arvet från flottans modellkammare: Sjöhistoriska museets modeller från åren 1600–1800', *Sjöhistorisk årsbok 1990–1991* (1990), pp. 9–44.
45. 'Den svenska linjeflottan, 1721–1860: en översikt av dess struktur och storlek samt några synpunkter på behovet av ytterligare forskning', *Forum navale*, 45 (1990), pp. 9–68.
46. 'En styrka mest på papperet? Historiografiska synpunkter på 1700-talets svenska linjeflotta', *Studier i modern historia tillägnade Jarl Torbacke den 18 augusti 1990* (Stockholm: Militärhistoriska förlaget, 1990), pp. 97–112.

47. Review of *I elektrotekniska industrins kraftfält: en studie av svensk lindningstrådsindustri 1946–1980*, by Robert Thavenius, *Historisk tidskrift*, 110 (1990), pp. 141–142.
48. Review of *Vetenskapen i försvarets tjänst: de nya stridsmedlen, försvarsforskningen och kampen om det svenska försvarets struktur*, by Wilhelm Agrell, *Historisk tidskrift*, 110 (1990), pp. 143–144.
49. 'Axel Ax:son Johnson', review of *Generalkonsuln: Axel Ax:son Johnson som företagare 1910–1939*, by Staffan Högberg, *Personhistorisk tidskrift*, 86, (1990), pp. 166–168.
50. 'Slaget vid Svensksund', review of *Svensksund: Gustaf III:s krig och skärgårdsflottan 1788–1790*, by Stig Jägerskiöld, *Nordisk tidskrift för vetenskap, konst och industri utgiven av Letterstedtska föreningen*, 66 (1990), pp. 518–520.

1991

51. 'Ägarkoncentrationen och den politiska demokratin', in: Rolf Eidem & Rolf Skog (eds.), *Makten över företagen*, Maktutredningens publikationer (Stockholm: Carlssons, 1991), pp. 201–244.
52. 'Örlogsflottorna som stora tekniska system: några långa perspektiv', *Polhem: tidskrift för teknikhistoria*, 9 (1991), pp. 61–77.
53. '1700-talets svenska flotta – en offentlig institution med omställningsproblem', *Historielärarnas förenings årsskrift*, 1990/1991 (1991), pp. 41–51.
54. Review of *Witchcraft and the Inquisition in Venice, 1550–1650*, by Ruth Martin, *Historisk tidskrift*, 111 (1991), pp. 145–146.
55. 'Stockholms handel på 1600-talet', review of *Mellan Torneå och Amsterdam: en undersökning av Stockholm som förmedlare av varor i regional- och utrikeshandel, 1600–1650*, by Åke Sandström, *Historisk tidskrift*, 111 (1991), pp. 445–450. — Thesis review; faculty examination conducted by Jan Glete.
56. 'Kungliga örlogsflottor, ett led i uppbyggandet av nationalstater', review of *Flådens fødsel*, by Jörgen H. Barfod, *Nordisk tidskrift för vetenskap, konst och industri utgiven av Letterstedtska föreningen*, 67 (1991), pp. 451–453.

1992

57. 'Coastal Defence and Technological Change: Technology, Doctrine and Organization Within Sweden's Coastal Defence', in: Göran Rystad (ed.), *The Swedish Armed Forces and Foreign Influences, 1870–1945* (Stockholm: Militärhistoriska förlaget, 1992), pp. 57–76.
58. 'Kriget till sjöss', in: Gunnar Artéus (ed.), *Gustav III:s ryska krig* (Stockholm: Probus, 1992), pp. 110–174.
59. 'The Oared Warship', in: Robert Gardiner (ed.), *The Line of Battle*, Conway's History of the Ship (London: Conway, 1992), pp. 98–105.

1993

60. *Navies and Nations: Warships, Navies and State building in Europe and America, 1500–1860*, 2 vols., Stockholm Studies in History, 48:1–2 (Stockholm: Almqvist & Wiksell, 1993) 752 pp.
61. 'Beredskap och vidmakthållande: varvet och linjeflottan 1772–1866', in: Erik Norberg (ed.), *Karlskronavarvets historia*, i (Karlskrona: Karlskronavarvet, 1993), pp. 145–252.

62. 'Från arsenalssystem till industriell omstrukturerare: FFV Ordnance och svensk krigsmaterielindustri', in: Ulf Olsson (ed.), *Aspekter på FFV, 1943–1992* (Stockholm: Institutet för ekonomisk historisk forskning, 1993), pp. 19–62.
63. 'The Foreign Policy of Gustavus III and the Navy as an Instrument of that Policy', in: *The War of King Gustavus III and Naval Battles of Ruotsinsalmi*, VIII International Baltic Seminar 5–7 July 1990, Julkaisuja/Kymenlaakson maakuntamuseo, 17 (Kotka: Provincial Museum of Kymenlaakso, 1993), pp. 5–12.
64. 'Swedish Managerial Capitalism: Did It Ever Become Ascendant?', *Business History*, 35 (1993), pp. 99–110.
— See also no. 65.
65. 'Swedish Managerial Capitalism: Did It Ever Become Ascendant?', in: Kersti Ullenhag (ed.), *Nordic Business in the Long View: on Control and Strategy in Structural Change* (London: Frank Cass, 1993), pp. 99–110.
— See also no. 64.
66. 'The Atlantic Battle Fleets and the Struggle for America, 1720–1790', in: *XVIII Congresso Internazionale di Storia Militare*, Turin, 30 August–5 September 1992 (Rome: *s.n.*, 1993), pp. 171–179.
67. 'Politik eller teknik? Drivkrafter bakom örlogsflottornas omvandling från 1500-tal till 1800-tal', in: Torsten Ryde (ed.), *... se över relingens rand! Festskrift till Anders Franzén* (Stockholm: Fischer, 1993), pp. 60–75.
68. 'Johan III:s stora skepp', *Forum navale*, 49 (1993), pp. 5–17.
69. 'Long-term Firm Growth and Ownership Organization: a Study of Business Histories', in: Richard H. Day, Gunnar Eliasson & Clas Wihlborg (eds.), *The Markets for Innovation, Ownership and Control* (Amsterdam: North-Holland/Stockholm: Industrial Institute for Economic and Social Research, 1993), pp. 155–177.
— Revised version of no. 41. See also nos. 38–39.
70. 'Bolidenbolaget', in: *Norrländsk Uppslagsbok: ett uppslagsverk på vetenskaplig grund om den norrländska regionen*, i: *A–Gästg* (Höganäs: Bra Böcker, 1993), p. 108.

1994

71. *Nätverk i näringslivet: ägande och industriell omvandling i det mogna industrisamhället, 1920–1990* (Stockholm: SNS, 1994) 374 pp.
72. 'Bridge and Bulwark: the Swedish Navy and the Baltic, 1500–1809', in: Göran Rystad, Klaus-R. Böhme & Wilhelm M. Carlgren (eds.), in: *Quest of Trade and Security: the Baltic in Power Politics, 1500–1990*, i: *1500–1890* (Stockholm: Probus, 1994), pp. 9–59.
73. 'Naval and Maritime History in Sweden', in: John B. Hattendorf (ed.), *Ubi sumus? The State of Naval and Maritime History* (Newport: Naval War College Press, 1994), pp. 345–352.
74. Review of *The sailing Navy List: All the Ships of the Royal Navy – Built, Purchased and Captured – 1688–1860*, by David Lyon, *The Mariner's Mirror*, 80 (1994), pp. 365–366.
75. Review of *Importing the European Army: the Introduction of European Military Techniques Into the Extra European World*, by David B. Ralston, *Historisk tidskrift*, 114 (1994), pp. 687–689.

1995

76. 'Hur stor var Wasa? Något om stora örlogsskepp under 1600-talets första hälft', *Forum navale*, 51 (1995), pp. 5–16.
77. 'Entreprenörerna som inte ville bli stora', *Risk & kapital*, 1/1995, pp. 25–30. — The article was written by a ghost-writer and approved by Jan Glete.
78. 'Regioner, nätverk, storföretag och grupper: något om mesonivån i finans- och företagshistorisk forskning', in: Hans Sjögren (ed.), *Aspekter på näringslivets historia*, Forskningsrapport, 5 (Stockholm: Ekonomiskhistoriska forskningsinstitutet, 1995), pp. 81–94.
79. 'Stat och samhälle: statsbildning, integration och identiteter i ett nordiskt/europeiskt perspektiv 1500–1850', together with Pär Frohnert, in: *Forskningsprogram vid Historiska institutionen, Stockholms universitet*, Meddelanden från Historiska institutionen vid Stockholms universitet, 2 (Stockholm: Historiska institutionen, 1995), pp. 10–15.
80. 'Fartygslistans hierarki: statsmaktens tillväxt och örlogsfartygens namn under 1600- och 1700-talen', *Historier från Frescati: en vänbok till Kerstin Israelsson*, Meddelanden från Historiska institutionen vid Stockholms universitet, 5 (Stockholm: Historiska institutionen, 1995), pp. 77–92.
81. 'Lex Boliden', in: *Norrländsk Uppslagsbok: ett uppslagsverk på vetenskaplig grund om den norrländska regionen*, iii: *Laap–Reens* (Umeå: Norrlands universitetsförlag, 1995), p. 35.

1996

82. 'Krigsvetenskapsakademien, försvaret och den industriella samhällsomvandlingen, 1870–1920', in: Erik Norberg (ed.), *Fäderneslandets försvar: Kungl Krigsvetenskapsakademien, 1796–1996* (Stockholm: Atlantis, 1996), pp. 141–260.
83. 'The European Navies 1688 to 1713: a Summary About Trends in Size, Structure and Technology', in: *Guerres maritime, 1688–1713* (Vincennes: Services historique de la Marine, 1996), pp. 283–303.
84. Review of *After the Deluge: Poland-Lithuania and the Second Northern War, 1655–1660*, by Robert I. Frost, *Historisk tidskrift*, 116 (1996), pp. 224–226.

1997

85. 'Absolutism or Dynamic Leadership? The Rise of Large Armed Forces and the Problem of Political Interest Aggregation From a Mid-Seventeenth Century Perspective', in: Marie-Louise Rodén (ed.), *Politics and Culture in the Age of Christina*, Acta From a Conference Held at the Wenner-Gren Center in Stockholm, May 4–6, 1995, Suecoromana, IV (Stockholm: Swedish Institute in Rome, 1997), pp. 23–28.
86. 'Axel Oxenstierna', 'Trettioåriga kriget', 'Byråkratins framväxt', in: Jan Melin, Alf W. Johansson & Susanna Hedenborg, *Sveriges historia: koncentrerad uppslagsbok – fakta, årtal, kartor, tabeller* (Stockholm: Rabén Prisma, 1997; rev. edn. Prisma, 1999). — See also no. 129.
87. 'Replik till Hans Sjögren', *Historisk tidskrift*, 117 (1997), pp. 256–258. [Response to Hans Sjögren's review of *Nätverk i näringslivet*, *Historisk tidskrift*, 116 (1996); Sjögren replied in the same issue: *Historisk tidskrift*, 117 (1997), pp. 259–260.]

88. Review of *Handelsflåten i krig 1939–1945: Nortraship – Profitt og patriotisme*, 1, by Atle H. Thowsen, *Scandinavian Journal of History*, 22 (1997), pp. 62–63.
89. Review of *Marchands du Nord: espaces et trafics à l'époque moderne*, by Pierre Jeannin, *Historisk tidskrift*, 117 (1997), pp. 522–524.
90. Review of *Sören Norby: sjökrigare i Östersjön på 1500-talet*, by Bo Graffton, *Historisk tidskrift*, 117 (1997), pp. 524–526.

1998

91. 'La construcción de un imperio con recursos limitados: Suecia y el desarrollo de las organizaciones militares', in: Enrique Martínez Ruiz & Magdalena de Pazzis Pi Corrales (eds.), *Espana y Suecia en la época del barroco (1600–1660)*, (Madrid: Fundacion Berndt Wistedt & Comunidad de Madrid, 1998), pp. 307–340.
    — Also published in English, see no. 110.
92. 'Entrepreneurs and Social Elites: Some Reflections on the Case of Sweden', in: Gunnar Eliasson & Christopher Green (eds.), *Microfoundations of Economic Growth: a Schumpeterian Perspective* (Ann Arbor: University of Michigan Press, 1998), pp. 83–93.
93. 'Maritim politik och krigsförberedelser', 'Sjökriget 1788–1790', in: Magnus Olausson (ed.), *Katarina den stora & Gustav III*, Nationalmusei utställningskatalog, 610 (Stockholm: Nationalmuseum, 1998), pp. 175–181, 184–194.
    — Also published in English, see no. 102.
94. 'Modernt samhälle eller bananrepublik? Det tidigmoderna Nederländerna i ny litteratur', review article of *A miracle mirrored: the Dutch Republic in European Perspective*, by Karel Davids & Jan Lucassen (eds.); *De republik tussen zee en vasteland: buitenlandse invloeden op cultuur, economie en politiek in Nederland 1500–1800*, by Karel Davids, Marjolein't Hart, Henk Kleijer & Jan Lucassen (eds.); *The Dutch Republic: its Rise, Greatness and Fall, 1477–1806*, by Jonathan I. Israel; *Nederland 1500–1800: de eerste ronde van moderne economische groei*, by Jan de Vries & Ad van der Woude, *Historisk tidskrift*, 118 (1998), pp. 199–206.
95. 'Voiles et rames: vaissaeux de guerre et marine dans la Baltique au XVIIIe siècle (1700–1815)', in: Martine Acerra, Jose Merino & Jean Meyer (eds.), *Les marines de guerre européennes, XVIIe–XVIIIe siècles* (Paris: Presses de l'Université de Paris-Sorbonne, 1998), pp. 381–414.
    — Previously published in English, see no. 23.

1999

96. 'Hur stor var Kronan? Något om stora örlogsskepp i Europa under 1600-talets senare hälft', *Forum navale*, 55 (1999), pp. 17–25.
97. 'Rapport om översiktlig undersökning av Svenska Handelsbankens arkiv mars 1998', in: *Sverige och judarnas tillgångar: slutrapport: bilaga*, Kommissionen om judiska tillgångar i Sverige vid tiden för andra världskriget, Statens offentliga utredningar 1999:20 (Stockholm: Utrikesdepartementet, 1999), pp. 201–223.
98. 'Den brittiska flottan 1793–1815', in: Knut Arstad (ed.), *Revolusjon, keiserdömme og statsomveltninger: et Europa i forandring, 1789–1814* (Oslo: Forsvarsmuseet, 1999), pp. 102–122.
99. 'Warfare at Sea 1450–1815', in: Jeremy Black (ed.), *War in the Early Modern World, 1450–1815* (London: Routledge, 1999), pp. 25–52.

100. 'Östersjön som maritimt operationsområde – ett historiskt perspektiv', *Tidskrift i sjöväsendet*, 162 (1999), pp. 272–280.
101. 'Direktörernas revolution och ägarnas kontrarevolution', in: Håkan Lindgren & Ulf Olsson (eds.), *Bevara och beforska: festskrift till Gert Nylander den 15 april 1999*, Forskningsrapport, 11 (Stockholm: Institutet för ekonomisk historisk forskning, 1999), pp. 54–75.
102. 'Naval Policy and Preparations for War', 'The War at Sea In 1788–90', in: *Catherine the Great and Gustav III*, Nationalmuseum exhibition catalogue, 610 (Stockholm: Nationalmuseum & St. Petersburg: State Hermitage Museum, 1999), pp. 175–181, 184–194.
— Previously published in Swedish, see no. 93.
103. Review of *Navies in History*, by Clark G. Reynolds, *International Journal of Maritime History*, 11 (1999), pp. 246–247.
104. Review of *Shipboard Life and Organisation, 1731–1815*, by Brian Lavery, *The Mariner's Mirror*, 85 (1999), pp. 367–368.
105. Review of *The Imperial Russian Army and Navy in Finland, 1808–1918*, by Pertti Luntinen, *Scandinavian Journal of History*, 24 (1999), pp. 221–222.

2000

106. *Warfare at Sea 1500–1650: Maritime Conflicts and the Transformation of Europe* (London: Routledge, 2000) 230 pp.
107. 'Vasatidens galärflottor', 'Den ryska skärgårdsflottan: myt och verklighet', in: Hans Norman (ed.), *Skärgårdsflottan: uppbyggnad, militär användning och förankring i det svenska samhället, 1700–1824* (Lund: Historiska Media, 2000), pp. 37–49, 78–89.
108. 'Axel Zettersten och "Svenska flottans historia"', in: *Historia, krig och statskonst: vänbok till Klaus-Richard Böhme* (Stockholm: Probus, 2000), pp. 27–44.
109. 'Makt genom organisation: Vasatidens stats- och imperiebygge som samhällsorganisatoriskt projekt', in: Kerstin Dahlbäck (ed.), *Att förstå det mänskliga: humanistisk forskning vid Stockholms universitet* (Stockholm: Natur och Kultur, 2000), pp. 82–108.
110. 'Empire-building With Limited Resources: Sweden and the Development of Military Organization', in: Enrique Martínez Ruiz & Magdalena de Pazzis Pi Carrales (eds.), *Spain and Sweden in the Baroque Era (1600–1660)* (Madrid: Fundación Berndt Wistedt, 2000), pp. 307–336
— Previously published in Spanish, see no. 91.
111. Review of *Dansk artilleri indtil 1600*, by Michael H. Mortensen, *Fornvännen*, 95 (2000), pp. 280–282.
112. Review of *The Making of a World Power: War and the Military Revolution in Seventeenth-Century England*, by James Scott Wheeler, *The Mariner's Mirror* 86 (2000), pp. 225–226.
113. Review of *Capitalists in Spite of Themselves: Elite Conflicts and Economic Transitions in Early Modern Europe*, by Richard Lachmann, *Historisk tidskrift*, 120 (2000), pp. 460–462.

2001

114. Review of *Birth of the Leviathan: Building States and Regimes in Medieval and Early Modern Europe*, by Thomas Ertman, *Historisk tidskrift*, 121 (2001), pp. 138–141.

115. Review of *Verkstadsmiljöer under 1800-talet: mekaniska verkstäder mellan hantverk och industri*, by Eva Dahlström, *Polhem: tidskrift för teknikhistoria*, 1999 (2001), pp. 109–112.
116. Review of *Albion Ascendant: English history, 1660–1815*, by Wilfrid Prest, *Historisk tidskrift*, 121 (2001), pp. 449–450.
117. Review of *In woelig vaarwater: marineofficieren in de jaren 1779–1802*, by Thea Roodhuyzen, *International Journal of Maritime History*, 13 (2001), pp. 339–341.

2002

118. *War and the State in Early Modern Europe: Spain, the Dutch Republic and Sweden as Fiscal-military States, 1500–1650* (London: Routledge, 2002) 277 pp.
119. 'Gustav II Adolfs *Äpplet*: två stora skepp som var samtida med *Vasa*', *Marinarkeologisk tidskrift*, 25:4 (2002), pp. 16–21.
120. 'Sheldon, af Chapman och de svenska linjeskeppen 1750–1800', in: Emma Having (ed.), *Modellkammaren 250 år: ett marinmuseums födelse* (Karlskrona: Axel Abrahamssons förlag, 2002), pp. 18–31.
121. Review of *Utiliteyt voor de Gemeene Saake: de zeeuwse commisievaart en her achterbaan tijdens de Negenjarige oorlog, 1688–1697*, by Johan Francke, *International Journal of Maritime History*, 14/1 (2002), pp. 304–308.
122. Review of *The Northern Wars: War, State and Society in Northeastern Europe, 1558–1721*, by Robert I. Frost, *Historisk tidskrift*, 122 (2002), pp. 380–382.
123. Fact check and preface to Alexej Smirnov, *Svensk historia under vattnet: vrak i Östersjön berättar* (Stockholm: Wahlström & Widstrand, 2002).
— Also published in Russian, see no. 124.
124. *Rasskazy zatonuvsich korablej: Svedskaja istorija so dna morja* (Stockholm: Svenska institutet, 2002).
— Also published in Swedish, see no. 123.

2003

125. 'Naval Power and Control of the Sea in the Baltic in the Sixteenth Century', in: John B. Hattendorf & Richard W. Unger (eds.), *War at Sea in the Middle Ages and Renaissance*, (Woodbridge: Boydell, 2003), pp. 217–232.
126. 'Naval Power and Warfare 1815–2000', in: Jeremy Black (ed.), *War in the Modern World, 1815–2000* (London: Routledge, 2003), pp. 217–236.
127. 'Hugo Raab och den samtida krigföringens utveckling (1848–71)', in: Gunnar Artéus (ed.), *Hugo Raab: förkämpe för ett modernt försvar* (Stockholm: Försvarshögskolan, 2003), pp. 115–161.
128. 'John Ericsson and the Transformation of the Swedish Naval Doctrine', *International Journal of Naval History*, 2 (December 2003) 18 pp (<http://www.ijnhonline.org/volume2_number3_Dec03/article_glete_ericsson_dec03.htm>).
— See also no. 147.
129. 'Snilleindustrier och entreprenörer', in: Jan Melin, Alf W. Johansson & Susanna Hedenborg, *Sveriges historia: koncentrerad uppslagsbok – fakta, årtal, kartor, tabeller* (Stockholm: Prisma, 2003; rev. edn. 2006), pp. 288–287.
— Also includes texts reprinted from no. 86.
130. Review of *Richelieu's Army: War, Government and Society in France, 1624–1642*, by David Parrott, *War in History*, 10 (2003), pp. 482–484.
131. Review of *Military Migration and State Formation: the British Military Com-*

munity in Seventeenth-Century Sweden, by Mary Elizabeth Ailes, *Scandinavian Journal of History*, 28 (2003), pp. 146–147.

132. Review of *Casa de Contratacion och spansk navigationsteknik, 1508–1606: en fallstudie i teknisk utveckling och tillämpad vetenskap under den moderna tidens början*, by Mats Kero, *Historisk tidskrift*, 123 (2003), pp. 665–666.

2004

133. 'Navy', in: *Europe 1450–1789: Encyclopedia of the Early Modern World*, 4 (New York: Scribner, 2004), pp. 259–264.
134. 'Navies and Power Struggle in Northern and Eastern Europe, 1721–1814', in: Rolf Hobson & Tom Kristianssen (eds.), *Navies in Northern Waters, 1721–2000* (London: Frank Cass, 2004), pp. 66–93.
135. 'Naval Power 1450–1650: the Formative Age', in: Geoff Mortimer (ed.), *Early Modern Military History* (London: Palgrave Macmillan, 2004), pp. 81–100.
136. Review of *By Order of the Kaiser: Otto von Diederichs and the Rise of the Imperial German Navy, 1865–1902*, by Terrell D. Gottschall, *Journal of Slavic Military Studies*, 17 (2004), pp. 355–357.

2005

137. 'Örlogsfartyg, flottor och flottbaser', and plate commentaries ('Lindholmsdockan i Karlskrona, 1718'; 'Svenska flottans seglingsordning, 1675'; 'Nederländarnas expedition till England, 1688'; 'Tvärsnittsritning av franskt linjeskepp, 1693'; 'Ritningar till akterspeglar, 1693'; 'Striden vid Vigo, 1702'; 'Linjeskeppet Nordstjernan, 1703'; 'Striderna vid ön Ruden, 1715'; 'Belägringen av Korfu, 1716'; 'Ritningar till skottpråm och roddfartyg'; 'Brittiska och svenska flottorna på linje, 1721'), in: Björn Asker (ed.), *Stormakten som sjömakt: marina bilder från karolinsk tid*, Karolinska förbundets årsbok 2004, Meddelanden från Krigsarkivet XXIV, Forum Navales skriftserie, 11 (Lund: Historiska Media, 2005), pp. 15–20, 88, 104, 109, 114, 116, 122, 124, 133, 135, 140, 142.
138. 'Armada 1588', in: Jeremy Black (ed.), *The Seventy Great Battles of All Time* (London: Thames & Hudson, 2005), pp. 118–121.
— Also published in Swedish, see no. 154.
139. Editor of *Naval History 1500–1680*, The International Library of Essays in Military History (Aldershot: Ashgate, 2005) 562 pp.
— Jan Glete was the author of 'Introduction', pp. xi–xxvi.
140. Review of *The Command of the Ocean: a Naval History of Britain, 1649–1815*, by N. A. M. Rodger, *The Mariner's Mirror*, 91 (2005), pp. 611–614.
141. Review of *The French Navy and the Seven Years War*, by Jonathan R. Dull, *International Journal of Maritime History*, 17 (2005), pp. 454–455.
142. 'Grekisk marinhistoria', review of *Greek Naval Strategy and Policy, 1910–1919*, by Zisis Fotakis, *Militärhistorisk tidskrift* 2005, pp. 142–144.

2006

143. 'Amphibious Warfare in the Baltic, 1550–1700', in: Mark Charles Fissel & D. J. B. Trim (eds.), *Amphibious Warfare, 1000–1700: Commerce, State Formation and European Expansion* (Leiden: Brill, 2006), pp. 123–147.
144. 'Operationer och administration: svenska sjökrig återspeglade i arkiven', in: *Inte*

bara krig – nio föreläsningar i Krigsarkivet, Krigsarkivet 200 år, Meddelanden från Krigsarkivet XXVII (Stockholm: Krigsarkivet, 2006), pp. 21–37.

145. 'The Sea Power of Habsburg Spain and the Development of European Navies, 1500–1700', in: Enrique García Hernán & Davide Maffi (eds.), *Guerra y Sociedad en la Monarquía Hispánica: política, estrategia y cultura en la Europa moderna (1500–1700)*, 1 (Madrid: Edicion del Laberintos, 2006), pp. 833–860.

146. Review of *Genoa and the Sea: Policy and Power in an Early Modern Maritime Republic, 1559–1684*, by Thomas Allison Kirk, *The American Historical Review*, 111 (April 2006) p. 583.

2007

147. 'John Ericsson and the Transformation of the Swedish Naval Doctrine', in: Andrew Lambert (ed.), *Naval History, 1850–Present*, 1 (Aldershot: Ashgate, 2007), pp. 185–202.
— See also no. 128.

148. 'Varför flyttade Sverige västerut?', in: Maria Sjöberg & Lennart Palm (eds.), *Historia: vänbok till Christer Winberg den 5 juni 2007* (Gothenburg: Historiska institutionen, 2007), pp. 105–116.

149. *The Oxford Encylopedia of Maritime History*, 1–4, editor-in-chief John B. Hattendorf (New York: Oxford University Press, 2007).
— Volume 1: 'Baltic Sea: an Overview', pp. 252–258; 'Baltic Sea: Regional Navies', pp. 258–262. Volume 2: 'Frigate', pp. 68–69; 'Karlskrona', pp. 292–294; 'Mediterranean Sea: Regional Navies', pp. 539–544; 'Naval Administration', pp. 640–648; 'Navies, Great Power: an Overview', pp. 677–688. Volume 3: 'Ship-of-the-line', pp. 608–609. Volume 4: 'Svensksund', pp. 72–74; 'Warships: Early Modern Warships', pp. 374–380.

150. Preface to reprint of Herman Wrangel, *Kriget i Östersjön 1719–1721*, Forum navales skriftserie, 1650–1837, 21 (Karlskrona: Marinlitteraturföreningen, 2007 [1906–1907]), pp. iii–xxiii.

151. 'The Swedish Fiscal-military State in Transition and Decline, 1650–1815', in: Rafael Torres Sánchez (ed.), *War, State and Development: Fiscal-military States in the Eighteenth Century* (Barañáin: Ediciones Universidad de Navarra, 2007), pp. 86–108.

152. 'Cities, State Formation and the Protection of Trade in Northern Europe, 1200–1700', in: Hanno Brand & Leos Müller (eds.), *The Dynamics of Economic Culture in the North Sea and Baltic Region In the Late Middle Ages and the Early Modern Period*, Groningen Hanze studies, 2 (Hilversum: Verloren, 2007), pp. 13–23.

153. 'Sjökrigens utveckling i Nord-Europa 1500–1800', in: Knut Arstad (ed.), *Sjömakt i Nord-Europa 1500–1800* (Oslo: Forsvarsmuseet, 2007), pp. 85–109.

154. 'Den spanska armadan', in: Jeremy Black (ed.), *Världshistoriens största slag*, translation: Per Lennart Månsson (Lund: Historiska Media, 2007), pp. 118–121.
— Also published in English, see no. 138.

2008

155. 'Europe and the Sea', in: Peter H. Wilson (ed.), *A Companion to Eighteenth Century Europe* (Oxford: Blackwell, 2008), pp. 418–432.

156. Preface to reprint of Oscar Nikula, *Svenska skärgårdsflottan 1756–1791*, Forum

navales skriftserie, 1650–1837, 27 (Stockholm: Sjöhistoriska samfundet, 2008 [1933]), pp. iii–vii.

157. 'Gustavus II Adolphus, Tilly, Wallenstein', in: Jeremy Black (ed.), *Great Military Leaders and Their Campaigns* (London: Thames & Hudson, 2008).

2009

158. 'Östersjön som krigsteater', in: Joachim Mickwitz (ed.), *Havet, minnet, slaget: kriget 1808–09*, Forum navales skriftserie, 33 (Stockholm: Sjöhistoriska samfundet & Kimito: Sagalunds museistiftelse, 2009), pp. 8–23.

2010

159. *Swedish Naval Administration, 1521–1721: Resource Flows and Organisational Capabilities*, The Northern World, 46 (Leiden & Boston: Brill, 2010) 816 pp.

160. 'Warfare, Entrepreneurship and the Fiscal-military State', in: Frank Tallett & D. J. B. Trim (eds.), *European Warfare, 1350–1750* (Cambridge: Cambridge University Press, 2010), pp. 300–321.

2011

161. 'The Dutch Republic as a Great Power: Political Action and Armed Forces', in: Jaap R. Bruin, Ronald Prud'homme van Reine & Rolof van Hövell tot Westerflier (eds.), *De Ruyter, Dutch Admiral: Protagonists in International Perspective* (Rotterdam: Karwansaray, 2011).

Jan Glete's unpublished reports, applications and other manuscripts, 1968–2009

Together with faculty examinations, lectures, and papers presented at conferences and seminars, 1975–2009

Compiled by Jonas Nordin

Manuscripts are marked with *. Many of Jan Glete's unpublished works can be accessed at <http://www2.historia.su.se/personal/jan_glete/> (22 June 2011). However, this is not a depository intended for long-time storage and conditions may change. Holdings in public archives are sometimes indicated, but these notes are not to be considered as complete.

Lectures, conference papers and the like, that have later been published are marked with ¤, and have a reference to the bibliography of printed works.

1968

162.* 'Unionsstridens betydelse för den svenska militära upprustningen, juni 1895–1899', extended term paper, presented at Elmar Nyman's proseminar, Department of Political Science, Stockholm University, spring semester 1968, 41 pp.

1969

163.* 'Stormakterna och Karlstadskonferensen 1905', extended term paper, presented at Hans Landberg's proseminar, Department of History, Stockholm University, spring semester 1969, 16 pp.

1970

164.* 'Socialdemokratiska Kvinnoförbundet och försvaret: från 1930-talets början till andra världskrigets slut', undergraduate dissertation, presented at Sven Ulric Palme's seminar, Department of History, Stockholm University, spring semester 1970, 59 pp.

165.* 'Svenska Träarbetarförbundets tidigaste verksamhetsår: centraliseringsprocessen intill 1897 års kongress', extended term paper, Department of Economic History, Stockholm University, autumn semester 1970, 18 pp.

1971

166.* 'Rapport till Riksbankens Jubileumsfond utarbetad av Arbetsgruppen för kartläggning och bedömning av historiskt källmaterial rörande Kreugerkoncernen.' Stockholm, November 1971, by Jan Glete, Björn Gäfvert & Anders Hiller, 123 pp. Appendix, special report I: Jan Glete, *Boliden*, pp. 122–123.

1972

167.* 'Boliden och Kreugerkoncernen', undergraduate dissertation, Department of Economic History, Stockholm University, autumn semester 1972, 55 pp.

1975

168. Lecture: 'Artilleritaktik eller bordningstaktik? Krigsfinansiering, teknik och taktik under 1500-talets flottrustningar', Sjöhistoriska Samfundet/Swedish Society for Maritime History, Stockholm, 5 November 1975.

1977

169. Lecture: 'Teknisk utveckling och flottrustningar i Nord- och Västeuropa under 1500-talet', Historiska föreningen, Stockholm University, 28 September 1977.
170. Faculty examination: Ulla Wikander, *Ivar Kreugers tändsticksmonopol, 1925–1930: fem fallstudier av marknadskontroll genom statsmonopol*, Department of Economic History, Uppsala University, 19 November 1977.
— Cf. no. 8.

1978

171. Faculty examination: Hans De Geer, *Rationaliseringsrörelsen i Sverige: effektivitetsidéer och socialt ansvar under mellankrigstiden*, Department of History, Stockholm University, 23 May 1978.
— Cf. no. 7.

1981

172. Lecture: 'ASEA och svensk starkströmsindustri – konkurrens eller organiserad specialisering?', Historiska klubben, Stockholm, 2 December 1981.
173.* Instructions for the graduate course 'Kapitalism och samhälle', Department of History, Stockholm University, 1981.

1982

174. Conference paper: (untitled) På väg mot en svensk teknikhistoria, Gothenburg, 16 November 1982.

1983

175. Faculty examination: Sven Lilja, *Kalmar under Gustav Vasa och hans söner*, Department of History, Stockholm University, 18 April 1983.
— Cf. no. 19.
176.¤ Lecture: 'Varför har svensk starkströmsindustri blivit högteknologisk?', Tekniska museet/National Museum of Science and Technology, August 1983.
— See no. 17.
177. Faculty examination: Olof Åhlander, *Staat, Wirtschaft und Handelspolitik: Schweden und Deutschland, 1918–1921*, Department of History, Lund University, 24 November 1983.

1984

178. Conference paper: 'High Technology and Industrial Networks: Some Notes on the Cooperation Between Swedish High Technology Industries and Their Customers', International Research Seminar on Industrial Marketing, Han-

delshögskolan/Stockholm School of Economics, Stockholm, 29–31 August 1984.

179. Lecture: 'Doktrin och materiel i svenskt kustförsvar 1850–1880', Sjöhistoriska Samfundet/Swedish Society for Maritime History, Stockholm, 1984.
— Cf. no. 180.

1985

180. Lecture: 'Doktrin och materiel i svenskt kustförsvar 1850–1880', Svenska militärhistoriska kommissionen, Stockholm, 1985.
— Cf. no. 179.

1986

181.¤ Conference paper: 'Demand Pull or Technology Push? Pre-Conditions for the Development of the Swedish Heavy Electrical Industry', Premier colloque international d'histoire de l'électricité, 15–17 April 1986.
— See no. 31.

182.* Instructions for the graduate course 'Militära rustningar och de europeiska staterna, 1500–1750', Department of History, Stockholm University, 25 September 1986, 6+5 pp.
— Copy held in the archives of Sjöhistoriska museet/Swedish Maritime Museum, Stockholm.

1987

183. Faculty examination: Michael Lindgren, *Glory and Failure: the Difference Engines of Johann Müller, Charles Babbage and Georg and Edvard Scheutz*, Departments of Theme Research: Technology and Social Change, Linköping University, 27 March 1987.
— Cf. no. 33.

184. 'Örlogsfartyg och örlogsflottor i Europa och Amerika 1500–1860: en jämförande studie om flottornas styrka, teknikspridning och doktriner för fartygsanskaffning: lägesrapport', November 1987, 12 pp.
— Copy held in the archives of Sjöhistoriska museet/Swedish Maritime Museum, Stockholm. Note by Jan Glete: 'Preliminary manuscript. May be used for research, but not to be cited without the author's permission.'

1988

185.¤ Trial lecture: 'Delen och helheten: något om möjligheterna att förena historiens makro- och mikroperspektiv', chair in urban history, Department of History, Stockholm University.
— See no. 35.

186. Lecture: 'Statsuppbyggande och permanenta flottbaser: centraliseringen av örlogsflottornas bas- och underhållsfunktioner under 1600- och 1700-talen', 16th Planning Meeting of the Nordic Museums of Maritime History, Karlskrona, 5–7 September 1988.

187.¤ Lecture: 'Ägande och skogsindustriell omvandling i Norrland 1850–1950', Västerrnorrland and Jämtland Counties' Chamber of Commerce, Härnösand, 7 December 1988.
— See no. 40.

1989

188.* 'Anteckningar om flottans äldre räkenskaper i Kammararkivet', memorandum for Riksarkivet/Swedish National Archives, 9 March 1989, revised and corrected 8 November 1990.
— Copy held in Riksarkivet/National Archives, Stockholm.

189.* 'Några anteckningar om Björn Landströms "Regalskeppet Vasan"', memorandum for Vasamuseet/Vasa Museum Stockholm, 13 March 1989, 4 pp.
— Copy held in the archives of Sjöhistoriska museet/Swedish Maritime Museum, Stockholm.

190.* 'Några anteckningar beträffande SSHMs register över örlogsfartyg', memorandum for Sjöhistoriska museet/Swedish Maritime Museum, Stockholm, 16 March 1989.

191.* 'Anteckningar om Oliva-slaget 1627', working paper for an exhibition at Vasamuseet/Vasa Museum, 15 May 1989.

192.* 'Några anteckningar om svenska flottan under 1500- och 1600-talen', memorandum for Vasamuseet/Vasa Museum, 15 May 1989.

193. Lecture: 'Statsuppbyggande och flottbaser: några perspektiv på Karlskrona som envältets svenska flottbas', University College of Karlskrona/Ronneby, Karlskrona, 22 November 1989.

1990

194. Trial lecture: 'Skyddskostnader, äganderätt och monopol på våld: ekonomisk teori', chair in history, University of Gothenburg, 1 February 1990.
— Cf. no. 195.

195. Trial lecture: 'Dominium Maris Baltici 1450–1650', chair in history, University of Gothenburg, 1 February 1990.
— Cf. no. 194. Jan Glete gave two trial lectures on the same day.

196.* 'Behovet av tillförlitliga fartygslistor', memorandum for Sjöhistoriska museet/Swedish Maritime Museum, Stockholm, 10 March 1990.

197.* 'Äldre fartygsmodeller vid Statens Sjöhistoriska Museum: sammanfattande rapport om undersökningen av äldre fartygsmodeller vid Statens Sjöhistoriska Museum 1989–1990', memorandum for Sjöhistoriska museet/Swedish Maritime Museum, Stockholm, 4 May 1990, 63 pp.
— Copy held in the archives of Sjöhistoriska museet/Swedish Maritime Museum, Stockholm.

198. Lecture: 'De deltagande flottorna: svensk och rysk sjömakt under 1700-talet', Sjöhistoriska museet/Swedish Maritime Museum, Stockholm, 15 May 1990.

199.¤ Conference paper: 'The Foreign Policy of Gustavus III and the Navy as an Instrument of that Policy', VIII International Baltic Seminar, Kotka, 5–7 July 1990.
— See no. 63.

200.¤ Conference paper: 'Swedish Managerial Capitalism: Did It Ever Become Ascendant?', 10th International Economic History Congress, Leuven, August 1990.
— See nos. 64–65.

201. Faculty examination: Åke Sandström, *Mellan Torneå och Amsterdam: en undersökning av Stockholm som förmedlare av varor i regional- och utrikeshandel,*

1600–1650, Department of History, Stockholm University, 7 December 1990.
— Cf. no. 55.

202.* Unpublished chapter: 'Bankgrupper, ägargrupper, företagsgrupper: drivkrafter och aktörer i svenska sfärer och grupper', written for the book *Vad betyder ägarna för bolagens utveckling?* (Stockholm: SNS).
— The book was never finished.

1992

203.¤ Conference paper: 'The European Navies 1688 to 1713: a Summary About Trends in Size, Structure and Technology', Maritime Warfare 1688–1713, The 4th Anglo-French Naval Historians' Conference, Portsmouth, 1–4 April 1992.
— See no. 83.

204. Conference paper: 'A Royal Navy in the European Periphery: Swedish Naval Policy in the Sixteenth Century', Nordic History Group meeting, Newcastle upon Tyne, 22–25 April 1992.

205. Conference paper: 'Drawings and the Bureaucratization of the Naval Design Process in Sweden 1650–1730', 1992 Annual Meeting of the Society for the History of Technology, Uppsala, 16–20 August 1992.

206.¤ Conference paper: 'The Atlantic Battle Fleets and the Struggle for America, 1720–1790', XVIII International Congress of Military History, Turin, 30 August–5 September 1992.
— See no. 66.

207.¤ Lecture: 'Politik eller teknik? Drivkrafter bakom örlogsflottornas omvandling från 1500-tal till 1800-tal', Historiska klubben, Stockholm, 12 October 1992.
— See no. 67 and cf. no. 209.

208.* 'Statsuppbyggande, marknad och hierarki: den svenska statsmaktens expansion i ett jämförande perspektiv 1550–1650', research programme for appointment at the Faculty of Humanities, Stockholm University, 1992.

1993

209.¤ Lecture: 'Politik eller teknik? Drivkrafter bakom örlogsflottornas omvandling från 1500-tal till 1800-tal', Sjöhistoriska Samfundet/Swedish Society for Maritime History, Stockholm, 22 April 1993.
— See no. 67 and cf. no. 207.

210. Lecture: 'Riket mest till en zirat? De stora skeppen i Gustav Adolfs flotta', Vasamuseet/Vasa Museum, Stockholm, 6 November 1993.

1994

211. Lecture: 'Drivkrafter bakom Östersjöimperier: medeltid till 1700-tal', Hässelby Castle, Stockholm, 6 March 1994.

212.¤ Lecture: 'Hur stor var Wasa? Något om stora örlogsskepp under 1600-talets första hälft', Vasamuseets vänner/Friends of the Vasa, Stockholm, 23 March 1994
— See no. 76.

213. Lecture: 'F. H. af Chapman – skeppsbyggare och industrialist', Marinmuseum/Naval Museum, Karlskrona, 12 April 1994.

214.¤ Lecture: 'Regioner, nätverk, storföretag och grupper: något om mesonivån i finans- och företagshistorisk forskning', Department of Economic History, Stockholm University, 14 November 1994.
— See no. 78.

215. Lecture on the book *Nätverk i Näringslivet*, SNS: Studieförbundet näringsliv och samhälle/Centre for Business and Policy Studies, Stockholm, 24 November 1994.

216.* Unpublished chapter: 'International Relations in the Baltic, 1660–1720', written for the book Thomas Riis (ed.), *The Baltic and the Baltic Region, 15th–18th Centuries*, 3. 20 pp.
— The book was never published. In manuscript the text has been used as course literature by IES, Institute for English-speaking Students, Stockholm University.

1995

217.¤ Conference paper: 'Absolutism or Dynamic Leadership? The Rise of Large Armed Forces and the Problem of Political Interest Aggregation From a Mid-Seventeenth Century Perspective', Politics and Culture in the Age of Christina, Wenner-Gren Center, Stockholm, 4–6 May 1995.
— See no. 85.

218.* Expert assessment for a lectureship in history, University College of Karlskrona, 29 November 1995.

1996

219. Lecture: 'Most Large Companies Have Product Concepts Older Than the 1920s in Their Business Ideas', Chalmer's Executive Seminar, Gothenburg, 26–27 September 1996.

220. Member of examining committee: Michael H. Mortensen, *Dansk artilleri indtil 1600*, doctoral dissertation, Department of Archaeology, Aarhus University, 1996.

1997

221. Lecture: 'Från inbördeskrig till imperium: Vasakungarna och den svenska vägen till nationalstat under 1500-talet, i: maktspel och militärorganisation', Föreningen Norden/Norden Association, Parliament, Stockholm, 6 September 1997.
— The second part of the lecture was Mats Hallenberg, 'Vasakungarna och deras förvaltning – när staten kom till lokalsamhället'.

1998

222.* Expert assessment for a chair in the history of technology, Chalmers University of Technology, Gothenburg, 1998.
— Partly co-written by Boel Berner and Bo Sundin.

1999

223. Lecture: 'Statsformering och eliter i det tidigmoderna Europa', Centre for Pacific Asia Studies, Stockholm University, 5 May 1999.

2000

224.* Expert assessment for a chair in history, Mid Sweden University College, 29 March 2000.

2001

225.* Conference paper: 'The Dutch Navy, Dutch State Formation and the Rise of

Dutch Maritime Supremacy', Anglo-American Conference for Historians, University of London, 4–6 July 2001, 7 pp.

226. Lecture: 'Stormaktstidens skeppsbyggnadskonst som arkitektur', Sjöhistoriska museet/Swedish Maritime Museum, Stockholm, 18 September 2001.

227. Lecture: 'Navies in Early Modern Europe: Function, Composition, Size and Fighting Tactics', Research Institute for History, Leiden University, 4 October 2001.

228.* Expert assessment for a chair in history, Uppsala University, 12 November 2001.

229.* Expert assessment of Maria Sjöberg's application to be appointed associate professor of history, University of Gothenburg, 2001.

2002

230.* 'Kontrakt, bestick och dimensioner: Vasa och de stora skeppsbyggnadskontrakten under Gustav II Adolfs tid. En sammanställning av data ur kontrakt, räkenskaper och administrativt källmaterial rörande flottan', report for Vasamuseet/Vasa Museum, 8 April 2002, 23 pp.

231.* 'Kronans artilleri: kort genomgång av arkivmaterial och data om bärgade kanoner', memorandum for the Kronan Project, Kalmar läns museum/Kalmar County Museum, 12 November 2002, 12 pp.

232.* 'Skeppsbyggmästare och konstruktionsofficerare i den svenska flottan 1680–1845', basic material for exhibition texts at the Marinmuseum/Naval Museum, Karlskrona, 2002.

2003

233.* 'Svenska örlogsfartyg 1571–1590', 29 April 2003 (later revised), 42 pp.
— Manuscript list of Swedish warships. Cf. nos. 236, 248, 249, 254.

234. Comments on Torbjörn Lundquist, 'Konkurrensvisionens framväxt: konkurrens, intressen och politisk kultur', Sekretariatet för Framtidsstudier, Stockholm, 27 May 2003.

235.* 'Cities, State Formation and the Protection of Trade in the Baltic, 1200–1700', lecture at an international workshop for doctoral students, University of Southern Denmark, Esbjerg, 9 October 2003, 11 pp.

236.¤ Lecture: 'John Ericsson and the Transformation of the Swedish Naval Doctrine', bicentennary of John Ericsson's birth, Försvarshögskolan/National Defence College, Stockholm, 14 November 2003.
— See nos. 128, 147.

237.* 'Svenska örlogsfartyg 1591–1599', 2003 (later revised), 35 pp.
— Manuscript list of Swedish warships. Cf. nos. 232, 248, 249, 254.

238.* Expert assessment for two project research posts, Department of History, Stockholm University.

239.* Expert assessment of Leos Müller's application to be appointed associate professor of history, Södertörn University College, 2003.

2004

240.* Seminar paper: 'The Swedish fiscal-military state and its navy, 1521–1721', Volos, 2004, 39 pp.

2005

241. Lecture: 'Den första globala världsmakten', lecture series Drottningarnas England, Senior University, ABF: Arbetarnas bildningsförbund/Workers' Educational Association, Stockholm, 21 February 2005.

242.¤ Conference paper: 'The Sea Power of Habsburg Spain and the Development of European Navies, 1500–1700', Guerra y sociedad en la monarquía hispánica: política, estrategia y cultura en la Europa moderna (1500–1700), Madrid, 9–12 March 2005, 45 pp.
— See no. 145.

243.* Working paper: 'Den svenska armén i Tyskland 1630–1632: storlek, sammansättning, geografiskt ursprung och förbandens ålder', 9 September 2005, 12 pp.

244.¤ Lecture: 'Operationer och administration: den svenska flottan återspeglad i arkiven', Krigsarkivet/Military Archives of Sweden, Stockholm, 29 September 2005.
— See no. 144.

245.* 'Värvade regementen i svensk tjänst 1618–1631', working paper, 30 September 2005, 14 pp.

246.* Conference paper: 'Local Elites and Complex Organisations: Interaction, Innovations and the Emergence of the Early Modern Fiscal-Military States', War and the Golden Age: the Netherlands in Comparative Perspective, *c.* 1550–1700, Rijswijk, 19–21 December 2005, 14 pp.

247.* Expert assessment for a chair in military history, Försvarshögskolan/National Defence College, Stockholm, 2005.

248. Unpublished chapter: 'Statsbyggande och entreprenörskap: Sverige som skattemilitär stat 1521–1721', written for the book Kent Zetterberg (ed.), *Sverige i Europa*, 35 pp.
— Undated manuscript, early 2000s. The book was never published.

2006

249.* 'Svenska örlogsfartyg1561–1570', February 2006 (later revised), 42 pp.
— Manuscript list of Swedish warships. Cf. nos. 232, 236, 249, 254.

250.* 'Svenska örlogsfartyg 1599–1610', March 2006 (later revised), 47 pp.
— Manuscript list of Swedish warships. Cf. nos. 232, 236, 248, 254.

251.¤ Conference paper: 'The Swedish Fiscal-Military State in Transition and Decline, 1650–1815', Mobilizing Money and Resources for War During the Early Modern period, 14th International Economic History Congress, Helsinki, 21–25 August 2006, 16 pp.
— See no. 151.

252.* Conference paper: 'Warfare and State Formation in Sweden, Spain and the Dutch Republic in the Early Modern Period: With Some Reflections on the Direction of Future Analyzes of State Formation and State Consolidation', Warfare and State Formation: Comparing States, Regions, and Theoretical Perspectives, Copenhagen Business School, 28–29 September 2006, 9 pp.

253.¤ Lecture: 'Sjökrigens utveckling i Nord-Europa 1500–1800', Sjömakt i Nord-Europa 1500–1800, Clio and Mars Seminar, Forsvarsmuseet/Defence Museum, Oslo, 2–3 November 2006.
— See no. 153.

2007

254.* Conference paper: 'War and Politics in Early Modern Europe: Spain', workshop on War and Politics in Early Modern Europe: England, France, Spain and the Dutch Republic, 5–6 May 2007, 11 pp.

255.* 'List of Swedish Warships 1521–1721', 2007, 42 pp.
— Based on nos. 232, 236, 248, 249.

2008

256.¤ Conference paper: 'Östersjön som krigsteater', Kimito, 1–2 August 2008.
— See no. 158.

About the Authors

Klas Åmark is professor emeritus in history at Stockholm University. He has published a number of books and articles on the Swedish labour market and its special interest organizations, the welfare state in Sweden and Norway, and Sweden's relations with Nazi Germany. His latest books are *Hundra år av välfärdspolitik: Välfärdsstatens framväxt i Norge och Sverige* (2005) and *Att bo granne med ondskan: Sveriges förhållande till nazismen, Nazityskland och förintelsen* (2011).

Gunnar Åselius is professor of military history at the National Defence College, Stockholm. His current research interests include the history of military command and control systems and the use of military history in the training of officers. Among his publications are his doctoral thesis *The Russian Menace to Sweden: The Belief System of a Small Power Security Elite in the Age of Imperialism* (1994), *The Rise and Fall of the Soviet Navy in the Baltic* (2005), *Krigen under kalla kriget* (2007), and numerous articles on military history and prosopography.

Jeremy Black is professor of history at the University of Exeter. He is or has been on a number of editorial boards, including *The Journal of Military History*, *The Journal of the Royal United Services Institute for Defence Studies*, *Media History*, *The International History Review*, and *History Today*, and was editor of *Archives*. He is the author of over a hundred books, especially on eighteenth-century British politics and international relations. Recent publications include *Maps and History: Constructing Images of the Past* (1997), *War and the World: Military Power and the Fate of Continents, 1450–2000* (1998), *The British Seaborne Empire* (2004), *George III: America's Last King* (2006), and *European Warfare in a Global Context, 1660–1815* (2007).

Jaap R. Bruijn is professor emeritus in maritime history at Leiden University. In his teaching, research, and publications he has concentrated on a number of themes: navies, East India shipping, whaling, and the social aspects of seafaring, mainly in the context of the Dutch Republic and the Netherlands from the seventeenth to the twentieth centuries. At present he is writing a book with Joost Schokkenbroek on Dutch whaling after the Second World War.

Christer Ericsson is professor of sport and sciences at the School of Health and Medical Sciences at Örebro University, Sweden. He is presently working on a project entitled 'Conditions of Democracy in the Shadow of Globalization – Male Football in Sweden'.

Anna Maria Forssberg is a senior curator at the Army Museum, Stockholm. She is currently working on a comparative study of war propaganda in France and Sweden during the Thirty Years War. Her publications include her doctoral thesis *Att hålla folket på gott humör: Informationsspridning, krigspropaganda och mobilisering i Sverige 1655–1680* (2005), *Army Museum: On war and people* (2009; editor and co-author), and 'Nationalist Arguments as Instruments of War Propaganda in Sweden, 1655–80', in Leos Müller & Linas Eriksonas (eds.), *Statehood Before and Beyond Ethnicity: Minor States in Northern and Eastern Europe* (2005).

Bo Franzén is a senior lecturer at the Department of Economic History at Stockholm University. Since his doctoral thesis in 1998 (on the Swedish late medieval monetary system), he has divided his time between teaching and project work on economic conditions and trends in medieval Sweden. His research interests include medieval prices, market institutions, and studies of how men and women acted in those markets from the mid thirteenth century to the Swedish Reformation.

Mats Hallenberg is a senior lecturer in history at Stockholm University. His research addresses the political and social history of early modern Sweden and Finland. His publications include *The King, the Bailiffs and the Realm: Local Administration and State-building in the Early Vasa Age* (2001; in Swedish), 'Organization, Legitimation, Participation: State Formation as a Dynamic Process – the Swedish Example, *c.*1523–1680', *Scandinavian Journal of History*, 33 (2008; with Johan Holm & Dan Johansson), and 'Peasants and Tax-farmers in seventeenth-century Sweden: Local Conflict and Institutional Change', in Wim Blockmans et al. (eds.), *Empowering Interactions: Political Cultures and the Emergence of the State in Europe, 1300–1900* (2009).

Marika Hedin has a Ph.D. in history from Stockholm University and is Director of the Vasa Museum in Stockholm. Her research interests include political history and the history of science. She has also been active in promoting popular history on radio and television, as well as in articles and books such as *Bilden av Sveriges historia* (2005) and *Vasa – The Story of a Warship* (2011).

Orsi Husz is an associate senior lecturer in economic history at Uppsala University. Her particular field is the cultural economy, and her publications include *The Value of Dreams: Department Store and Lottery in Swedish Consumer Culture 1897–2004* (2004; in Swedish), 'The Morality of Quality: Assimilating Material Mass Culture in twentieth-century Sweden', *Journal of Modern European History* (forthcoming), and 'Collapse of a Bourgeoisie? The Wealthy in Stockholm, 1915–1965', *Scandinavian Economic History Review*, 57 (2009; with Johan Söderberg & Martin Gustavsson).

Arne Jarrick is professor of history at Stockholm University and Secretary General for the Humanities and Social Sciences at the Swedish Research Council (2007–2012), and he has worked internationally with the likes of the European Science Foundation (2001–2007) and the European Commission. He has published widely on the history of mentalities in early modern Europe and is involved in collaborative research together with natural scientists on the cultural dynamism of human society. He is presently working on the long-term history of law-making. His latest book is *The Need to be Needed: An Essay on Humankind, Culture, and World History* (2010).

Ulf Jonsson is professor emeritus in economic history at Stockholm University. In recent decades his research has been devoted to different aspects of the history of agro-food systems. Recent publications include 'Flexibilty in Peripheral Communities: An Asset or Brake', in Marie Emanuelsson et al. (eds.), *Peripheral Communities: Crisis, Continuity, and Long Term Survival* (2008), and 'Wine in the New Global Food Order: Perspectives from the Southern Cone', *Territorio del Vino* (2008; with Paulina Rytkönen).

Gunner Lind is professor of early modern history at the University of Copenhagen. His publications include *Hæren og magten i Danmark 1614–1662* (1994), *Dansk Forvaltningshistorie*, 1 (2000; with Tim Knudsen et al.), *Konger og krige: Dansk udenrigspolitiks historie*, 1 (2001; with Esben Albrectsen & Karl-Erik Frandsen), and *Danmarks krigshistorie*, 1 (2008; with Kurt Villads Jensen & Knud J. V. Jespersen). At present his main research interest is the establishment of the social division between military and civilians, armed and unarmed.

Enrique Martínez Ruiz, professor of modern history at the Complutense University of Madrid, is the author of more than two hundred and fifty published works on military history, institutional history, and the history of security and public order. His latest works are *The Soldiers of the King: The Hispanic Monarchy Armies 1480–1700* (2008; in Spanish), and *The Church Against Napoleon: The Ideological War* (2010; in Spanish).

Leos Müller is professor of history at the Centre for Maritime Studies, Stockholm University. His books include *The Merchant Houses of Stockholm, c.1640–1800: A Comparative Study of Early-Modern Entrepreneurial Behaviour* (1998), and *Consuls, Corsairs, and Commerce: The Swedish Consular Service and Long-distance Shipping, 1720–1815* (2004). He has published extensively on the history of Swedish trade and shipping, and edited a number of volumes, most recently *The Rise of the Atlantic Economy and the North Sea/Baltic Trades, 1500–1800* (2011; with Philipp Robinson Rössner & Toshiaki Tamaki).

Jonas Nordin is associate professor of history at Stockholm University and researcher at the National Library of Sweden. His research focus is the seventeenth and eighteenth centuries, and as well as numerous articles he has published books on national consciousness, public rituals, and monarchy in the early modern period. He has also been the editor-in-chief of *Historisk tidskrift*, Sweden's leading history journal.

Magdalena de Pazzis Pi Corrales is a lecturer in modern history and Vice-dean of Students and Institutional and International Relations at the Complutense University of Madrid. She is the author of more than two hundred and fifty published works, with a particular focus on military and naval history and on the history of security and public order in the sixteenth to eighteenth centuries.

Johan Söderberg is professor of economic history at Stockholm University. His research has mainly dealt with medieval and early modern economic history. Among his books are *A Stagnating Metropolis: The Economy and Demography of Stockholm, 1750–1850* (1991; with Ulf

Jonsson & Christer Persson), *The Agrarian Economy of sixteenth-century Sweden* (2004; with Janken Myrdal), and 'Servants and Bourgeois Life in Urban Sweden in the early twentieth Century', *Scandinavian Journal of History*, 35 (2010; with Therese Nordlund Edvinsson).

Maria Wallenberg Bondesson is a historian and researcher at the Centre for the Study of Cultural Evolution at Stockholm University. She is currently working on a comparative study of the development of legislation in China, France, and the Middle East. Her publications include her doctoral thesis *Religiösa konflikter i norra Hälsingland 1630–1800* (2003), and articles on religious and legal history.